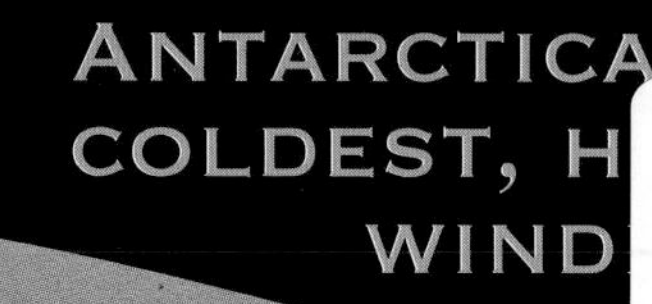

C000177529

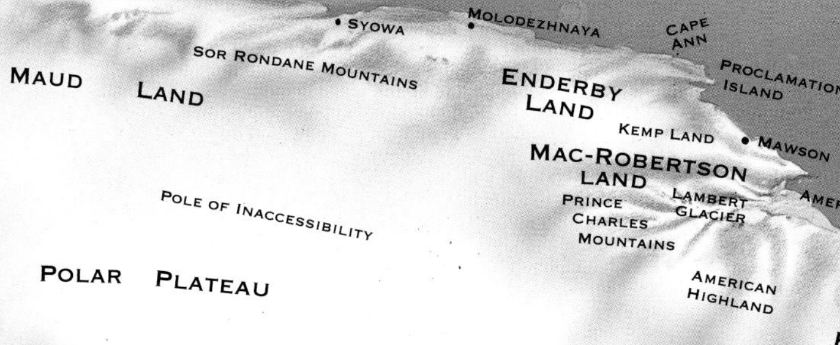

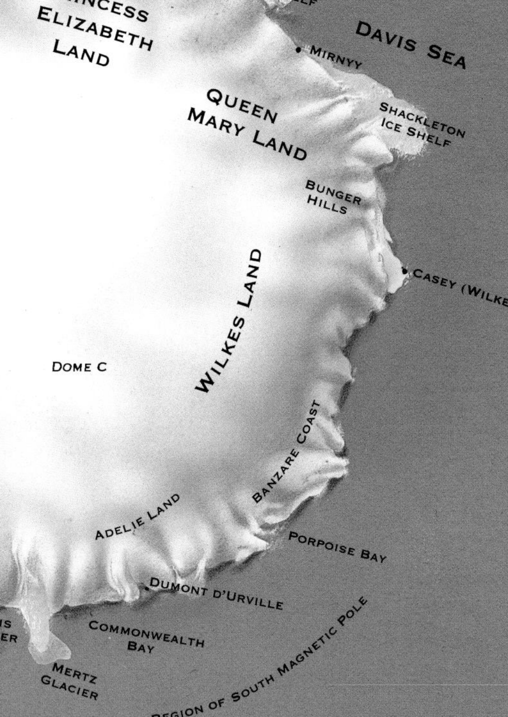

GLOBEMASTER, PIONEER 'WORKHORSE' OF
ICANS IN ANTARCTICA

F FLOAT PLANE PREPARING FOR ANARE FLIGHT

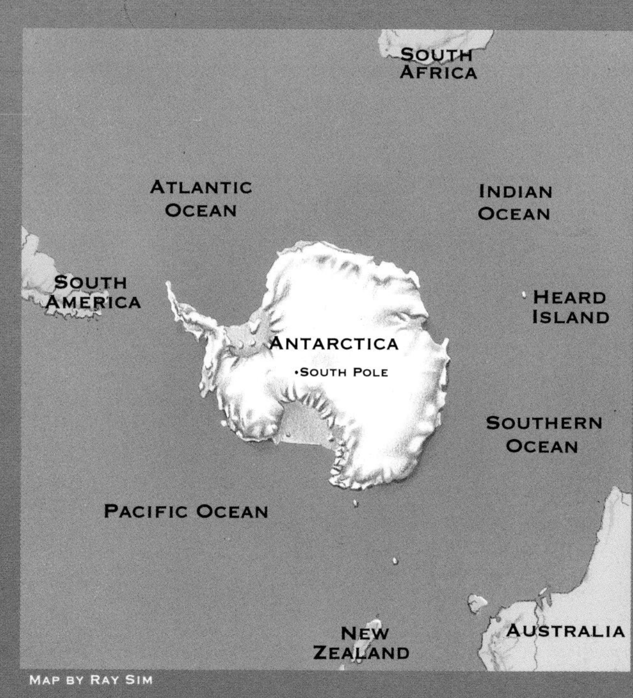

MAP BY RAY SIM

MOMENTS OF TERROR

Antarctica's first aeronaut — the balloon *Eva* prepared for Captain Scott's ascent at the Bay of Whales on 4 February 1902.

To C. J. X.

and all those brave Antarctic airmen

Aviation in Antarctica consists
of hours of boredom punctuated
by moments of stark terror
— old South Polar Airmen's proverb displayed in air operations hut, Williams Field, McMurdo Sound

DAVID BURKE

MOMENTS OF TERROR

THE STORY OF ANTARCTIC AVIATION

ROBERT HALE • LONDON

Other Books by the Author

Monday at McMurdo
Come Midnight Monday
Darknight
Railways of Australia (with the late C.C. Singleton)
Great Steam Trains of Australia
Full Steam Across the Mountains (with artist Phil Belbin)
Changing Trains
The Observer's Book of Steam Locomotives
Kings of the Iron Horse
Man of Steam
With Iron Rails
Road Through the Wilderness

Some Conversion Factors

1 in = 25.4 mm
1 ft = 304.8 mm
1 m = 3.28 ft
1 sq ft = .093 sq m
1 sq m = 10.76 sq ft
1 mile = 1.61 km
1 km = .62 mile
1 lb = .45 kg
1 kg = 2.20 lbs
1 ton = 2240 lbs = 1.016 tonnes
1 tonne = 2205 lbs

© David Burke 1994

First published in Great Britain 1994

Published in Great Britain by
ROBERT HALE LIMITED
Clerkenwell House
Clerkenwell Green
London EC1R OHT

ISBN -0-7090-5309-6

The right of David Burke to be identified as author of this work has been asserted by him in accordance with the Copyright, Designs and Patents Act 1988.
Printed by Kyodo, Singapore
Designed by Di Quick

CONTENTS

AUTHOR'S NOTE

THIS AUTHOR was fortunate in being able to discuss Antarctic exploration of earlier years with many of the men who are quoted in these pages. Most memorable was an association with Professor Griffith Taylor, first occupant of the Chair of Geography at the University of Sydney, who was a living link with Captain Scott's last expedition in which he had served. Dr Phillip G. Law, first director of the Australian government's Antarctic Division and first leader to the continent of the Australian National Antarctic Research Expedition (ANARE), was an invaluable source of information. Among the expedition leaders of other nations who contributed their knowledge and experiences were Dr Paul Siple (when he was science attaché at the American Embassy, Canberra), Dr M. M. Somov, director of the Institute of Arctic and Antarctic Affairs, St Petersburg (Leningrad in those years), and Rear Admirals George W. Dufek and James R. Reedy of the United States Navy, in charge of Operation Deep Freeze, based on McMurdo Sound. I remain particularly grateful to Admiral Reedy for being given the opportunity to participate in the first direct flight from Australia to the South Pole.

Among the aviators who gave details of epic journeys were Commanders William ('Trigger') Hawkes and Fred S. Gallup, of the U.S. Navy's VX-6 detachment, Squadron Leader John Lewis, of the Royal Air Force, Mr John Seaton, a now retired early member of the Royal Australian Air Force's Antarctic flight, and Dick Thompson, former Administrative Officer, ANARE. Nameless but not forgotten are the many other aircrew with whom the writer had the opportunity of travelling while on his visits to Antarctica. Thanks to you all!

During the preparation of this story, exceedingly helpful assistance was received from the staff of the Antarctic Institutes of Argentina and Chile; Arctic and Antarctic Museum, St Petersburg; Scott Polar Research Institute, Cambridge University; Norsk Polarinstitutt, Oslo; Lockheed Aircraft Corporation, Georgia, USA; National Air and Space Museum, the Smithsonian Institution, Washington, D.C.; Byrd Polar Research Centre, Ohio

The wild ice of Oates Land viewed from an Australian expedition aircraft.

State University, Columbus, Ohio. Likewise, acknowledgement is made of the valuable assistance of Australia Post, Melbourne; Australian National Library (Mawson papers) and Australian Archives (Commonwealth records) in Canberra; the Antarctic Division of the Australian government in Hobart; Barr Smith Library (holder of the Mawson collection), Adelaide University; the Mitchell Library, Sydney; and Mr Colin Monteath, Christchurch, New Zealand. Among the many overseas individuals to whom the writer is indebted are Mr Mort Beebe, San Francisco; Dr R. Pardoe, Eureka, California; Mr Damien Smith, Stavanger, Norway; Messrs James Winbigler and Paul Finley, of the Aero Products Division, Litton Industries, California. At home, special thanks are extended to Mr Jonathan Chester, Ms Elizabeth Chipman, Mr Jim Harvey, Mr Ray Honisett, Group Captain Keith Isaacs, RAAF (ret.), the late Dr Fred Jacka, Mr Dion Makowski, Renate Metraux, Lufthansa German Airlines (Sydney), Mrs Bet Quick, Mr Dick Smith and Ms Gillian Manning, *Australian Geographic*; Sr Joan Spruson, rscj. Manuscript deciphering and typing has been in the experienced hands of Paddy Elworthy, to whom the writer ever stands in deep respect; Russian translations by Xie Xiao Qiang.

The story of the first 50 years of Antarctic aviation is essentially that of fixed-wing aircraft; the contribution of the helicopter, especially in more recent times, would require another account, yet to be written. This is also a story that spans an era both imperial and metric in its values. As a result, measurements are given together in metres and feet, kilometres and miles; however, in the cause of smoother reading, the figures have been rounded off where possible (and in certain instances, the original numbers were approximate). Various precise figures are provided in the table of Antarctic data at the end of the book.

INTRODUCTION

SOMEHOW it seems appropriate that Captain Robert Falcon Scott, his name ever-synonymous with Antarctic exploration and Antarctic tragedy, should also have been the first to ascend the Antarctic skies. At the edge of the Great Ice Barrier on 4 February 1902 he went up in a reconnaissance balloon named *Eva*, which had been obtained from British Army stores. Nineteen cylinders were needed to fill the bag with 240 cubic metres of hydrogen gas, and once the wind dropped and after mending several tears, it was readied for taking 'the owner' (as they called Captain Scott) aloft.

Captain Robert Falcon Scott

'The honour of being the first aeronaut in Antarctica, perhaps somewhat selfishly, I chose for myself', he recorded in the diary of the Discovery expedition. From a winch placed on the ice, his men paid out the wire cable which allowed *Eva* to reach a height of 500 feet (150 metres), at which point the nervous 'aeronaut' commented: 'As I swayed about in what appeared to be a very inadequate basket and gazed down on the rapidly diminishing figures below, I felt some doubt as to whether I had been wise in my choice'.

Sir Ernest Shackleton

An unbelievable world of glittering white awaited him: on one side the undulating snowy face of the Barrier, reaching endlessly towards the far southern horizon; on the other a deep blue sea littered with the fragmented pack ice and the drifting fortresses of mighty icebergs.

When Scott's inexperience caused the balloon to rise abruptly by another 300 feet (90 metres), the explorer's upward journey may well have ended in a more immediate Antarctic tragedy. 'I heard the word "sand" borne up from below', he wrote, 'and remembered the bags at my feet. With thoughtless inexperience I seized them, wholesale, and flung them out, with the result that *Eva* shot up suddenly and, as the rope tightened, commenced to oscillate in a manner that was not at all pleasing'. However, he hung on until the rocking ceased and after an hour's observation signalled the crew to haul him down.

Next to go aloft was Ernest Shackleton, another man destined for leadership in the heroic age of polar exploration. Shackleton, who served as a sub-lieutenant from the merchant marine in Scott's first expedition, was also about to make a mark on history: from his precarious perch in the swaying

Deflating *Eva* after Scott and Shackleton's observation of the Great Ice Barrier in February 1902. The balloon was never used again; *Discovery* is moored behind, with seal carcass hanging from the rigging.

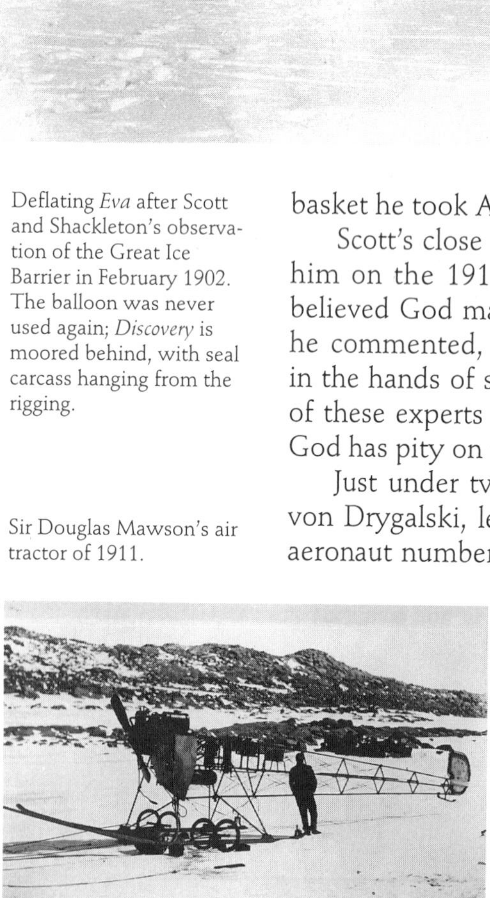

basket he took Antarctica's first aerial photographs.

Scott's close companion, Dr Edward Wilson, who would perish alongside him on the 1912 march from the South Pole, seemed of the school that believed God made angels to fly, not men. 'The whole ballooning business', he commented, 'seems to me to be an exceedingly dangerous amusement in the hands of such inexperienced novices as we have on board . . . if some of these experts don't come to grief over it out here, it will only be because God has pity on the foolish.'

Just under two months later, on 29 March 1902, scientist-explorer Erich von Drygalski, leader of the 1902–03 German expedition, became Antarctic aeronaut number three. With his ship held fast in the pack 90 kilometres (56 miles) from the coast of Kaiser Wilhelm II Land, Professor Drygalski went ballooning to an altitude almost twice that of the Britishers. 'It's so warm up here I can even take off my gloves', he reported to his crew over the telephone attached to the basket. Emile Philippi, a fellow expeditionary, made the next ascent to take a series of memorable pictures.

Sir Douglas Mawson's air tractor of 1911.

Professor Ferdinand von Mueller, the eminent Melbourne botanist and Antarctic protagonist, had told a meeting of the Royal Geographical Society back in 1886—'no future polar exploring expedition should be without an experienced aeronaut'. Yet ballooning had its limitations, for observations were anchored to one point, were very much subject to prevailing weather and, once the gas supply was exhausted, the deflated envelope had to be stowed away. Wobbling in the wind on the end of a thin wire cable, these fragile gas bags nevertheless delivered a singular lesson which would endure far beyond the aeronaut's passing phase; if a man wanted to see the length and breadth of Antarctica, he must take to the skies.

A year after Scott and Drygalski's exploits, the Wright brothers launched their aeroplane at Kittyhawk, U.S.A. Dr Wilson would not have been overly impressed at that historic flight, for in another comment that proved wide of the mark, he exclaimed: 'When polar exploration becomes possible to a flying machine, its attraction to most people will be finished'. In fact the flying machine was to change the face of Antarctic exploration — and never would the attraction fade.

When the British and Colonial Aeroplane Company, of Bristol, offered Captain Scott a Zodiac monoplane for inclusion in his 1911 expedition, the offer was declined on the grounds of being 'too experimental'. However, had he taken the Zodiac, one wonders if it might have flown out beyond One Ton Depot to save the luckless leader and his dying companions, Wilson among them. Scott did hope to employ wireless telegraphy, but found the equipment too cumbersome for his expedition to manage.

In the lee of an iceberg north of Princess Elizabeth Land, Mawson's more successful aircraft, a de Havilland Moth, is prepared for take-off in 1931.

Looking down on the vessell *Gauss* during Erich von Drygalski's ascent on 29 March 1902. The German balloon reportedly went almost twice as high as that of the Britishers.

The lesson of reaching for the sky was not lost on that other giant of the south, Douglas Mawson, whose career would reach from the heroic to the mechanical age of Antarctic exploration. Mawson was first to utilise wireless telegraphy to communicate from the Antarctic, and he planned to be first with an aircraft.

In fact it was Kathleen Scott, the bohemian sculptor wife of the British explorer and an early woman flying enthusiast, who offered to find Mawson 'a good aeroplane

Flying above the Beardmore Glacier, an American C-124 Globemaster heads for a parachute drop at the South Pole Station.

and a good pilot'. However, when he left her side at the Hendon air show of May 1911 to talk with Shackleton, she regarded his action as ill-mannered and his disinterest in her aviation promise as ungrateful. She added, 'the man is an ass'. Not an altogether surprising outburst, perhaps, because the Scotts regarded Shackleton as an upstart rival (not 'navy', of course) — and Mawson had declined an invitation to join the second Scott expedition. The Vickers company supplied Mawson with his REP monoplane for the 1911 Australasian Antarctic Expedition. It was a typical 'strings and wire' contraption of the era, with open cockpit, exposed crisscross struts, minuscule motor and big propeller. But on a practice flight at an Adelaide racecourse, prelude to a proposed series of fund raising flights for AAE's coffers, the plane's wings suffered irreparable damage. Not wholly dismayed, or perhaps wanting to redeem some of his investment, Mawson decided to use the flightless craft as Antarctica's first air tractor — a role in which it proved to be short-lived and fairly useless.

Kathleen Scott

Antarctica's pioneer aviators pose with the Lockheed Vega aircraft in which they began flights above Graham Land in November 1928. Their leader, Australian-born Sir Hubert Wilkins, is second from left.

Flying was no longer considered a funny business after World War I. The fragile craft that had worn the roundels or iron cross of battle was now sufficiently powerful and proven to commence a twentieth-century revolution in the way society looked at time, travel and distance. Furthermore, young men with wings demanded the chance to pursue the skills they had learned in dog-fighting or straffing over the Western Front. With a fledgling industry backing them, they were ready to start airlines, to carry passengers, mail and parcels; to race, to offer joy flights and resort to daredevil stunts to win public support. And they volunteered to take the aeroplane to distant frontiers where ship or land vehicle could not easily venture, whether over desert, jungle or ice.

Lincoln Ellsworth, pioneer of trans-Antarctic aviation, at his first camp during the long flight of November 1935.

Of the icy domains, Alaska and the Arctic were first to lure the new breed of aviators; but after air conquest of the North Pole and its surrounds, eyes turned south to the greatest challenge of all — to Antarctica, where lay 90 per cent of global ice.

George Hubert Wilkins, like Mawson a South Australian, led the aerial assault upon the frozen continent. November 16, 1928, should rank with other memorable dates in the calendar of man's conquest of the world around him. On that little-recognised day, Wilkins in his Lockheed Vega, with Carl Ben Eielson at the controls, took off from a rough airstrip on Deception Island and flew, albeit briefly, above the southern ice. Other flights by the pair soon followed, and the age of Antarctic aviation began.

Left: Admiral Richard E. Byrd. *Right*: Professor E. von Drygalski

Wilkins was one of the most outstanding explorer adventurers Australia ever produced. Son of a sheep farmer, he was engineer, cinematographer, reporter, World War I hero ('the bravest man I ever met', said General Monash), secret agent, submariner, pilot, navigator, expedition manager, government adviser. His exploits covered both North and South Poles and no horizon went unchallenged.

Wilkins' path through the clouds was soon followed by airmen-leaders of the next age of Antarctic exploration. Best known among them were the Americans, Richard E. Byrd and Lincoln Ellsworth; Mawson again, from Australia, with his air force crews; the Norwegian whalers and their spotting planes, and from Germany, the Luft Hansa men and their big flying boats. Pilots whose names belong to that early polar hall of fame include Eielson, Crosson, Balchen, Hollick-Kenyon, Campbell, Murdoch, Douglas, Schirmacher, Wahr and Riiser-Larsen.

A Russian IL-14 aircraft ferrying expedition members from Mirnyy.

The heady excitement of flying the Antarctic skies induced explorers, or the governments directing them, to unleash a rash of territorial claims upon the 14,000,000 square kilometres (5,400,000 square miles) of that empty con-

Australian Beaver and Auster aircraft meet during a depot supply run at King Edward Gulf during the 1950s.

tinent. Under instructions from Whitehall, Wilkins dropped the Union Jack to reassert Britain's claim to the disputed region of the Antarctic Peninsula (Graham Land). Norwegian whalers raised the flag on behalf of King Haakon, at one stage in potential conflict with Australian aims. At Adolf Hitler's direction, the Schwabenland expedition spiked swastika emblems into the ice and claimed part of Norway's territory as a Nazi domain. Byrd and Ellsworth both frequently dropped, or raised, the Stars and Stripes, marking out the huge Pacific sector of Antarctica for the United States. We have the comic episode of Wilkins paddling ashore to proclaim Australian territory while his employer, the millionaire Ellsworth, was above him in the plane dispensing the American flag. Congress, incidentally, has never ratified the United States' territorial claims in Antarctica, nor have they been discarded.

World War II put but a temporary halt to the southern adventure. However, as with the aftermath of the Great War before it, the end of World War II released a Pandora's treasure of technological achievements, particularly in aviation, navigation and communication and in a host of scientific disciplines, including a better understanding of how man could survive under extreme climatic conditions. Two years into the peace, the aviators were back

Against the backdrop of Mount Erebus, an Operation Deep Freeze LC-130 takes off from Williams Field, McMurdo Sound.

The era before aviation: An ice grotto frames *Terra Nova*, and pack ice surrounds the ship during Scott's 1911 southward voyage.

in Antarctica. Never in global history had the aeroplane dominated exploration as it was now to do. Jet-propelled, high-flying, long-range, capable of landing on skis and of vastly improved instrumentation — over the coming decades it was to supply explorer and scientist with unique and indispensable wings in probing the mysteries of the seventh continent. Indeed, the use of the aeroplane would prove finally that Antarctica was a continent and not a giant archipelago held in an icy grip.

An icebreaker leads a tanker carrying aviation fuel into present-day McMurdo.

So a fascinated world would learn of the spectacular achievements of the Russian airmen, of Britain's trans-Antarctic flight, of the missions flown by Argentines and Chileans, and of the massive American airlift known as Operation Deep Freeze. They would penetrate to the furthest corner of the Antarctic mountains, touchdown on the chilling heights of the plateau, fly many rescue missions and untold numbers of supply missions, even through the darkness of the Antarctic night. All of this took place above that 'great white terror' that is the coldest, windiest, driest, loftiest continent on earth: the most remote, the most uninhabited and as many an aviator would find — some to survive, others to perish — the most hostile.

◀ Views of historic McMurdo Sound: Scott's 1911 hut at Cape Evans; expedition members at mid-winter dinner; and the preserved hut today.

The early aviators might look for whales that could be killed and turned into oil. They raised the flag because of hints that much wealth lay beneath the ice cap. The militarists among them sometimes spoke blithely of air or naval bases along the forbidding coast. Their brave achievements in the sky reflected an age when uninhibited exploitation and territorial ambition were not seen as peculiar.

One could properly say that the coming of the modern aircraft has helped to settle a different age upon Antarctica. It is one of international treaty, cooperation in science, free exchange of data and an expressed desire for environmental integrity. But who can tell what more distant times will hold? The riches of Antarctica, the food chain of the polar seas, the known or suspected mineral deposits in the ground beneath the ice, and the assumed reserves of off-shore oil...none of these will go away. So, realistically, who can tell what demands may be made by a changing world upon that most beautiful, peaceful and unharmed continent?

Regretfully, the great flights that opened up Antarctica are all accomplished and aviation across the South Pole has become a more regular and routine affair. The private flyers have arrived and in the South American sector, at least, airborne tourism is an ongoing business. 'Regretfully', we say, because in man's apparent subordination of Antarctica to the comings and goings of the aeroplane lies the very seeds of exploitation.

A memorable and historic flight...one prosecuted with the highest competence.

— *Dr P. G. Law*

Prepare for crash landing.

— *Commander Fred Gallup*

1

FOR THE HELL OF IT

At the conclusion of the pioneering flight from Australia, the U.S. Navy LC-130 *Adelie* with fuel almost exhausted, waits on the Byrd Station skiway. Behind it is a 7,110-kilometre (4,420-mile) journey via the South Pole.

I remember holding a piece of cardboard over my head and trying to bury myself among the survival kits and sleeping bags. The crew knew the drill better; they had pulled on hard hats and belted themselves to the rear seats. It was the end of the first direct flight from Australia to the South Pole. We were coming in for a crash landing.

We weren't landing at the Pole itself. It was far too cold for us to land our 70-tonne Hercules at the bottom of the world; we'd never get off again. Minus 67°C (–90°F) when we opened the hatch for dropping the mail and newspapers to the twenty-two men living in blizzardly isolation at Amundsen-Scott Station. Nor were we at McMurdo Sound, site of the main United States base in Antarctica, though it was supposed to be our ultimate destination. Williams Field (named after the first American to die at McMurdo) had been ruled out, reporting an 85-knot crosswind on the skiway and failing visibility.

Instead we were headed 900 kilometres (560 miles) across the wilds of the Rockefeller Plateau, making for Byrd Station, the Americans' 'city of science' hidden beneath the ice cap.

Two navy flight crews manned *Adelie* for the long journey to Antarctica. Commander Fred Gallup, in full uniform, stands in the centre of the group.

Normally, no one in their right mind would want to fly to Byrd with winter barely over. Can we make it? Lucky, if we do. Not because there was anything wrong with our original fuel and weight computations; the U.S. Navy crew led by Commander Fred Gallup, who heads the VX-6 Antarctic aviation detachment, had been doing their sums for the past four months, practising for this day. But planning presupposed a regular 8,000 metre (26,000 foot) cruising altitude (give or take a few thou), and no crazy detours. Fuel reserves now are running low, the mountain crags seem barely beneath our wings — we're flying unpressurised.

Did I tell you how we lost cabin pressure? Why we began to go wobbly at the knees, talk funny and me to write all squiggly in my reporter's notebook? The culprit is that mail drop over the South Pole a few minutes before. The side hatch was open only for about 30 seconds, but long enough for rime ice to form around the frame, instant condensation when the heated air inside the cabin met the cold blast outside. The hatch seemed to close, but it didn't, not for the last few centimetres. Leaking pressure, the Hercules climbed back through 5,500 metres (18,000 feet), which is when things turned nasty.

Emergency procedure up on the flight deck. Fred Gallup (thank heavens he was breathing oxygen) smartly brought us down to a level where we didn't want to vomit; an oxygen cylinder was broken out and, like members of an oriental opium gang, we took turns to suck from the mask. Just about this time, one of the crew started crawling on all fours, not gone giddy but purposefully attaching a cargo chain to the drop hatch and passenger door.

Conquering the Pole

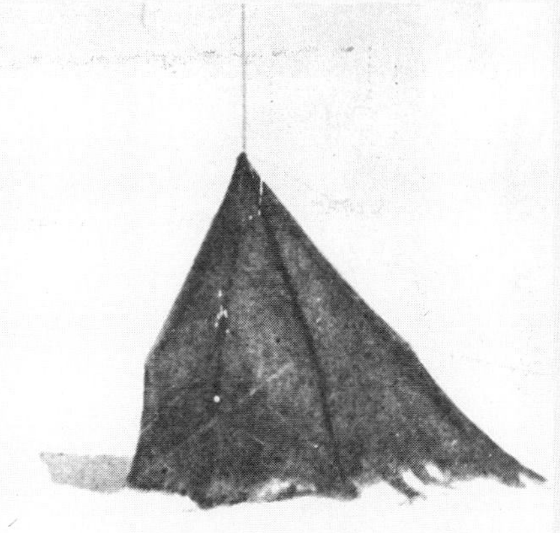

'And so, farewell, dear Pole. I don't think we'll meet again.'
Roald Amundsen, first at the South Pole, 14 December 1911.

'One gets there and that is all there is for the telling. It is the effort to get there that counts.'
Commander Richard E. Byrd on the first flight over the South Pole, 29 November 1929. He holds a stone from Floyd Bennett's grave which will be dropped as his flight reaches the bottom of the world.

An international group gathers at the South Pole to commemorate the 50th anniversary of the Amundsen and Scott expeditions.

'Great God, this is an awful place!'
Captain Robert Falcon Scott, second to the Pole, 17 January 1912.

We were told to belt up and stay put until he completed the exercise. With the pressure change, there was just a chance that the openings might suddenly pop and all of us could be sucked out... as sometimes happens to James Bond's enemies.

The snowy surface we've been flying above for the past seven hours might look white and soft from aloft, but it's not. It is creased with diabolical sastrugi — icy ridges hardened by the wind — and scarred with blue and sinister crevasses. No place for a free fall. No place to land. No place to live.

We level out and are approaching the vast chain of mountains that guard the rim of the polar plateau. If we're at 3,700 metres (12,000 feet), some of these unfriendly fangs must be just as high — and maybe more. We have a close-up view of every rock-faced peak, of every sheer ice fall, and of the vast serrated glaciers that wind through the ranges, one day to reach the edge of

Untrodden peaks and glaciers of the Trans-Antarctic Mountains lie beneath *Adelie's* flight path on the long haul from Australia to Byrd Station.

the Great Ice Barrier where the mighty tabular 'bergs are born.

Fine view, but no place to land. Half an hour away from the Pole, our course is changed for Byrd Station. We're flying further and lower, and using up the fuel reserves. Worse is to come.

Rear Admiral Jim Reedy, commander of the Navy's Antarctic support force known as Operation Deep Freeze, a very American name, sits up there on the flight deck beside Fred Gallup. Reedy has dearly wanted to make this flight. 'Dear David', he wrote while en route to New Zealand, 'am counting on you to keep it quiet until we are ready to release the news ...I intend to fly in from Melbourne and if possible pass over the Pole and back to McMurdo. Weight is quite critical ...but send me your clothing and hat and shoe sizes. If we can fit you in, would you like to come?' I replied 'Yes please!'

Why did I say, 'Yes, please!'

Rear Admiral Jim Reedy at *Adelie*'s controls while preparing for the flight to Antarctica. The co-pilot and plane commander (*above*) carry out a pre-flight study of available navigation aids.

Reedy is an adventurer in aviator's rig. He wears the ribbon of the British Flying Cross. In World War II he commanded the squadron in which Joseph Kennedy, Jr, was one of the pilots. Reedy had to visit old man Kennedy and tell him of his son's last flight. Some say John Kennedy would not have been the candidate for presidency if his big brother had survived.

'We regard the crossing between Australia and the South Pole as the last great long-distance flight to be made on this earth between two continents', is how the admiral announced our venture to the press. And then, to a deep and meaningful inquiry I hear him quip: 'Ah ... for the hell of it!' Last season he pioneered the Cape Town–Pole–McMurdo flight which covered 7,520 kilometres (4,700 miles) in 14½ hours, non-stop. Reedy described it as 'a routine flight'. (Not like *this* one, I bet he's thinking.) For 1964, his last year in the Antarctic command, he's planned this big aerial fling. We fly in across the Pole from Australia. Then another C-130 comes in via the Pole from Punta Arenas in Chile, that'll be 4,660 kilometres (2,900 miles) in 11½ hours, while a third C-130 commences the regular 'milk run' of 3,860 kilometres (2,400 miles) from Christchurch, all of us scheduled to reach McMurdo at about the same time in late September, which is asking a lot of Antarctic weather.

We're leaving the mountains behind. The immense glistening ramparts of the Queen Mauds, the La Gorce and the distant Horlicks. To get across Mt Johansen we climb to 5,300 metres (16,000 feet) and the oxygen bottle is passed around again to keep us sane. Sobering to ponder that ours are among the few eyes privileged to view this remote corner of Antarctica in all its startling, forbidding grandeur. Amundsen came this way, first to reach the Pole, dog-sledging on the surface, and Scott and his plodding, tragic band followed. Away to the left was Mount Fridtjof Nansen, rising almost to 4,300 metres (14,000 feet), and named by Amundsen after the great Norse explorer, his own polar hero. Further off lies the vast Beardmore Glacier, a name that Ernest Shackleton bestowed in honour of his backer. Shackleton, 'the boss', who had the guts to turn back just 155 kilometres (97 miles) short of being first man to the Pole. And on the horizon to the right, the marvellous chain of the Horlicks named, of all people, after the malted milk king who contributed to Richard E. Byrd's historic exploits that stirred the hearts and minds of all America. But since then, except maybe for a Deep Freeze flight, who else has passed this way ... who else to gaze down upon the tortured surface of the Robert Scott and Leverett Glaciers, to see the beginnings of the gigantic slab of the Ross Ice Shelf ?

This is my second Antarctic excursion with Admiral Jim Reedy. Last time it was aboard icebreakers; our ship, USS *Glacier* of 21,000 horsepower, led the earliest convoy ever to reach the McMurdo Sound. Somewhere in the Ross Sea pack we had a collision with the thin-hulled freighter following in our wake. Not quite of *Titanic* proportions, but a collision at sea all the same. The admiral had been asleep, and after a while emerged from his cabin blinking. 'What was the bump?' he asked. 'Ah, just an oversized bergy bit, Admiral,' someone replied. No one was willing to say what.

There's always the sniff of adventure when Jim Reedy is around, he of the tufty red hair and beguiling Irish grin. Unlike a Deep Freeze predecessor, Admiral George Dufek, he hasn't been twice dunked in Antarctic seas; instead he's taken it upon himself to don a scuba suit and go swimming with the seals in that weird world of half-light beneath the ice crust on McMurdo Sound.

Aviation history in polar flight

From DAVID BURKE, the only journalist on the flight.

BYRD STATION, Antarctica, Friday. — Aviation history was made today when a United States Navy aircraft completed the first direct flight from Australia to the South Pole.

The giant, ski-equipped Hercules transport had covered 4.420 miles from Avalon, Victoria. in 15 hours 39 minutes — the longest flying time ever known in Antarctica.

It reached the South Pole, 3,600 miles from Melbourne in exactly 12 hours, with outside temperatures at minus 85 deg. farenheit.

Bad weather at McMurdo Sound caused a last minute change of flight plans after leaving the Pole.

Rear-Admiral James R. Reedy, Commander of Operation Deep-Freeze on board the aircraft. ordered the course changed to Byrd Station, 900 miles further east.

At Byrd the Hercules landed on a 14000ft. snow strip, with heavy chains holding the nose ski, gear in position following failure of the automatic locking device.

The pilot, Fred S. Gallup brought the 65-ton Hercules to a skilful halt with the main skis bearing the weight of the plane.

Twenty-two men who staff the lonely Amundsen-Scott Scientific Station stood in swirling ice fog to receive a 50-lb. mail sack parachuted to them as the Hercules passed 500ft. above the South Pole.

The surface temparature at the Pole was minus 64 deg. Fahrenheit and the chill swirled into the Hercules for the brief 15 seconds the hatch was opened to drop the parachute.

Dr. Phillip Law, Director of the Australian National Antarctic Research Expedition, representing the Australian External Affairs Department on the flight, had his first sight of the Pole, where the base is almost entirely hidden by snowdrift beneath the surface of a blizzardly, desolate plateau.

Last great long flight

Inside the Hercules' belly huge metal tanks the size of a locomotive boiler carried 3,600 gallons of fuel required to nearly double the normal capacity of aircraft for an epic flight.

At Byrd Station Admiral Reedy said, "We regarded the air crossing between Australia and the South Pole as the last great long-distance flight to be made on this earth, connecting two continents.

"That was the challenge and I am glad we took it."

Bad weather at McMurdo yesterday caused a postponement of two other long distance Navy Hercules flights — one from Christchurch and the other across the Pole from Punta Arenas, in South America.

As Director of the Australian National Antarctic Research Expedition, Dr. Law congratulated Rear-Admiral Reedy on the completion of the first flight from Australia to the South Pole.

Antarctica is the loftiest continent on this globe. It is like a great upturned saucer, of 1,800 metres (6,000 feet) average elevation and rising to around 4,200 metres (14,000 feet) in the region of the Pole of Inaccessibility in eastern Antarctica. Now we've crossed to western Antarctica and we're flying above one of these limitless ice deserts, that of the Rockefeller Plateau, another name left behind by Admiral Byrd in tribute to a powerful friend. Byrd's early aircraft were over this area through the 1930s and the turn of the '40s, leaving behind the Edsel Ford Ranges, the Wrigley Gulf, Cordell Hull Bay, Executive Committee Range and, after a man who owned the New York Yankees, the Ruppert Coast. Byrd and his crews dropped the Stars and Stripes at numerous locations, he named the whole vast Pacific sector Marie Byrd Land after his wife, and submitted to the State Department that the region should be claimed as United States territory — an action still awaiting Congressional blessing.

A report from Byrd Station tells of the arrival of the first flight.
Right: Deep Freeze chief meteorologist, Commander Ken Allison, examines the trans-ocean route to the Pole.
Below: Behind a crew member is the 3,600 gallon auxiliary fuel tank which fills the cargo space.

At last, with the mountains well astern, there's a plateau surface on which we might reasonably land if the fuel shortage brings us down. Lincoln Ellsworth, the restless millionaire, and his Canadian pilot Hollick-Kenyon managed to survive during their epic journey across Antarctica in 1935 when they ran out of gas. They finally camped at Byrd's old headquarters of Little America until rescue teams arrived — an Australian government party from the west, and from the east almost simultaneously, Ellsworth's own vessel, the *Wyatt Earp*, commanded by another indomitable Australian aviator-explorer, Sir Hubert Wilkins.

The memory of all those courageous men who lived to tell the tale sure gives you heart. Why don't I write a book about them, some day: providing there is a 'some day'? Anyway we've been lucky enough to get this far. First

A Mobiloil tanker pumps extra fuel to the LC-130 in the last moments before take-off from Avalon airfield, outside Melbourne.

of all, McMurdo's adverse weather report almost ruled out the try for the Pole from Australia. Then, after consultation with his chief aerographer, Commander Ken Allison, the admiral's decision was to push on and we all went down to Avalon airfield, on the Geelong Road outside Melbourne. 'Why pick Avalon to start from?' I asked, knowing of airfields closer to the city.

'Well,' the Admiral replied thoughtfully, 'with all this fuel aboard, there's not too many houses around here, and if we came down . . .' Ask a dumb question. The rest of the answer was unsaid.

The Hercules awaited us, all silver fuselage, four big Allison turboprops and high orange tail — 'survival orange', according to the Americans. Juliet Delta 318 is an LC-130F, configured for Deep Freeze operation, with long, fat skis slotted over its wheel landing gear and the name *Adelie* on the cockpit nose. We have a double crew of 14 men, plus the admiral and the two Australians, Dr Phil Law, head of the Antarctic Division, and myself, the lone reporter.

A message arrives from Paul Hasluck, Minister for External Affairs. It reads: 'Your flight across the South Pole from Melbourne to McMurdo Sound will be the first from Australia to the Antarctic mainland. On this historic occasion I send you all best wishes on behalf of the Australian Government'. Phil Law and I say hear-hear! We're rather proud to be the two Australians who will share this slice of aviation history. The amount of fuel aboard lifts our confidence, JD318 is well equipped to come to grips with history. Our wing tanks carry about 7,000 gallons (31,500 litres) of JP4; within the fuselage, a huge cylindrical tank of almost the proportions of a locomotive boiler, holds another 3,600 gallons. Of course there's fuel enough to get us, via the Pole, to McMurdo Sound . . .

Down to the end of the runway, the Mobil truck follows, topping up our tanks right to the take-off moment. Our fuel load is 68,000 pounds (31 tonnes) our all-up weight 156,000 pounds (70 tonnes) which is 10,000 above the recommended. But with all four Allison turboprops making a fearful roar, we do it comfortably, wheels up little more than halfway down the long runway. At six o'clock on a pleasant spring evening we're over Port Phillip Bay, climbing steadily above Bass Strait, across Tasmania and heading south, into the clouds.

We drone on all night, which is a polite way of describing the ear-shattering noise of the turboprops. We're doing a steady 480 kph (300 mph), altitude somewhere around 8,500 metres (28,000 feet). Sleep is fitful on rudimentary bunks slung along the vibrating cabin sides. Three hours beyond Tasmania, through the inky darkness ahead, the Antarctic hangs out the welcome sign; I wake Phil Law and from the flight deck we watch the eerie blue-green curtain of the aurora beckoning us south.

A slouch hat is a memento of the stop-over in Australia for the crew member checking radio equipment.

At 12.20 a.m. and 2,900 kilometres (1,800 miles) from Avalon we cross the Antarctic coast; a dim sheet of white far below marks our entry to Australian Antarctic Territory. Reedy is reaching his first objective, to overfly the South Magnetic Pole which we're doing right now at 145° East longitude. Mawson, Edgeworth David and McKay were the first to raise the flag at that elusive point on our globe, when they went south with Shackleton in 1908. One of Antarctica's best yarns is spun around Professor Edgeworth David, then aged over 50, falling into a crevasse close by their camp, only hanging on by his finger-

Pre-flight checks of fuel system controls and tail section (below) on the tarmac at Avalon.

Byrd station, the unscheduled final destination of the flight from Australia, is situated at an elevation of 1,525 metres (5,000 feet) on the plateau of Marie Byrd Land. Scientists at the observatory have their huts built inside a series of tunnels excavated in the ice cap (*below*) and covered with sections of arch roofing (*left*).

tips and too polite to ask Mawson (who was in the tent changing camera plates) to hurry up and rescue him. 'All right, Mawson, don't rush, just when you're finished.' Somewhere below, too, is the Mertz Glacier Tongue, a gigantic outpouring of the ice cap, named after the second man to die with Mawson on their ill-fated push from Commonwealth Bay in 1912. Lieutenant Ninnis had been first to perish, down a crevasse with his whole dog team and sledge and never seen again. And then poor Xavier Mertz, the Austrian mountaineer, wasting away on the sledge, dragged by Mawson across the ice; dying remote, frozen, helpless.

The radar altimeter tells of a steadily rising plateau surface beneath our wings: 1,800 metres (6,000 feet) :2,100 metres (7,000 feet) as we head across the ice dome that rises through Wilkes Land and reaches forever towards the Pole. We cross the 77th South parallel, the latitude on which lies Vostok, the Russian station established at the coldest inhabited place on earth; –89°C (–129°F) in the dead chill of August, before the sun returns.

I guess our course is in the right direction, forever south. The navigators, Lieutenant Wright and Sergeant Hester, are poring over their astro calculations, taking star shots and plotting our grid progress, relying entirely upon the celestial bodies with no landmarking help from the radar.

Did I tell you about the radar? Not more than an hour out of Melbourne, the radar went 'out'. Don't ask me what 'out' means because when you're a privileged guest, it's not good manners to ask nosey questions about what is 'out' with 'out'. I just heard the admiral mumble something

Byrd Station skiway—a welcome stop after crash-landing procedure at the close of the marathon flight. Crew members inspect the faulty wheel-ski gear which had held together as *Adelie* set down on the rough snow surface.

Admiral Reedy (*inset*) opened the new Deep Freeze exploration season with his flight into Antarctica.

about 'the Navy's paid for all this fuel, I ain't for dumping it and turning back'.

Dawn was an orange fireball, straight in the eyes of the flight deck. The polar plateau, now rising above 2,600 metres (8,000 feet) takes on a weird rose-purple glow and the ice-fog clouds traversing it assume massive boomerang shapes, as if sign-pointing the direction of the Pole. At our altitude of around 7,000 metres (23,000 feet), we have visibility for 320 kilometres (200 miles) which is why, far on the left (port) horizon we can sight the saw-toothed peaks on the eastern rim of the polar plateau. Ridge upon ridge, range after range, they parade for us in a cold pinkish light; another rare treat for human eyes.

The GCA and TACAN at Amundsen-Scott station, to repeat the navy idiom, like our radar are also 'out'. Across the featureless white blanket of the plateau, who can expect to pinpoint a minuscule base held in a snowy embrace! Nothing seems to perturb the admiral. He sits there, firm-jawed, eyes searching the horizon, and tells Fred to have them build a bonfire. Fire on the snow — at the South Pole? What a joke. But they get our radio message, and somehow they manage the impossible. As we begin our long, slanting descent from 96 kilometres (60 miles) out, at the bottom of the globe a

New Flight To Pole

From Our Staff Representative

MELBOURNE, September 30.

The first aircraft to fly direct from Australia to the Antarctic is due to reach the South Pole at 6 a.m. EST tomorrow.

On the ice, the 22 Americans who have been isolated at the pole scientific station since February will be waiting in a temperature of minus 65 degrees Farenheit, to receive their mail, dropped by parachute.

The aircraft is a US Navy ski-equipped Hercules transport plane which left Avalon airfield near Geelong late today on the record, 4,100-mile flight.

Rear Adml. J. R. Reedy, USN, commander of Operation Deep Freeze, is aboard the Hercules, with a 14-man crew.

He is due to reach McMurdo Sound at 9 a.m. tomorrow where he will open the Americans' 1964-65 programme of exploration and research.

With him is the Director of the Australian National Antarctic Research Expedition (Dr. P. G. Law), who is making his first visit to the South Pole.

Ocean Hop

The flight will take the Hercules across 2,000 miles of the Southern Ocean and vast uncharted areas of the Antarctic continent.

The discovery of mountain ranges and other geographical features may result from the crossing, which will be one of the longest ever made in polar aviation.

Rear Adml. Reedy, who has led Operation Deep Freeze for the past three years, said:

"The open space of water, and part of the Antarctic to the south of Australia towards the pole, has not been flown over before but we want to take a look at it.

"Although the Hercules cruises at 26,000 ft., we will be studying the Antarctic surface intently on our radar and a number of interesting findings may result."

Fuel Reserve

A 3,600-gallon auxiliary tank fitted to the interior of the Hercules will give sufficient range for the 14½ hour journey and a 2½ hour reserve.

However, headwinds of up to 100 m.p.h. could reduce the reserve and in emergency Rear Aml. Reedy could order the Hercules to make straight for McMurdo Sound.

The ski gear fitted to the Hercules makes it possible to set the 65-ton aircraft down on a reasonably level patch of snow.

One of the only two Australians on the flight is David Burke who is writing a story of the journey for "The Advertiser."

Over The Pole From Melbourne

(From N.Z.P.A. Special Correspondent, DAVID BURKE. Copyright.

BYRD STATION. October 2.

The United States Navy aircraft flight from Australia to the South Pole was described here today by Rear-Admiral J. R. Reedy as "the last great long-distance flight to be made on this earth connecting two continents."

Admiral Reedy, commander of the United States Naval Antarctic support force, was aboard the ski-equipped Hercules which landed today at Byrd Station on a 14,000ft snow strip.

"We regarded the air crossing between Australia and the South Pole as the last great long-distance flight to be made on this earth connecting two continents," Admiral Reedy said upon arrival at Byrd Station. "That was the challenge and I am glad we took it."

The Hercules covered 4420 miles from Avalon, Victoria, in 15 hours 39 minutes—longest flying time ever known in Antarctica.

It reached the South Pole, 3600 miles from Melbourne, in exactly 12 hours. The outside temperature upon arrival was minus 85 degrees Fahrenheit.

Bad weather at McMurdo Sound had caused a last-minute change of flight plans after leaving the Pole.

Admiral Reedy ordered the course changed to Byrd Station. 900 miles further east.

At Byrd Station the Hercules landed with heavy chains holding the nose ski gear in position after the failure of the automatic locking device. The pilot, Commander S. Gallup, commander of VX6 Squadron, brought the 65-ton Hercules to a skilful halt with the main skis bearing the weight of th- plane.

Twenty-two men who staff the lonely Amundsen Scott scientific station at the Pole stood in swirling fog to receive the 50lb mail sack parachuted to them as the Hercules passed 500ft above them.

Copies of the "Sydney Morning Herald" were among a few Australian newspapers dropped to the Pole base, which last received mail and papers eight months ago.

Surface temperature at the Pole was minus 65 degrees Fahrenheit. Chill swirled into the Hercules for the brief 15 seconds the hatch was opened to drop the parachute.

Dr. Phillip Law, director of the Australian National Antarctic Research Expedition, representing the Australian External Affairs Department on the flight, had his first sight of the Pole—where the base is almost entirely hidden by snowdrifts.

After leaving Avalon on Wednesday night the aircraft headed due south across the Southern Ocean with the aurora flickering eerie greenish white in the darkness.

The coast of Australian Antarctic territory was crossed at a point near the South Magnetic Pole, and at dawn the aircraft was flying into the eye of a returning summer sun which bathed the jagged peaks of the Western Mountains in a frigid orange glow.

Beyond the Pole the aircraft crew looked down on enormous snowclad peaks rising to 15,000 feet, and the immense breadth of the Robert Scott glacier.

Inside the Hercules, huge metal tanks the size of a locomotive boiler carried 3600 gallons of extra fuel required for this epic flight. This nearly doubled the normal capacity for the aircraft.

Battle by crew to refuel in Antarctica

From DAVID BURKE, the only journalist on the flight.

McMURDO SOUND, Antarctica, Friday. —The crew of the first plane to fly from Australia to Antarctica today battled in bitter minus 40 degree weather today to get the big ski-equipped Hercules transport back into flight.

The aircraft, after flying over the South Pole in an outside temperature of minus 85 degrees, was forced by bad weather to divert from McMurdo Sound to Byrd Island, 900 miles east.

A relief Hercules which had just arrived at McMurdo Sound was urgently diverted to the icy plateau with extra fuel.

With bitter winds at minus 40 degrees sweeping across the ski runway, crews from both planes struggled to lay a pipeline from one Hercules to the other in an operation which lasted a paralysing two hours.

The United States Navy aircraft, which had Rear-Admiral James Reedy, Commander of Operation Deep Freeze aboard, departed from Avalon, near Geelong, on Wednesday night.

It was forced by adverse weather to divert to Antarctica's Byrd Station after completing the parachute mail drop at the South Pole in minus 85 degree Fahrenheit temperatures.

This is the coldest temperature in which aircraft has ever crossed the Pole.

The flight to Byrd, 900 miles east of McMurdo, lasted 15 hours 39 minutes —the longest in the history of Antarctic aviation.

sickly, anaemic column of black smoke struggles against the polar air; but it's all the beacon we need.

The swoop on the Pole doesn't take all that long, at a sink rate of 915 metres (3,000 feet) per minute and with the plateau at this point being 2,800 metres (9,200 feet) elevation and all but the last few hundred of it being solid ice underfoot. So, at nearly mast height we buzz the good folk of Amundsen-Scott, open the hatch and tumble out a fat parcel of letters and Sydney and Melbourne newspapers — yesterday's news today, fellers. You don't see that much for all the effort; the outline of half-buried huts, figures clustered by them, the feeble glow of the bonfire, and on the radio the base leader trying to talk with us from down there, except that his voice sounds as though he's being throttled. No wonder. The temperature outside is –62°C (–90°F), and Reedy has two more records to his credit: the earliest flight ever to reach the South Pole, and the coldest.

Far too cold for us to land, of course, except that we might have eyeballed the place in a very unscheduled way. That was when the windscreen shattered. Did I mention the windscreen? One of the large panes at floor level on the left-hand side of the flight deck broke as we descended in the immense

Press reports of the flight from Australia, which was airborne for 15 hours and 39 minutes in completing a total 8,580-kilometre (5,330-mile) journey via the South Pole and Byrd to McMurdo Sound. A flight engineer (*below*) checks controls. Beyond the Australian coast, the route lies across a no-man's-land of ice and ocean.

cold above the South Pole; it went all 'crazed' as an automobile windscreen sometimes does when struck by a stone, but it held in place which is what they're designed to do. The alternative was a window that had disintegrated into little pieces and a coldest ever landing at the Pole, adding a record that Admiral Reedy would not really relish.

And so, having passed the parcel, we said farewell to the hardy inhabitants of Amundsen-Scott and, at that point on the bottom of the world from where all directions are north, began our return. Well, you know how the hatch iced-up and wouldn't close, and we found suddenly that we couldn't breathe. And then having the hatch and door chained fast, so we wouldn't do a James Bond. And then, 30 minutes away from the Pole, receiving the bad weather report from McMurdo and changing course for Byrd Station, the only alternative landing spot for us in all of Antarctica. And the peak-skipping flight across the mountains, so we could stay low enough to breathe at the cost of our fuel running out faster than computed. And with the worst yet to come.

FIRST AIR MAIL DELIVERY
AUSTRALIA TO ANTARCTICA
OVER SOUTH POLE

DEEP FREEZE 65

Byrd Station is located in a series of tunnels ploughed 10 metres (30 feet) deep into the ice cap. The huts and laboratories are located within the tunnels which have been roofed over, then covered with snow. The inhabitants of this 'city of science' lead their whole year surrounded by walls and floor and ceilings of ice. They need never see the sun, or the sky or the stars, unless they want to climb to the openings of the tunnels which in winter can be a trifle risky, as men in Antarctica can be blown away without a trace.

After two hours of flying across the Rockefeller Plateau, we approach the base, seeing only a few radio masts protruding above the surface, a couple of

Hercules JD318, otherwise *Adelie*, landed at Byrd with tanks close to empty. Engines are uncharacteristically silent as the big transport awaits the arrival of replenishment fuel from McMurdo.

smokestacks from the diesel power plant and an auroral observation tower. No one braves the cold to wave to us, because no aeroplane is expected for another month or more ... least of all not one carrying the admiral.

When we start flying in endless circles above Byrd's skiway (which finally brings out the blokes down below) and the chief mechanic produces a fat Lockheed manual labelled *Landing Gear* and laboriously starts thumbing through the pages: and we keep circling with the fuel reserve surely touching the bottom of the tank, that's when you start thinking oh-ohhh.

That super deepfreeze at the Pole really was murder, not to put too fine a point on it. Not only did the cargo hatch ice-up. So did the nosewheel-ski landing gear. Moisture in the compressed air lines has turned to ice, blocking vital valves. It, too, is 'out', which means the gear hangs beneath the nose of the aircraft like a broken foot. Not the sort of equipment to try your luck with in landing a hefty Hercules in the nether regions of Antarctica. Here they don't have a fire brigade. Don't have a rescue crew: don't have an ambulance: don't have anything.

Entrance to Byrd Station is through a tunnel driven under the ice. Snow from the frequent blizzards has to be cleared from the footway. The base is now reserved for 'summer season only' operation.

Next thing, trapdoors in the C-130's floor are pulled apart. One of the crew uncoils a very big metal chain (bigger than the one put on the doors so we wouldn't get sucked out), clambers into the aircraft's bowels and attaches a hook at the end of the chain to the elbow of the frozen arm — hey, aren't we just about out of gas — and 10 of us, all who can be mustered, lie on the floor, grasp the chain, dig our heels in and, like Volga boatmen, pull-pull-pull. The chain is clamped tight, but whether all this exertion actually helps is rather academic. After an hour and twenty-five minutes of going round in circles, Fred Gallup doesn't dare keep our *Adelie* aloft any longer. A bell shrills. His voice comes crackling over the intercom yet quite calmly. 'Prepare for crash landing'.

Last time I visited Byrd Station it was much more comfortable. And wasn't it only last night I was in sensible, warm, predictable Australia? I think about my wife and kids, they're probably having breakfast, getting ready for school. Why did I ever say, 'Yes, please'?

Byrd Station is situated on the 80th South parallel at a height of 1,525 metres (5,000 feet) but the depth of the ice beneath it is equal to twice the elevation. Everything is ice, including the 3,650-metre (12,000-foot) skiway, which is full of bumps and ridges, not having been used for eight months past. And it's fast coming closer.

'Hold on,' announces Fred. 'We're going in.' All the crew not needed on the flight deck have their hard hats on, belting themselves to the benches in the rear of the plane. And me with my trusty shield of cardboard, trying to burrow among the survival sacks and wondering what sort of a deadly projectile that 3,600-gallon (16,200-litre) tank will make when it breaks loose.

Accomplishment of Admiral Reedy's spectacular flights from South America, South Africa and Australia raised the question that commercial traffic might one day follow the south polar route.

Fred has the big plane almost standing on its tail as he prepares to take the landing impact on the main gear only, leaving the nose up in the air until the final possible moment. I can see the plateau surface racing by a window, rough and terribly unfriendly. 'Hold on ... ' This calls for a prayer! 'Mother of God, pray for us sinners now, and at the hour of our—' Hey, what am I saying!

Commercial flights to Antarctic?

From
DAVID BURKE
at McMurdo Sound, Antarctica

COMMERCIAL air routes across the South Pole are being discussed in Antarctica this week following the success of Rear Admiral James R. Reedy's record-breaking flight from Australia.

Admiral Reedy's flight, the first from Australia to the Antarctic, covered 4,420 miles form Avalou, Victoria, to Byrd Station in 15 hours 39 minutes.

His ski-equipped transport crossed the 3,600 miles from Australia to the Pole in exactly 12 hours.

Hailed as "the last great long-distance flight to be made on this earth connecting the two continents," it was joined almost simultaneously at McMurdo by another U.S. Navy Hercules flying-in from Punta Arenas in South America.

The second Hercules covered 2,900 miles from South America to McMurdo in 11½ hours, including time spent on a photo-mapping mission.

Between them, the two giant Navy planes in effect forged a 5,700 mile air link across Antarctica between southern Australia and the southern tip of South America.

Polar aviators now assembled here for the 1965 season of exploration and science believe that Admiral Reedy's accomplishment of his imaginative inter-continental fly-in plan will hasten the day of commercial air traffic to the Antarctic and across it.

Commander Fred S. Gallup, captain of the special "Operation Deep Freeze" Air development Squadron (and who plotted the historic Australia-Pole flight) said: "Trans-polar commercial aviation will follow the trails that are being pioneered across the bottom of the world.

"Jet aircaft, flying faster, higher and in longer hops than we have done, will cross the Antarctic to bring the nations of the Southern Hemisphere much closer together.

"At the rate civil aviation is progressing, the day of these services is much closer than we realise:"

Aircraft engineers regard the cold, dry Antarctic air as ideal for powerful jet engines. One expert said: "Science can find a solution to all the problems and stresses an aeroplane will encounter in Antarctic skies.

"Admiral Reed's plane on the journey from Melbourne, for instance, crossed the South Pole in temperatures of minus 90 degrees, F. — colder and earlier (on October 1) than an aircraft has ever reached the Pole before.

"New radio and navigation aids have been installed and ice landing fields improved and much more is known of the weather. Aircraft have penetrated the polar "night."

"These are the guarantees that give commercial aviation the OK to go ahead."

Mr. Philip M. Smith, the United States Antarctic Research Programme representative at McMurdo, believes that a Trans-Antarctic route linking Australia and South America is the one which will bring the best rewards.

"A glance at the map shows that there isn't a single direct flight route between Australia, South America and South Africa," Mr. Smith said. "Every air journey between these two continents, particularly Australia and South America, has to be made in an enormous 'zig zag' fashion that is costly in time and money and frustrating to the development of trade and tourism.

"Operation Deep Freeze has shown what modern airplanes can do in Antarctica — it is only a matter of time before the commercial operators catch up."

From Sydney to Buenos Aires, the Trans-Antarctica air route measures 6.400 miles, which is almost 2000 miles shorter than the trans-Pacific direct route proposed via Tahiti; it is less than half the distance of the only Australia-Sou h America route currently available, viat San Francisco.

Last year Admiral Reedy made the first direct flight across the Pole from Capetown to McMurdo — 4,700 miles in 14½ hours, with the link to Christchurch occupying another 2,400 miles and eight hours. Via the regular Cocos Is.-Australia route, the same journey would have measured 12,000 miles and at least 30 flying hours.

From Sydney to Capetown across the Antarctic is about 6,000 miles.

The development of the Deep Freeze airfield at McMurdo is a pointer to the future.

Apart from a 14,000 ft. skiway for the Hercules, the base has a 6,000 ft. ice runway, and a 7,000 ft. crosswind runway under construction, which can support the weight of a Globemaster and Super Constellation.

McMurdo field has GCA and TACAN, homing beacons and direction finders and a weather station that makes a 24 hour surveillance of Antarctica and Southern Hemisphere conditions.

Cold weather engineers are visiting McMurdo this season to conduct further snow and ice compaction experiments that are designed to make the runways impervious to all conditions and wind and melting.

McMurdo's store holds three million gallons of aviation petrol and turbo prop fuel

Already the Navy aircraft have made two emergency dashes to Antarctica during winter darkness without ill effect and lighting is to be fitted to what is normally a 24 hour-daylight field.

Thus, the gap between the possible and impossible in polar aviation is gradually being closed.

Jets have yet to set down on the field — that is something for the future; engineers speculate about the effect of jet exhaust on the ice.

Experts here say that the other venture which will bring commercial planes to Antarctica is opening up the 24,00 Christchurch-McMurdo "milk-run" to tourist business, which is forecast in many quarters.

which have been the
years.

Perhaps his tho
have been in line wi
the N.C.D.C., whic
that the Kingston
centre was not in
Plan, and so should
ted.

It might be well to
Minister that nine
the Department sub
that land in the Gr
area together with a
of Jardine Street, an
an auction sale for
leases.

These subdivisions
to investors at a c
premium, and mor
million was invested
velopment.

These people ha
look forward to in t
the present polic
N.C.D.C. continues
of Canberra.

By increasing t
population in the Ki
this excellent shop
will survive.

John
Kingston.

Varying p
of brea

Sir, — Isn't it abo
had some action on
price situation! Gr
are promised but lik
in Canberra words on
and no actions taker

I went into a
shop in Civic Centr
.bread — I boug
of a brand of star
bread which I alway
mally at the Ainslie
1/9½ a loaf (since t
ous 1d. was added) b
today I was charged
1/11 per loaf). Wh
extra 1½d. in Civic —
keeper or the manu

Why doesn't somec
definite statement
bread prices or pub
of the correct price
ous types of bread s
public can stand on
when making a pur
have some concrete p
price we should pay.

Pro Bono M
Ainslie.

VICE-REG

The Governor-Ge
Canberra yesterday n
an official visit to We
tralia.

The main gear touches the ice. More of a kiss than a hit. What a pilot is this man Gallup! Gradually, despite the awful rattling, the speed drops, the nose tilts forward and touches the surface. The chain holds... *it holds*. Fred has brought us in at 85 knots, just above the stalling rate, and not put the nose down until 40 knots. (These are the sort of figures you learn afterwards, which rather gives the plot away. Yes, there is an 'afterwards'.) We shudder to a halt and the engines go to dead stop, something they never normally do out here in Antarctica; a lesson on how low is our fuel. All together, we breathe out. The first flight from Australia via the South Pole has arrived. In minus forty, welcome to Byrd.

Phil Law and I congratulate the admiral. We congratulate Fred Gallup and each and every member of the bleary-eyed crew. And we congratulate each other. We're not just the first two Australians to have flown direct from the Sunburnt Country to Antarctica. We have survived.

'A memorable and historic flight,' says Phil, 'and one prosecuted with the highest competence...a remarkable demonstration of modern aviation technology applied to Antarctic transportation.' In an aside I hear him tell the admiral: 'The last time I crossed that stretch of sea we covered last night was in a small polar vessel, chartered by the Australian government. We spent 10 days of misery, rolling and pitching in a stormy ocean. Aboard your aircraft, after the take-off from Avalon, it took us just 6 hours and 24 minutes to cover the same distance'.

We camped in the sub-ice world of Byrd until a relief Hercules could be flown down from Christchurch and come, via McMurdo, with fuel for our empty tanks. Eventually we farewelled the troglodytes and flew back to McMurdo, our original destination.

Jim Reedy was happy to haul down his flag, justifiably proud of having made aviation history despite all the odds. Our flight had covered 7,110 kilometres (4,420 statute miles or 3,860 nautical miles) from Melbourne, across the South Pole to Byrd Station, being airborne for 15 hours and 39 minutes, in time the longest Antarctic flight on modern record. Including the final leg from Byrd to McMurdo, the total distance covered was 8,580 kilometres (5,330 miles) with the time aloft of 19½ hours.

He had pioneered the air route from Australia to Antarctica and set the multiple records of first direct flight over both the South Magnetic and South Geographic Poles, earliest flight ever to reach the Pole in the coldest-ever weather, and earliest flight to Byrd.

And the other remarkable thing about the journey was that we all came home again. Phil Law later wrote an article for a travel magazine in which he said: 'After many years of Antarctic experience, I had approached this journey as a pretty routine exercise . . . expecting little in the way of excitement. As it turned out the whole experience was full of incident and one of the really memorable episodes of my life'.

What a master of understatement.

A fuel line lies across the ice at Byrd to refill the tanks of JD318. The relief LC-130 has flown from New Zealand, via McMurdo, to enable *Adelie* to resume the final leg of the journey to Deep Freeze headquarters.

I rank him with the greatest…first man in history to discover new land from the air.

Vilhjalmur Stefansson of the indomitable George Hubert Wilkins

Graham Land

Panel indicates flight area

Deception Island

2

BROTHERS TO THE EAGLE

Dog teams are harnessed to the Lockheed Vega in which Sir Hubert Wilkins made aviation history in the skies above the Arctic and Antarctica.

On 16 November 1928 George Hubert Wilkins, son of a South Australian sheep farmer, and Carl Ben Eielson, an Alaskan bush pilot, took off from the volcanic sands of Deception Island, flew about for 20 minutes and then returned. So was made aviation, and Antarctic, history.

For seven years Wilkins, engineer, photographer and war hero, had been planning to bring an aeroplane to Antarctica. As an ultimate objective, he envisaged aerial exploration leading to the establishment of a string of observatories around the Antarctic coastline which would assist meteorologists to forecast and warn of the weather cycles that in bad times brought drought and ruin to men like his father. 'The probable seasonal conditions in Australia might be anticipated if observatories were established in the Ross Sea area,' he told a newspaper in 1920. 'With wireless communications, not only weekly predictions of comparative accuracy, but seasonal forecasts with practical certainty might be available.'[1]

Wilkins' entrée to the poles began when he accompanied Vilhjalmur Stefansson's expedition to the Canadian north in 1913. True to his style, Wilkins on at least one occasion saved his leader's life. He emerged from World War I with the Military Cross and Bar, awarded for bravery under fire, and with recognised ability as airman and navigator. They were just the qualifications for living dangerously at the poles.

Dr J. L. Cope, the physician and biologist who had served with Shackleton in 1914–17, invited Wilkins to come with him to Graham Land as deputy leader of the high-sounding British Imperial Expedition of 1920–22. He intended to buy 12 surplus bombers from war disposals and leapfrog his way to the South Pole.

The doubtful distinction of Antarctica's most incompetent expedition surely belonged to Cope. The planes were never purchased. He rowed with the Norwegian whalers who provided his transportation. His mismanagement almost cost his three-man party their lives. He forgot to take material for a hut, or a cooking stove, and his main rations seemed to consist of boxes of donated crème de menthe lollies. Wilkins endured the fruitless expedition for a season and then got out.

Undaunted and full of energy and enthusiasm at the age of 34, he found opportunity soon knocking again in an invitation to take two new Junkers aircraft on a flight to Antarctica — an offer he was on the point of accepting when Sir Ernest Shackleton cautioned him that to use German machines would be a very un-British act. Instead, said Shackleton, 'come fly with me' in his 1922 expedition which he hoped would navigate long stretches of the Antarctic coast.

A New Zealand pilot, Major C. R. Carr, had been recruited and an Avro Baby seaplane was waiting in Cape Town. But a change of plan left the aircraft sitting on the docks and the chance of Wilkins and Roddy Carr pioneering Antarctic aviation slipped away. Nor need Shackleton have worried about distracting Wilkins from setting off on a rival expedition, whether with German aeroplanes or not; for 'The Boss', that giant of three south polar expeditions, died in his bunk of a heart attack as his ship approached South Georgia.

Wilkins next proposed the Australasian Polar Pacific Expedition of 1925.[2] To fly from the Ross Sea across King Edward VII Land to Graham Land, he sought a loan of £15,000, most of which would be spent on an aircraft

The two men who wrote their names as air explorers at both ends of the globe: American pilot Carl Ben Eielson (*left*) and the Australian-born explorer, Sir Hubert Wilkins. Their Lockheed Vega cabin monoplane, *San Francisco*, carried them down the Graham Land Peninsula in the famous flight of 20 December 1928.

together with fuel and provisions. Despite local interest, the South Australian branch of the Royal Geographical Society appointed a sub-committee to raise funds, the money was not forthcoming. He had wanted to obtain a Dornier N25 from Amundsen's Arctic exploit, but the Norwegians turned him down. Never abashed, never set back, Wilkins switched his sights elsewhere. If Antarctica could not satisfy his restless ambitions, the top of the world offered a more substantial opportunity to have someone else pay to make flying history — which arrived in the shape of a commission from the North American Newspaper Alliance to report on unknown regions beyond the Arctic seas.

Stefansson introduced Wilkins to a quiet young American of Norwegian parentage, known to the Eskimos as 'Brother to the Eagle'. He was Carl Ben Eielson, aged 26, a former U.S. Army flier with the rank of lieutenant and now an Alaskan bush pilot who almost daily flew through blizzardly weather and landed his ski-plane in the roughest places. In trust and temperament the two men proved to be ideally suited and over a period of three years from 1925 they would achieve some memorable Arctic flights. Together they survived crashes, forced landings, miscellaneous injuries, falling into freezing water and endless trudges home across the snows.

The Arctic exploits climaxed in the great journey of April–May 1928, when they took a little Lockheed

Wilkins' many exploits made world news and won him important support for his polar ventures — including a valuable contribution from the Vacuum Oil Company.

'The runway ran in three directions, with two sharp turns', wrote Wilkins of the improvised volcanic cinder strip which they named Hoover Field. The whaling station of Deception Island lies in the distance.

Vega high-wing monoplane from Point Barrow in Alaska to the Norwegian Island of Spitzbergen, for a flying time of 20 hours and 20 minutes across a distance of 4,000 kilometres (2,500 miles), most of it above uncharted northern wastes. Pioneers of the first aerial crossing of the Arctic from the New World to the Old, the pair were hailed as heroes on their return to civilisation. In Oslo, Berlin and Paris, medals and trophies were theirs. In London a knighthood awaited Wilkins who, because his first name was also that of the reigning monarch, chose to be called 'Sir Hubert'.[3]

Fame won at the top of the world inspired Wilkins again to chase his dream of being first to fly an aeroplane across the other end of the earth: about Wilkins a saying had been woven that the man had the ability 'to make his dreams come true'. As an Australian, he turned for help to Major R. G. Casey, an official at the High Commission office in London, pointing out that Commonwealth support for his expedition would do much to assist Australia towards gaining a chain of meteorological reporting stations around the Antarctic perimeter. Casey, who was known for his deep interest in Antarctic matters, tried to extract £10,000 from the government purse but the hard-headed Federal politicians refused.[4]

Fortunately for Wilkins, the United States' outlook was more encouraging. The American Geographical Society voted in his favour, the Detroit

Ben Eielson receives the good wishes of Captain Marius Hansen, of their Norwegian transport, *Hektoria*. 'What do you think?' said Wilkins to his pilot. 'Whatever you say', Eilson replied. 'I thanked God for the courage of my companion', Wilkins added before they took off into an unknown sky.

Aviation Society, which had been one of his Arctic backers, opened an appeal, while the millionaire publisher William Randolph Hearst subscribed $25,000 for exclusive press and radio reports; the new age of aviation must cater for the new age of broadcasting, too.

Now that Australia had dropped out and the Americans were in, Wilkins prepared to concentrate his operation on Graham Land, or the Palmer Peninsula as anyone in the U.S. camp must call it. Deception Island in the South Shetlands would be their base, as it had been for the disorganised Dr Cope of seven years earlier. From here, if a suitable jumping-off point could be found in the shadowy region towards the Weddell Sea, it might be possible to achieve a major flight — not to the Pole, which Wilkins regarded as too much of a stunt at this juncture, but possibly across Antarctica, at a tangent to the coast.

Wilkins, who never renounced his nationality, carried a miniature Australian flag in the pocket of his flying suit.

Wilkins had reckoned on taking only one aircraft — the wooden-framed Lockheed Vega of Arctic fame which, in tribute to Hearst, now bore the name *Los Angeles*. The smart little machine was fondly described by Wilkins as

> a beauty, a bird of paradise compared with the clumsy-looking one I had flown . . . It had no flying wires or exposed controls to offer wind resistance — simply a sleek, shiny, bullet-shaped body coming to a sharp point at the nose, with a trim radial engine and a shimmering wing extending outwards from the top of the fuselage like the wings of a soaring seagull. (Thomas: 201)

Despite Wilkins' faith in the single monoplane, his backers insisted on two aircraft for the sake of safety, which posed no problem to Wilkins' cheque book. Immediately he ordered a second Vega to the identical Jack Northrop design, which the Lockheed people built at cost, recognising the publicity value to be gained. The second aircraft they named *San Francisco*; at the same time Lockheed took in *Los Angeles* for a complete overhaul.

The Vacuum Oil Company of Australia donated $10,000 in product value. The Norwegians of the N. Bugge Hektor Whaling Co. agreed to provide transport to the ice as well as accommodation; for Wilkins, no expensive shore or winter bases! For the aircraft they obtained a short-wave radio made by the San Francisco house of Heintz and Kaufman; weighing less than 50 pounds (25 kilograms) it would give them long-range communication and, by holding down the key, they gained an added bonus of a direction-beacon, allowing the home base operator to trace their progress. Ben Eielson joined as chief pilot and, on his recommendation, Wilkins engaged a second intrepid Arctic aviator by the name of Joe Crosson, who had the first open-cockpit return flight between Fairbanks and Point Barrow to his credit. Their mechanic was Orval Porter, an old hand from the 1926 flights, and Victor Olsen, a Norwegian, was radio operator.

Five men in all — which was exactly how Wilkins wanted to run his expedition, mean and lean but never short-changing his men in pay or on vital equipment. The pilots were to receive US$500 a month, plus expenses, the mechanic and the radio man $400 and $200 respectively. Ever conscious of the need for a good team relationship, especially after the Cope debacle, Wilkins paid the expedition funds into a bank on which would be automatically drawn the monthly payroll and expenses for the duration of the expedition. He wanted his men to have the security of knowing their wage was assured, regardless of achievement or what might befall the leader himself.

The Wilkins-Hearst Expedition (sometimes known as the Hearst-Wilkins Expedition) sailed from New York on 22 September 1928. In October they left Montevideo with the two aircraft loaded aboard the 16,000-tonne whaling vessel *Hektoria*, a converted White Star liner which for the next five months would furnish Wilkins and his men with living quarters of faded first-class comfort.

Before leaving their last port of call on the Falkland Islands, Wilkins said he had received a confidential message from the British governor, authorising him at the direction of the Foreign Office to make territorial claims on behalf of His Majesty's government. Britain's claim to the Falklands Island Dependency, of which Deception Island was a part, sat unhappily with the South American neighbours who believed this region of Antarctica rightfully to be theirs. As *Hektoria* ploughed southwards into the ice, leading five catcher boats, Wilkins the diplomat, with American aircraft and under American patronage, now was called upon to play his part in reaffirming British sovereignty.

Deception Island is a mere speck of land nestling, as if for comfort, close by the western rim of the Antarctic Peninsula at 62° South latitude. Sharp-peaked mountains and bare and black rocky cliffs, like the remnants of a broken tooth, rear above the sheltered harbour that fills a once fiery volcanic crater.

Hektoria and her convoy tied up at the whaling station on 4 November. The Norwegians immediately set about reopening their dormant factory in

ANTARCTICA.

Flights Delayed.

MISHAP TO 'PLANE.

LONDON, Dec. 3.

Sir Hubert Wilkins, in a message from Deception Island, dated November 30, reported that a mishap to an aeroplane had forced another postponement of the expedition's effort to make an Antarctic flight.

"All day long," his message states, "we slaved against heavy odds, trying to get off the treacherous ice shore. However, it proved too much for us. Everything looked fine, but Deception Island is well named. Conditions are changing daily. Before we can fly again we must fit our waiting aeroplanes with skis and take the gasoline ashore in a motor boat, which the treacherous ice hitherto has prevented."

A second message, despatched on December 1, reads: "Marring a day of otherwise excellent progress, an accident, which was the climax of the transfer of two 'planes from the ship to the icefields, resulted in the 'plane Los Angeles damaging her propeller, and receiving a hole in one of the wings. Pilot Eielson received a ducking in the icy sea. This accident will delay aerial operations for a week.

"We took what we thought to be a fifty-fifty chance, but it turned out to be a 50 to 1 chance against the 'planes. With only a pilot and a few gallons of gasoline the Los Angeles rose in the air at 5:30 a.m. for the purpose of landing on the ice with its wheels, after which it was to be equipped with skis. The Los Angeles came down beautifully and taxied several hundred feet. Then the wheels struck a hole in the ice, through which the 'plane sank until the wings and the fuselage held it. The machine slowly nosed over. Eielson fell through the ice, but clambered out none the worse for the wetting. With the help of the Norwegians he jacked up the machine, slipped on the skis, and hauled the aeroplane to safety. We must overhaul part of the engine, which was immersed for two hours."

A later message from Sir Hubert Wilkins says: "The 'plane is now salvaged and is on the beach, little the worse for an unfortunate ducking. The weather is fine but treacherous. We are concerned at our inability to leave, but the actual salvage work has not worried us."

Newspapers around the world kept in touch with Wilkins' progress. The *Sydney Morning Herald* report of 4 December 1928 tells of Eielson's plunge in *Los Angeles* through the weakened bay ice.

Two modern Vega high-wing cabin monoplanes were purchased for the Wilkins-Hearst expeditions. *Los Angeles*, which had carried Wilkins and Eielson on their Arctic crossing, taxis on floats across the ice-free bay of Deception Island.

preparation for the summer slaughter. Wilkins, Eielson and the others turned to readying their two aircraft for the flights ahead. The Lockheed landing gear kit allowed them three options — rubber-tyred wheels, floats or skis. The wheels were the least desired choice, the floats could be suitable for flying off the coast, but skis would be the most useful in allowing them to penetrate the interior and to set down anywhere that the surface seemed reasonable.

As Wilkins looked around him, however, he realised something was emphatically amiss with the season on Deception Island. Thin and drifting ice filled most of the bay while recent rainfalls — it did rain on Deception Island — had washed snow away from the shores. The scene was utterly different from his visit with Cope in 1921; the icesheet covering the water had reduced to less than half the two-metre (seven-foot) thickness he expected to find. All of them agreed the Wilkins-Hearst Expedition could not have chosen a more inauspicious month to go flying at a most uninviting location.

Wilkins planned to explore the peninsula as far south as range, weather and safety allowed him. Such flights could be made on either of the three landing gear modes, except with wheels the payload would probably need to be reduced. Though he did not formally commit himself to it, the opportunity of achieving a really long newsworthy, indeed sensational, journey from the peninsula across to the Ross Sea 3,200 kilometres (2,000 miles) away, where Amundsen had set up his camp of Framheim in 1911, was always in the back of his mind. It was a plan that required the two planes, one to land and refuel the other for the final stage to the edge of the Great Ice Barrier. With wheels, such a venture was obviously impossible, not only because less fuel could be carried but once the aircraft set down they would probably never get off again.

In the meantime, the volcanic sands of the island's narrow twisting beach gave them a toehold for flying, albeit within the limitations of using the wheel gear. They cleared off some of the rocks, filled the most obvious depressions and on 16 November, Wilkins agreed they should take *Los Angeles* up. Carrying minimal fuel, Eielson flew about in circles; the weather looked threatening and within 20 minutes the plane was down again. Hardly to the dimensions of a Wilkins' grand plan, hardly deserving of champagne, but an historic first Antarctic flight notwithstanding.

Within a week, the twin Vega was ready for the air; it was Joe Crosson's turn to wheel *San Francisco* a few circuits above the island and bump back across the sandy strip. Emboldened by these initial excursions, on 26 November both planes went up, Eielson in *Los Angeles* taking off on his wheels from the bay ice which appeared to have thickened and Crosson flying *San Francisco* from the beach. Again they flew around the island, watching for any alternative strips, giving wide berth to the peaks and generally turning on something of a public relations show for the watching Norwegians.

Antarctica had quietly bared the first of many moments of terror that would await its aviators. When Eielson came in to land and touched down on the firm bay ice, *Los Angeles* skidded forward on its wheels, rushing him towards the edge where the surface was thin and brittle. The horrified watchers saw the aircraft plunge downwards, engine and forward fuselage splashing into the water, tail rearing in the air, held above the deep only by the edge of its wings.

Wilkins, Porter and Olsen rushed towards the plane, followed by the whalers who had further to run. They saw Eielson clamber from the cabin as *Los Angeles* sank lower into the chilly sea. Eighteen hours of toil finally retrieved the aircraft; with ropes attached to tail, wings and fuselage they hauled it back to solid land. The bay was found to be 400 metres (1,300 feet) deep at the point where Eielson crashed. Crosson, who had been circling the harbour, brought *San Francisco* safely back on the sand.

Wilkins was a man of modest disposition, though in his aims ever questing and ambitious. He was distinguished in bearing, tall and well built; as his hair receded he began to sport the dark shovel-shaped beard that would always be a feature of his later portraits. He had an even temperament and a ready, friendly smile; and despite how desperate his plight might sometimes seem, he had a healthy regard for safety, which helped to explain how he had survived into his fortieth year.

Yet even the leader's forbearance began to wear thin as the adverse weather continued to turn Deception Island into an aviator's prison.

The Wilkins-Hearst crew leaving Montevideo to begin the flights of 1928 (from *left*) — Joe Crosson (pilot), Sir Hubert Wilkins (leader), Carl Ben Eielson (chief pilot), Orval Porter (mechanic). Behind them, *Los Angeles* is lashed to the deck while the products of one of their sponsors are well displayed (in the foreground.)

Unwrapping the stored aircraft was an early task when Wilkins returned to Deception Island on his second expedition of Novemer 1929; Al Cheesman and Parker Cramer were now the pilots. Wilkins named a feature of Graham Land 'Cape Northrop' after the gifted designer of the Lockheed Vega which, in 1927, was the first machine to incorporate both a monocoque fuselage and cantilevered wing. Wilkins' *Los Angeles* was third from the production line.

December had arrived and temperatures remained unseasonably warm, once reaching 10°C (50°F) with steam rising along the shoreline from the long-silent volcanic core. There was no sign of thickening bay ice, no hint of impending snowfalls. Wilkins knew that by the month's end he could farewell his exploratory program for another year — provided his backers were still forthcoming.

They tried towing an aircraft to open water and flying away on floats. Hordes of seabirds immediately surrounded the taxiing machine, hurling themselves into the path of the propeller, making any take-off attempt suicidal for bird and man.

It had to be wheels or nothing, and maybe nothing if rough stones and cinders shredded the tyres of a laden aircraft. For 36 hours they laboured along the beach with tools borrowed from the Norwegians, pick and shovel, wheelbarrow and crowbar and sometimes with bare hands to rake the surface, lever away the rocks and fill the potholes. By the time they were ready to fly, Deception Island airstrip measured 700 metres (2,300 feet) in length, was 12 metres (40 feet) wide, included a couple of 20-degree bends and ended in a steep bank above the watery deep.

Following *Los Angeles'* dunking, *San Francisco* was their choice for the long flight. They filled the tanks with fuel sufficient for the powerful Wright Whirlwind radial engine to carry them 2,250 kilometres (1,400 miles) at a cruising speed of 200 kph (125 mph). Their emergency rations included biscuits, pemmican, chocolate, nuts, raisins and malted milk tablets. In the rescue kit was a block and tackle, should either of them need to be pulled from a crevasse in the event of a forced landing.

Crosson, who remained behind to fly *Los Angeles* in case of an emergency, with Porter and Olsen watched the bright little orange monoplane go racing down the beach in a series of bone-jarring bumps, shoot up the final rise and lift into the air, making for the harbour gap between the surrounding mountains. They guessed that a rather more historic moment than the previous circuits they had witnessed had just passed them by.

The flight that began from Deception Island at 8.20 a.m., five days short of Christmas 1928, signalled the start of a new chapter in the young and lusty flying age — that of the exploration of the last unknown continent from the air. To quote Professor Griffith Taylor: 'Just as 1841 and 1903 were wonderful years in Antarctic exploration, so 20th December 1928 was the most wonderful day, for in ten hours Sir Hubert Wilkins settled more problems and sketched more new coastlines than any other expedition had accomplished in West Antarctica'. The plan was to fly eastwards across the waters of Bransfield Strait and then head down the peninsula of Graham Land — the Antarctic Peninsula. Skirting the mountains that barred their progress to the left, Eielson took *San Francisco* to 1,830 metres (6,000 feet). But with the plateau behind the peaks rising still higher, Wilkins directed him to keep going south, flying in parallel with the peninsula's craggy spine.[5]

Newspapers frequently repeated Wilkins' call for the establishment of a chain of Antarctic weather observatories. 'I hope to make every effort to encourage the governments of the Southern Hemisphere to inaugurate an international weather bureau which would maintain permanent stations,' he said.

WILKINS'S PLANS.

Forecasting the Weather.

EFFECT OF POLAR ICE.

LONDON, May 5.

Sir Hubert Wilkins, who has reached London from New York, in an interview with the Australian Press Association, said that he was at present marking time until September when he would return to the Antarctic to pick up equipment stored at Deception Island.

In the meantime his immediate purpose was to visit France, Norway, and Germany, where he proposes to see Captain Bruns and Professor Berson, of Berlin, both members of the Aero Arctic Society, which exists for the establishment of meteorological stations within the Arctic circle. They aim at sending a new Zeppelin on an Arctic tour in the summer of 1930.

Discussing his own plans Sir Hubert said: "It must be recognised that the present work is of a preliminary character. The task which I have set myself involves 10 or 15 years' labour. After the completion of the geographical work this year and the making of one more trip to the Arctic I will be able to proceed with my real plans. My ambition is to establish 12 observation stations. With such a chain in the Antarctic for a decade it should be possible to forecast whether the seasons will be early or late, wet or dry.

"It has long been my theory that the Antarctic ice affects the weather in Australia, Africa, and the Argentine," he said. "This is supported by the United States Meteorological Society, which is now proposing to control the weather by redistributing icebergs of the Antarctic by towing them from one place to another and so promoting rainfall in the desired areas. A tremendous amount of labour is required, and also a close study of the distribution of the air currents."

Sir Hubert Wilkins will sail from New York in September to join the Norwegian whalers at Montevideo on their trip southward, and will reach his headquarters in November. He expects to commence his flight between December 15 and 20, when conditions are best. There will be two aeroplanes, and the party will again include Lieutenant C. B. Eielson.

It is proposed to explore 2500 miles of the coast between Graham's Land and the Ross Sea. Prior to setting out on the flight Wilkins will chart the detail of the country discovered last year, consisting of 1200 miles of coastline, 20 islands, one strait, and two channels. He points out that he was working 2500 miles distant from Byrd's party, but the next flight will bring him to Byrd's headquarters, thus joining up the work.

THE MAWSON EXPEDITION.

NEW YORK, May 5.

In an editorial the New York "Times" says: "Sir Douglas Mawson's outline of his second penetration of the Antarctic as a scientist gives promise, to those who studied his expedition of 1911-14, of still greater achievement."

Wilkins was busy with their navigation, with making notes for the press and photographing the scene on a hand-held Kodak 3A and two movie cameras. He sketch-mapped a distance of 65 kilometres (40 miles) in 20 minutes, knowing it would take three months by surface travel to record the same area. 'I felt liberated,' he wrote. 'I had a tremendous sensation of power and freedom.'

They droned above Hughes Bay, covered Gerlache Strait and neared the Danco Coast where Wilkins glanced up from his chart and motioned Eielson to take the Vega to 2,750 metres (9,000 feet) and cross the peninsula from west to east.

From within the closed and warmed cabin, they watched a magnificent unfolding panorama of rolling white-capped mountains, stark rock faces glinting green and black, shadowy crevasses that surely could swallow them, and immense ice-filled fjords intersecting the icy slopes. Whereupon Wilkins made another exciting diary note: 'For the first time in history, new land was being discovered from the air'.

Beyond the Antarctic Circle at 67° South they came closer to the surface and saw a group of the fjord-like channels cutting deeply between the mountains. To Wilkins these features were the support for his growing theory (but mistaken, as the work of John Rymill, a fellow South Australian, would prove seven years later) that the peninsula was actually divided into three major islands, making it an archipelago rather than an extension of the mainland. To one of these features he gave the name of Casey Channel, reflecting his friendship for R. G. Casey at the Australian High Commission in London. Another he called Stefansson Channel, after the man who had introduced him to the Arctic; to these he added the Crane and Lurabee Channels. On other features, names were freely bestowed as icy tributes to those who assisted with the expedition ... Hearst Land, Mobiloil Bay, Scripps Island, Lockheed Mountains and at the most south-easterly point, Cape Northrop after the Vega's gifted designer.[6] Inevitably they also marked the map with the Wilkins Coast and Eielson Peninsula.

Here the Vega is taxied alongside the ship and then loaded aboard. Wilkins, however, was frustrated in his objective of flying across Antarctica to the Bay of Whales.In search of better flying grounds, the 1929 expedition sailed further south along the peninsula aboard the British research vessel *William Scoresby*.

Against gale-force winds, Wilkins opened the hatch and dropped the territorial proclamation on behalf of the British government. Enticing mountains and plateau went on rolling southward to merge into the far horizon, but at 71°20' South, with their fuel gauge hovering close to the halfway mark, Wilkins reluctantly nodded it was time to turn around. They headed north across the vast Larsen Ice Shelf, still keeping to the east of the peninsula and filled with the satisfaction that their ten hours in the air had taken them across at least 1,600 kilometres (1,000 miles) of previously unrecorded Antarctica.

Storm clouds obliterated the horizon at the end of the journey. Wilkins' navigation said Deception Island must lie somewhere below, but a dark, boiling cauldron of vapour was all they could see. Eielson, forever cool at the controls, began to bank the Vega knowing that if they were above the island, somewhere in the same cloud mass must lie the sharp peaks of the guardian mountains. Tense moments went by as they watched a descending fuel gauge and tried to fix on an exact position. Abruptly, a parting of the cloud revealed the airstrip on Deception Island almost directly below. Eielson quickly sent *San Francisco* into a steep descent to get them down before the cloud again closed in.[7]

Wilkins, the Man

Of George Hubert Wilkins, the man who brought the aeroplane to Antarctica, a newspaper article once said 'he feeds on perilous adventure as a Child does on milk'.

Sir Hubert Wilkins: 'He feeds on perilous adventure as a child does on milk,' said a *Sydney Morning Herald* editorial of 14 November 1928.

During World War I he hung by his fingers from the basket of an observation balloon while a German aircraft straffed the gas-filled envelope above his head. For some unaccountable reason it did not explode and Wilkins hauled himself back into the safety of the basket; as he recalled, 'the hardest physical effort of my whole life'.

He was an enthusiast for airship travel but missed the final trip of the new British dirigible R38 which broke up over the Humber with heavy loss of life. During his Arctic exploits, after a shipwreck he survived for six days in freezing temperatures while marooned on an ice floe.

Of the number of crashes, forced landings, near misses, injuries and miscellaneous accidents that involved him, one almost loses count. As if in a replay of World War I, the aircraft on which he was escaping from Nazi-occupied France was machine-gunned by an enemy fighter — again, he survived.

Being the thirteenth child of a South Australian sheep-farming family obviously was no obstacle. He was born at Mount Bryan East, South Australia, on 31 October 1888. As a young student he secured a place to study engineering part-time at the School of Mines in Adelaide. However, photography became his absorbing interest, particularly the fairly new pursuit of cinematography. These qualifications were to write the passport to an amazing career which in an official biography is listed as war correspondent, polar explorer, naturalist, geographer, climatologist and aviator, to which might rightfully be added (apart from photographer) author, balloonist, war hero, reporter, secret agent, submariner and navigator.

Wilkins stowed away in 1908 and when off-loaded in Algiers found himself involved with a gang of desperadoes who were gun runners, kidnappers, drug dealers and operators of a spy ring. It was a swift introduction to life beyond Mount Bryan — the more so when as a 24-year-old, the Gaumont Film Company assigned him to join the Turkish side and report the Turko-Bulgarian war of 1912. His footage was reputedly the first ever taken in battle.

Wilkins had the uncanny knack of turning up in the remotest places. He was second in command of Stefansson's 1913 expedition to the far north of Canada. Having learned to fly an aeroplane in the meanwhile, he returned to Australia in 1917 to join the Australian Flying Corps with the rank of lieutenant.[8]

For him the impact of war, however, was not as aviator but official AIF photographer assigned to capture the grim and bloody reality of fighting in the trenches. Captain Frank Hurley, his superior officer who had gained fame in Mawson and Shackleton's expeditions, filled the controversial role of depicting battle through the eyes of a 'camera artist'. Together they were plunged into the Third Battle of Ypres, when at Passchendaele allied forces suffered 250,000 casualties. For fearlessly going into no-man's-land to rescue wounded soldiers, Wilkins won the Military Cross. In a later episode, he regrouped and temporarily led a company of American soldiers whose officers had been killed, an action which added a Bar to his MC. He was, in the words of the Australian commander, General Monash, 'the bravest man I have ever seen'.[9]

After his discharge, Wilkins entered the much publicised England – Australia Air Race of 1919, only to crash-land against the fence of a lunatic asylum in Crete. Next it was Russia, still gripped in the turmoil of the 1917 revolution, where he was assigned to report on the fighting and famine sweeping the country as well as gathering confidential intelligence for the British government.

Wilkins with (Sir) Charles Kingsford Smith, to whom he sold the aircraft which became known as the famous *Southern Cross.*

Behind all this derring-do, he gained a solid reputation as naturalist and ornithologist which in 1923–24 took him to North Australia on behalf of the British Museum, to collect rare native fauna and report on Aboriginal tribal life. He awoke in his tent one night to find marauding natives, in full warpaint, gazing down on him with their spears aimed at his stomach.

However, the time spent with Hurley on the Western Front rekindled Wilkins' interest in Antarctica; the visionary in him, always seeking new horizons, said this was the place where the aeroplane, allied with aerial photography, could reign supreme as the instrument of exploration. But he would have to make his name at the top of the world to find the fame to attract supporters for schemes at the other end of the earth. His Arctic flying, with his close companion Ben Eielson from 1925 to '28, earned them both a place in the aviators' hall of fame. Wilkins received the Patrons Medal of the Royal Geographical Society, the Morse Medal of the American Geographical Society and a knighthood from the King.

At the end of his first Arctic exploits, it is interesting to recall that to purchase the new model Lockheed Vega, he decided to sell *The Dakotan*, a heavy Fokker F7 tri-motor which had an unfortunate history; it had beheaded a young reporter who stepped too close to a spinning propeller, none of the pilots liked it and it was partly wrecked in a crash. But the big machine was repaired by Boeing and Wilkins sold it at half his asking price of £3,000 to an eager fellow-Australian who wanted to make the first air crossing.[7] Charles Kingsford Smith renamed the plane *Southern Cross.*

In a pause from his 1928–30 Antarctic exploits Wilkins paid a dollar for a surplus World War I American submarine, renamed it *Nautilus* and tried to sail beneath the ice to the North Pole. The aged submarine broke down and the venture failed, which earned Wilkins some unkind publicity: in reality, as so often happened, he was just a man ahead of his time. The submarine represented his last individual and private venture, from here on he accepted the post of manager to his friend and supporter, the American millionaire Lincoln Ellsworth, in an Antarctic association, ever full of drama and disappointment, that continued until 1938.[11]

Wilkins was essentially a 'big picture man' — questing, imaginative, innovative. Yet it would be doing him a gross disservice to portray his role peculiarly as that of explorer-adventurer, for throughout his career he was always responsive to the challenge of nature in its wildest environment.

Remembering his boyhood on his father's sheep farm at Mount Bryan and the recurring droughts which almost drove them from the land, he made his life's abiding goal the advancement of the science of meteorology. To this end he continuously campaigned for a string of observatories around the Antarctic coast which would radio their reports back to Australia and other Southern Hemisphere countries, to forewarn of changing weather patterns and assist in the perfection of long-range forecasting.

Towards the end of his days—he made his last visit to Antarctica in 1957 as a guest of Operation Deep Freeze—Wilkins had the reward of seeing one more of his dreams partly realised with the involvement of many nations in weather studies of the International Geophysical Year.

Wilkins always carried a miniature of the Australian flag in the cockpit of his aircraft. Though he settled in the United States and worked mainly under American patronage, and in World War II for the American government, he never surrendered the Australian citizenship of which he was intensely proud. Within his native land, unfortunately, the government could not afford him or, to be more brutal, was disinterested in his imaginative schemes, which rather reflected political attitudes towards understanding Antarctica.

At the New York celebration after his epic 1928 flight, he met a pretty young actress who, because she was also Australian, had been talked into handing him a bouquet. She was Suzanne Evans from Walhalla in Victoria (her stage name was Suzanne Bennett) and they were wed the following year. Despite Wilkins' long absences, they appear to have been a loving couple; they were childless but brought to the marriage the satisfaction of knowing that each supported the other in the achievements of their separate careers.

Perhaps it was the Australian in him that inspired Wilkins with an impish delight in playing David against an Antarctic Goliath. One cannot help but wonder whether he knew or cared about the consternation his slim expedition, being first in the field with aeroplanes, was causing on that other side of the continent where an expensive American contingent led by Commander R. E. Byrd had reached the Bay of Whales at the end of 1928.

Unveiling an Antarctic emblem at a party in New York hosted for Sir Hubert and Lady Wilkins by the Ford Motor Company. Wilkins' vivacious wife was the Australian actress Suzanne Bennett.

The episode is better understood from within the Byrd camp, where an anxious leader had every published word from the Hearst press radioed to him, and who sweated over the seemingly deliberate haziness of his rival's flight plans. Would Wilkins beat them to the South Pole? Would he fly across the unknown area where Byrd wanted to be first? Maybe the man from down-under enjoyed the game.

Wilkins was a spiritual man, religious in the less formal sense of the term, acknowledging dependence on a Creator, emphasised in his thankfulness for his many escapes from sure disaster. He once composed his own version of the Lord's Prayer and later on became interested in experiments with telepathy, about which a book was written.

Vilhjalmur Stefansson, the explorer who had first taught him the art of polar living and survival, wrote: 'Wilkins, the Australian I rank with the greatest...the first man in history to discover new land from the air, the first to demonstrate the feasibility of wheel and ski descents and take-off from pack ice remote from land...first to cross the Arctic by airplane, first to navigate a submarine beneath the floating polar ice....'

Wilkins died suddenly of a heart attack, aged 70, in 1958.[12] His ashes were taken on the nuclear submarine *Skate* and scattered at the North Pole.

The account of Antarctica's first exploratory flight best concludes with the final entry for that memorable day from Wilkins' diary: 'We had left at 8.30 [*sic*] in the morning, had covered 1,300 miles — nearly a thousand of it over unknown territory — and had returned in time to cover the plane with a storm hood, go to the *Hektoria*, bathe and dress and sit down at eight o'clock to dinner as usual in the comfort of the ship's ward-room'.

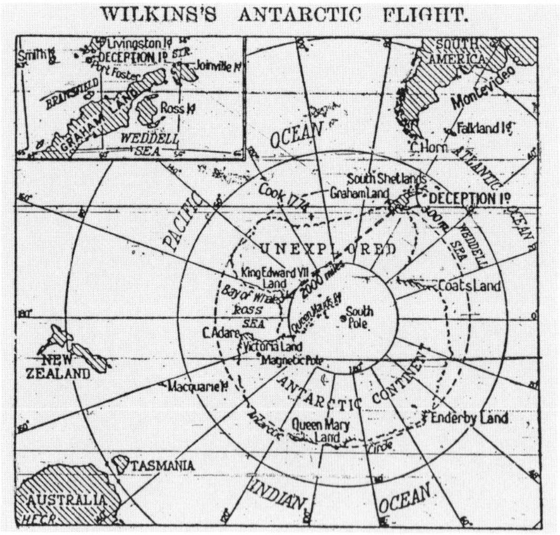

Finding a break in the cloud which led them to the airfield was one of those fortunate happenings — difficult to call them luck — that often sustained Wilkins' life in moments of danger. He was not a religious man in the formal sense, but he had an intense sense of the spiritual and a strong realisation of the Almighty, in whom he frequently professed his belief and his thanks. What's more, within an hour of their return, the storm over Deception Island intensified and continued to rage until the end of December.

Wilkins made one more flight before the aviation season closed; on 10 January 1929 his aircraft reached 400 kilometres (250 miles) to the south, following part of December's route to check on their sightings. With both planes dismantled and stored in the whalers' shed, they farewelled the Norwegians and joined a patrolling British warship, HMS *Flerus* to take them to Montevideo. The press reports Wilkins had been radioing to Hearst served them well, New York turned on another heroes' welcome.

WILKINS'S ANTARCTIC FLIGHT.

Newspaper map depicting Wilkins' proposed trans-Antarctic flight.

The second Wilkins-Hearst Expedition returned to Deception Island aboard the factory ship *Melville* in late November 1929. Their equipment now included an outboard motor boat, a caterpillar tractor and a Baby Austin automobile fitted with eight wheels and chains. The British government again authorised Wilkins to make territorial gestures on behalf of the Crown. To assist the expedition, which seemed only fair if he were being asked to carry the Union Jack, the Colonial Office voted £10,000 and the services of the Discovery Committee's research ship, *William Scoresby*.

With one plane loaded aboard *Scoresby*, a converted catcher, they sailed just below the 67th South parallel in a vain hunt for a better flying base. However, by using floats to take-off alongside the ship a number of flights were completed between December and February of 1930 but never leading to the opportunity of a trans-Antarctic venture. The most rewarding journeys were those of 27–29 December when the area known as Charcot Land revealed itself to be a large island, over which Wilkins duly parachuted the flag and document of proclamation in the name of King George V. The final flight of 1 February reached 73° South in the vicinity of Peter Island, but in terms of discovery returned empty-handed.

Wilkins' pilots of the second expedition were both experienced Arctic men, Al Cheeseman and Parker D. Cramer. Ben Eielson did not come south a second time, preferring the Arctic skies where he had obtained a mail contract.[12] While the expedition was reorganising on Deception Island, a radio message informed them that Eielson had taken off on a mercy mission to locate a stranded fur-trading vessel and had not returned. Shortly afterwards they heard that Joe Crosson had found the wreckage; Eielson had flown into a fog-shrouded Siberian hillside and was dead. The grieving Wilkins said he felt the loss of a brother — a Brother to the Eagle.

SOUTH POLAR FLIGHT

Wilkins's Great Plan.

(BY CAPTAIN J. K. DAVIS.)

[Captain Davis, now Commonwealth Director of Navigation, was chief officer of the Nimrod in Shackleton's expedition of 1907-9, second-in-command of Mawson's expedition in 1911-14, and commanded the Ross Sea relief expedition, which picked up the survivors of Shackleton's expedition in 1916.]

In thrilling regions of thick-ribbed ice;
To be imprisoned in the viewless winds,
And blown with restless violence round about
The pendent world.
Shakespeare (Measure for Measure).

Less than 300 years ago Australia was still within the vague region called by geographers the "Great South Land." Now an Australian, Sir George Wilkins, M.C. and Bar, Gold Medallist of the Royal Geographical Society of London, will be the first to attempt a flight by aeroplane across the South Polar Continent, the remains of the "Great South Land," from sea to sea.

The white area at the southern extremity of the globe still embraces a practically unknown region as vast as the whole of Australia itself. Men, it is said, go to the Polar regions to seek gain, fame, or knowledge. Sir George Wilkins can certainly be acquitted on a charge of going there for the first; he has no need of the second; so he must receive credit for attempting his trans-Antarctic flight with the genuine desire of acquiring knowledge.

A 2000-MILE FLIGHT.

The late Lord Curzon, speaking as president of the Royal Geographical Society in London, of the late Sir Ernest Shackleton's proposal to cross the Antarctic Continent in 1913, referred to it as "a Napoleonic conception." It is a similar undertaking that Sir George Wilkins has now set himself to accomplish. He will use a monoplane of special design in the place of dog-sledges, hitherto the only resource of explorers in these regions.

Few men have the mind to conceive, and the energy and courage to carry out, undertakings of such magnitude. The entry of an Australian into the list of those who, in these regions "set the goal above renown, and love the game beyond the prize," is something which should claim the attention of his fellow countrymen. Australia is never indifferent to the labour of her sons, but so little news has yet reached us from Wilkins himself that an outline of his plans as gathered from scattered notices of his intention is of more than usual interest.

Wilkins proposes to fly across the Polar Continent from Graham's Land to the Ross Sea, a distance of approximately 2000 miles, over territory which no man has yet seen. He has already proved his capacity for similar work in the Arctic, where for three years he struggled against hostile fortune before he and Eilson successfully accomplished their magnificent flight from Point Barrow to Spitzbergen. Wilkins left Monte Video (South America) on October 15, in the whaler Ronald, with two Lockhead Vega aeroplanes, fitted with Wright engines. One of them is the machine in which his Arctic flight was made. Carl Eilson is with him again as chief pilot, and the machines are capable of being fitted with floats, skids, or wheels.

PLAN OF OPERATIONS.

The Ronald will probably land the party at Deception Island (a whaling station in the South Shetland group) about the end of November. The two machines will be flown over about 70 miles of water to Graham's Land, and continue southward down the eastern side of this land, which is unknown, possibly mapping 300 miles of new territory in the first and preliminary step of his great flight across the Antarctic Continent. It is here at once that the aeroplane exhibits its superiority as a means of exploring the Antarctic. This particular region has always been unapproachable in ships.

Antarctic. This particular region has alwa been unapproachable in ships.

A suitable area for landing having be chosen, both machines will land at some co spicious point three or four hundred mi south of Deception Island. Further ferry flights will depend on discoveries made, a on local conditions. Eventually one mach will be filled with a full load of petrol, a Wilkins and Eilson will set out for the Ro Sea. Arrangements have been made for whaler, carrying supplies from Tasmania, meet them in that locality, on receipt of wi less instructions. The map published in a other column, shows the region the explore propose to cover.

UNKNOWN REGION.

So much for the plans. But what will ha been done if they are successful? While flight of this nature can only be a reco naissance, the map of the South Polar regio will show at a glance that nearly the wh of the route will be over absolutely unkno territory—territory which, moreover, h hitherto defied the efforts of the explorers every nation. Cook, Bellingshausen, G lache, and Charcot have carried the flags Britain, Russia, Belgium, and France respe ively southward in this region without be able to determine the nature of the land m that exists within and southward of the pa ice. That pack-ice has always barred appro by sea in this sector. If Wilkins is success he will not only have carried out a great f of aviation, but, more important, he will the first human being to look upon and descr for us one of the few remaining extensive u known portions of the world. He will ha made a definite contribution to geographi knowledge of first importance, which must n cessarily prove once and for all whether t lands believed to exist between Graham's La and King Edwards VII. Land are insular continental.

The hazards of such an enterprise are gre but if ever two men were well-equipped training and experience to undertake such flight, and to measure its risks, those t men are Wilkins and Eilson. In his n book, "Flying the Arctic," we get a glimp of some of the perils they encountered a the difficulties which they overcame in t northern ice. This gallant Australian h already shown how the sternest forces nature can be overcome by the courage, pow and firm resolve of man.

Like all polar explorers, Sir Hubert Wilkins depended on contracting with newspaper chains to raise money for his exploits. The American press baron William Randolph Hearst was Wilkins' chief supporter.

You must not forget that Wilkins is out to lick us…
don't forget that he was offered $50,000 by Hearst to beat us to the South Pole.

Commander Richard E. Byrd to Hilton Railey, his fund manager

3

LORD OF THE ICE

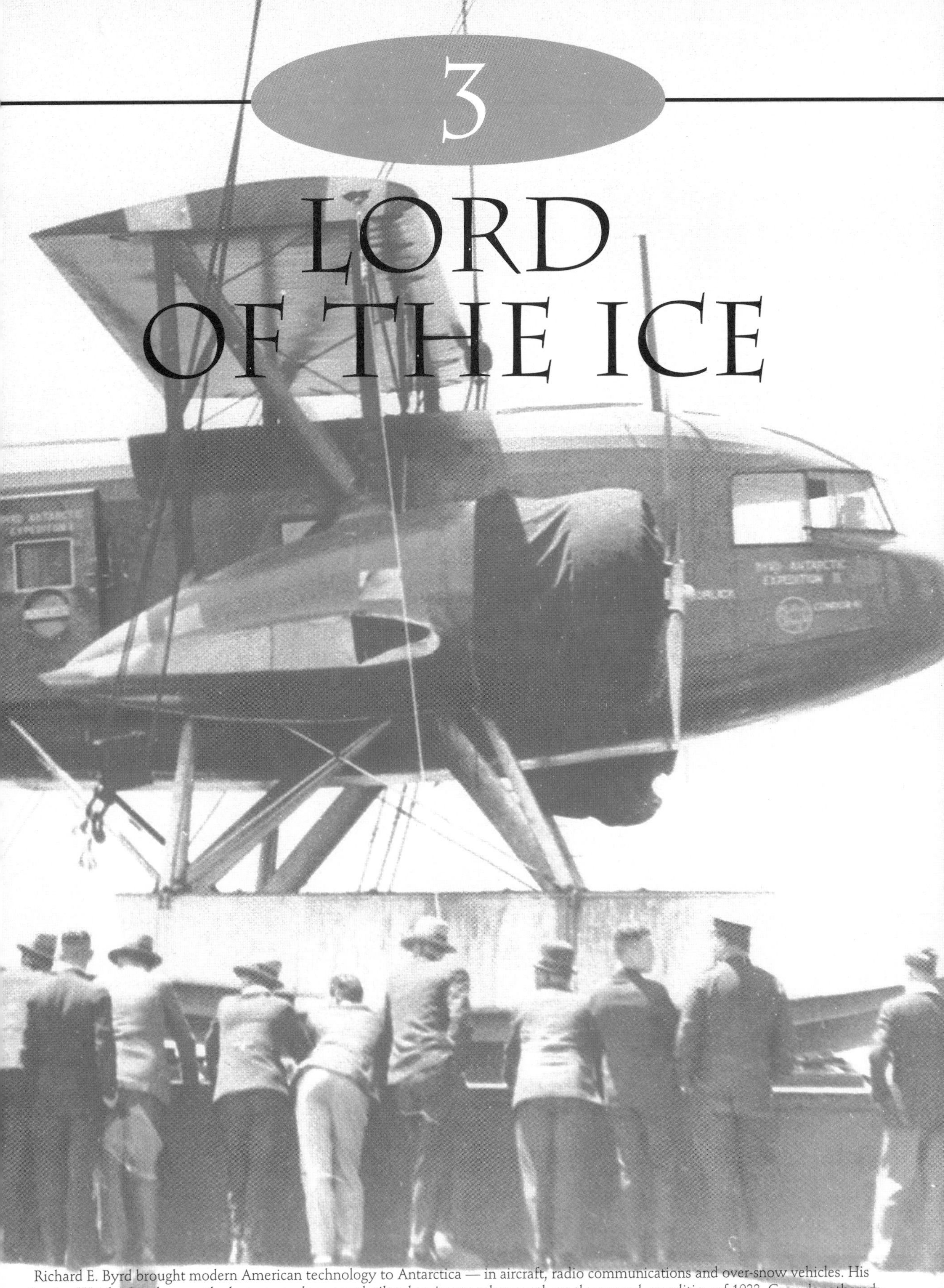

Richard E. Byrd brought modern American technology to Antarctica — in aircraft, radio communications and over-snow vehicles. His Curtiss-Wright Condor was the largest seaplane ever built when it was taken south on the second expedition of 1933. Crowds gathered in Wellington, New Zealand to gape at the big machine — named *William Horlick,* after the malted-milk magnate — with its 25-metre (82-foot) wingspan and twin 700-horsepower Wright Cyclone engines.

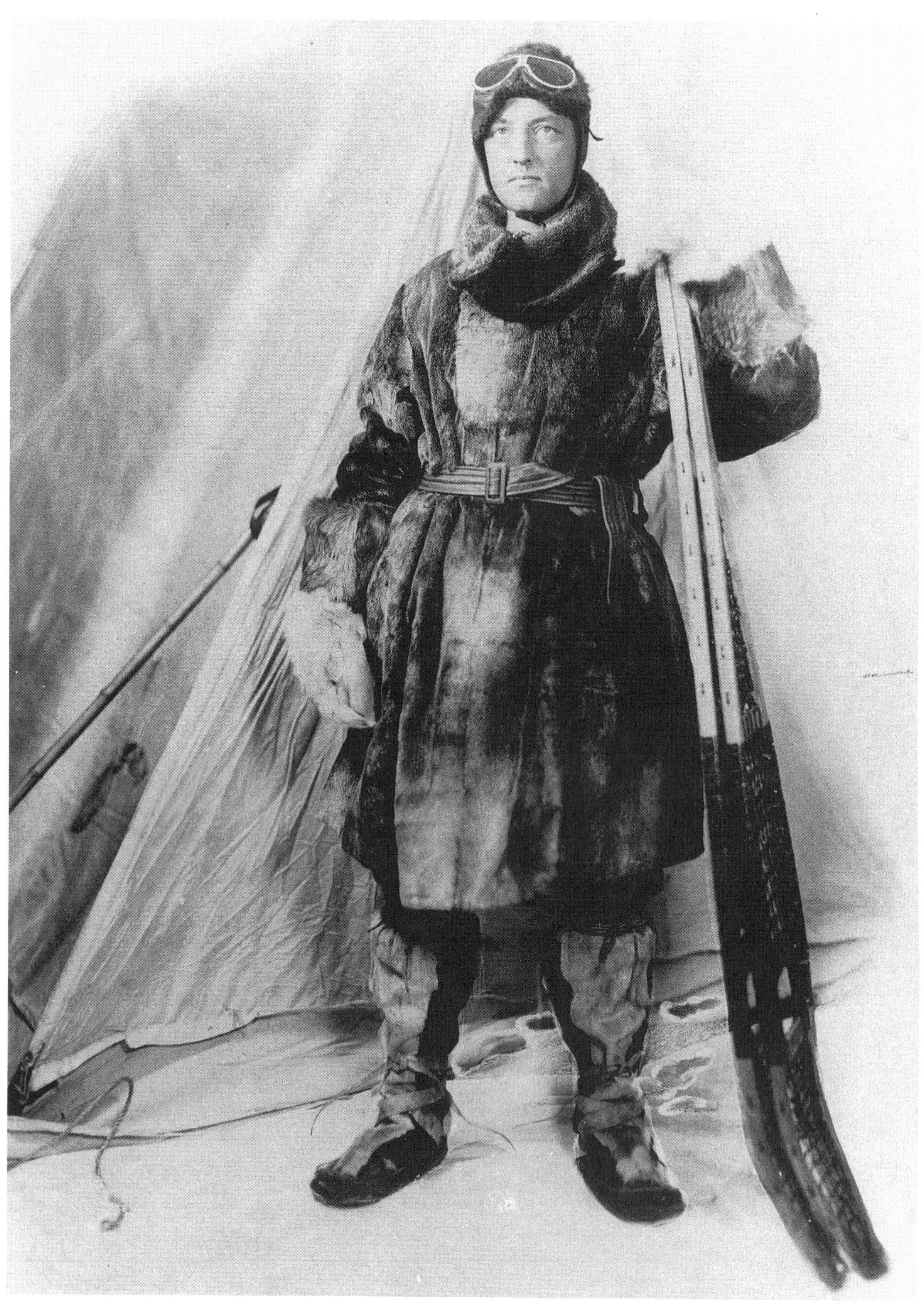

Ever a master of public relations, Commander Byrd stands in front of a studio 'tent' in New York, wearing his full sealskin flying suit. He holds a pair of snowshoes, to be used in the event of a forced landing.

Richard Evelyn Byrd's worst fear as his ships ploughed through the Ross Sea pack in the December of 1928 was that an Australian would beat him to the prize. The whole expedition buzzed with the rumour — William Randolph Hearst, the newspaper magnate, had promised their rival, Hubert Wilkins, a $50,000 bonus if he got to the South Pole first. 'You must not forget that Wilkins is out to lick us,' Byrd told Hilton Railey, his fund manager, 'and he is going to make every effort to beat us...'

Byrd, a commander of the United States Navy and national hero, acclaimed as first man to fly to the North Pole, could not abide the thought of losing. For his name, his career, his very bankroll, he could not afford it.

Drawing upon the generosity of friends like Edsel Ford and John D. Rockefeller, Jr, this slight figure, a Southerner with wavy hair, neat features and a formal manner, had spent nine months in raising almost a million dollars to finance the largest private expedition ever sent to Antarctica. Other heavyweights on his subscription list were the American Geographical Society, the National Geographic Society, Tidewater Oil, Todd Shipbuilding Yards and the New York *Times*, which paid US$60,000 for exclusive story rights, having its own reporter included with the expedition.

In June, in the midst of his campaigning for funds and bringing together all his men and ships, his planes, stores and tractors, the very worst news reached Byrd's office in the Biltmore Hotel, New York. The man once pitted against him to gain the North Pole first by air had announced he was taking aeroplanes to Antarctica. Wilkins, his rival, was deserving of respect. He was a seasoned polar aviator. He was now 'Sir Hubert', a man of stature. His team was small, mobile, equipped with very able aeroplanes, and William Randolph Hearst would surely drool over beating the New York *Times*. What was most worrying, Wilkins was leaving first.

The very size of Byrd's expedition might prove its own downfall. One of the old Arctic hands described it as 'too ponderous, too cluttered up with safety plans and specialised experts'. Yet for Byrd, through his upbringing and career, it was very hard to do anything but 'think big'.

The largest previous expedition south, Sir Ernest Shackleton's ill-fated Trans-Antarctic venture of 1914–17, set out when Byrd was a young cadet at Annapolis Naval Academy. Shackleton had no radio or aeroplane, either of which could have prevented disaster. The hero of the North Pole resolved to change it all. 'The dog sledge must give way to the aircraft; the old school has passed,' he announced to the press as his 83 men and their 100 dogs sailed from Hoboken, New Jersey, in August 1928.

Scene at Little America camp in 1929 as the Byrd expedition prepared for its first Antarctic winter. Snows gather around the aircraft and the three tall radio masts that will carry the story to a waiting American public.

The ships carrying the expedition were *City of New York*, a square-rigged vessel of 515 tonnes built in 1883, and a converted minesweeper of 800 tonnes named *Eleanor Bolling*, after Byrd's mother. Consigned as separate deck cargo to New Zealand were three high-wing monoplanes: a large metal Ford tri-motor, a single-engine Fairchild with folding wings and a single engine Fokker, all equipped with radio. Other radios were packed for use by the trail parties which would also have the use of the snowmobile, a Model A Ford on skis — the first automobile in Antarctica.

The Ford tri-motor was the aircraft which Byrd nominated to fly him to the South Pole. Edsel Ford himself had authorised, at Byrd's request, the fitting of the more powerful 525-horsepower Wright Cyclone central engine; adding the two wing-mounted Wright Whirlwinds gave a total output of 975 horsepower.[1] The aircraft had a top speed of 195 kph (122 mph), could heave aloft a seven-tonne bulk and was reputed to be the largest flying machine ever mounted on skis. Endurance was the tri-motor's major problem, as its range of 13 hours certainly demanded a refuel stop if they were to complete the 2,800-kilometre (1,750-mile) round trip. Another question mark related to its altitude limit of around 3,650 metres (12,000 feet). Byrd's men referred to the big all-metal machine as the 'tin goose'

Byrd's three mechanics, Demas, Bubier and Roth, beside the *Floyd Bennett*. The corrugated metal fuselage earned the Ford tri-motor the nickname of the 'flying washboard'.

Sir Hubert Wilkins and his men demonstrate their exhilaration on heading back to Antarctica in 1929. With Wilkins, from left, they are Parker D. Cramer (pilot), Orval Porter (mechanic) and Al Cheesman (pilot). It was a portent of the moment most feared by Byrd that Wilkins would beat him to the South Pole. 'Shorty' Cramer died in 1931 while flying the Atlantic.

or, because of its corrugated duralumin fuselage, 'the flying washboard'. Officially it was the *Floyd Bennett*, in tribute to Byrd's close companion and North Pole pilot who had died of pneumonia earlier in the year; had he lived Bennett was to be the expedition's second-in-command. Of the other two machines, both with 525-horsepower Wasp engines, *Stars and Stripes* was the name given to the Fairchild while the Fokker was *The Virginian* after Byrd's beloved home state. All three aircraft bore the legend 'Byrd Antarctic Expedition' painted along the fuselage.

The ticklish operation of unloading *Floyd Bennett* at the Bay of Whales. Byrd called the spot Ver-sur-Mer after the French beach where he had crashed in 1927 at the end of his flight over the Atlantic Ocean.

Rather than lose time in his slow-moving ships, Byrd crossed the Pacific in the big Norwegian factory ship *C. A. Larsen*, which they had contracted to batter a path for them through the Ross Sea ice. Byrd, now turned forty, set up an advance office in Wellington, New Zealand, where for a month he was also feted by government, business and councils. One stroke of good fortune awaited his visit. Sir Douglas Mawson was in town to discuss plans for his forthcoming combined British, Australian and New Zealand expedition, BANZARE. Mawson willingly gave time to spend an afternoon and, over dinner, an evening with Byrd, who was at his most charming self to extract every morsel of advice from the man he regarded as the greatest living authority on Antarctica. And this, at least, was an Australian from whom he feared no competition for the Pole.

Commander Byrd and Sir Douglas Mawson at their meeting in Wellington, New Zealand. Byrd holds his fox terrier, *Igloo*, which he took to Little America.

By mid-December the expedition ships were in tow of the 15,000-tonne *Larsen*, probing the Ross Sea pack, to find a way into the Bay of Whales. As they approached the eastern extremity of the Great Ice Barrier, Byrd received a message he knew had to come, but whose contents he still feared. On 20 December, reported the Hearst chain's San Francisco *Examiner*, Sir Hubert Wilkins had completed the history-making first long flight of Antarctic exploration. Ever a stickler for protocol and good manners, Byrd immediately radioed Wilkins with a message of congratulations and offering him the hospitality of his camp.[2]

Fortunately Byrd was distracted from this sobering news by the problem of reaching the ice edge, of mooring his ships to discharge the cargo, especially the tricky process of unloading the three aircraft, not to speak of their narrow escape when the barrier cliff broke away and sent a couple of hundred tonnes of ice crashing around the decks of *Eleanor Bolling*, almost capsizing the vessel. One sailor was thrown into the water and Byrd promptly leapt in to save him, thus putting the leader's life at some risk even though another dozen men stood by equally ready to jump. Such, they would find, was Byrd's unpredictable and peculiar style, one in which he frequently appeared to find it necessary to 'prove himself'.

Surely in the quiet hours of his cabin, Byrd, given to aloofness from his men, would ponder Wilkins' modest expedition, his versatile aeroplanes and, most of all, the fact that he had located himself almost two months earlier on the Palmer Peninsula (Graham Land), a base far less exhausting to reach than the struggle to the Ross Ice Shelf. Already the Australian had beaten him to

Final test in the United States of the Fairchild *Stars and Stripes*, one of the three aircraft included in Byrd's first expedition. The neat cabin monoplane which was painted orange and blue and had folding wings, is at Farmingdale field, Long Island. The second aircraft, a Fokker Super Universal, would be lost in a blizzard.

the first Antarctic flight and, though Wilkins had dismissed such an intention, surely an irresistible next step, keeping in mind the fame, Hearst's promised bonus and the fact that 'Aussies' were known gamblers, would be an attempt on to the Pole.

Byrd would well recall that the last race to the South Pole had ended in disaster for one of the two parties. Perhaps in the back of his mind lurked the spectre of that brief cable Captain Scott found waiting for him in Melbourne in 1911. 'Beg leave to inform you proceeding Antarctic — Amundsen'. Could history repeat itself? To fail like Scott, Byrd did not necessarily have to die; just be ruined in his career, in glory and fortune. The spectre of the expedition's outstanding $300,000 debt would certainly occupy his mind.

While Wilkins denied reports of a 'competition', Jack Northrop said he believed the desolate South Polar regions 'will see a race between Wilkins and Byrd.' Possibly Northrop, who should have been privy to the flying plans, hoped to see his slim Vega out-perform Byrd's heavier machine.

With *City of New York* and *Eleanor Bolling* finally moored to the ice, unloading continued through January 1929. Four dog teams and scores of men were needed to drag the partly assembled Ford tri-motor up to the level of the ice shelf and then the 12 kilometres (8 miles) to the site of the base. Byrd named it Little America, and in a touch of showmanship added 'the loneliest city in the world'.

The *Stars and Stripes* made the expedition's first flight on 15 January 1929. Byrd was anxious to get hits on the board before any gloomier news arrived of Wilkins' successes. Over the next few weeks, while reasonable flying weather continued, he had the Fairchild and Fokker both aloft, wanting to

Floyd Bennett, main aircraft of the first expedition, waits for clearing weather.

hurry them into a program of aerial exploration of the immense slice of unknown territory to the east of their base.

Soon American names began to fill blanks in the map. The Rockefeller Mountains resulted from a five-hour exploratory flight on 17 January… not dedicated to the oil baron, cracked one irreverent soul, but in honour of his $100,000 cheque. Byrd, who went along as navigator and flight commander, originally thought the range contained fourteen peaks but a later count went up to at least twenty-five. Flights of 18 February produced a name for the vast lofty plateau to the east, of which they sighted only the barest edge — Marie Byrd Land, after the leader's wife 'the best sport and noblest soul I know'.[3] Clearly the leader's kith and kin and his big supporters were first in the queue to have their names immortalised on a huge and mysterious white continent which most of them would never see.

March brought the good news and the bad. Good news in that Wilkins had closed up his Deception Island operation and returned to America. The flight of 7 March was the bad. Dr Larry Gould, the deputy leader, flew to the edge of the Rockefellers on a geological investigation. A sudden blizzard pinned down the three-man party. Helplessly from their tents they watched a demoniac wind, gusting to 240 kph (150 mph), tear the Fokker from the anchoring cables and hurl it to destruction. They waited six days before Byrd and Dean Smith, a hulking young Arctic pilot, reached them in the Fairchild. They recorded that Byrd fell to his knees and prayed when he saw that all three were alive. Antarctica's first aircraft loss and first air rescue had happened.

Wreck of the second expedition's *Blue Blade* at Little America II in 1934. The high-wing Fokker, piloted by Ike Schlossbach, crashed on take-off. Byrd retained his good record — no one was injured.

The two ships sailed for New Zealand, leaving the wintering-over party of 43 men to watch the last sunset on 17 April. Through the following five months of winter darkness they studied the aurora, experimented with radio signals, overhauled the equipment and off-duty limbered up in the gymnasium, borrowed from a 3,000-book library and watched re-runs of 75 specially selected non-provocative movies. With the gradual return of daylight, Byrd and his crew concentrated their effort on planning the great journey. 'I

When shall we make for the Pole? What is Wilkins doing? The 1929 conference in Little America's library no doubt had these urgent considerations on the agenda. Bernt Balchen stands at Commander Byrd's left shoulder.

want,' said the commander, 'to explore and make an aerial survey of the line of vision between our base and the South Pole.'

First they had to begin the heavy labour of digging out the aircraft from the encrusting snow, with particular care being given to the *Floyd Bennett* for the attempt to reach the Pole. They analysed the weather pattern, studied Amundsen's diary and photographs, pored over the charts for their likely route; the mechanics checked and rechecked the aircraft, on one scary occasion having to douse the flames when the central engine caught fire under test.

Then, from Byrd's office in America, came the very worst news. Wilkins was returning once again to fly his two planes. And with an auxiliary ship supplied by the British to help him find a more southerly base, one clearly suited to long-range aviation. Again the leader faced despair. They had lived through the difficult, blizzardly months of eternal night, now having to immerse themselves in the laborious task of de-winterising the aircraft and the rest of their mechanical gear. Meanwhile the Australian prepared to outsmart them for a second season, not worried about digging out tonnes of ice, his men completely fresh, all his equipment doubtlessly up-to-date and in first-rate order.

The news items copied from the Hearst press did not mention the South Pole. Indeed, Wilkins said he intended to concentrate his flying on the Pacific sector that lay between the Weddell Sea and the Ross Sea, the very region where Byrd's objectives lay. Paul Siple, the tall Eagle Scout chosen to accompany the expedition, recalled the rage that flared among the men of Little America upon learning of Wilkins' intentions. They used the same term that Scott employed 18 years earlier in denouncing Amundsen — 'interloper'. All of them knew that the Vega's advertised 24-hour endurance could enable the Australian to encompass the Pole on a marathon triangular route that would generate a world sensation and — hard to swallow — bring him to visit them (as Byrd had invited him!) at Little America.

Byrd vented his feelings in a radiogram despatched to Hilton Railey, his fund-raiser and agent in America:

> You must not forget that Wilkins is out to lick us. I wish to impress upon you that the flight he proposes is even more important than a flight to the south pole. He is flying over the area that we are most anxious to explore and which is most important to science. As he starts much farther north than we do, he can start early and he is going to make every effort to beat us to it. Don't forget that he was offered $50,000 by Hearst to beat us to the south pole and that he will now possibly fly here by way of the south pole. In spite of this we have got to be sports and have got to be square with him, but do not give any information as to when we start flying. If he thinks we are going to start early he will naturally hurry the more ...We must be very careful not to do anything that is lacking in sportsmanship. (Rodgers 157)

Much of Byrd's frustration lay in the fear of being thwarted at being first with the news. He had contracts with the New York *Times*, with a book publisher, with *National Geographic* and with Paramount films. The whole American public watched him and waited. Yet Wilkins, so much closer to the outside world, could hire a whaler or obtain the help of a friendly British ship to take his still pictures and movies to a South American port, from where Hearst, through his powerful Universal News and King Features Syndicate, would achieve a world scoop.

To outsmart his rival, Byrd instructed Railey to investigate the chartering of one of the Norwegian catcher boats, once the summer ice allowed, to reach New Zealand with his pictures and film, en route to the States. Reduced to this level, the exploration of Antarctica seemed to embody a circulation battle between the interests of the *Times* and those of the competing Hearst press. Yet the episode is illustrative of Byrd's total absorption with the news that would portray his leadership and success. Some accused him of self-aggrandisement, a criticism rather borne out by his insistence on vetting, censoring and not infrequently rewriting the reports of a distressed Russell Owen, the *Times*' own correspondent.

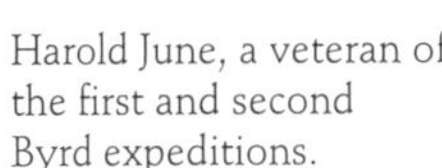

Harold June, a veteran of the first and second Byrd expeditions.

Byrd also fumed over Wilkins' avoidance of specifics in flight plans and dates. From the *Examiner* towards the end of September, the man of Little America gleaned that his rival would have the two Vegas airworthy around mid-November when, if conditions permitted, he hoped to penetrate 'much further south'. Again, a Pole attempt was denied but this statement did not help to assuage anxiety and suspicion in the American camp. Byrd considered sailing *City of New York*, once it returned from Dunedin, eastwards in the direction of the Amundsen Sea where some flights could be made to counter Wilkins' intrusion. Perhaps their sponsors could obtain more intelligence, Byrd suggested in another message to Railey, which continued:

> Have repeatedly asked Wilkins for his plans, which he does not give me. All he says is that he is going to fly to us December 15. Since we are publishing our plans, it is only fair that he should give us his. If he is going to fly to the south pole, I want to know it. Please make urgent request to him for his plans.

Which one will take me to the Pole? Byrd's three aviators (from left) Harold June, Dean Smith, Bernt Balchen.

In the midst of all this anguish, the leader at Little America — it must have hurt him as if written in his own blood — handed his radio operator a message which, in the Virginian's cherished code of sportsmanship and cooperation, wished Wilkins good fortune and invited him to call in for Christmas dinner 'to share a penguin leg'. Wilkins cryptically replied that he looked forward to joining them for the meal.[4]

From the high anger directed towards Wilkins (he was always portrayed as 'the Australian', even though his endeavours were American-sponsored), the sentiment in Byrd's camp slumped to an uneasy depression as the tense waiting weeks passed. Other reports reached them that the Norwegian Riisser-Larsen was on the far side of the continent with his float plane, and Mawson had announced that BANZARE would take an aircraft on its forthcoming cruise. These were operations quite distant from the Pole, perhaps, but newsworthy enough to reduce the American leader

Floyd Bennett preparing for take-off on the historic first flight to the South Pole of 28 November 1929. Byrd, who will emerge from the expedition as a Rear Admiral, had the power of the tri-motor increased by his friend and supporter, Edsel Ford. He claimed the big aircraft had 'a load capacity of 15,000 lb'.

A view (*inset*) from *Floyd Bennett*'s cabin of the Axel Heiberg Glacier on the flight home.

from Emperor Penguin to just another bird in the polar rookery.

Byrd's procrastination at launching the aerial program was sometimes attributed to the man's own phobia of flying. Even though he raised one of history's most courageous aircraft expeditions, he was never relaxed at the controls. Sitting in the pilot's seat never came easy; it was more of the test of 'proving himself'. Using his meteorologists' advice, he planned to hold back until early December before undertaking the Pole attempt, but with the news of Monday, 25 November, a change was forced on him. Wilkins had achieved his first flight of the season. As he fingered Railey's radiogram, the leader knew it had to be full ahead for South Pole.

With skis hissing down the snow strip and three engines roaring at full power, the *Floyd Bennett* took off from Little America at 3.29 p.m. on Thursday, 28 November 1929 — America's Thanksgiving Day.

Byrd appointed himself flight commander and navigator, relying on a drift indicator and mariner's sextant with compensating bubble-level. The mid-afternoon departure would bring the sun abeam of the aircraft for both outward and return journeys, allowing him to take his sights for true heading through the cabin side windows. Begrudgingly he had chosen his chief pilot, the 28-year-old Bernt Balchen, to fly the plane. The two did not much like one another but Byrd knew the stocky, powerful Norwegian, a naval aviator and internationally ranked boxer and skier, had the coolest and most experienced hand of any of his airmen, and coolness and experience were the qualities he needed that day.[5] Harold June, deputy to Balchen, was radio operator and general crew, a duty which included operating the Paramount newsreel camera. Ashley McKinley, ex-army photo-survey expert, managed the heavy Fairchild K5 mapping camera aimed through one of the celluloid windows of the stripped and packed passenger compartment.

They were 640 kilometres (400 miles) across the Ross Ice Shelf when Balchen sighted Larry Gould's dog-sledge team. At noon Gould had radioed the clinching message: 'Weather clear above the Queen Maud Mountains'.[6] They zoomed lower to drop chocolates, cigarettes and photo charts to the waving men who had taken four weeks to travel the distance they had covered in four hours.

With the sun on their left shoulders, to the far right they began to see the peaks of the Great Antarctic Horst glinting at them like burning glass. At 160 kilometres (100 miles) out, Balchen turned *Floyd Bennett* more sharply to the west. Two glaciers were their options in striving for the polar plateau, both mapped and named by Amundsen: one was the Axel Heiberg, honouring his backer; Liv was the other, for Fridtjof Nansen's daughter. The Heiberg crested with the plateau at around 3,200 metres (10,500 feet), the Liv at about 300 metres (1,000 feet) lower. 'Take the Liv', shouted Byrd.

The big aircraft of the long blue fuselage and bright orange wing shrunk to a merest dot against the overpowering mountains that crowded the entrance to the Liv. They came in at 2,500 metres (8,200 feet), Balchen urging the motors at full throttle. Ahead of them the glacier slanting mercilessly upward in a chaos of gigantic icefall and crevasse-scarred snowfield. Towards the southern end, where the heavily laden aircraft panted at a bare 130 kph (80 mph), their path became even steeper. For every length *Floyd Bennett* lifted its nose, a torrent of headwind from the plateau seemed to drop it again, almost as far. At least 500 metres (1,500 feet) stood between them and the final crest; white-flanked mountains closed in, the glacier grew narrower; hardly space to turn, no alternative but to press on, with an aircraft about as responsive as a bucketful of lead.

From the cabin, looking forward through the cockpit window at a solid wall of ice, Byrd described what followed:

> Balchen began to yell and gesticulate, and it was hard to catch the words in the roar of the engines echoing from the cliffs on either side. But the meaning was manifest. 'Overboard — overboard — 200 pounds.'
>
> Which would it be — gasoline or food?
>
> If gasoline, I thought, we might as well stop there and turn back. We could never get back to the base from the Pole. If food, the lives of all of us would be jeopardized in the event of a forced landing. Was that fair to McKinley, Balchen and June? It really took only a moment to reach the decision. The Pole, after all, was our objective. I knew the character of the three men. They were not so lightly to be turned aside. McKinley, in fact, had already hauled one of the food bags to the trapdoor. (Byrd 335–6)

Byrd nodded and the precious provisions splattered across the glacier floor. The straining machine lifted, but still not climbing fast enough against the relentless downdraft. They stared into another obstacle, the whitened hump of a mountain peak rising from the middle of the Liv; no way around it, only over the top.

'Drop more,' the pilot shouted. 'Another bag, unload!' McKinley grabbed a second sack and, with barely a glance at their leader, sent it plummeting out; goodbye to enough rations to let them survive for a month.

Like an act of madness, Balchen abruptly threw the bucking aircraft sideways, aiming them at the glacier wall, the right-hand wingtip close to touching the unfriendly face of brown and blackened rock. No reply to their shouts of warning. His final gamble guessed at catching an eddy of the updraft that might lurk by the cliff on the very fringe of a ceaseless headwind.

Suddenly a lightened *Floyd Bennett* roared skywards, rising on the current as if propelled by an unseen boot. To whoops of joy and relief from those in

the cabin, they were over the crest with 150 metres (450 feet) to spare. In that moment of terror, a cool head in the cockpit had saved them all.

The top of the Liv delivered them to the vast white desert of the polar plateau. The icy peaks of the Queen Mauds fell away with Byrd's comment 'the parade of mountains, the contrast of black and white, the troughs of the glaciers...something never to be forgotten'. At about 300 metres (1,000 feet) above the surface, the steady beat of the motors carried them through unbelievably low and oxygen-starved temperatures outside. Byrd had sometimes warned: 'any small failure could spell an end to it all, a flaw in a piece of metal, a bit of dirt in the fuel lines or in the carburettor jets'.

Above the remotest place on this globe Byrd's most dreaded moment struck: the aircraft began to vibrate with the spluttering and backfiring of the right-hand engine. June reached for the fuel dump lever, ready to drain the tanks to save them from a fireball if they were forced to ditch on the sastrugi ridges below. McKinley twisted the flow valve — this way, that way, trying to correct a possibly over-lean mixture before the stuttering propeller stopped altogether. Then another loud backfire and the erratic motor resumed its full-throated roar. All eased back in their seats conscious of the slender margin between them in *Floyd Bennet's* cabin and a cold hell below.

Another four hours of the eternal plateau: at 89° and 20° South, Balchen studied his slide rule and sent a scribbled note along the wire that connected to Byrd's position aft. 'According to my reckoning we should be over the South Pole in 14 minutes.' 'My reckoning agrees', Byrd replied, though Balchen privately wondered if their leader, with his inadequate sextant, really had any clue to where they were.

At 10.08 a.m. on 29 November 1929, the triumphant aviators landed at Little America. Byrd and his crew were chaired to the base by the jubilant ground party. President Hoover declared that America's conquest of the Pole was 'proof that the spirit of great adventure still lives'. *Floyd Bennett* had covered the 2,800 kilometres (1,750 miles) in a flying time of 17 hours and 28 minutes.

In the full daylight of 1.14 a.m. they made a broad circle above the lofty ice. Byrd handed June his signal:

> Aboard Airplane *Floyd Bennett* in flight, 1:55 p.m. Greenwich time, Friday, November 29. My calculations indicate that we have reached the vicinity of the South Pole, flying high for a survey. The airplane is in good shape, crew all well. Will soon turn north. We can see an almost limitless polar plateau. (Byrd: 340–22)

They dropped the American flag, weighted with a stone from Floyd Bennett's grave. Byrd's parting comment was probably one of the truest observations he ever made: 'One gets there and that is all there is for the telling. It is the effort to get there that counts'.

Byrd chose the Axel Heiberg for their return to the Ross Ice Shelf. At the foot of the mountains they sought the cache of 350 gallons (1,500 litres) of gasoline which had been brought out aboard *Floyd Bennett* eleven days before. Balchen noted with some displeasure while he and his two companions lugged the chill five-gallon drums to replenish near empty tanks, that Byrd, who had been swigging liberally from his cognac flask, chose to dance about yelling 'We made it! We made it!'. (Montague: 261–3)

After another four and a half hours they sighted the landmark of three tall radio towers. At 10.08 a.m. they were climbing from the aircraft, into the arms of Little America's jubilant welcome. Hoisted on many shoulders, they were carried to the mess hall for a postponed Thanksgiving dinner.

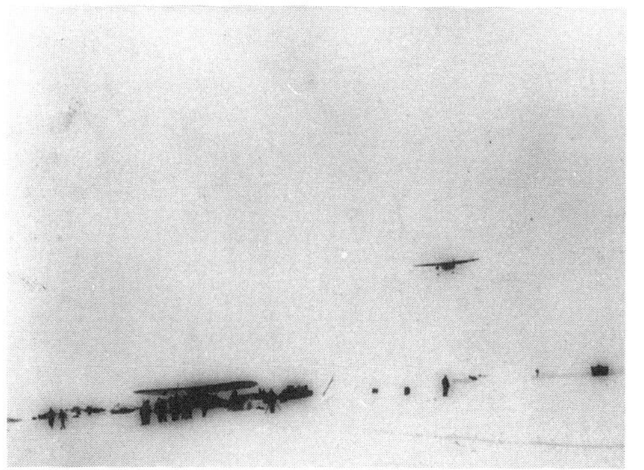

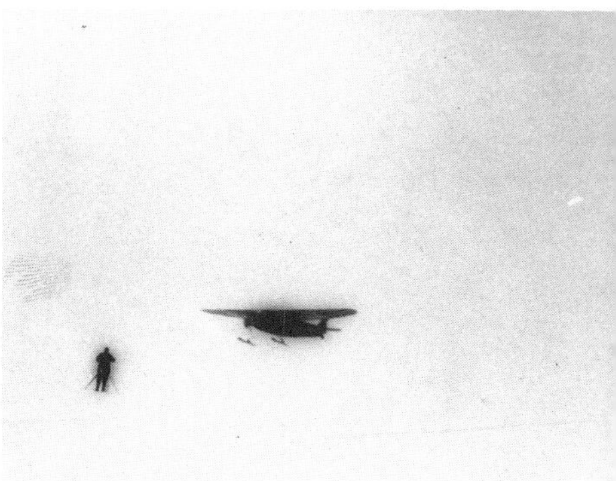

Watched by the eager men of Little America, the *Floyd Bennett* circles the airstrip, preparing to land.

Floyd Bennett had carried them 2,800 kilometres (1,750 miles) in a flying time of 17 hours and 28 minutes or a total absence of 18 hours and 41 minutes. During those hours, announced McKinley, he had exposed 1,600 frames on the K5 camera, covering an area of some 388,000 square kilometres (150,000 square miles) of Antarctica, much of it previously unseen. President Hoover greeted their feat as 'proof that the spirit of great adventure still lives'. Congress prepared legislation that would elevate commander Richard E. Byrd to the rank of rear admiral (retired). In New York, a cheering crowd gathered in Times Square to watch the illuminated bulletin flash the news that America had conquered the South Pole. Who the hell was Wilkins?

Like the 1928 venture, Byrd's next exploit was also private. The 1933 expedition, by which time he wore the Congressional Medal of Honour and could exercise his lofty rank, was perhaps easier to organise, despite the gloomy depression years. Byrd's fame was unassailable. He knew the power game, spoke with the President. His brother had become Senator Harry Flood Byrd of Virginia; so, he was able to win the support of numerous wealthy men.

Once again Edsel Ford was a backer, as was John D. Rockefeller, Jr, and Joseph Pulitzer, publisher of the St Louis *Post Dispatch*. To their names could be added those of William Horlick, the malted-milk king; C. R. Walgreen, head of a big drug company; and Jacob Ruppert, a brewer and owner of the New York Yankees along with the corporate support of General Motors, International Business Machines, American Airways and many others from 'Who's Who' of American industry. Ralston Purina Cereals donated 50 tonnes of dog food for the huskies.

With aerial conquest of the South Pole behind him, Byrd now set out to explore in more detail what he termed 'the Pacific quadrant' — that vast, uncharted and unclaimed region lying between the 80th and 150th West meridians where his 1928 expedition had barely picked at the edges.[7]

Byrd's expedition consisted of two ships, *Bear of Oakland* and *Jacob Ruppert*. To carry his aerial survey parties he brought four aircraft, supported by five tractors, two of them developed originally for desert travel by the French automotive genius, Andre Citröen. Foremost among his aeroplanes was Curtis Wright's new Condor, a large twin-engine biplane, given the name *William Horlick*.[8] In appearance the Condor looked slow and cumbersome, its top wing some six metres (20 feet) above the ground, but in operation it proved extremely useful, being adaptable to either skis or floats and having a 2,600-pound payload. The other aircraft were a high-wing Fokker, *Blue Blade*, a Fairchild, *Miss American Airways*, and a Kellet K-4 autogyro, which was the first rotary wing machine to operate in Antarctica.

The expedition, including 56 men of the wintering-over party and 153 dogs and three cows and a calf (born during the voyage south) went ashore at the Bay of Whales in December 1933. Little America I had to be dug out before they could reoccupy Byrd's old base, and new buildings put up to connect with those that were half-buried, thus bringing into existence Little America II.

Byrd was a canny showman, quite a master of public relations. To bring Antaractica into the homes of the American people, or to be specific, the amazing and heroic deeds of Admiral Byrd's expedition, he began the first direct-voice broadcast from Little America II to listeners in the United States on 1 February 1934. Weekly programs from 'the ice' were then featured on the Columbia Broadcasting System's network. Newspapers received almost daily bulletins by radio. From Boston to Bakersfield, no one was likely to be unaware of what 'the Admiral of the Ends of the Earth' was doing among all those cute little penguins.

Rear Admiral Byrd (third from left) preparing for the return to Little America with his seond expedition of 1933–35. To Byrd's left stands his pilot, Harold June. His large Condor aircraft (which also flew on skis) had a camera bay installed in the cabin.

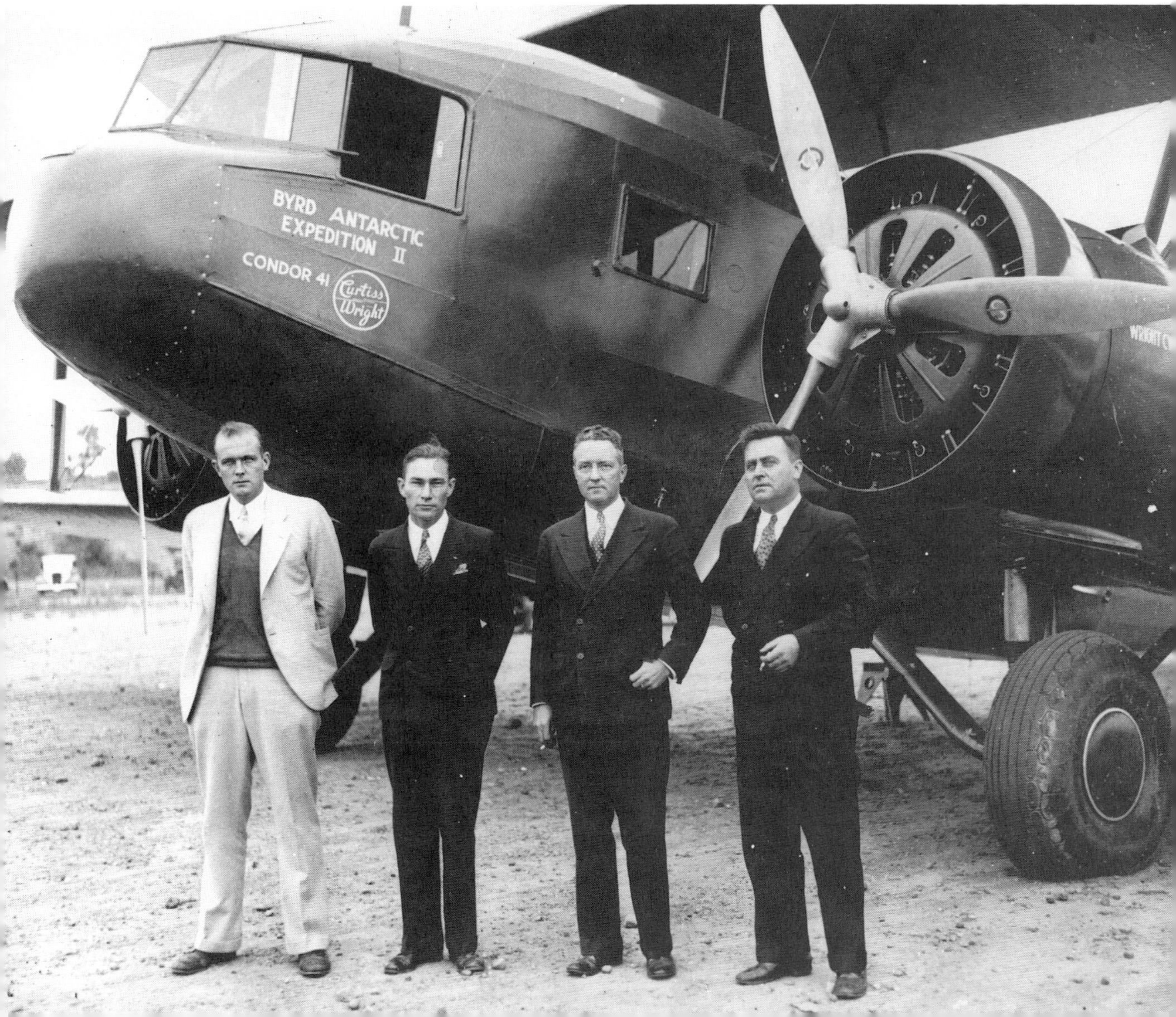

The 1933–35 expedition placed greater emphasis on science and surveying. Was Antarctica in reality two continents? Did a strait extend from the Ross Sea to the Weddell Sea? Did the mountains of the Antarctic Peninsula link up with the Queen Maud Range? Long distance flights were planned to unravel these mysteries. With Harold June as chief pilot, the Condor covered 1,240 kilometres (770 miles) on a mission to define the eastern edge of the Ross Ice Shelf; in the process, Byrd named the William Horlick Range. Another flight of 720 kilometres (450 miles) to the north-east penetrated the immense ice dome which he had previously called Marie Byrd Land, in honour of his wife. Territorial claims to the region were volunteered on behalf of the U.S. government.

Lowering the flag at the conclusion of the first expedition to Little America. Byrd (right) watches the blizzard - torn Stars and Stripes fluttering down.

The ease of performing aerial photography was advanced through having a special camera bay built into the Condor's cabin. Byrd's crew refined the technique of dropping smoke bombs to detect surface winds and the elevation of the ice before attempting a landing. Seismic soundings were carried out to determine the depth of the ice crust; the improvement in radio technology enabled his men to communicate freely between base, aircraft and field parties. The Kellett autogyro, which had made its first flight on 1 February 1934 and proved an extremely useful workhorse, was lost when it spun into the ice on 28 September. The Fokker also crashed during an attempted take-off. Men were injured, but Byrd's remarkable record endured and there were no fatalities.

The second expedition saw and surveyed some 1,165,000 square kilometres (450,000 square miles) of Antarctica, of which more than half had never been previously sighted. Such was the record when Byrd and his men closed up Little America II and sailed for home in February 1935.

Byrd had made a sound investment in lifting the awareness of the American people to a new zone of national interest, far to the south in remote Antarctica.[9] Approaching 1939 he planned his third private expedition, to 'fill in some of the blanks in the map', as he put it. However, times were changing. The world was a much more uncertain place than in the bright summers of the 1920s and even the slumped depression years at the turn of the decade. Big Norwegian whaling fleets were on the polar seas, reaping a rich harvest and using light aircraft to explore the coast on which they had already raised King Haakon's flag. What might the French do next? They had claimed Adelie Land, directly south of Australia in 1924. At Adolf Hitler's orders, two Luft Hansa flying-boats were making for the ice.

...Byrd 1933-34
—USAS 1939–41

Alerted to these events, particularly because the Germans were intent on exploring Antarctica, President Roosevelt decided to establish the United States Antarctic Service around which a government-sponsored expedition would be organised. Congress authorised a budget of $350,000 to underwrite the venture, which signified the end of America's official 'disinterest' in the frozen South. Byrd's ten-year investment in public opinion had paid a dividend.

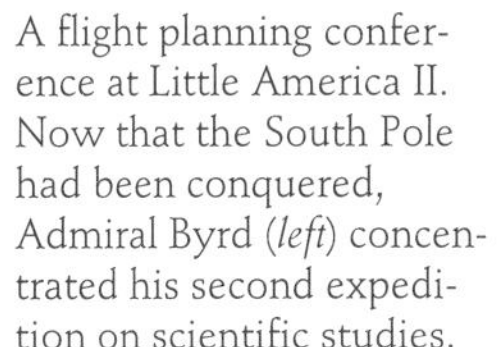

A flight planning conference at Little America II. Now that the South Pole had been conquered, Admiral Byrd (*left*) concentrated his second expedition on scientific studies.

Byrd's Condor aircraft (below) manoeuvring on floats.

Byrd quickly threw in his lot with the government initiative and was appointed commander on 30 June 1939 of the first officially sponsored American Antarctic expedition since Commander Wilkes of the U.S. Navy had sailed a century before.

The Antarctic Service expedition consisted of two ships, *North Star* and *Bear*, to carry the 59 men, 160 dogs and eight aircraft. Government finance permitted two establishments — once again at Little America on the Bay of Whales, commanded by Paul Siple, and a second outpost, in charge of another Byrd veteran, Richard Black, known as East Base on the Antarctic Peninsula, just to the north of Alexander I Island. A Condor was allocated to each base.

Miss American Airways flying beside the *William Horlick* above Marie Byrd Land.

Another significant difference allowed under government auspices was the declaration of America's official territorial desires upon the Antarctic continent. These focused specifically on the vast quadrant of Marie Byrd Land which, to one side was bordered beyond 80° West by British Graham Land, and to the other beyond 150° West by the Ross Dependency, administered on Britain's behalf by New Zealand. Roosevelt instructed Byrd, as expedition commander, to show the American flag at a series of points during exploration sorties. In the words of the presidential instruction 'so that in the event of Congressional action, the region explored by the United States may be claimed as a national territorial area.'[10]

Further east, in vindication of Byrd's previous work, the expedition's purpose was 'to give America full and up to date knowledge of Antarctica, especially the hitherto unknown sector [beneath] the extreme south-west part of

Byrd's proposed third return to Antarctica became merged in the American government's official expedition of 1939–41. The Admiral did not stay at Little America III, but participated from shipboard on aerial exploration of the Marie Byrd Land coast by Barkley-Grow float plane.

the Pacific Ocean. It is incumbent upon us to be prepared with information for whatever policy concerning territorial rights the government may decide upon'.

Noteworthy, too, is Byrd's response to the President's instruction. On his 1935 return he referred to Antarctica in the context of 'let there be no boundaries here. Let the Antarctic stand as a symbol of peace and a beacon for the world'. Now he was to modify that view, and Antarctica became potentially 'a base for commercial and naval aircraft, a key to weather forecasting and a source of huge mineral deposits'. Further, America should regard any attempt by another country to establish a base west of 180° as 'an unfriendly act'.

At the Bay of Whales, a new Little America III had to be built on firmer ice to the east of the original site, now covered close to the tips of the tall radio towers placed there in 1929. The attitude of the government expedition was much more workaday, more serious and disciplined than in the era of the privateers. Likewise the list of sciences represented had expanded impressively over the intervening 10 years, now embracing geology, glaciology, meteorology, geomagnetism, auroral observation, seismic and cosmic ray studies, biology, physiology and radio communications.

Three aircraft comprised the expedition's aviation wing at Little America — again, a heavy Curtis-Wright Condor biplane; a Barkley-Grow seaplane used in three important flights during *Bear's* cruise off the Marie Byrd coast in February 1940; and a small Beechcraft monoplane, intended to be carried on the roof of the snow cruiser, a 35-tonne oversnow vehicle which proved a total failure. In the summer of 1940 the Condor completed two lengthy missions, one across a remote part of Marie Byrd Land and the next in a survey of the eastern flank of the Queen Maud Range. During the second flight the crew discovered another huge river of ice, the Shackleton Glacier, flowing from the plateau and were able to check on the 4,600-metre (15,000-foot) height of Mount Alton Wade, which Byrd had sighted in 1929 on his way to the Pole.

In the following summer both aircraft made lengthy flights in the vicinity of the remote coast to the east of Little America III. When returning from assisting a tractor party, the Condor's right (starboard) engine caught fire soon after take-off. The crew turned off the fuel and guided the big machine safely to the ice, where, with a shattered cylinder and piston, it had to be abandoned. The second Condor, flown from East Base near the Antarctic Peninsula, met a similar but more passive fate; after ferrying the outgoing expedition to the awaiting *Bear* it was simply left to the mercy of the next Antarctic storm.

Upon the change of command at McMurdo Sound, naval officers shake hands beside the monument to Admiral Byrd, who died in 1957. Ironically, McMurdo was an Antarctic base that Byrd never used.

During one cosmic ray observation flight, the Beechcraft reached an altitude of 6,400 metres (21,000 feet), a record for Antarctic aviation. One of the longest flights of 1940 brought back a photo-survey of 1,600 kilometres (1,000 miles) of the Great Antarctic Horst. Photo-surveying had reached high accuracy while aerial colour photography was also introduced experimentally to Antarctica. Map definition was heightened through radio bearings and position reporting to base and, through radio communication, in greater co-ordination with surface parties.[11]

Though Roosevelt intended a permanent American presence in Antarctica, the third expedition closed up Little America III and East Base on the Peninsula in March 1941.[12] The ice once again returned to its lonely silence. Another catastrophic world war had already commenced. Before the year's end, the Japanese would attack Pearl Harbor and an America at battle filed away its potential involvement in the seventh continent for another day.

Byrd returned twice more to Antarctica, but the days of the derring-do commander were finished. Future American expeditions were of such lavish proportions that only a military machine could support them.

Byrd, the Man

Little America has long disappeared. Calved out to sea in the inexorable process of an ever-moving icecap, its aeroplanes and tractors and buildings and all else remaining dropped into the depths of the polar sea.

Monuments to Admiral Byrd stand in Washington D.C., at McMurdo Sound, the present-day American base, and in Wellington and Christchurch, his New Zealand points of departure on the great southern adventure. Before the space age, he led the United States in the race to uncover the newest of worlds and unravel its ice-shrouded mysteries. To look at the map of 'Pacific' Antarctica is to witness the extent of his exploits in the host of names that he and his men left behind, all of them wholly American. As far as Americans were concerned, he dominated Antarctic exploration; over three decades, he headed five expeditions and explored more than 3 million square kilometres (2 million square miles) of the great white southland, a record on this globe which can never be duplicated. To his countrymen, he was indeed 'the Lord of the Ice... Admiral of the Ends of the Earth'.

An official portrait of Rear Admiral Richard Evelyn Byrd (ret.), taken in 1942. Among his decorations are the Congressional Medal of Honor, the Navy Cross and the Distinguished Flying Cross.

Byrd, who came from an old Southern family, was born at Winchester, Virginia, on 25 October 1888. At the age of 12 he was sufficiently mature to have his parents send him off alone by ship to visit friends in the Philippines.

At 24, he joined the United States Navy, only to be invalided out four years later because of a recurrent leg injury. World War I brought his recall to the mast, except for him it was to be a desk in Washington until he practically browbeat his superiors into letting him train for a combat role where not so much store was put on strong ankles. He entered the Pensacola flying school in Florida and, as hostilities ended, obtained his wings.

Byrd emerged from his wartime training with the goal of exploration; to make a name for himself as the aviator who rolled back the curtain of mystery above far-away places. His early ventures included flying the Atlantic, though mishaps robbed his chance of beating Charles Lindbergh's history-making crossing.

Backed with a $100,000 fund provided by his friend, Edsel Ford, he set out to be the first man to fly an aeroplane to the top of the world. With Floyd Bennett, an experienced Arctic aviator, as his pilot and Byrd himself filling the role of navigator, he claimed the North Pole on 9 May 1926. An American hero, he was promoted by order of Congress from lieutenant to commander (he is said to have refused rear admiral as too much of a leap). New York welcomed him home with a ticker-tape parade.

A meeting with Roald Amundsen at Spitzbergen airstrip on return from the North Pole may have determined his next path to glory. 'Where to now, Byrd?' asked the famous Norwegian explorer. Almost involuntarily, Byrd replied 'the South Pole, of course'.

Richard Evelyn Byrd's place is secure as one of the foremost explorer-leaders in the twentieth century's new age of technology. He was a gifted organiser, had access to the corridors of power, be it politics or commerce (his brother was Senator Harry Flood Byrd) and for him, thinking big was as natural and American as apple pie. His organisation

As a modern American hero, Byrd became a close friend of many leading businessmen and politicians. President Roosevelt was Governor of New York State at this homely meeting in the Roosevelt living room. Members of the Byrd and Roosevelt families surround the pair.

brought enormous advances in the use of aircraft, radio and tracked vehicles in Antarctica — literally lifting south polar exploration from the heroic to the age of the mechanical. His other attribute was a superb sense of showmanship. He knew how to employ public relations to make his American public sit up and take notice; he signed contracts for books, magazine articles, newsreels, radio programs and personal appearances.

The same R. E. Byrd was indeed a complex individual, some of his critics would say only a publicity-grasping figurehead, propped up by the labours of other men. Among his expedition members were those who would refer to him as jealous, aloof, ill-tempered, and where flying and navigation were concerned, of questionable ability. In his own service he was never highly popular, because of his rapid, even 'political' rise to two-star rank.

Russell Owen, the correspondent for the New York *Times* which was paying for an exclusive service on the 1928 expedition, is reputed to have lapsed into a deep depression and retreated to his bunk for several days when Byrd demanded the right to censor and change his newspaper copy. Shortly after the first expedition reached Little America, Byrd aroused the ire of another man, his dog team leader, whose chain of authority he arbitrarily altered.

Stories such as these, particularly centred around the first expedition, were recounted by Bernt Balchen, whose relationship with his leader appeared to have been far less than easy. Though Balchen was chief pilot, other pilots were privately told by Byrd that they would be his preference for the prized South Pole flight. Balchen complained of Byrd's utter aloofness towards him, yet he was the one on whom Byrd ultimately depended to get *Floyd Bennett* to the Pole. On that epic flight, said Balchen, it was he who had to tell the leader they were nearing the Pole, for Byrd himself had lost his sense of direction. For his part, Byrd once admitted, almost in annoyance, that Balchen 'can do more things well than any man I ever knew.'

'Little America is the most peaceful spot in this world, due to the absence of women', said Admiral Byrd before he made his last trip to Antarctica in 1955. Women protesters were waiting in ambush when he reached Dallas airport, en route to New Zealand.

Byrd was further accused by Balchen of having wilfully sown the seeds of jealousy among the mechanics who were entrusted with the vital task of aircraft maintenance. Each one of them was apparently taken aside by the leader and told that he alone had Byrd's confidence and that the others should be severely watched. The incident led to bad blood in the workshop until detected by Balchen, who had no wish to fly across Antarctica in an aeroplane fixed by disaffected men.

Strangest of all was Byrd's decision on the 1933 venture to subject himself to 19 weeks of isolation in what was called the Bolling Advance Weather Station, located 200 kilometres (125 miles) south of Little America. Byrd proposed to transmit daily weather reports from this tiny hut, buried in the ice. His lone vigil began on 24 March 1934, but within a few months the stumbling and partly incoherent radio signals made it obvious that something was seriously amiss. An oil stove with a faulty flue and a petrol generator leaking fumes were in fact, killing Byrd, who could not turn off either when the outside temperature hovered around –52°C (–62°F).

On 11 August, after several futile attempts, a three-man party set out on a hazardous drive using a Citröen tracked vehicle through the freezing darkness. At the advance base they found their leader emaciated, debilitated and close to death from carbon monoxide poisoning. They remained with Byrd for another two months before he was well enough to return to Little America, where he underwent a further spell of recovery. Strange behaviour indeed.

Why Byrd would want to place himself in such utter isolation from the men he was supposed to lead remains hard to fathom. Byrd detailed the almost fatal experience in his book, *Alone*, which became a bestseller. Recounting that he was prompted to maroon himself because of an 'interest in the experience for its own sake' seemed to be another way of saying that by some strange quirk in his nature he was forever trying to prove himself; that he was perhaps instinctively hostile to some of his rivals or subordinates for fear of being overshadowed in the hall of fame. One notes, for instance, that Byrd's writing never gave credit to Hubert Wilkins for the first flight in Antarctica. Indeed the Australian's exploits are barely mentioned.

As other evidence of that need to push himself, Balchen recalled Byrd's leap into icy water at the Bay of Whales to rescue a sailor. Other men were ready to go in, but it was Byrd who jumped first. In the rescue of Larry Gould from the Fokker wreck in the Rockefeller Mountains, Byrd again added himself on this dangerous flight when one person fewer would have made the return journey so much easier.

Though the late 1920s were prohibition time in America, Byrd ensured that the expedition stores contained an amount of liquor for medicinal reasons. 'Booze' became a serious problem among some of the men of Little America, not helped by the leader's own drinking habits. On the Pole flight, Balchen recounts that Byrd helped himself liberally to a flask of cognac he usually carried because of a supposed heart ailment.

On the occasion of a seven-hour flight on 5 December to study the Queen Maud Range, Balchen describes the unseemly posture of the commander as the aircraft doors were opened at the return from the long journey. Assembled base personnel beheld their leader pinned to the floor by June and McKinley, struggling and cursing loudly; in short he seemed to be 'raving mad'.

Balchen himself could be temperamental and bad tempered, and to some degree like natures may have collided. Yet the reason for Byrd and Balchen's falling out may have come from the darker side of exploration and its practitioners. According to Balchen, his friend Floyd Bennett — Byrd's pilot on the first epic flight that gained his national fame — confessed to him before his death from pneumonia in 1928 that, in truth, they had never reached the North Pole. (Montague: 289–90. Rodgers: 91–4). Byrd's resentment may have been directed at the man who knew his secret, if indeed such a secret did exist. Again, that other American polar leader, Commander Finn Ronne, told much the same story which disputed the admiral's moment of glory.[13]

America's adulation of the explorer-hero is evident in his ticker-tape welcome through the streets of New York. But did Byrd really reach the North Pole in 1926 — the first achievement that won him fame? Critics of the controversial Admiral continued to pursue him as the years went on.

Byrd's long term associate, Paul Siple, noted a growing antagonism towards America's hero figure. Reviewing the start of Operation Highjump, he wrote:

> Certainly the attitude of the uninitiate towards veterans was to haunt both Admiral Byrd and myself as well as other old timers in the operations ahead. (Siple: 94)

And when Byrd and Siple participated in the launching of Operation Deep Freeze:

> But times had changed. The small discourtesies exhibited towards the Admiral by Task Force officers who felt Byrd represented the past continued without abatement ...[they were] almost insultingly willing to have Byrd and me take our leave. (Siple: 123)

Byrd may have been a strange character, audacious, theatrical and ambitious. Yet he was generally careful for the welfare of his men, to which the record of few accidents or major injuries on his expeditions is testimony. He also showed himself to be divisive in his dealings with those he placed in authority and unpredictably moody. Perhaps his erratic nature embodied those characteristics that are sometimes inseparable from an indefinable charisma, the strange stuff of leadership.

Whatever the truth of these matters, the Byrd family succeeded in having sections of Balchen's 1956 book, *Come North With Me*, suppressed. But Byrd's descendants have nothing to fear. His name stands high and unassailable as a great American explorer of the twentieth century. In the words of the then president-elect, John F. Kennedy, at a time when New Zealand authorities were planning a Byrd memorial in Wellington: 'You are honouring a great man and one of whom this nation is very proud'.

I am not going to take any risks for that bloody rubbishing business of raising the flag ashore.

Captain J. K. Davis to Sir Douglas Mawson

4

BANZARE—A TALE OF TWO LEADERS

In the cockpit of their de Havilland Moth, BANZARE leader Sir Douglas Mawson (left) and pilot Stuart Campbell wait to begin the flight of 5 January 1930 which led to the naming of Mac-Robertson Land, a major part of Australian Antarctic Territory.

'I have left the Antarctic coast with great regret,' wrote a frustrated Sir Douglas Mawson: 'another week here with the aeroplane would have completed the mapping of MacRobertson Land and added detail of Scott Mountains...if I was in full authority over the handling of the vessel, I would not leave these shores'.

The entry of 26 January 1930 in Mawson's diary reflects a conflict between the expedition leader and ship's master that came close to marring the outcome of the British, Australian and New Zealand Antarctic Research Expedition (BANZARE) of 1929–30.

Mawson was the leader. Tall, bearded, handsome, he stood unchallenged as the world's greatest living polar explorer. At the age of 47, he was on leave from the Chair of Geology at Adelaide University to take BANZARE to the little-known ice coast far to Australia's south. John King Davis, captain of their vessel, *Discovery*, proved to be his unrelenting adversary. A veteran polar mariner, Davis had served (as had Mawson) with Shackleton, been master of the steam yacht *Aurora* in Mawson's previous 1911–14 Australasian Antarctic Expedition (AAE) and now held the post of Commonwealth director of navigation. In the years between, the thin, almost gaunt, red-haired skipper who 'lived on corn beef and pickles' had grown testy, sour, argumentative. In Mawson's view, as BANZARE progressed from one obstructionist outburst to another, he was 'mentally unbalanced'.

BANZARE'S little biplane, VH-ULD, with Flight Lieutenant Campbell at the controls, wings away from *Discovery* above a drifting iceberg at a position identified as 78° South longitude.

Both of them — Mawson (or 'Dux' to his fellow expeditionaries) and Davis (behind his back, 'Gloomy') — watched from *Discovery's* deck as two young air force pilots, Stuart Campbell and Eric Douglas, climbed into the open cockpit of the de Havilland Moth VH-ULD. Lowered into open water between the floes, they fired the engine and turned the little float plane into the wind, ready for the flight that would mark the beginning of Australia's aerial exploration of Antarctica.

'After lunch we fly the aeroplane,' Mawson noted on the last day of 1929. 'It rises to 5,000 ft . . . from that height they see what may be land to south near the horizon, over 40 miles of ice at least, then 10 miles of water'. The expedition's Moth biplane, a fragile thing of fabric and wood, was fortunate to reach Antarctica intact. Exposed on deck to the wild Southern Ocean, it had survived the long and stormy voyage from Cape Town, only to face destruction from a fusillade of icicles dropping from the rigging. Campbell recalled:

> I was up on deck early, basking in the calm sunlight and looking to see if we had enough [open] water to take off and rather proud of the way our aeroplane had stood up. A couple of bits of ice fell from aloft and crashed at my feet and then in a few minutes it had started. The masts and rigging were thickly coated with ice and as the morning sun came up and started to melt it, it came crashing down in great chunks all over the ship, mostly it

Taken from a lofty perch on *Discovery's* mast, photographer Frank Hurley recorded a view of the de Havilland Moth stowed on the crowded deck below.

seemed to me on our poor little unprotected aircraft. I have a vivid recollection of one long sliver about six feet long pointed like a dagger going straight through both upper and lower port mainplanes. In about a minute gaping tears began to appear all over the mainplanes and tail and seeing this disintegration going on in front of me I felt completely helpless.

After a near disastrous ice cascade, aviators Campbell and Douglas set to patching the torn wing fabric. At one stage, Campbell had to work beneath the aircraft while roped in a cradle.

After 10 minutes of bombardment the Moth presented a sorry picture with some 60 tears up to half a metre long in the fabric and about 10 ribs stove in and flattened. To calm Mawson's dismay, Campbell assumed an air of confidence and said 'Oh, it's only some tears; we can mend them all right'. For Campbell and Douglas, the mending took 10 days of non-stop patching, splicing, joining and sewing. For their next problem, the young pilots found that with a wet magneto, due to frozen seaspray, they could not start the 85-horsepower Gipsy Mark I engine. Cooking the magneto in the oven to dry it out was their simple solution. Flight-Lieutenant Campbell, one of the RAAF's new seaplane pilots, and Flying Officer Douglas, a fresh graduate of the Pilot Training School, Point Cook, lacked neither enthusiasm nor initiative.

Eighteen flights were made during BANZARE, none exceeding two hours' duration. None was the stuff of headline-making aviation, except for the distinction of leading the explorers into new territories. None was intended to compete with the aerial heroics of Wilkins, Byrd or Ellsworth. This was no reflection, of course, on the courage and professionalism of Campbell and Douglas, but simply a consequence of BANZARE's acute starvation for funds. Aware of Wilkins' historic flights over Graham Land the year before, Mawson also aimed to be a pioneer of Antarctic aviation and, but for the mishap to his Vickers monoplane in 1911, he might well have led them all to the polar skies. While his fellow South Australian, courtesy of generous American patrons, operated two modern cabin aircraft, Mawson had to be content with a little machine which was low in speed, short of range and burdened with a feeble radio. To add to his disadvantage, the expedition was crammed aboard a rolling, lumbering old ship — the same *Discovery* that had carried Scott's first expedition to McMurdo Sound — whose master, besides being 'sulky, pig-headed, damned rude, uncouth', also wanted no part in the flying operations, declaring 'I leave that for those who are fools enough to do so'.[1]

Despite the antagonism of Davis whom Mawson still regarded as 'a very old friend' (Davis had been best man at his wedding) – Mawson's patience allowed the rest of the expedition to go about its business more or less undeterred. Among the 39 scientists, airmen and seamen aboard *Discovery* were a few who had soldiered beside 'Dux' on AAE. Mort Moyes, the cartographer, was one, as was Frank Hurley, the irrepressible photographer and a survivor of Shackleton's abortive Endurance expedition of 1914. That same patience must have been tested, however, on New Year's Eve 1929 when Mawson sought the captain's permission to hand out drinks to the ship's company:

But for a crash at Adelaide racecourse, Mawson's REP monoplane could have been flying above Antarctica in 1911. The machine is at the Vickers workshop, prior to delivery to the Australasian Antarctic Expedition (AAE).

> I found him in bed. He replied very sulkily and testily 'No, certainly not, what do you take me for? I am not going to give them anything of that kind to make a row about all night, waking everybody.' Later he said 'If I do anything of that kind it will be for their dinner tomorrow.' The men were disappointed when I told them they could have nothing tonight but possibly something tomorrow.

The Antarctic Committee set up in Australia to plan BANZARE had issued Mawson with his marching instructions: 'to attempt to chart the Antarctic coastline from Enderby Land (45°E) to King George V Land (160°E), making landings to plant the flag; carrying out inland surveys by plane; mak-

ing hydrographic surveys; and studying meteorological conditions, geological formations, and the fauna of the region, especially the numbers, species and distribution of whales'.[2] In fulfilment of this order, weather balloons were sent up to 15,000 metres (50,000 feet), the ocean bottom sampled with *Discovery's* trawl nets, and a lookout kept for whales and all other forms of wildlife. But the main goal was new land — and raising the flag before the Norwegians came.

The issue of territorial rights sparked another angry denunciation from the skipper. If this seemed an odd posture for a man who had been born in England, served on British ships and in British expeditions, it was in keeping with the expressions of the 'most utter rubbish, fiction and impudent assertion' recorded in Mawson's diary:

> January 3, 1930
>
> Today at lunch he argued strongly that the Norwegians had every right to try and anticipate us at Enderby Land. He said we had been most disgracefully secret about our plans. He went on in this disloyal way, trying to find fault with our expedition where there was no fault, forgiving the faults of others. I pointed out that ours was a scientific expedition. He said that was all eye wash, we were out to grab land. If we were really scientific, we would certainly not leave Australia where there was a much better field for scientific work. Scientists who were really devoted to science... would not come down here. He had everybody at the table laughing to themselves, and Dr Ingram went over to the gramophone and turned it on to drown Davis' twaddle.

Sir MacPherson Robertson, the Melbourne philanthropist whose £10,000 donation helped to launch Mawson's BANZARE in 1929.

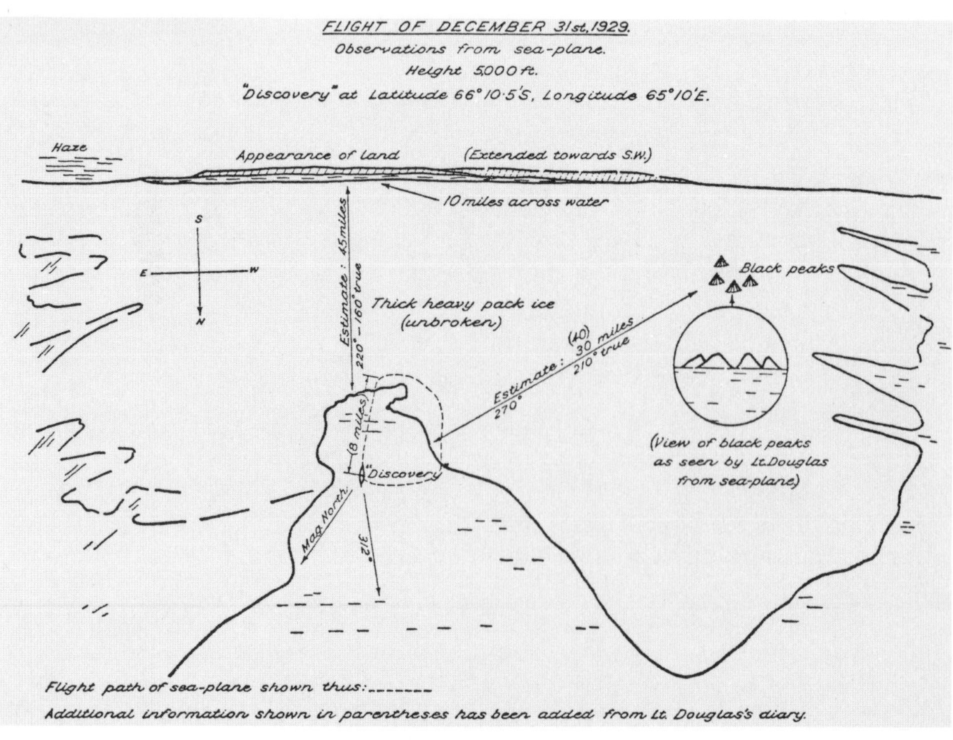

A sketch of Antarctic territory made from 1,525 metres (5,000 feet) by Campbell and Douglas during their first flight of 31 December 1929.

When the weather cleared two days later, Flight Lieutenant Campbell, with Mawson as his observer, took off after lunch to investigate the rising plateau and rocky peaks that had been sighted to the south. Following a triangular course, they rose to 1,220 metres (4,000 feet) in an outside temperature of –7°C (20°F). Looking from the open cockpit on his first Antarctic flight, Mawson contemplated the enormity of the continent he strove to explore, a white world of jagged coastal cliffs and swelling icesheet pierced by blue and black-faced mountains. It was new land! The diary continued:

> January 5, 1930
>
> Heavy laden with wireless gear, which would not act when tried — evidently wire connection wrong...Took camera but after exposing first plate could not operate changer in box, something wrong inside. I pulled so hard that pulled back [box] off and spoiled exposed plate...
>
> As we rose, a wider and wider view of the land unfolded. A black, rugged mountain appeared to the east of the rising plateau slopes. Tips of peaks rose from the plateau elsewhere. Rock mountain outcrops appeared at intervals right around to even north of west. A few dimly seen black mountain masses showed up to extreme W, even beyond what had previously appeared to be the end of field of vision...
>
> Were in air just over 1 hour. On arrival at ship plane taken on board and left on floats as hoped for another flight further to west tomorrow. Simmers [the meteorologist] however, later reported conditions developing suggestive of a blizzard coming soon. I anticipate sufficient warning if weather changes to get plane off floats.

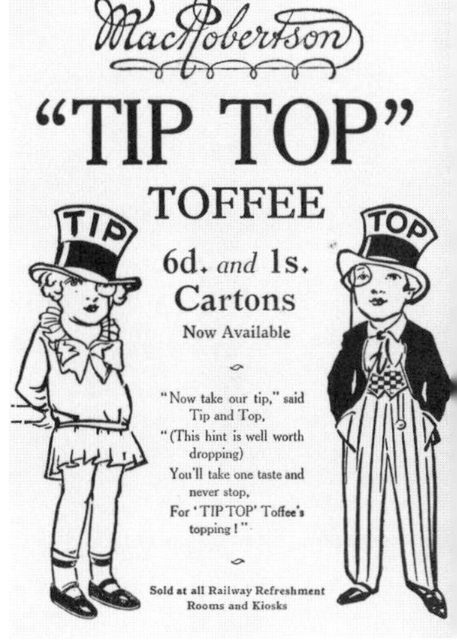

A MacRobertson advertisement of the 1930s. Sir Macpherson's confec-. tionery fortune was the source of his contribution to the two BANZARE voyages.

The flight of 5 January resulted in the naming of Mac-Robertson Land, and the Casey, David and Masson ranges. Mac-Robertson Land was in tribute to the Melbourne confectionery manufacturer whose substantial contribution had helped to make BANZARE a reality.[3] The three lonely mountain ranges were likewise in honour of men who had helped to put BANZARE in the field.

The Antarctic weather forever lay in wait, unpredictable in its swing from moments of calm to hours of violent assault upon the small ship that plodded laboriously through the pack on a south-westerly heading. From a 5 January entry of 'evening was magnificent. Placid water, scattered picturesque ice, plentiful emperor penguins', to the elemental havoc that followed:

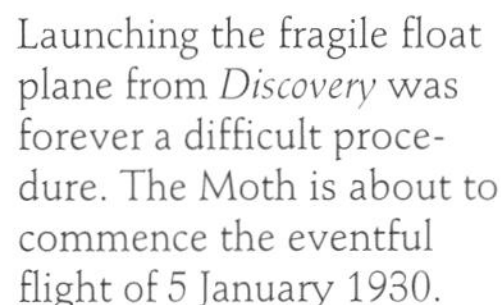

Launching the fragile float plane from *Discovery* was forever a difficult procedure. The Moth is about to commence the eventful flight of 5 January 1930.

January 6, 9 p.m.

A hurricane has been blowing all day, with very nasty short, steep sea. In fiercest times ship practically out of control as engines not strong enough to steer her . . . Spindrift flying off steep wave tops. Ship's deck snow, ice slush. Aeroplane coated with ice. Aviators stood by all day bracing and doing best for it . . . Ship pitched greatly and made confusion below. Doctor ill in bed. Hurley is making proclamation tablet. He photoed from topgallant crosstrees this morning at great risk, also from various parts of ship.

The menu for Christmas Day as the first BANZARE voyage headed through the pack ice.

The Canberra Times

SERVE THE NATIONAL CITY AND THROUGH IT THE NATION

CANBERRA, FRIDAY, FEBRUARY 22, 1929.

EXPEDITION

... THIS YEAR

... MAWSON TO LEAD

... BY BRITAIN

...ent has decided on an Aus... Antarctic immediately to ... and equip an expedition to ... this year. ... nted to lead the expedition, ...hip "Discovery."

ART EXHIBITION

Canberra Society's Progress

FINE COLLECTION HUNG

COAL INDUSTRY

ROYAL COMMISSION PROMISED

MR. BRUCE TO MEET REPRESENTATIVES

OF OWNERS AND MINERS IN CANBERRA

During a discussion of the coal industry in the House of Representatives, yesterday, the Prime Minister (Mr. Bruce), stated that preparations were being made for the appointment of a Royal Commission to inquire into the coal industry.

He announced that he had invited representatives of the colliery owners and of the coal miners to meet him in Canberra on Monday.

Broadcast From 3LO

BY HINKLER IN LONDON

BERT HINKLER

DISARMAMENT

BRITAIN CONSIDERING

Dominions to be Admitted

NORTHERN TERRITORY

Electoral Act Amended

AERIAL SEARCH

For Missing Boat

Aeroplanes To Be Used

Cost Of the Expedition

AIR FORCE PLANES

For Defence of London

LUMBER WAR

U.S. Capturing Trade

GOVERNMENT AIDS WITH BOUSES

PRIMARY INDUSTRIES

Full Inquiry Urged

THE ...

Improve... Contin...

WANTS ... OUTDO...

THE SEN...

Award Dis...

ON PARTY

SELECT COM...

FINANCIAL AG...

First Reading

TO CARRY EXPEDITION TO ANTARCTIC.

The "Discovery," which returned to Falmouth in 1927 after cruising for two years amid the ice-flows and islands that litter the Antarctic Seas south of Cape Horn, South America. The ship was specially built for Captain Scott's first expedition, and was "frozen in" in the Ross Sea for nearly two years. Since that time the vessel has been identified with many voyages of discovery and adventure. During her last mission the crew of scientists was engaged in oceanographical, meteorological, and other scientific investigation.

The decision to send another Australian expedition south made front-page news, as evidenced in a newspaper of 22 February 1929. Mawson contracted to transmit reports of BANZARE's progress back to the press.

Before the expedition left Cape Town the previous October the local and overseas press had speculated about the territorial intentions of the Norwegian government. 'Another race to the Pole?' asked one editorial, reflecting on the massive investment in that country's whaling fleet. 'What are the Norsemen up to? Secret orders to claim more land...intruding on British preserves...?'[4] To which Norway's editorial writers replied, in essence, that they had as much right as anyone to any no-man's land which might be discovered.[5]

While *Discovery* gradually nosed westwards, a radio message had arrived near midnight on 2 January from R. G. Casey in London, advising Mawson of a Norwegian claim upon the Antarctic sector between Enderby Land and Coats Land.[6] Mawson asked that the message be taken to Captain Davis. In his diary he added: 'Not long after I heard the engines chugging faster and guessed that JK had got a hustle on'.

A week later a second message reached the ship from Dr Henderson (secretary of the External Affairs Department) reminding Mawson of the urgency of his territorial mission. In a correction to the previous dispatch, the new Norwegian claim had been identified as 100 kilometres (62 miles) of coast between Enderby and Kemp Lands, near where *Discovery* was then positioned. Mawson expressed obvious dismay at the turn of events:

January 9

This is most exasperating, for they [the Norwegians] have evidently made a direct voyage here to raise their flag, and they knew this was in our itinerary. This sort of thing is not helpful to science, for it means to compete with such 'explorers' an expedition should not arrange any organised programme of detailed scientific work but just rush to most likely points of coast to make landing and raise flags. When we heard at Cape Town that the Norwegians had on foot, [ie in progress] an Antarctic expedition with sealed orders I cabled London to get in touch with Norway and inform them of our plans and ask for their programme. All they replied was that theirs was a scientific expedition. They knew that we were going to Kemp and Enderby Land. They did not inform us that they were making for vicinity of Enderby Land.

MAWSON PARTY.

Coast of Enderby Land.

OBSERVATIONS FROM 'PLANE

(By Wireless From Sir Douglas Mawson on Board the Discovery.)

(All Rights Reserved.)

Jan. 27.

"We spent January 24, 25, and 26 along the north coast of Enderby Land, adding detail to maps by aid of the aeroplane, piloted by Lieutenant Campbell and Lieutenant Douglas. On one occasion, at an elevation of 4000ft, some 73 peaks, the highest rising to 7000ft, were observed protruding through the ice plateau, which was observed still to be rising to the south to a greater elevation than 4000ft.

"From the aeroplane, our photographer, Captain Hurley, secured cinematograph views of the coastline and the land ice and sea ice formations. Hereabouts the land ice slopes are generally of the nature of glistening ice to a height of 2000ft, above which level they are composed of hard, compressed surfaces, offering the best possible conditions for sledging.

"The whole region is most attractive for land operations. The meteorologist, Mr. Simmers, made good use of recent fine weather, on several occasions observing test balloons to a height of 4000ft. Professor Johnston, using both Monagasque and Otter trawls, made extensive collections of the marine bottom life of the continental shelf. In some of these catches, sponges, bristling with long siliceous spines, were so abundant that the biologists and their enthusiastic assistants soon found their hands and clothing loaded with irritating invisible glassy spines. Now, every time we bend or sit down, a hope is registered that further dredgings will be free from such prickly objects.

"The position of the Discovery is 62.51 degrees south by 54.16 degrees east."

Sir Douglas Mawson has telegraphed stating that he is making for Kerguelen Island to replenish the Discovery's coal supply.

(Reproduction in whole or in part outside Australia forbidden.)

For polar expeditions in the Mawson era, finding new whaling grounds was one of their declared objectives. The story appeared in the *Sydney Morning Herald* of 8 February 1930.

Mawson was on the lookout for a landing place at which he could make his first territorial proclamation. However, he received short shrift on visiting the captain's cabin. To his suggestion of a closer approach to the MacRobertson or Kemp Land coasts, Davis refused and added: 'I am not going to take any risks for that bloody rubbishing business of raising the flag ashore'.

On 13 January Mawson achieved BANZARE's first landing in Antarctica.[7] At a rocky outcrop off Enderby Land which he aptly named Proclamation Island, they raised the British flag (always the British flag, not Australia's) while Mawson read from the document of possession:

In the name of His Majesty King George the Fifth, King of Great Britain, Ireland and the British Dominions beyond the Seas, Emperor of India.

Whereas I have it in command from His Majesty King George to assert the sovereign rights of His Majesty over British land discoveries met with in Antarctica. Now, therefore, I, Sir Douglas Mawson, do hereby proclaim and declare to all men, that, from and after the date of these presents, the full sovereignty of the territory of Enderby Land, Kemp Land, MacRobertson Land together with off-lying Islands as located in our charts constituting a sector of the Antarctic Regions lying between longitudes 73° East of Greenwich and 47° East of Greenwich South of Latitude 65° vests in His Majesty King George Fifth His Heirs and successors for ever. Given under my hand on board the Exploring vessel

The men who gave Mawson his sailing orders gather around the BANZARE committee table in Melbourne. Mawson sits second from left, Major R. G. Casey stands third from left; at the end of the table is Sir MacPherson Robertson. On Robertson's right is Sir Edgeworth David who, with Mawson, had climbed Mount Erebus and reached the South Magnetic Pole in 1908.

Discovery now lying off the coast of this annexed land, in Latitude 65° 50'S, longitude 53° 30'E. The Thirteenth Day of January, 1930.
Witness:

Signed J. K Davis	Douglas Mawson
Master	Commanding Antarctic
S.Y. *Discovery*	Expedition 13.1.30
13.1.30	

Scientific pursuits apart, this 'bloody rubbishing business' of Davis' outburst was indeed the key action for which BANZARE had been dispatched; an action designed to demonstrate emphatically, and to all comers, that Britain held sway over this enormous sector of the ice continent.[8] Again, we turn to Mawson's notes for the background to this historic day:

January 13

Practically all staff embark in launch. On way in the motor broke down several times and had to get out oars. As [we] neared shore on SW end of island found large areas of lower slopes covered with Adelie Penguins. Sides of island all smoothed by ice. Landed . . . main party hastened to summit of island to fly the flag . . .

Very steep climb to top, but rewarded by magnificent view over grounded bergs — over 100 large ones in sight. Can observe many ice-capped islets in immediate vicinity. We erect flagpole, stacking rocks about the foot to make it secure. The tablet on pole faces south. Proclamation read at noon. Three cheers given for King, and God Save King sung. Hurley takes photo . . . On way down I collect quantity of rocks, making a very heavy load. Had rucksack of rocks, camera case with rocks inside, rocks in pockets and hands, and pick. Had very arduous descent . . . The pack ice had closed around island whilst we were ashore, so that we [were] gradually becoming isolated from *Discovery*. On this account could no longer remain on island but need to push off and join ship. Launch broke down several times on way to ship.

The day after their Proclamation Island landing, Mawson had a first-hand opportunity to find 'what the Norsemen were up to'. As *Discovery* sailed close by the rocky promontory of Cape Ann, out from between 'bergs and drifting floes a small vessel was seen to approach. Binoculars showed it to be low in the water and loaded with two largish aircraft, one in the well deck, the other at the stern. '*Norvegia*' cried the lookout.[9] Mawson instructed Davis to hoist a friendly signal, 'wish you pleasant voyage'. As the two vessels closed, through a megaphone the question was asked: 'May Captain Riiser-Larsen come aboard to meet Sir Douglas Mawson¿' In reply to their shouted response *Norvegia*'s launch bore the visitor to a lonely rendezvous amid the ice floes of the Antarctic coast.

January 14

Davis received Larsen at gangway and introduced him to me. We went to chart room and Davis' cabin to talk. Larsen said 'There has been much said in the newspapers about our expedition. I want to tell you what we have been doing'. So he told us that the *Norvegia*, in company with the mother ship, had come down from Bouvet to Valdivia Bay where held up by ice; that aeroplane reconnaissance had shown open water inside; that aeroplane alighted in water alongside coast, taxied to shore, pulled itself out of water with own power. They then set off on skis with object of reaching a nunatak inland where to raise flag as shore [was] ice only. After 2 hours the nunatak appeared as far off as ever and, seeing cloud forming on it, suggesting blizzard, they retreated.

He said that they had been warned from Norway against doing many things which they were told would be resented by Great Britain. I judged from what he said that they had been instructed from Norway not to raise Norwegian flag on Enderby Land or Kemp Land. I did not ask him exactly what they had done. I merely listened to what he volunteered. I then told him what we had mapped in coast approximately from about 73°E longitude to present position, that we had been right along Kemp-Enderby Land coast...said we were very sorry to learn in Cape Town that there was the possibility of a Norwegian expedition operating in an area that might overlap ours ...we were hoping that the Norwegian expedition would keep W of 40°E longitude, and that Norway had been informed that we would not go west of that line...Riiser-Larsen is a very fine fellow. When they departed we all gave them 3 cheers for the *Norvegia*.

Companies which donated supplies to the expedition, or sold them at discounted prices, won the opportunity of advertising that their wares were enjoyed in the frozen south.

ANTARCTIC exploration still thrills the world, for it demands courage and real stamina of those who brave its hardships. Profiting by his experience with Shackleton and the previous Australian expedition to the South Pole, Sir Douglas Mawson, who this year will lead the Australian Government Expedition to the Antarctic, is leaving nothing to chance.

"The successful work of an expedition," he says, "depends on the health of the men who form its members, and *good and suitable* food reduces to a minimum the danger of scurvy which has marred many polar enterprises." In provisioning *The Discovery* with the supplies upon which the fitness and lives of his men will depend for two hard years on the ice, Sir Douglas has selected CROSSE & BLACKWELL'S foods from all others as those in which he can place absolute confidence.

In his choice Sir Douglas Mawson has confirmed the judgment of Commander Byrd, whose expedition to the Ross Sea has for many months enjoyed Crosse & Blackwell's foods. He has confirmed the choice of a million careful housewives, too.

Famous for two hundred years, Crosse & Blackwell's foods still maintain the old-time standards of quality and purity. Prepared in spotless kitchens, from the finest ingredients, they are at once wholesome and delicious. You will find Crosse & Blackwell's foods at your grocers —identical in quality with those chosen by Mawson, by Byrd and by knowing chefs and housewives the world over. Serve them regularly on your table and you will experience new delights each day.

When
Good Food
means everything

WAY back in 1845, when Sir John Franklin undertook an expedition to the North Pole, there was no precedent from which to draw experience. Consequently every man of Sir John's party perished of scurvy. There was plenty of food, *but it was not of the right kind*. Since then science has shown us how to select foods of definite dietetic value. No longer is it necessary for us to experiment, but no matter whether we are providing for an Antarctic expedition or for the family table it must still be remembered that danger—just as tragic in the long run —lies in wait for those who do not discriminate in the choice of foods.

Crosse & Blackwell
famous for quality

All good grocers sell Crosse & Blackwell's famous products. Among the many delicious varieties you will find—

POTTED MEATS, SOUPS, FISH, FISH PASTES, SAUCES, PICKLES, CHUTNEY, ESSENCES, CALVES' FEET JELLY, OLIVES, CAPERS, PUDDINGS, JAMS, MARMALADE, and a host of other good things.

SUPPLIERS OF GOOD FOODS FOR TWO HUNDRED YEARS

BGLE — Rymill's Way

An Antarctic pathfinder — John Rymill.

South Australia claims three most notable figures in the annals of Antarctic exploration — Mawson, Wilkins and Rymill. Mawson (admittedly born in England) is certainly the most famous, while Wilkins, the first man to fly over Antarctica, deserves much more recognition. But what of John Rymill? Outside a narrow circle of the polar fraternity his exploits are almost entirely unknown.

Born at the family homestead on Old Penola estate in 1905, John Riddoch Rymill had the bushman's natural attributes of innovation and survival; it was said 'he could fix most things'. After leaving Australia, his tertiary education gained in London and Cambridge was gauged at preparing him for polar exploration. In 1928, at de Havilland's Hendon establishment, he obtained British Ministry Licence No. 1611, qualifying him for 'all types of flying machines'. He was a pilot in the British Arctic Air Route Expedition of 1930–31, where he and fellow aviator Wilfred Hampton showed their skills in using pieces of driftwood steamed into shape to repair two damaged Tiger Moths.

Yet it was the leadership of this man of accomplishment and quiet authority that enabled his work to make a lasting impression on the pattern of much future polar exploration. His British Graham Land Expedition (BGLE) of 1934–37 was austere, deliberately limited in its scope and superbly self-reliant. A budget of £20,000 proved sufficient to support the BGLE over three seasons in Antarctica. Rymill's objective was equally concise: to penetrate and survey the coast of the Weddell Sea which, because of the fastness of the pack ice, had proved invincible to seaborne approaches. He reckoned to reach the Weddell coast by finding a way to the eastern side of Graham Land through one of the channels which supposedly intersected the peninsula, or by scaling its sheer-sided mountains.

Rymill's ship, *Penola* (named after his

birthplace), mirrored economy itself. Bought for £3,000, this 130-tonne oak-hulled Brittany fishing schooner, equipped with two auxiliary 50-horsepower diesels, would voyage to and from Antarctica over a distance of 43,000 kilometres (27,000 miles), half under sail alone. Rymill attracted a team of young and enthusiastic scientists, all of them seasoned volunteers. Four of his companions had been with him on previous Arctic expeditions; his captain, Lieutenant R. E. Ryder, RN, later won the Victoria Cross for his role in the British raid on German forces at St Nazaire.

BGLE's one aircraft was equally austere, yet ideal for the task. The de Havilland Fox Moth, powered by a 120-horsepower Gipsy Major engine, carried a survey camera, a radio and could accommodate a three-man crew. It gave them a range of about 650 kilometres (400 miles). Packed into *Penola*'s limited deck space was a motor boat, a tractor and a bunch of husky sledge dogs — 64 when they set out and 15 still alive on reaching Graham Land, though another 43 were bred during their stay.

The sixteen men of the BGLE, five aboard ship and the rest on the ice, were organised into small specialised teams dedicated to surveying and mapping, atmospheric and auroral studies, magnetism, meteorology and geology. They built their own two-storey 'house' and aeroplane hangar at two separate locations. As an example of Rymill's attention to detail, each team member was assigned to cooking duties on the AGA fuel stove for a week in turn.

Though BGLE intended no epic flights, the Moth, equipped either with floats or skis and piloted by Wilfred Hampton, achieved a satisfying record of reconnaissance and ground party support. The southerly sweeps of February 1935 were perhaps the most rewarding; two observers sat forward of the pilot to operate the Eagle III vertical camera in photographing 1,600 kilometres (1,000 miles) of Graham Land's west coast. Rymill wrote of 'magnificent views of awe-inspiring scenery'.

The British Graham Land Expedition (BGLE) established its first base at the Argentine Islands in 1934. The de Havilland Fox Moth carried a three-man crew and was equipped for aerial photography in conjunction with securing strict ground-control fixes.

In their first year the expedition operated from a base on the Argentine Islands at 65°15' South. For the second season they moved to a more southerly position at Marguerite Bay when Rymill realised that the mountainous spine of the peninsula would restrict their work to the western shore. His aerial surveyors and ground control parties, the latter travelling by dog sledge, made one especially important contribution to Antarctic knowledge in traversing the massive strait, later named King George VI Sound, which separated Alexander I Land from the peninsula proper. In failing to find a path to the peninsula's east coast, they were also able to disprove the existence of the channels — the Casey, Lurabee and Stefansson — which supposedly divided Graham Land from the rest of the Antarctic continent. Though it took one South Australian to show another wrong (for it was Wilkins' pioneering flights that had reported Graham Land as a detached archipelago), the correction was hardly a black mark against the aviation pioneer of eight years earlier who had relied on aerial sightings to deliver his finding; nor had Lincoln Ellsworth's flights of 1935 disputed Wilkins' observations.

In the words of the Australian polar authority, Arthur Scholes:

Treaty Series No. 73 (1938)

EXCHANGE OF NOTES

between His Majesty's Governments in the United Kingdom, the Commonwealth of Australia and New Zealand and the French Government

regarding

AERIAL NAVIGATION IN THE ANTARCTIC

Paris, October 25, 1938

Presented by the Secretary of State for Foreign Affairs to Parliament by Command of His Majesty

LONDON

PRINTED AND PUBLISHED BY HIS MAJESTY'S STATIONERY OFFICE

To be purchased directly from H.M. STATIONERY OFFICE at the following addresses: York House, Kingsway, London, W.C.2; 120 George Street, Edinburgh 2; 26 York Street, Manchester 1; 1 St. Andrew's Crescent, Cardiff; 80 Chichester Street, Belfast; or through any bookseller

1938

Price 1*d.* net

Cmd. 5900

Development of Antarctic aviation called for new regulations. The multi-nation navigation papers appeared in 1938.

Rymill established that no useful mapping is possible in the Antarctic regions by aerial survey alone; any observations from the air have to be followed up, checked and fixed by accurate ground reconnaissance. Rymill was the first of modern Polar explorers to realise this fact and put it into practice. In his accounts of the expedition describing the journeys over the death-filled crevasses and treacherous glaciers Rymill, in his modest style, made them appear as simple excursions into suburbia. However...Rymill worked over shorter ranges, but his mapping and observations were accurate to a degree and contained no guess-work. He mapped nothing that he could not confirm by personal exploration. His aim was always to concentrate on certain defined objectives and to make a good job of those before attempting anything further. An important result of Rymill's expeditions was that he eliminated the terrible privations which always seemed to form such a large part of the early experiences of Antarctic travellers. Rymill and his companions undoubtedly struck hardships, but... they carried out their work with more efficiency than their predecessors, because they were better sheltered, better clothed and better fed. (Scholes: 186, 194.)

The British government did not acknowledge BGLE as an official venture because of the risk of confrontation with Argentina over the contested Antarctic claims. The Colonial Office, however, did contribute £10,000 to Rymill's effort while certain leading institutions and industrialists, among them Lloyds Bank and Lord Leverhulme, also provided support in cash or kind.

The BGLE completed its work in March 1936 and returned to England with accurate maps of the wild southern end of Graham Land where only supposition, at best, had previously existed. When the Australian government considered sending another expedition to continue the work of Mawson's BANZARE, Rymill offered himself as leader but World War II intervened.

On the role of the aviator, he had written:

> It would appear from experience in other parts of the Antarctic that aeroplanes can be of the utmost importance in scouting for exploring ships or discovering positions for possible winter quarters on land. When, but not until, machines are available which can land on and take off from a rough surface of land or ice, they will become available for all the purposes of exploration. Meanwhile, astronomical observations, without which no useful mapping is possible, must be made from the surface. (Rymill: 20)

Rymill lived the rest of his life as a South Australian grazier. He was a giant of a man, physically and in the breadth of his exploration. As a young man he had studied anthropology at London University, then worked at the Scott Polar Research Institute under Professor Frank Debenham, a veteran of Scott's second expedition. He had explored the Arctic regions, climbed alpine mountains and added to his proficiency with qualifications from cook to aviator, surveyor to bookkeeper. An automobile accident in 1968 ended the life of this modest man who had recast the map of Western Antarctica and in so doing proved himself an outstandingly successful pathfinder of Antarctic exploration.

The BGLE float plane goes in search of open water. Rymill ran an efficient expedition that was limited in objectives, but highly effective in the goals it achieved.

Mawson's diary suggests the two strong men of Antarctica met as friends and farewelled as friends in an atmosphere respectful of one another's polar exploits. Would anything else have been folly? They agreed it was not sensible for their exploration to overlap. An outcome of the meeting was that Norway limited its national claims to the western side of 45° East longitude, for the Norwegian government accepted Britain's right to Enderby Land. Mawson showed his appreciation in volunteering that a 1,830-metre (6,000-foot) mountain in the Tula Range of Enderby Land should be named Mount Riiser-Larsen and that another peak bear the title of the Norwegian whaling magnate, Mount Consul Lars Christensen.

After *Norvegia*'s departure, Davis struck his inevitable discordant note at the wardroom table:

ANTARCTICA.

Mawson Expedition.

THE SCIENTIFIC STAFF.

MELBOURNE, Wednesday.

The personnel of the scientific staff of the Australian Antarctic Expedition was announced to-day by the chairman of the Australian committee (Sir George Pearce) as follows:—

Commander: Sir Douglas Mawson, Professor of Geology (Adelaide).

Medical officer: Dr. W. Wilson Ingram, of Macquarie-street, Sydney

Senior zoologist: Professor Harvey Johnston, Professor of Zoology (Adelaide).

Assistant zoologist (with special duties in taxidermy): Mr. H. O. Fletcher (Australian Museum, Sydney).

Assistant zoologist (specialising in ornithology and taxidermy): Mr. Falla.

Chemist: Mr Alfred Howard, M.Sc.

Plankton expert: Mr. Marr,

Meteorologist: Mr. H. G. Simmers. (New Zealand).

Survey officer: Instructor-Commander H. Moyes.

Echo-sounding and wireless expert: Petty-officer Williams (appointed in England).

Official photographer and cinematographer: Mr. Frank Hurley.

Pilot: Pilot S. Campbell, of H.M.A.S. Albatross, seconded to the expedition by the Australian Air Force.

Sir George Pearce said that the selection of a second pilot woud be made shortly, and if it was possible to find the necessary accommodation, another physicist would be added to the party

PERSONAL SKETCHES

THE COMMANDER.

Sir Douglas Mawson, C.B.E., D.Sc., F.R.S., Professor of Geology at Adelaide University, and commander of the expedition, was born at Bradford, Yorkshire, in 1882.

Entering Sydney University at the age of 18 years, he graduated Bachelor of Mining Engineering three years later, and B.Sc in 1904. In the next year he was appointed lecturer in Mineralogy and Petrology at Adelaide University, where he obtained his D.Sc. degree in 1909. He accompanied Sir Ernest Shackleton's expedition to the Antarctic in 1907, and was one of the discoverers of the South Magnetic Pole. He was leader of the Australian Expedition to the Antarctic in 1912-14, discovering and mapping 1000 miles of new Antarctic coastline. In 1914 he was knighted. For three and a half years of the war he was engaged in work for the British Ministry for Munitions, resuming his work at Adelaide University in 1919. He holds the special medal of the Royal Geographical Society, founder's medal Royal Geographical Society, 1915, King's Polar Medal (two bars), gold medals of the America and Chicago Geographical Societies, Bigsby gold medal of the Geographical Society of London, and is also Officer of the Order of St. Maurice and St. Lazarus, and Commander of the Order of the Crown of Italy.

INSTRUCTOR-COMMANDER H. MOYES.

Instructor-Commander H. Moyes, of H.M.A.S. Penguin, who has been seconded to the expedition as survey officer, by the Navy Department will make his second trip to the Antarctic with Dr. Mawson. He was born in South Australia, and received his early education at St. Peters College, Adelaide. He took the engineering course at the Adelaide University, and, after graduation, returned to St. Peters College as science master, and later held similar positions at Townsville and Rockhampton Grammar schools. In 1911 Instructor-Commander Moyes was appointed to the scientific staff of the Australasian Antarctic expedition under Dr. Mawson, and acted as meteorologist with the second base party for eighteen under Mr. Frank Wild, returning to Australia in 1913. In January, 1914, he was appointed instructor in navigation at the Royal Australian Naval College, Geelong, and later at Jervis Bay. During the war he served in H.M.A.S. Encounter.

Instructor-Commander Moyes proceeded to the Antarctic in October, 1916, with the relief expedition which searched for Shackleton's party, acting as navigating officer.

Since the war Instructor-Commander Moyes has served in various ships of the Australian fleet, including H.M.A.Ss. Encounter, Sydney, Melbourne, and Australia, and at the Flinders Naval Depot. He was promoted to his present position in 1924, and is senior officer of this branch of the Navy. He is well-known in athletic circles, having held the high and broad jump championships of South Australia for four years. His wife was formerly Miss Miriam King, of Strathfield.

present position in 1924, and is senior officer of this branch of the Navy. He is well-known in athletic circles, having held the high and broad jump championships of South Australia for four years. His wife was formerly Miss Miriam King, of Strathfield.

PROFESSOR T. H. JOHNSTON.

Professor Thomas Harvey Johnston, senior zoologist of the expedition, was born at Sydney in December, 1881, and was educated at Sydney University. At present he fills the Chair of Zoology at the University of Adelaide. Prior to coming to Adelaide he was on the staff of the Queensland University. In 1912 he was lent to the Queensland Government as scientific controller of the investigations conducted in New South Wales and Queensland by the Commonwealth Prickly Pear Board. He travelled extensively abroad on the work of the commission, and collected much valuable data on the destruction of the pest. From 1920 to 1923, Professor Johnston was scientific controller of the Commonwealth prickly pear investigations which were conducted in New South Wales and Queensland. He was awarded the Syme Research medal and prize by the University of Melbourne, and since going to Adelaide has occupied the position of honorary curator of helminthology in the South Australian museum. He is the author of numerous publications on parasitology and entomology in Australian, Indian, and European journals.

DR. W. WILSON INGRAM.

The medical officer of the expedition, Dr. W. Wilson Ingram, who is in private practice in Sydney, came to Australia in 1919. He was born in Scotland in 1889, and graduated M.B., with honours at the University of Aberdeen. He carried out research work at the Lister Institute, London, and was assistant to the late Dr. E. C. Hort, of Harley-street, London. Dr. Wilson Ingram had a distinguished war career, being one of the "Old Contemptibles," and is vice-president of the Fellowship of Mons in Sydney. He was severely wounded, and was awarded the Military Cross and the Mons Star, and was mentioned in despatches. From 1920 to 1926 Dr. Wilson Ingram was lecturer in physiology at the Sydney University. He is honorary director of the Institute of Medical Research associated with the Royal North Shore Hospital, and is also honorary physician to that institution.

MR. ALFRED HOWARD.

Mr. Alfred Howard is 23 years of age, and has been engaged for two years in research work in the chemistry school at the University of Melbourne. He obtained his Master of Science degree in March, 1928, and has already proved his ability in research work, and has made some original contributions on problems of organic chemistry. He has had a full training in physical and general chemistry, and this has qualified him for the work which he will be called upon to undertake in the Antarctic. Mr. Howard will investigate oceanography, studying the composition of the sea water (which has an important bearing on the food supply of fish).

MR. FRANK HURLEY.

Mr. Frank Hurley, official photographer and cinematographer, has had much Antarctic experience. He was photographer to the Shackleton expedition, and also to the Australian Antarctic expedition led by Sir Douglas Mawson—1912-14. Mr. Hurley, who is a specialist in aerial photography, has also carried out exploration work in Papua.

FLYING-OFFICER CAMPBELL.

Flying-Officer S. A. C. Campbell is a member of No. 101 Flight of the Royal Australian Air Force, which is on board the seaplane carrier Albatross. He is a young man with the reputation of a skilful pilot, and has been in the Air Force for three years, during which time he has flown almost every type of machine. He has been in the Albatross since its commissioning, and is accompanying the vessel on her cruise to New Guinea.

MR. H. O. FLETCHER.

Mr. H. O. Fletcher, the assistant zoologist with the party, will have also special duties in taxidermy. He is 26 years of age, and is attached to the staff of the Australian Museum, Sydney. He joined the staff as a boy, and has had extensive experience in collecting specimens. He attended classes in geology at the University, and was a member of the Lake Eyre (South Australia) survey party.

MR. FALLA.

Mr. Falla, (who was nominated by the Government of New Zealand for the position of assistant zoologist), will specialise in ornithology and taxidermy. He has had much experience in zoological expeditions.

MR. W. MARR.

Mr. W. Marr, the plankton expert, was on the Discovery in a former expedition, and is thoroughly familiar with the methods adopted for plankton work. Plankton is a collective name for all forms of floating of organic life found at various depths of the ocean.

MR. H. G. SIMMERS.

Mr. H. G. Simmers, meteorologist, was nominated by the New Zealand Government. He is a member of the staff of the Meteorological Bureau, Wellington, which is at present under the control of Dr. Edward Kidson formerly of the Meteorological Bureau, Melbourne.

In the 1930s, polar expeditions were in the news. Byrd, Ellsworth, Mawson, Wilkins, the Norwegians and Germans were on the ice; BGLE, despite its small size, also reached the headlines.

January 16

JK was most voluble in his praises of Norwegians, referred to their flying in to shore in plane as a wonderful execution, said we could never do anything like that — they are real explorers, we are just novices. He went on in this sort of strain until I had to tell him that they might be able to put it over us in matters of seamanship, he could judge that but that in other departments we are equal or better than anything on the *Norvegia*. He then went on with a lot of drivel about our work, said it was nothing but a cinema show. He applauded the Norwegians for their flag raising effort, and then said we were nothing but a lot of flag raising humbugs and that he had no time for 'this bloody flag waving business'. I mention these things so as to be able later to recall how utterly imbecile JK is. He is not mentally balanced.

They rode out a stormy week in the vicinity of Proclamation Island until the next flight of 24 January when Campbell took off from the lee side of a stranded iceberg. Mawson and Frank Hurley next day put on helmets and goggles to go flying. Hurley took still and movie pictures while Mawson's flight was the one in which he made a second territorial claim. His diary of 25 January reported:

Flying over land-ice for a couple miles inland at 3,000ft I passed Campbell the flag attached to mast, and he stalled engine and passed [it] over side. I retained the proclamation, claiming once more all the land discovered, and this time including the newly

> discovered slice at our farthest west. Campbell spotted the flag lying on the ice surface and drew my attention to it. We then flew back to ship.

When an edgy and pessimistic Davis refused to take *Discovery* close to the shore Mawson reported 'all the members of the staff were broken-hearted' that the irascible skipper had denied them the chance of setting foot on the Antarctic continent. 'His attitude', declared Mawson, was 'one in charge of a passenger ship in regular service...on no account will he take even a slight risk...he should not be sailing an exploring expedition.'

In the rewarding though final aerial journeys of the following day, some 200 peaks were sighted rising from the ice sheet, at an average estimated height of 2,140 metres (7,000 feet).[10]

> January 26
>
> All that can be done is to arrange with him [Davis] that he allow us all day to carry out flying...Aeroplane got out, and Hurley, Douglas made flights for photographs, both cine and still. They went to 4,200 feet, saw further extension of mountain peaks to south over ice plateau. They saw peaks rising much higher than plane, estimated at 7,000 feet anyway. Also saw ice slopes of plateau going higher than aeroplane. Saw small patches of water in west lee of ice cliff projections all along coast. Finally Moyes, with his sketch pad, went up with Campbell to get idea of the coastline and inland peaks. Both flights of 4,000 feet.

Davis would not allow time for further exploration. His attention was concentrated on the heap of coal remaining in the bunkers, an amount Mawson thought sufficient to permit at least another week's westerly cruising. He recorded his resentment at Davis' intransigence and the decision to head northwards for Kerguelen Island:

> I have left the Antarctic coast with great regret — another week here with aeroplane would have completed mapping MacRobertson Land and added detail of Scott Mountains. I am sure we could have spared another 20 tons of coal for this; in fact, if I was in full authority over the handling of vessel, I would not leave these shores until down to 80 tons. As it is, JKD boasts openly that he will leave not later than this evening no matter what I say. As it is JKD is frightfully pessimistic of our ever reaching Kerguelen. He says the westerly gales will be so bad that we will neither be able to accomplish any marine work nor land at Kerguelen — we will be blown past Kerguelen and lucky if can make Australia.

Though some aerial surveying was made above the French possession, the Antarctic phase of the first BANZARE had abruptly concluded. Yet they returned to Australia with 'several tons' of geological samples together with records of 750 deep sea soundings, detailed hydrological records, charting of pack ice movement and meteorological records and observations, especially with regard to movement of cold surface water which could influence Australia's weather conditions.

The Proclamation document, bringing King George V Land and Oates Land under the British flag, read by Sir Douglas Mawson at Cape Denison on 5 January 1931.

Proclamation

In the name of His Majesty George the Fifth King of Great Britain, Ireland, and the British Dominions beyond the Seas, Emperor of India.

By Sir Douglas Mawson.

Whereas I have it in command from His Majesty King George the Fifth to assert the sovereign rights of His Majesty over British land discoveries met with in Antarctica. Now, therefore, I, Sir Douglas Mawson, do hereby proclaim and declare to all men that, from and after the date of these presents, the full sovereignty of the Territory of King George V Land and its extension under the name of Oates Land situated between Longitudes 142 and 160 degrees east of Greenwich and between Latitude 66 degrees south and the South Pole. Included herein are the following Islands: Curzon Archipelago: Way Archipelago: Dixson Island: Mackellar Islets: Hodgeman Islets, vests in His Majesty King George the Fifth, his heirs and successors, for ever.

Given under my hand at Cape Denison on the Fifth day of January, 1931.

Douglas Mawson 5.1.31

Fitting floats and propeller to their aircraft is the discussion topic of Campell (*left*) and Douglas beside VH-ULD. Mawson wrote of 'the determination and skill' of his young air force aviators, 'whose capacity is of the highest order'.

Mawson, the Man

The man on the $100 note. Sir Douglas Mawson was of world stature among polar explorers.

Douglas Mawson came to Australia from Yorkshire as a boy. With degrees in mining, engineering and science from Sydney University, he was appointed a lecturer at Adelaide University and as a physicist, at the age of 25, he won a place in Shackleton's 1907–08 expedition. He was in the first party to climb Mount Erebus on McMurdo Sound, and was one of the three men first to reach the South Magnetic Pole.

Awarded a Doctorate of Science for his exploits, he conceived the idea of raising an Australasian Antarctic Expedition. His AAE brought a group of 25 young scientists and seamen in the steam yacht *Aurora* to establish a main base at Commonwealth Bay in December 1911. While *Aurora* completed three lengthy voyages which added King George V Land and Queen Mary Land to the knowledge of Antarctica, and surface teams probed south and west, Mawson himself led an eastern party for 500 kilometres (315 miles) along the edge of the continental plateau. The journey ended in tragedy when the young Belgrave 'Cherub' Ninnis was lost in a crevasse and Xavier Mertz died of exhaustion, leaving Mawson to fight his way back to the base alone.

Knighted in recognition of his outstanding leadership and discoveries, Mawson became Professor of Geology and mineralogy at Adelaide University from where, in 1929, he organised and led his second exploit, the British, Australian and New Zealand Antarctic Research Expedition — BANZARE.

A photograph of his benefactor, Sir MacPherson Robertson, hangs above Mawson's desk in his cabin on *Discovery*.

Captain Frank Hurley, who participated in AAE and BANZARE (as well as with Shackleton), made popular films of Mawson's work for theatre audiences of the 1930s.

In his 1930 report to the Commonwealth government, Mawson said:

> The Antarctic Continent has been either charted, or its location approximately indicated, through 28° of Longitude between 45°E and 73°E of Greenwich. Evidence deduced indicates that this land is portion of the great continental mass which occupies the major portion of the Antarctic regions. The land seen and charted includes the new area designated Mac-Robertson Land together with lands further to the west known as Kemp Land and Enderby Land, portions of which though vaguely reported 100 years ago were never since confirmed. The whole of this land and the offlying islands have been claimed for the Crown.

And further:

> it can now be definitely asserted that off the coast of Enderby Land there exists a very valuable whale fishery... From that fishery no doubt millions of pounds worth of products will be recovered during the next few years. That discovery alone is worth far more than all the cost of our exploring expedition.

By 30 April 1930 they had docked at Port Adelaide, whereupon the exasperated Hurley vowed 'never again to sail on a ship commanded by J. K. Davis'.

The result of Mawson's 1911–14 expedition had been overshadowed by the outbreak of World War I. From BANZARE he returned to find Australia sunk deeply into the worldwide depression. Despite the adverse economic climate he achieved the near impossible, raising a further £6,000 from Sir MacPherson Robertson who had already donated £10,000, and securing joint government agreement to let a second expedition go south.[11] He was thus able to win approval for the plan to explore westwards from his old stamping ground in the vicinity of King George V Land to the boundary of the area covered by BANZARE I.[12]

Of no small consequence, especially in generating public interest, was the arrival from the Antarctic waters in Tasmanian and New Zealand ports of four Norwegian ships, laden with record cargoes of whale oil. On 22 May 1930 Prime Minister Scullin announced to the House of Representatives: 'The Government has decided that the work in the Australian sector of the Antarctic, which is of considerable national interest and importance to the Commonwealth for economic, scientific, and other points of view, will be continued during the coming Antarctic summer season'.

In his article published in the *Sydney Morning Herald* on 10 December, Mawson described some aspects of the next expedition:

Norvegia, loaded almost to the gunwales with two aircraft, held a strange rendezvous with *Discovery* in the Antarctic seas. The Norwegian expedition had sailed 'under sealed orders', Mawson declared, and was intent 'on raising King Haakon's flag on as many lands as possible'.

> Since her return from last year's Antarctic cruise the *Discovery* has been thoroughly overhauled, and further improvements have been effected in the scientific fittings and equipment. Facilities for oceanographic work are now more comprehensive than ever.
>
> Our tiny aeroplane, the 'eye' of the *Discovery*, has been overhauled and again rendered good as new. With it we shall be able to see beyond the pack ice and to investigate many places inaccessible to the ship. Profiting by last year's experience, small modifications have been made to the aeroplane and to its wireless and camera equipment.
>
> We plan to complete so far as possible a survey of the broader features of the region more directly south of Australia, thus completing the work begun by our 1911 to 1914 expedition. Provisioned and adequately equipped with scientific instruments, the ship will be occupied throughout all the summer working from east to west through the ice-infested southern seas.

The second voyage left Hobart on 22 November under a new master, Captain J. K. MacKenzie, who had been first mate on the previous voyage. While he was not of Davis' defiant nature, Mawson soon found to his dismay that he had inherited a skipper with the same super-cautious leanings. Adequacy of fuel reserves continued to be a source of friction between the expedition leader and a master who seemed plagued with fear of sailing *Discovery* into some sort of dangerous predicament that would leave a blot on his career.

They headed due south from Tasmania, through the roaring forties and furious fifties, this time in the direction of the Balleny Islands, where coal was taken from the factory ship *Sir James Clark Ross*. Observing the directive 'to chart from King George V Land at 160° East', they swung about off the Oates Land coast and pushed their way through a region which Mawson had last sighted during the AAE 19 years previously. On 5 January 1931 they went ashore briefly at Commonwealth Bay; for Mawson what memories there must have been of the lost companions, Ninnis and Mertz, and his own lone struggle against starvation to reach the hut at Cape Denison, only to sight J. K. Davis sailing *Aurora* back to Australia...

Davis — the Gloomy Captain

John King Davis, born Kew, Surrey, on 19 February 1884, served for four years on the fully rigged sailing vessel *Celtic Chief*, gained first mate's certificate in 1906 and his extra master's certificate in 1908. He was appointed chief officer of steam yacht *Nimrod*, which took Shackleton's British Antarctic Expedition to McMurdo Sound; in 1909, as master of *Nimrod*, he brought Shackleton's party back to England. Two years later, as master of steam yacht *Aurora*, he was second in command of Douglas Mawson's Australasian Antarctic Expedition; during the three years until 1914 he completed five difficult voyages, which included oceanographic research, in establishing and relieving AAE's wintering-over parties at Macquarie Island, Commonwealth Bay and the Shackleton Ice Shelf.

In World War I he commanded the troop ship *Boonah* and towards the end of the war, with the rank of lieutenant commander, was Australian representative in London, dealing with repatriation of the AIF. In between, he again commanded *Aurora*, which in 1916–17 broke through into the Ross Sea to retrieve the 'shore party' survivors of Shackleton's failed trans-Antarctic expedition from McMurdo Sound.

In 1920 he was appointed Commonwealth Director of Navigation, a position which he held — except for the 1929–30 break as master of BANZARE's *Discovery* — until his retirement in 1949. A member of the Commonwealth's planning committee on Antarctic matters until 1962, he was twice invested with the King's Polar Medal as well as receiving the CBE and other distinguished awards for his Antarctic services. The Davis Sea, west of the Shackleton Ice Shelf, bears his name, as does Australia's second Antarctic base, established in 1957. He and Mawson were lifelong friends, and the bond between them continued despite the difficulties of divided control between ship's captain and expedition leader, evidenced in *Discovery*'s 1929-30 voyage. Davis' account of the earlier expeditions appeared in his book *High Latitude*, published in 1962. His side of the BANZARE affair, however, has yet to be heard. Davis died in Melbourne in 1967.

Captain John King Davis. As skipper of *Discovery*, he frequently clashed with Mawson during the first BANZARE voyage.

Wilkes Coast was added to the map when the new season's flights commenced on 7 January, just beyond the western boundary of Adelie Land.[13] Bad weather interrupted operations until 15 January when Stuart Campbell and Lieutenant Oom, the navy hydrographer who had replaced Moyes on the second cruise, climbed to 2,400 metres (8,000 feet) in search of open water close by the coast. Douglas and Oom flew again the following day at 65°5' South and 120°36' East when an ice-shrouded plateau, a continuation of the previous day's survey, was sighted. To all of this fresh discovery Mawson, on his 18 January flight with Campbell, gave the name of BANZARE Coast in commemoration of their passage.

Cloud and storms of blizzard intensity continued to interrupt flying. Chafing under the delays and knowing that they were fast losing what was supposed to be good aviation weather, Mawson persuaded Eric Douglas on 27 January to take up the Moth with himself as passenger. They climbed to 1,800 metres (6,000 feet) and saw a distant coastline:

> Ascended from sea with difficulty on account of big swell and some wind from E. Kept bumping the machine — bang bang, etc. She would nearly rise off top of wave, then fall into sea again with smack...Rose to 5,300 ft. Below a billowy sea of cloud. At about 4,700 ft could see line on S horizon coming above cloud stratum. Many large bergs aground. This particularly so a few miles to west of ship where counted about 40 bergs in small area, some very large. These must be aground. Many of the bergs heavily serracked, many also appear to be very decayed. When low, flew over large tabular berg near ship. It was seen to be riven by broad parallel crevassed lines [filled with snow] as if, from crown of berg, strips have been let down in steps to the sides. Many seals seen to be on the pack, should say about 100 to the square mile of pack from edge of 1 m inland. On reaching ship [we had] difficulty getting on board on account of swell and wind — end in smash! Penguins and whales view the catastrophe. Matheson, in dinghy, recovering gear was object of interest to whales — he was scared.

Strong wind and rising waves had awaited the Moth's return. Mawson's dismissal of the episode with the few words, 'end in smash!', excused near disaster to himself, Douglas and the plane. For agonising moments, the Moth hung half upside down from the ship's derrick, spilling petrol and secured only by one cable, while he and his pilot, tipped from the cockpit, clung to a pontoon to save themselves from being swept away in an angry sea.

Ritchie Simmers, the meteorologist gave a rather more detailed account of the incident, while Hurley captured the makings of catastrophe with his cine camera in a sequence that remains gripping even to this day:

> After about three-quarters of an hour's flight a good landing was made but great difficulty was experienced getting alongside, as with the ship moving slowly forward to keep head on to the swell, the plane had to taxi so slowly that she would not steer. In the end Dux got the hoisting line attached and then troubles came thick and fast. A roll tilted the plane backwards, one of the hooks holding the wire lifting cradle straightened out and the starboard wing and tail got under water. The sway we had on promptly canted the bus on her tail and she began to swing about bumping into the side of the ship and finally turned completely upside down. Dux, who was on top of the petrol tank, held himself as well as he could on the metal spreader on the cradle and ended up hanging upside down under the plane with his feet and legs dipping down into the water at each roll. A further difficulty was that the propeller was still revolving, so we couldn't secure her and as every roll meant something else broken, she was lowered into the water again a hopeless-looking cripple. Dux and Eric Douglas were soon in the pram, which had been sent away as soon as trouble seemed imminent and rope slings were rigged to replace the broken wire ones. What a wreck when we did get her aboard! However, things aren't as bad as they appeared likely to be as Stuart and Doug. say she can be mended alright and tonight have

> been hard at work on repairs...Hurley, by the way, was aloft with his camera as she came alongside and got a film of the whole ghastly business.

In his litany of damage done to VH-ULD, Campbell included that the float booms were buckled, petrol tank badly crumpled and torn and all the ribs on the port lower wingtip crushed in by immersion. Once again he and Douglas took the aircraft to pieces, straightened the metal booms and struts in the furnace, made ribs from packing cases and spliced and sewed and patched the mainplane. 'The petrol tank was my main worry,' Campbell continued, 'but Frank Hurley, that master of all trades, took it over and hid himself in a corner and after about three days of beating and riveting and soldering produced us a most admirable petrol tank again right back to its former streamline shape.'

Popular interest in the Antarctic expeditions led to the inevitable cartooning of 'life at the South Pole'.

On 6 February they were able to load 16 tons of coal from the *Lestris*. That evening Douglas and Campbell made another flight and from 425 metres (1,400 feet) reported seeing a faint line on the horizon, though uncertain whether it was land or cloud. To the day's events Mawson added, 'A wonderful red sunset, big red moon rose in SE'. During the next five days they were among the factory ships, tankers and catchers of the Norwegian fleet.[14] They came alongside Christensen's *Thorshammer* and Captain Klarius Mikkelsen invited Mawson aboard, whereupon he showed the Australian a chart of Enderby to Coats Land and indicated *Norvegia*'s position.

A few more flights were accomplished before the nervous MacKenzie advised the leader that he intended to turn *Discovery* homebound.

On 9 February, from 1,500 metres (5,000 feet) at 66°30' South and 76° East off the King Leopold Coast (as named by the Norwegians), Campbell with Mawson as observer looked down on a graveyard of stranded icebergs and, on the horizon, far to the south, saw more icebound territory. Once it was confirmed by sightings from the ship, Mawson named this region Princess Elizabeth Land after the young member of the royal family and future monarch.

Accompanied by Lieutenant Oom, Campbell made flights on 10 and 11 February. The second mission almost ended in tragedy when, close to takeoff, one of the floats struck a glancing blow against a slab of semi-submerged ice. The Moth faltered but remained upright and the float survived without a puncture as Campbell rapidly pulled up the nose to get them airborne. Mawson reported the air crew's close call in his usual matter-of-fact manner: 'Campbell cannot rise off water — no wind and no sea. Runs so far gets into water with brash [ice] narrowly escapes big piece and death'. Once safely overhead, the pilot reported a southerly bearing coast. Mawson continued: 'We steam for the open again...drink champagne toast as we are now close to new land. Campbell dropped flag on the land.' They came through a labyrinth of grounded tabular 'bergs, one close to them estimated at 52 metres (170 feet) above the waterline for which Mawson estimated total depth of about 280 metres (920 feet).

In these exciting few days towards the conclusion of BANZARE II, the explorer-aviators discovered the Amery Ice Shelf (which they mistook for land) and then, having reached Mac-Robertson Land of the first expedition, came upon notable outcrops of rock, two of which rose almost 300 metres

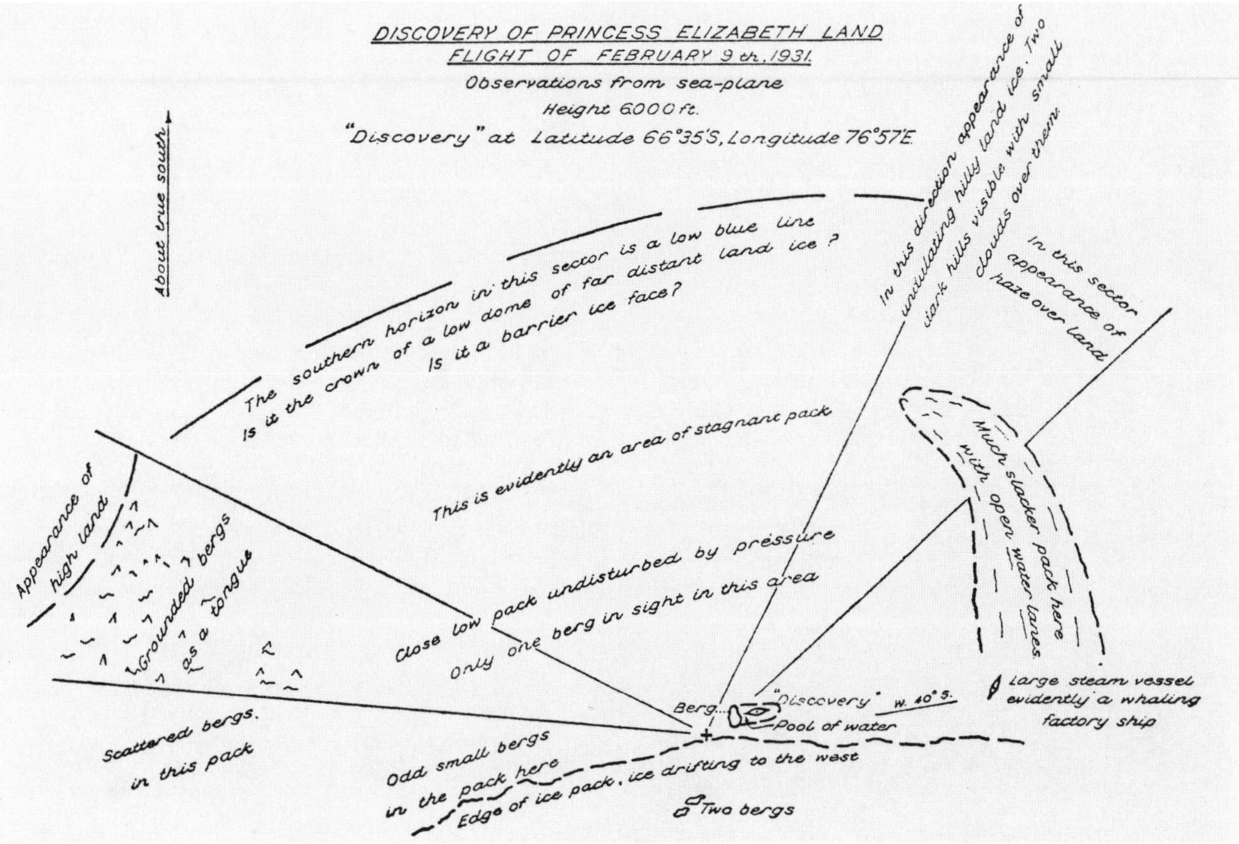

DISCOVERY OF PRINCESS ELIZABETH LAND
FLIGHT OF FEBRUARY 9th. 1931.
Observations from sea-plane
Height 6000 ft.
"Discovery" at Latitude 66°35'S, Longitude 76°57'E.
About true south
The southern horizon in this sector is a low blue line
Is it the crown of a low dome of far distant land ice?
Is it a barrier ice face?
In this direction appearance of undulating hilly land ice: Two dark hills visible with small clouds over them.
In this sector appearance of haze over land
This is evidently an area of stagnant pack
Appearance of high land
Grounded bergs as a tongue
Close low pack undisturbed by pressure
Only one berg in sight in this area
Much slacker pack here with open water lanes.
Large steam vessel evidently a whaling factory ship
Berg
"Discovery"
W. 40° S.
Pool of water
Scattered bergs. in this pack
Odd small bergs in the pack here
Edge of ice pack, ice drifting to the west
Two bergs

Sketches made from 1,850 metres (6,000 feet) by Mawson, Campbell and the meteorologist, Simmers, in flights of 9 February (*above*) and 11 February 1931 (*below*).

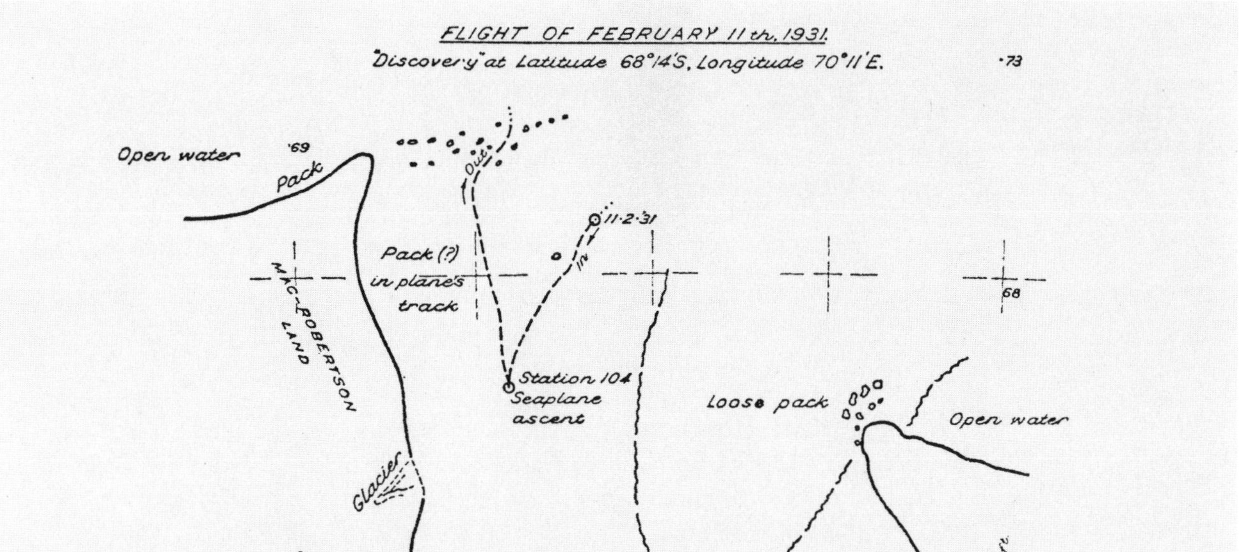

FLIGHT OF FEBRUARY 11th. 1931.
"Discovery" at Latitude 68°14'S. Longitude 70°11'E.
·73
Open water
·69
Pack
Out
11·2·31
In
Pack (?) in plane's track
MAC-ROBERTSON LAND
68
Station 104 Seaplane ascent
Loose pack
Open water
Glacier
Slopes rising to 2000 ft.
Open
2000 to 3000 ft. ice covered.
·69

(1,000 feet). To these they gave the name of the Scullin and Murray monoliths. After one misadventure in approaching Murray Monolith, Mawson decided to land at Scullin Monolith for another flag raising and proclamation ceremony. He repeated the action at their final landfall of Cape Bruce. His initiatives of possession were timely perhaps because, unbeknown to him, just a day or two behind came Mikkelsen in his ship *Torlyn*, apparently on the lookout for new territory:

February 13

First called Murray Monolith. We got off in boat before breakfast. Swell bad and no shelter, sea breaking. Examine coast. Ice-polished slopes up which penguins scrambling . . . We touch rock with oar then throw cylinder with proclamation on amongst boulders above beach after reading, then throw wood plate with copper inscription — it strikes rocks and tumbles into sea. Matheson throws flag on pole — it strikes rock and falls into sea. Chief Officer kept boat too far out — he could easily have taken it in closer.

We steam on to Scullin Monolith to west for landing. Go ashore before lunch. Best landing offering at rocky boulder shore . . . Campbell jumped out with line, I followed. We secured line from ship to rock, buried an end. Stanton sagged boat in to beach and a number of us jumped out into shallow water — Campbell and I, Hurley, Falla, Cherub. We erected flag and repeated taking possession. Hurley takes photographs.

All was not plain sailing on the voyage home. Mawson believed MacKenzie had deceived him in reporting 50 fewer tonnes of coal than *Discovery*'s bunkers actually held. 'I see it is not a good thing to have a beginner as master on an exploring vessel,' he wrote, though one assumes he hardly wished for a return to the argumentative veteran of his previous exploit. As for MacKenzie, he considered the BANZARE members were 'always thinking of yourselves, never of us':

March 18

At 7.40 found Captain on deck. He came up to me and immediately started accusing me and scientists of holding ship. This is just parallel with several cases earlier in the voyage, particularly just after leaving Mac-Robertson Land, returning, when without any warrant whatever MacKenzie launched out in accusing the scientific staff of being entirely selfish and not helping the ship in a critical time. Such talk is, and always has been, balderdash arising from his own hot head and limited viewpoint. I had been fed up with this sort of talk from him on other occasions but held my peace, or was otherwise diplomatic in order not to make a breach. Now I flared and said 'It is all damned rubbish you are talking' and I turned on my heel and went below.

Flights of the second *Discovery* voyage added significantly to BANZARE's report on the hazy coastline between 45° and 160° East longitude and the continental icesheet that swelled beyond it. In one of his reports Mawson went on to say:

The work conducted in Antarctic waters through the two summer seasons, 1929–30 and 1930–31, resulted in the amassing of an immense amount of data regarding the region lying south of Australia and the Indian Ocean. The collection of this vast amount of scientific data makes concrete our knowledge of a wide arc of the Antarctic formerly but little known.

The information will, when published, have a direct and immediate economic value in connection with the development of the fisheries. Long stretches of new coastline were discovered. The area claimed by Royal Decree, for Britain, comprises 2,250,000 square miles [*sic*]. There have been added to the map Mac-Robertson Land, Princess Elizabeth and Banzare Land, also Kemp Land and Enderby Land were rediscovered and mapped.

The Union Jack was raised over much of Antarctica. It was the flag that Mawson flew, just as had been done by Carstens Borchgrevink, from the vessel *Southern Cross*, upon making the first Antarctic mainland camp at Cape Adare in 1898.

> Thus perhaps the most important outcome of the expedition is that, in conjunction with the discoveries made on the former Australasian Expedition to the same sector, and observations by British and other expeditions elsewhere, *the presence of a real continent within the ice* [author's italics] has been finally established, with its main bulk towards the Indian Ocean, as prognosticated by Captain James Cook 160 years ago.

Two years later, the immense Australian Antarctic Territory was formally declared and created by a United Kingdom Order-in-Council of 7 February 1933.[15] The consequent Australian Antarctic Acceptance Act (1933) was ratified on 24 August 1936. The Act gave Australia 'all the islands and territories other than Adelie Land which are situated south of lat. 60° of South latitude and lying between the 160° of east longitude and the 45° of east longitude'.[16] With its axis at the South Pole, the claim constitutes some 42 per cent of the Antarctica — an area of almost 5,840,000 square kilometres (2,472,000 square miles), nearly as large as Australia itself.

Mawson returned to the Chair of Geology at Adelaide University to write up his many scientific reports. He was also planning new expeditions, but would never go south again as leader. World War II put a stop to those ambitions and after the war, while a key member of the government's new Antarctic advisory organisation, he agreed that leadership was a task for younger men. But the Mawson who died in Adelaide in 1958, the man whose face is on Australia's 100 dollar note, could look back with a high degree of satisfaction on his Antarctic days, acknowledging that a fragile little aeroplane had assisted him in the quest of science, and in putting more territory under the Australian flag than any other explorer before or since:

> The aeroplane proved a most important factor in the success of the geographical operations. That so much use was made of the machine, operating under difficult conditions, is owing to the determination and skill of the aviators, Campbell and Douglas whose capacity and ability is of the highest order.

Frank Hurley's memorable photograph of three cheers for the British flag at Proclamation Island on 13 January 1930. Enderby, Kemp and Mac-Robertson Lands were all made subject to King George V in the document read by Mawson. *Discovery* waits among gathering ice floes in the distance, where Captain Davis would refer to 'that bloody rubbishing business of raising the flag ashore'.

From the time of his return from the 1911-14 expedition, Mawson tried to have Britain declare sovereignty over the 'Australian sector' of Antarctica.[17] His representations to the British government, based on British exploration and his own Australasian Antarctic Expedition, made no progress. Nor did his several approaches to the Australian Prime Minister, W. M. (Billy) Hughes. Hardly was it an opportune time to be talking about the remote bottom of the globe when Britain and the Empire were plunged into a world war and Hughes, for his part, was soon absorbed in a divisive conscription debate.

Postwar years allowed Mawson to begin his Antarctic campaign afresh, working from his post as Professor of Geology at Adelaide University. A world at peace in the 1920s was able to turn its attention once again to the normal pursuits of agriculture, manufacturing and trading. Production of whale oil from harvesting the southern seas was on the rise again. Even in the dark days of 1915–16, sub-Antarctic waters were host to no less than 57 catcher boats, 11 floating factories and seven shore stations, which resulted in the kill of some 12,000 whales and a yield of 360,000 barrels of oil.

Technology came to the aid of the whalers, contributing the aeroplane, radio and improved mechanical devices of all kinds. Whales could be sighted, tracked, destroyed and flensed faster and more efficiently than ever before. The blue, the right, the sperm, humpback and finback — all were prey to the harpooner's gun and bomb. Britain and Australia were vitally interested in whaling, where it was being carried out, and how pursued. Britain was an imperial power, with historic connections with the Antarctic region reaching back to the voyages of Captain Cook; it also maintained a whaling industry and charged royalties to foreigners for hunting in its waters. Australia was one of the three Southern Hemisphere nations with the

Antarctic seas, so to speak, in its own backyard. In 1908 Britain had proclaimed the Falkland Islands Dependencies region; in 1923 it extended sovereignty to the Ross Sea region (150° West to 160° East longitude), in the latter instance giving control and administration to the Governor-General of New Zealand.

'Getting up on the step', as aviators termed a float plane take-off, close to the pack ice off BANZARE Land. The small de Havilland Moth — 'our tiny eye' Mawson called it — was responsible for much of the exploration that would lead in 1933 to legislation establishing the vast area of Australian Antarctic Territory.

From 1910 to 1920, some £15 million had been won in the production of whale oil. Britain's Falkland Islands region and the coasts of Graham Land had been the home to shore whalers for many years, while Australia's principal ventures were those of the shore-based whalers.

As early as 1838 a meeting of Sydney merchants considered 'the subject of a secret expedition towards the South Pole', surely for whale or fur seal hunting.[18] Eleven years earlier, a man of Sydney Town wrote in his memoirs:

> We see the London and American ships congregating at our doors, as it were, by the dozens, and carrying off yearly thousands upon thousands of the rich harvest which the bounty of Providence had placed within our grasp.

One of the first industries in Sydney Harbour was Archibald Mosman's whaling station on the bay that carries his name, while Ben Boyd's men and their successors were busy with the hand-held harpoon at Twofold Bay on the New South Wales far south coast. Sydney, Hobart and other east coast ports sometimes swarmed with American whalers in the 1840s, and the feeling lingered that Australia was missing out on reaping a substantial fortune from harvesting the deep. When American whalers appeared off the southern coast of Western Australia in 1837, a Perth journal made the comment: 'it is painful for us to see strangers sweeping from us one of our richest harvests — the whale fishery — while we are indolent spectators'.

Large factory ships ushered in the era of pelagic (ocean-going) whaling. To encourage national participation in the profits of the kill the Commonwealth government in the 1930s established a subcommittee to study the development of an Australian whaling industry, based on private investment. If hard facts were needed to provide an incentive, by 1929 in Antarctic waters 170 catchers and 24 factory ships were harvesting close on 30,000 whales for a yield of 20 million barrels of whale oil at a price of around £20 per ton. No nation was more expert at whaling than the Norwegians. From the distant end of the earth, their factory ships, tankers and scurrying catcher boats each summer season descended on the southern seas. Far from satisfied with the notion that Britannia ruled the Antarctic waves, the Norwegians with their zest for exploration began to look further afield. Their fleet moved westwards, into the Ross Sea, towards the Balleny Islands and Macquarie Island, and then around the empty and unclaimed ice coast to Australia's south. That the Norsemen were on the march was the warning of Captain John King Davis to the deputy prime minister, Dr Earle Page, in 1923.

Speaking with authority as Commonwealth Director of Navigation and a man who had sailed with Shackleton and skippered Mawson's *Aurora*, Davis pointed out that much of the coast to Australia's far south lay wide open to any intruder. A great deal of it had not been sighted, much less landed upon. For instance, who was known to have visited Enderby Land, between 45° and 55° East longitude since the British sealer John Biscoe had flown the Union Jack at Cape Ann in 1831?

With the 1923 Ross Dependency proclamation as something of a catalyst, the British and Australian governments began discussing the idea of extending British dominion to the adjoining westward portion of Antarctica — the 'Australian sector' through to 45° East longitude.[19] Such a control would accomplish the dual objectives of developing and policing whaling, while simultaneously excluding foreign interests. But despite the weighty talk and exchange of views between Melbourne and London, and prompting from such respected experts as Douglas Mawson, no action was forthcoming.

The remoteness and irrelevancy, to many, of Antarctica came suddenly back into focus in March 1924, when by presidential decree the French declared their sovereignty over the narrow sliver of Terre Adelie, the closest part of Antarctica to Australia, lying due south of Hobart. Within a year, supported by his old polar comrade Professor Edgeworth David (together they had climbed Mount Erebus and reached the South Magnetic Pole), Mawson led a deputation to the Prime Minister from the Australian National Research Council urging the Commonwealth to challenge the French action on the grounds that the Republic had done nothing to justify its claim since Dumont d'Urville visited and named the coast in 1840. The French were not interested in arguments and Britain and Australia backed-off, preferring not to provoke a polar confrontation over Adelie Land.

The 1926 Imperial Conference in London issued a communique that Britain, by virtue of discovery, exercised prior rights of sovereignty over large sections of Antarctica, particularly between Enderby, Kemp and Queen Mary Lands and Wilkes, King George V and Oates Lands. Yet, as Mawson hastened to advise the government, a weakness existed in this statement for nothing could be said about that unknown region to Australia's south-west lying from 60° to 86° East longitude.[20] This area (the future Mac-Robertson and Princess Elizabeth Lands) truly was a no-man's land. And what had the press of Norway to say about Britain's territorial sensibilities? That 'Norway had as much right as anybody else to any lands which might be discovered'.

Clearly the dual issue of whaling and annexation of territory continued to figure in British government thinking. Australia was again consulted for expert opinion which in 1927 allowed Mawson another chance to advance his cause. The Commonwealth's request for the views of the scientific community went to the Australian National Research Council which formed a special Antarctic Committee whose members included Mawson, Edgeworth David, Davis and Professor Orme Masson. They recommended that the vessel RRS *Discovery* should be obtained without delay and sent to Antarctica with a Commonwealth-financed expedition to carry out scientific investigation and make a formal territorial claim.

Through the committee, Mawson repeated his warning that the region between 60° and 86° East longitudes was still wholly unknown, unexplored, and not covered by the 1926 Imperial statement. Norway was obviously free to raise the flag there, to pursue unimpeded whaling from a rich and fresh hunting ground which, as all the evidence showed, is just what the magnate Lars Christensen seemed intent on doing.

Despite her anxiety over the Norwegians, Britain declined to support a new expedition and notified the Commonwealth that *Discovery* would be fully occupied on oceanographic cruises over the next few years. Partly at Mawson's urging, the Prime Minister then suggested immediate annexation of the whole Australian sector (with the exception of Terre Adelie), presumably without prior visit or exploration. The British government again preferred not to act, citing two grounds: the inevitable cost and the risk of antagonising friendly powers, a statement which, if properly analysed, would make the London ruling of 1926 seem rather pointless.

Mawson made a widely reported statement from Hobart on 18 January 1928 that annexation of the Australian sector of Antarctica was vital to national interests. The following day came news from London that the Norwegians had claimed Bouvet Island, though a French discovery and later used by Britain. On 20 July Mawson wrote to (Sir) David Rivett, the deputy chairman and chief executive officer of the Council for Scientific and Industrial Research (forerunner to CSIRO). Mawson's letter stated that the Norwegians 'were preparing an expedition to seize Enderby Land in the ensuing summer, and that their ship would continue year by year to explore the Antarctic and would take possession of the lands visited'. He added that the Antarctic Committee should again try to have *Discovery* made available for an expedition to Enderby Land, raising the British flag along the coast and concluding the voyage in Melbourne.

The question mark hanging over Australia's sector of Antarctica began to reach the public mind. The press published news of the latest whaling harvest gathered by alien fleets. From Mawson's home city, the Adelaide *Advertiser* frequently questioned Australia's relationship to Antarctica. A spokesman for the Royal Geographical Society of Australasia urged the Commonwealth to accept Mawson's advice and move into Antarctica before another nation forestalled the British flag. As Sir Hubert Wilkins had often proposed, the society also recommended setting up weather stations which would fulfil the condition of territorial occupation.

Prime Minister Stanley Bruce chided Mawson for his outspokenness in Hobart, suggesting that the government was quietly following a course of action to settle the Antarctic question — one in which public controversy would not be helpful. To an angry and frustrated Mawson, the Prime Minister's statement might well have sounded like typical political footwork to dodge public scrutiny of the Commonwealth's vacillating attitude towards raising a new expedition, and to avoid having Britain exposed to the embarrassing revelation that release of RRS *Discovery* had been denied.

Certainly, a message of November 1928 delivered by the Norwegian ambassador in London had somewhat assuaged British anxiety. The Norwegian government stated it had no territorial designs over those lands listed in the communique of 1926. For this undertaking Britain 'did a trade' in accepting the Norwegian claim over Bouvet Island, which it had hitherto opposed. But for Mawson, the Norwegian undertaking only served to heighten the vulnerability of the 'unknown lands' to a foreign flag.[21] The fragility of the situation was emphasised in the news that Christensen had sent his *Norvegia* on another (1929–30) Antarctic cruise, this time equipped with two quite powerful aircraft, manned by expert polar aviators.

Suddenly Mawson found his 15 years of ceaseless energy directed at petitioning and public speaking had begun to pay off. The implication of Christensen's second cruise was too much for governments to ignore. So was the lavish flag-dropping American expedition under Richard E. Byrd at the Bay of Whales; as was France's entrenched hold over Adelie Land; and so too was the rising price of whale oil and the number of whale hunters sailing south.

In January 1929 the British government agreed to free *Discovery* from its earlier schedule, if the Commonwealth would mount an expedition to raise the flag at selected points from Oates Land to Enderby Land, and undertake to administer the control of this vast sector of Antarctic territory, combining the region from 45° East with Mawson's oft-quoted sector to reach 160° East longitude. Mawson was en route to England, determined to convince the British to give him *Discovery* when the good news broke. From the Prime Minister he received a message asking him to head the new expedition and on 4 February he cabled his acceptance. An official committee was immediately established to organise the expedition. New Zealand agreed to participate. The name would be BANZARE, an acronym (which Mawson did not relish) for the British, Australian and New Zealand Antarctic Research Expedition.

On 21 February 1929 Prime Minister Bruce announced to the House of Representatives the launching of an Australian Antarctic expedition under the leadership of her foremost polar figure, Sir Douglas Mawson.[22] Captain J. K. Davis would command RRS *Discovery*, which was being made available as Britain's contribution. BANZARE would 'complete and crown' the work of Mawson's first expedition in a voyage of the 1929–30 south polar summer. On learning of the reference to 'one summer', Mawson once again put an emphatic pen to paper from London on 1 March, stressing that two seasons were needed to achieve the goals of his planning.

A famous Antarctic foursome at a dinner, complete with an ice-sculptured penguin, to celebrate Mawson's embarking on BANZARE. From left, Captain J. K. Davis, Sir Douglas Mawson, Vice-Admiral R. W. Skelton (of Scott's expedition) and Sir Hubert Wilkins.

At a meeting of 12 March in Melbourne, the government's Antarctic Committee defined BANZARE's aims. In effect, they gave the absent Mawson his 'marching orders':

> To chart the Antarctic coastline from Enderby Land at 45° East longitude to King George V Land at 160° East longitude:...making landings to plant the flag; carrying out inland surveys by plane; making hydrographic surveys; and studying meteorological conditions, geological formations, and the fauna of the region, especially the numbers, species and distribution of whales.

Public interest was high. The Adelaide *Advertiser* of 8 April editorialised on 'A Scramble for Antarctica' and questioned America's possible territorial ambitions, as well as those of Norway. If Mawson's courageous and unremitting campaign to send another expedition south had at last achieved the first objective, he was now about to face the difficult part. When asked in 1927 to estimate the cost of the venture, his reply suggested £60,000, an amount which proved quite close to the mark. No longer did he have to negotiate with the British government over a ship. Now, he believed, his energies in London could be directed towards the real business of organising the expedition. He was mistaken.

If the availability of *Discovery* was the good news, the bad came from Prime Minister Bruce; the world was sinking deeper into economic depression and the Commonwealth had precious little money to spare on Antarctica. Mawson and his associates would have to be the fund-raisers. It was a bizarre and anti-climactic note. Australia was about to dispatch an expedition to the frozen wastes of Antarctica, with the principal objective of raising the British flag over an enormous empire of unclaimed territory — and Mawson was being asked to finance much of it through his own endeavours.

From the polar coast to a factory in Fitzroy was a long jump, yet not too far to dampen the enthusiasm of a Melbourne philanthropist whose generosity would almost certainly save BANZARE from oblivion. In a statement he made on 14 July 1930, between the first and second expeditions, Mawson described his unofficial ultimatum from the Commonwealth: 'the proposal was put to me that I should raise funds where possible from private sources, and if possible largely from one individual'. This 'one individual', whose picture hung above the desk in Mawson's cabin was Sir MacPherson Robertson, confectionery manufacturer and self-made millionaire. He had begun business making lollies in an old nail tin in a Melbourne back street. He now owned an impressive factory in Fitzroy, employed hundreds of white-clad workers, delivered his products with white draught horses and often himself wore a fine white suit. He had invested in an airline, sponsored an around-Australia motor race and donated thousands of pounds to charity.

Mawson wrote to 'Mac' Robertson from Colombo while en route to England. A cheque for £10,000 was the reply, a most substantial sum of money. The Royal Geographical Society made 'Mac' Robertson a member; the kindly confectioner's other reward was to have his name immortalised on the Antarctic coast.[23] Ironically, other 'wealthy Australians' to whom Prime Minister Bruce personally addressed a letter of appeal collected the princely sum of £1,750. Mawson's ally in London, Major R.G. Casey, the Australian liaison representative in the Dominions Office, used his influence to gather a further £9,948 by selling newspaper rights to BANZARE's reports. An amount of £8,200 came from the Hearst press in America (which had also supported Wilkins), an arrangement which dismayed Mawson who preferred not to build the expedition on foreign money. He named a promontory Cape Hearst as a gesture of appreciation, but later it was changed to Cape Wilkins.

Major R. G. Casey (later Lord Casey), the Australian politician who worked to further Mawson's and Wilkins' polar objectives. A base in Australian Antarctic Territory now bears his name.

In all, Mawson's personal efforts raised £27,627, to which should be added a further £4,000 for the goods and services he obtained from British sources, either as gifts or at reduced prices. Mawson undertook all this organisation and travel on an honorary basis: 'I wanted to put the least possible call on the government', he admitted. He paid for his own three trips to London. The University of Adelaide cooperated by allowing him three years leave of absence. The Commonwealth's contribution was £12,000 while that of the British, in making *Discovery* available free of cost, was put at £11,714. New Zealand paid in £2,500. The grand total of government contribution thus reached £26,214, approximately £1,400 less than Mawson's unpaid efforts achieved.

The Commonwealth also provided the bureaucratic framework to handle the formalities of raising the expedition. Captain Davis came on leave from the Department of Navigation and two RAAF airmen were seconded to BANZARE in a quasi-civilian role. Mawson had been determined to employ air reconnaissance, and hoped to afford two aircraft to assist his exploration; however the dearth of funds forced him to settle for the cheapest and smallest machine that could be expected to survive polar conditions, a de Havilland Moth float plane with an 85 horsepower engine, top speed of 75 mph (120 kph), cockpit accommodation for two crew and a modest radio.

But when Bruce and other politicians kept referring to BANZARE as a 'Commonwealth expedition', Mawson could not contain his anger. 'In no stretch of the imagination was it a "Commonwealth expedition",' he said. 'The only true description was a "Commonwealth-backed expedition"'. How else, he asked, could he have gained the support of willing helpers, obtained gifts or stores and services and sought the private donations which amounted to thousands?

There are some men who are born to champion lost causes and I am one perhaps. I was not to be defeated. I would cross Antarctica by air.

Lincoln Ellsworth, on his third attempt to fly across Antarctica

5

ONE OF OUR MILLIONAIRES IS MISSING

To reduce landing speed, *Polar Star* featured the employment of wing flaps which the designer, J. K. Northrop, had devised from observing seagulls setting down. Lincoln Ellsworth used the advanced low-wing monoplane on three of his Antarctic Expeditions. His original pilot, Bernt Balchen (*left*) and Sir Hubert Wilkins (*right*) autographed the photograph for a friend.

Lincoln Ellsworth, the American millionaire, is remembered as the first man to fly across the Antarctic, a feat of remarkable courage and daring. He should also be recalled as the American who tried to steal a slice of Australian territory for the Stars and Stripes — a claim which has never been formally rejected by the United States. Two men figured in the Ellsworth heroes' gallery. One was Wyatt Earp, the old-time marshal of the Wild West who blazed his way to storybook legend through the shoot-out at OK Corral. Ellsworth wore Earp's wedding ring and, like a lucky charm, carried his gun belt and holster wherever he went. 'He was the bravest man I ever heard of,' said Ellsworth who, in almost a paraphrase of General Monash's 'the bravest man I ever met', placed Sir Hubert Wilkins in the same exalted company. Of Wilkins he declared: 'I have often told him that had he lived in our own West during the pioneer days, he would most certainly have been a frontier marshal two-gunning some wild district into law and order'.

The American millionaire, Lincoln Ellsworth, owned a castle in Switzerland and a villa in Italy. Sir Hubert Wilkins and his Australian-born bride, Suzanne, were honeymooning when he entertained them amid the Swiss Alps.

Achievements of the polar kind drew the two men together. Wilkins for his record breaking Arctic flight, his three Antarctic sorties and his attempt of 1931 to reach the North Pole by submarine, an exploit which Ellsworth financially supported. For his part Ellsworth, who qualified as a U.S. Army pilot in World War I, was no polar undergraduate. He and Roald Amundsen, with Riiser-Larsen, combined in 1925 to fly to the North Pole and were lucky to escape with their lives when the aircraft crashed; he saved two of their crew from drowning in the icy sea. Again with Amundsen, he returned to the Arctic the following year as 'navigation adviser' to Umberto Nobile in the crossing of the Pole by the dirigible *Norge* just three days after Byrd's acclaimed flight of 9 May 1926.

Apart from being a civil engineer and expert navigator, Ellsworth possessed one other qualification — money. Wilkins contributed experience combined with organising ability, itself a priceless track record. So they met in a New York club during the summer of 1932. On one side of the table sat Ellsworth, an average sort of fellow with short college-cut hair, salt and pepper moustache, quiet and retiring in manner. Across from him rested Wilkins' powerful figure, a man of keen eyes, dark pointed beard, also of mild demeanour, yet rather more like the popular image of a daring explorer. Ellsworth at 52 was seven years the older, but the difference in age mattered little. They sensed mutual respect and comradeship and from that moment began an association which, for them, would make the thirties a decade of extraordinary adventure.

Ellsworth was to pay for the expedition, Wilkins would manage it as 'technical assistant', and Antarctica was their goal. Specifically, Ellsworth wanted to concentrate on the same unclaimed sector between British

Graham Land and the Ross Dependency that Byrd had entered in 1929 but never crossed. The choice suited Wilkins ideally, for he had much unfinished business with the vast icesheet that stretched from the Weddell to the Ross Sea, especially as it would further his objective of planting a series of weather monitoring stations along the Antarctic coast.[1]

At first Ellsworth proposed a 5,500-kilometre (3,400-mile) round trip between Little America (Byrd's camp site) and the Weddell Sea. He would use a catapult-equipped vessel to fire off a reconnaissance aircraft then make the grand transcontinental dash. Upon more mature consideration they decided on a one-way flight, the round trip smacking too much of a stunt. En route, a number of landings would allow time to be devoted to genuine science and exploration. This one-way journey between the limits of Wilkins' and Byrd's last flights theoretically should be around 3,200 kilometres (2,000 miles), most of it over the unknown interior. In a small, heavily laden aircraft only two men could make the crossing, Ellsworth and his pilot.

Finding a suitable ship was Wilkins' first task. Arctic intelligence led him to Norway where, with the owner's open cheque, he chose a wooden vessel that had been built for the herring fleet. She was of 400 tonnes, with a length of 41 metres (135 feet), driven by a Bolinder semi-diesel engine capable of seven knots, maybe reaching nine knots with the sails unfurled, and a cruising range of 17,000 kilometres (11,000 miles). Wilkins had the accommodation areas rebuilt, rigging moved to fore and aft and metal sheathing and oak planking fitted from stem to amidship to withstand the Antarctic pack.

Lifting *Polar Star* to a take-off position on the bay ice. After one successful flight, the first Ellsworth expedition of 1933 came to an abrupt halt.

Ellsworth and Balchen (*right*) in the cockpit of *Polar Star*. The frustrations of the second expedition would terminate their association.

Ellsworth required one other alteration: the original name of the vessel, *Fanefjord*, was changed to that of his wild west hero. 'One of my whims was to imbue the whole enterprise with the spirit of Wyatt Earp,' he declared.[2]

If Ellsworth sounded slightly eccentric, his was a peculiarity that bought them only the best. 'A Rolls Royce of aeroplanes,' is how Wilkins described his owner's choice of the Gamma 2B low-wing monoplane, the latest product of J. K. Northrop who had recently resigned from Lockheed to open his own works at Inglewood on the outskirts of Los Angeles. A 600 horsepower Pratt and Whitney Wasp powered the sleek all-metal machine which had an advertised top speed of 368 kph (230 mph). Wing flaps, allowing a low approach speed of 66 kph (42 mph), were among the Gamma's refinements that appealed to Ellsworth, for they gave the pilot time to study the plateau surface before setting down. Likewise he and Wilkins favoured the low-wing design because it allowed the machine to be dug into the snow to lessen the impact of a howling wind. On 29 November 1932 Ellsworth signed the $37,000 contract for his *Polar Star*.

Next, to find a pilot. As with the aircraft itself, Ellsworth's choice was for the tops. He offered a contract to Bernt Balchen, the man who had taken Byrd to the South Pole three years before and now worked as a test pilot for Tony Fokker. Balchen accepted with two stipulations: first, no catapults — he did not relish returning to the ship in a float plane to find the ice had closed-up — and second, the employment of a meteorologist to refine their weather readings. He then went to Northrop and stood by during the Gamma's construction.[3]

Wyatt Earp sailed from Dunedin, New Zealand, on 10 December 1933, bound for the Bay of Whales. The crew of 14 were mainly Norwegian, as Wilkins had been anxious to secure men with polar service and, in some instances, whaling experience in the Ross Sea region. Six small but well-appointed cabins had been provided. In the owner's cabin hung the cartridge belt of 'the bravest man I ever heard of', and in the next the manager's phonograph and collection of light and classical records was laid out. 'ELLSWORTH ANTARCTIC EXPEDITION' read the large letters along *Wyatt Earp's* timbers, and also down the fuselage of his carefully stowed *Polar Star*.

Punching for 720 kilometres (450 miles) through the Ross Sea pack, they reached open water early in January 1934 and began preparations for Balchen's first flight on skis from the Bay of Whales. Perhaps the entry in second mate Olsen's diary should have warned them all was not well:

> Suddenly, from within the deep caverns far below the surface of the ice barrier, came ominous sounds like the tuning up of a mighty orchestra. It was as if the whole universe itself had begun to vibrate. We all stood rooted to the spot, so great was the terror which engulfed us. As the ominous sound continued, it was as if a mammoth organ began to play accompanied by gigantic 'cymbal' crashes.

Balchen and Ellsworth took *Polar Star* on a trial flight lasting 30 minutes on 12 January. They parked the machine overnight on a gently rocking floe and all retired to the sound of soft music from Wilkins' cabin. In the early hours of the morning the watch summoned them on deck. They beheld their precious aircraft suspended above the sea by only its wings where the floe had split apart. Six hours of all hands labouring with ropes and winches brought *Polar Star* to safety. There was to be no more Antarctic flying for the 1934 summer, and there was nothing but gloom in the radio messages Wilkins had contracted to send the New York *Times* and the North American Newspaper Alliance.

Watching the broken machine lowered to the deck, Ellsworth recorded, '*Polar Star* was swung aboard, a pitiful sight, skis fractured, one wing bent, unfliable'. Nothing for it but on 17 January to retreat across the storm-tossed 4,000 kilometres (2,500 miles) of ocean to New Zealand where, on the voyage south, they had to don Wellington boots while eating in the mess.[4] To add a touch of irony to their defeat, Byrd's second expedition arrived off Little America only three days later. To Byrd's credit, on learning of Ellsworth's misfortune he radioed his fellow American an offer to use either the Fokker or Fairchild which were aboard his ships. Ellsworth politely declined, as neither had the range to make trans-Antarctic history. Perhaps Byrd was relieved at the answer — particularly to see Wilkins depart.

Wilkins (*right*) had much faith in the designs of J. K. Northrop who had gained his experience at Lockheed and Douglas. The Gamma 2B was Northrop's latest creation from his own Californian plant.

In September 1934 Ellsworth returned to Antarctica to make his second attempt at the transcontinental flight. Except for a couple of crew changes it was much the same team — Wilkins as manager and Balchen the pilot. *Polar Star* had been rebuilt at the Northrop works, permitting various improvements to the airframe, and *Wyatt Earp* overhauled in New Zealand. What could be done when money was no object! This time, however, the plan of operations underwent an important change, in fact a complete reversal.[5]

Wilkins had persuaded Ellsworth to start his journey from the Antarctic Peninsula, using his old facility at Deception Island and from there, via the Weddell Sea, to attempt the crossing to the Ross Sea. The manager's reasoning was simple. Byrd's Little America II awaited them at the Bay of Whales. There the fliers could shelter for weeks, even a couple of months, while *Wyatt Earp* broke through the pack to retrieve them and the aircraft.[6] By flying in the opposite direction, their destination would be much more uncertain, and by ship perhaps impossible to reach.

At *Wyatt Earp*'s farewell on 19 September 1934, the mayor of Dunedin declared they were 'the most popular of any expedition that had ever visited the town'.[7] Ahead lay a wallowing 6,400 kilometres (4,000 miles) and 26 days across the high latitudes of the Pacific before Wilkins would sight the familiar ramparts of Deception Island, an apt destination for Ellsworth as the 'Yankee harbour' of America's sealing days. Seventeen men were packed into the little ship. Balchen had brought a pig from New Zealand; a plague of rats was a less welcome contribution from the Kiwis. They carried enough Texaco gasoline to fly *Polar Star* on four trans-Antarctic journeys and sufficient rations to keep the whole expedition alive for two years.

Once again unbelievable ill-fortune dogged Ellsworth and his *Polar Star*. On Deception Island, outside the old whaling station, a loud metallic 'crack' came from within the engine as they fired it up for the first test run. Heavy lubricating oil used as a preservative had not been drained from a cylinder and a connecting rod had snapped in two. Worse, among the hundreds of parts and pieces in *Wyatt Earp*'s hold, there was no spare conrod.

End of an expedition: With skis and wing tip severely damaged, the Gamma 2B is rescued from the fractured ice floe and hoisted aboard *Wyatt Earp*.

Wilkins sent off an urgent message to the Pratt and Whitney plant. The replacement rod was placed on a Pan American-Grace airliner and flown to South America, which was the quick part of the exercise. *Wyatt Earp* meanwhile sailed the 1,600 kilometres (1,000 miles) north to Magellanes, the nearest port in southern Chile. By the time the ship returned on 17 November (Ellsworth while exploring in the meantime had almost perished in a crevasse) and the engine was reassembled 10 days later, the ice on Deception Island had broken out. To make a flight, they must search elsewhere.

A cruise to the other (eastern) side of the Peninsula located a possible take-off surface on Snow Hill Island where, for relaxation, the ever-inquiring Ellsworth collected 150 fossil specimens. Then on 3 January 1935, practically the last day of flying weather, the sky cleared, the sun shone brightly and the snow stayed firm. A meteorological balloon with transmitter attached was sent up. The expedition's weatherman, in contact with Byrd's weather office at Little America, gave an encouraging report.[8] Conditions at both ends of Antarctica were inviting. On an impulse, Ellsworth said to Balchen: 'Let's make a try! What do you say?' 'All right,' answered his pilot and they began to warm up the engine. Wilkins insisted on serving them a hot meal before the sudden take-off, and cooked a dish of pemmican stew and brewed coffee on a primus stove beside the plane. An excited Ellsworth dictated his message for the North American press: 'Flash — Balchen and I took off at seven this evening, heading for the unknown. The great adventure so long awaited is at hand.'

Ellsworth's Rescue Plan

To whom it may concern

It is my intention to fly from Dundee Island to the Bay of Whales, Ross Sea, on a more or less great-circle course. In case of a forced landing from which no communication by wireless and no further progress by our own plane can be made, before reaching Lat. 69:30, I would expect to follow the Larsen ice barrier to Robinson Island and Robertson Island, then follow through the Crown Prince Gustave Channel and reach Hope Bay as a rendezvous, possibly looking for depots and leaving notes on the southwest corner of Robinson Island and on the southeast corner of Robertson Island and on Cape Longing.

Future Antarctic exploration is the topic at a meeting in Sydney of the three eminent polar figures – Sir Douglas Mawson (*left*), Lincoln Ellsworth (*centre*) and Sir Hubert Wilkins.

In case of a forced landing from which no communication by wireless and no further progress by our own plane can be made, after passing Lat. 69:30 and before reaching Lat. 72, I would make for Cape Pierre Baudin, Marguerite Bay, passing through Bourgeois and Lallemand fjords, thence along Martha Bay to Cape Evensen and expect to find notes or depots at each or one of these places. If by chance the route to Pitt Island is impassable on foot, I should expect to make the southeast corner of Beascochea Bay the rendezvous.

In case of a forced landing, etc., between Lat. 72 and Lat. 75, I would expect to make for Mount Martha, Charcot Island, and remain there until relieved, looking for a depot on the southeast corner of Charcot Island.

In case of a forced landing, etc., between Lats 75 and 89, I would turn north to the edge of the land-fast ice and then eastward to Mount Monique, Charcot Island, expecting to remain there until relieved and looking for a cache on the southwest corner of Charcot Island.

In case of a forced landing, etc., between Lats 80 and 81 and before reaching Long. 130, I would make for Mount Mabelle Sidley to leave a message and look for a depot and possibly remain there with the expectation of being relieved. However, if there is no food obtainable at Mount Mabelle Sidley and we have food sufficient to enable us to reach Mount Grace McKinley, I might decide to leave a note at Mount Mabelle Sidley and proceed to Mount Grace McKinley.

In case of a forced landing, etc., after passing Long. 130, I would make for Little America, following the course laid down for the airplane. At Little America last year, through the courtesy of Admiral Byrd, I laid down 500 gallons of gasoline and some lubricating oil, and with these supplies there is twenty or thirty days food rations. I have no information from Admiral Byrd as to the amount or disposition of his supplies or if any were left at Little America; and I am not much concerned about that, for once we are at the Bay of Whales we will find many seals and penguins, and with our own supplies we will be able to live until the latter part of January or later, if the Wyatt Earp should be delayed in reaching us.

(signed) Lincoln Ellsworth

Polar Star, the small silvery plane which flew across Antarctica, on view in the United States.

Bernt Balchen — a picture taken later in life of the famous Norwegian-born aviator.

Packed with fuel and rations to nearly four tonnes all-up weight, the aircraft at first hesitated to lift from the snow until Balchen sent them at full throttle down a precipitous slope. *Polar Star* banked to the south and headed into a clear blue sky. They flew down the peninsula's east coast at 1,830 metres (6,000 feet) seeing the Weddell Sea ice-free to 69° South. Above Hearst Land, beyond the limit of Wilkins' previous flight, snowy peaks began to stretch across their flight path. 'Scenes like this come only once in a man's lifetime,' noted Ellsworth, head down in the cockpit as he wrote in his log. When he glanced up to check their position he suddenly realised the mountains had retreated behind them. They were heading north again.

'What's going on?'

'Heavy cloud and storm', was Balchen's answer. 'We're going back.'

Ellsworth could see only a single bank of dark cloud with the sun shining beyond it. When the aircraft landed at Snow Hill Island, the great adventure into the unknown had lasted only two and a half hours. Ellsworth stamped away from *Polar Star*, furious and frustrated. 'Two years of work and planning going by the board,' he muttered. Wilkins took Balchen aside and asked what had happened. 'Ellsworth can commit suicide if he likes,' Balchen replied coolly, 'but he won't take me with him.'

The voyage back was a somewhat tense affair with two strong personalities, the millionaire and his pilot, at loggerheads. Balchen told Wilkins he had decided, when Ellsworth refused to take a third man in the cockpit, not to continue unless they faced a 100 per cent chance of a non-stop flight. In Ellsworth's view, the third man would cost so much fuel and provisions as to make the transcontinental flight virtually impossible. Balchen retorted that, once forced down, they would be unlikely to dig the plane out if they were minus a third man. So came the inevitable point-of-return decision. Ellsworth later said he never lost his esteem for Balchen, but at Montevideo docks on 21 January the two men said farewell for keeps.

Wyatt Earp was laid up, the crew paid off, the aircraft stored away. 'Could I ever hope to find a pilot willing to make the flight?' Ellsworth asked as he contemplated an indefinite future. By this stage, having survived two costly failures, one might expect he was ready to call it quits, especially when his accountant analysed the balance sheet. Back in New York the head of the

North American Newspaper Alliance, sensing Ellsworth's indecision, sought to counsel him with the advice: 'You'll lose your life, Lincoln. Try something else, something easier'. This remark possibly made the turning point. In Ellsworth's own words: 'There are some men who are born to champion lost causes, and I am one, perhaps. I was not to be defeated. I would cross Antarctica by air'.[8]

He contacted Wilkins who was holidaying with his Australian-born wife, the actress Suzanne Bennett, and asked him to prepare a third expedition. Ellsworth and his wife went on the annual visit to their Swiss chalet.[9] Then they took the Graf Zeppelin to South America to go exploring in the Mato Grosso. His one firm appointment was with Wilkins on the wharf at Magallanes, where they left for Antarctica on 28 October 1935. Across stormy seas, *Wyatt Earp* tossed its way towards Deception Island where *Polar Star* again would be reassembled. One odd incident occurred during the voyage when their new physician, who seemed obsessively talkative, accused the stoic Norwegians of being 'clannish' whereupon the second mate floored him with a blow to the chin. The doctor refused all efforts at reconciliation and posted a notice on his door which read: 'For the rest of this voyage no professional care will be extended to members of this expedition'.

Off the peninsula's north-east tip they came upon snowfields of Dundee Island — so wide, smooth and firm that Wilkins was moved to tell Ellsworth: 'If we had known of this surface in 1928, you'd now not be planning the first flight across Antarctica'. Unloaded from *Wyatt Earp*, the aircraft was able to taxi straight to a natural skiway where the pilots started preparing for the long-awaited flight.

In Balchen's place came Herbert Hollick-Kenyon. 'Kenyon', aged 38, married with two children, was a taciturn, inveterate pipe smoker and reputedly a whiz in the air with 6,000 hours to his credit, mostly in the Arctic. He was the quintessential casual Englishman, London-born, served in the Canadian Expeditionary Forces of World War I and had been twice wounded before joining the Royal Flying Corps.[10]

The advertisements Ellsworth placed to recruit a successor for Balchen who had returned to airline flying in Norway attracted another highly qualified polar aviator, Jack H. Lymburner. Like Kenyon, he was also a Canadian Airways pilot at the time of his application. Married and aged 31, his particular expertise lay in keeping aircraft engines turning under polar conditions. Ellsworth decided to hire him, also.

'This time we must succeed,' Ellsworth wrote as they warmed and loaded *Polar Star* for the flight of 20 November 1935. Two hours out from Dundee Island, Hollick-Kenyon noticed a leaking fuel gauge which at any moment might vent a stream of petrol into the cockpit. Two hours later they were back on the island. Their second attempt on 21 November brought reasonable going until they were 960 kilometres (600 miles) to the south, sighting the new range of high mountains and climbing to 3,650 metres (12,000 feet) to escape a buffeting headwind. Ellsworth began to rejoice at being the first man to set eyes upon these Antarctic wonders when Hollick-Kenyon indicated he was turning the aircraft around. The darkening clouds ahead, in Ellsworth's view, were not particularly threatening; no reason why they could not land and wait for the storm to pass, such was his casual attitude to their ability to set down *Polar Star* on the Antarctic surface and take off again whenever the need arose. But vital fuel had been consumed and with it went all hope of completing a transcontinental flight.

When, after 11 hours, they landed before the dismayed ground party on Dundee Island, even the quiet-tempered Wilkins was heard to exclaim: 'If I'd known this was to be a one-day flight, I would never have joined the expedition!' Ellsworth stamped away, his anger against Hollick-Kenyon boiling over, his frustration at the limit. Aboard *Wyatt Earp*, Wilkins, ever the peacemaker, tried to placate his leader. 'Tomorrow I'm trying again,' Ellsworth replied from between clenched teeth, 'but I don't want Hollick-Kenyon. I'm going to take Lymburner.' Wilkins reasoned that Lymburner was exhausted from working on the engine and did not know the route along the peninsula as his senior man did. Still puffing his pipe, the phlegmatic Hollick-Kenyon came on deck and said quietly to Ellsworth: 'I understand that you would prefer Lymburner on the next flight. That's quite all right with me'.

On Dundee Island before take-off, Ellsworth surveys his national flag and the banners of four organisations which had supported his determined ventures; they are (from left), the National Geographic Society, Yale University, The Quiet Birdmen and the New York Athletic Club.

Ellsworth was not one to bear a grudge, or to act irrationally to satisfy a hurt pride. The quiet man to whom he gave the responsibility of piloting his aircraft was right. They had burned up excess fuel in bucking wind above Hearst Land; and if *Polar Star* had landed in the narrow cloud-obscured Strait, might they ever have taken off again? Certainly not without discarding all fuel and provisions. He realised that in Hollick-Kenyon he had a masterful aviator, and a few hours later told him to prepare for the next day's attempt. 'But,' he added emphatically, 'this time we won't turn back.' (Ellsworth: 299, 315–6)

Adverse weather grounded them throughout the day. Then at one o'clock on the following morning the slumbering Ellsworth felt a tug at his shoulder. The Norwegian steward was standing by his bunk and, as Ellsworth remarked, with that look of great respect the Norsemen have for the explorer, that most exalted of all creatures, told him of a clear sky. Hollick-Kenyon was already dressing, Ellsworth could hear the noise of his electric shaver for, no matter their circumstance, his pilot always wore carefully pressed clothing and shaved every day. Wilkins and Lymburner had been out at the airstrip for some hours, preparing *Polar Star*. This was 22 November, the day when Antarctic history had to begin.

Ellsworth carefully donned his Antarctic flying rig. On his feet, first went a pair of moose-hide moccasins, then a pair of rubber-soled canvas boots with a drawstring to keep out the snow (a misguided footgear combination that caused serious trouble later). He wore underclothes of silk and wool, on top of them an 'under suit' of camel's hair, then thick trousers and over his flannel shirt a Siberian squirrel parka, fur side turned in, that Amundsen had given him. A knotted woollen cap covered the ears, then helmet and goggles, fur gloves and heavy reindeer parka worn fur side out. Separately he carried an extra pair of sealskin breeches in event of extraordinarily low temperatures and woollen face masks for the same emergency.

After a breakfast of bacon, five fried eggs and coffee, they climbed the slope to the skiway, walking slowly on their snow-shoes to avoid raising a perspiration. Wilkins, mindful of the long hours ahead sitting in a cramped cockpit, an experience he had shared, handed them lunch boxes and a thermos of tea. Back in April, they had contacted Admiral Byrd asking for disposition of the food remaining at Little America II, which the Byrd expedition had evacuated a year before. No reply came from the rear admiral, so at Wilkins' urging they loaded an extra 100 pounds (45 kilograms) of rations — 40 pounds of pemmican, 20 pounds of oatmeal, 10 pounds each of sugar and butter and 20 pounds of biscuits, raisins, nutmeats and tea.[11] Their heavy skis were offloaded to compensate for the added burden; for walking they would depend only on their metre-long snow-shoes.

In making his farewells, Ellsworth composed a formal note of appreciation for Wilkins' loyalty to his expedition:

> I wish to pay tribute to the man whose single-hearted devotion to my Antarctic enterprise contributed so much to its ultimate success. It was a fine stroke of fortune when I secured the services of Sir Hubert Wilkins . . . his conscientiousness had no limits. The expedition and its great object came first with him and nothing else — not sleep, food or personal comfort counted. (Ellsworth: 318)

For camping beside the aircraft, they carried a silk tent and reindeer sleeping bags. Their emergency gear included a collapsible sledge that Balchen had built for Ellsworth two years before and a pistol in case they were forced down on the coast and had to shoot seals. Two radios, one of 100-watt power, the other of 400 watts, would let them report progress to *Wyatt Earp* and included the back-up of a manual generator. Navigation gear, charts and maps were loaded together with their only reading matter, a small Bible, packed in Ellsworth's rucksack. A message was written for the North American press. Final discussions were held with Wilkins on the details of their flight.

After the take-off from Dundee Island, the flight plan sounded all very logical and uncomplicated. Because of the difficulty or inaccuracy in taking sextant sunsights once airborne, they would land on the icesheet at various places to plot their progress. Landings could also be made to rest, or avoid bad weather, or to map surrounding features; then they would push on to the Bay of Whales. If some untoward incident did arise, a detailed rescue had been agreed upon and documented. Their journey was to proceed quite smoothly, regardless of hostile and treacherous Antarctica with its wild and sudden blizzards, whiteouts, tearing winds, gaping crevasses and sharp-ridged surface.[12] To the best of their knowledge, they would be the only two humans abroad on a continent larger in area than the United States. If they were forced down or crashed on an icecap which no man had crossed before, in reality the chances were one in a zillion that they could ever be found again. So went the unspoken part of the scenario.

They took off at 4.20 a.m. local time, with the sun low on the far horizon and the snow still cold and hard enough to speed the skis of the little silver and bright orange aircraft, laden with 7,000 pounds (3,175 kilograms) of fuel, supplies and crew. Again they followed down the east coast of the peninsula, enjoying a perfect morning of blue sky, sunshine and light breeze. Beyond Hearst Land, the last monument to Wilkins' pioneering of seven years before, the course carried them into unknown territory, the visibility of maybe 240 kilometres (150 miles) revealing open water in the Weddell Sea and white and rock-tipped ramparts of the mountain chain rearing up again.

Conditions were so gentle that Hollick-Kenyon remarked he was flying 'hands off'. Ellsworth smiled with the satisfaction of the explorer who knows the wonders of an unknown world are his reward. Turning south-west, onwards they calmly flew, and into the silence, vanishing.

Ellsworth, the Man

Lincoln Ellsworth was born on 12 May 1880 into a family of Chicago wealth. His father, James Ellsworth, owned a string of coal mines which fed fuel to the thousands of steam locomotives on America's eastern railroads. Upon his father's death, Lincoln inherited a fortune — as a multi-millionaire, he had no cause ever to work again. His, however, was a character of different fibre, tinged with a nostalgia for the Wild West and tough hombres like the gunslinging marshal of Tombstone and Dodge City.

Having graduated in civil engineering from Columbia and Yale Universities, and possessing a strong interest in anthropology and archaeology, he found himself drawn to the remotest corners of the earth. For a couple of years he took a job as an axeman in the survey party of a Canadian transcontinental railroad; as an engineer he then moved to distant mining camps. His wealth allowed him to raise a geological expedition into the Andes, reaching the headwaters of the Amazon River. Later in life he returned to South America, to search for the lost tombs of Inca emperors.

As with the other polar leaders of his era, exploration of the Arctic posed the greatest challenge until he turned to Antarctica. Upon reaching Sydney at the close of his fourth expedition in 1939, he told a newspaper reporter:

> The Antarctic attracts me because of all the world it is the only place left where there is so much trailblazing still to be done — nearly a whole continent left where you can put out into the unknown, and land no man has seen before.
>
> When I was a boy I used to lie on the floor gazing at the blank spaces on the map. I was still a boy when I was taken to the memorial service for Scott in London. That was when I first decided I was going to be an Antarctic explorer. To my mind, there are three men in exploration — the trailblazer, the mapmaker and the man who looks out for the resources of the country. I have been a trailblazer since boyhood and I always will be.

Ellsworth wanted his endeavours to be remembered for their value to exploration and science, not just as another stunt in this new age of the aeroplane. He had discovered and been able to report reliably upon a huge and hitherto unknown portion of Antarctica. He had made position fixes of the features he found and fulfilled a duty to fly the United States flag across the unknown ice. He reasoned that the highlands of the Antarctic Peninsula must be regarded as a continuation of the South American Andes, possibly linked with the Queen Maud Range and the mountains of Victoria Land that girded the Polar plateau. Allowing that this lofty chain formed a backbone across Antarctica, he questioned whether a sea-level channel was likely to reach between the Weddell and the Ross Seas. These were mysteries of Antarctica that he wanted his work to solve.

His 1935 flight was Antarctica's longest aerial journey until the Deep Freeze missions of two decades later. No single flight had revealed so much of the seventh continent; it permitted a new map to be drawn by the American Geographical Society, proof of Ellsworth's dedication to the task. He frequently in times of peril repeated his favourite words from an old hymn: 'So long Thy power has blest me, sure it still will lead me on'. And from another verse, the final line that gave testimony to his restless nature: 'Who has trodden stars seeks peace no more'.

Ellsworth died in New York on 26 May 1951.

Ellsworth with his new third expedition pilot, Herbert Hollick-Kenyon, before setting out on their triumphant flight in November 1935. Of the taciturn Britisher, Ellsworth said, 'He was the quietest man I ever knew'. But he also paid supreme tribute to the airman who finally flew him to the Ross Ice Shelf: 'Kenyon's control of our machine was miraculous'.

I say, it's awfully decent of you fellows to drop in on us like this.

Pilot Herbert Hollick-Kenyon to his Australian rescuers

6

AUSTRALIA TO THE RESCUE!

Crew members push drifting floes away from *Discovery II*'s steel hull as the vessel approaches the Antarctic coast in search of the millionaire, Lincoln Ellsworth. *Discovery II* had to be modified and loaded within ten days to reach the Ross Sea before the ice closed in.

On 5 December 1935 the Prime Minister of Australia, Joseph Lyons, announced that a rescue attempt was being organised to locate the missing aviators, Lincoln Ellsworth and Herbert Hollick-Kenyon. *Wyatt Earp* had received the last radio message from their aircraft, *Polar Star*, eight hours after take-off. The message itself was garbled but did not seem to indicate anything amiss with the flight; then it suddenly broke off and nothing more had been heard.

From the anchorage off Dundee Island, the expedition's manager, Sir Hubert Wilkins, had been sending hour-by-hour reports of the flight to the North American Newspaper Alliance. Once the radio schedule was lost, he had no option but to report the silence. Immediately the world media took notice. Wire services hummed with dire speculation. Ellsworth and his pilot were missing. Ellsworth was feared to have crashed. References were soon made to the 'ill-fated Ellsworth expedition'.[1]

In a private message to the millionaire's wife, Wilkins reassured Mrs Ellsworth that the cessation of messages was no cause for alarm. There was nothing to indicate that the two aviators were in any peril. Moreover, their rescue plan was being followed. Mrs Ellsworth called together a committee of New York luminaries and they began to launch their own rescue effort, starting with the quest for an amphibian aeroplane equipped with skis that could operate on the sea or the interior ice.

No doubt Wilkins feared that the furore in the press could cause matters to get out of control.[2] He and Ellsworth had evolved a perfectly sound contingency plan. To have outsiders called in, or rather 'buying in' to attempt a rescue, was the last thing either of them wanted. But the publicity had provoked considerable alarm; American newspapers editorialised on 'what was being done?' *Time* went so far as to suggest that Ellsworth may have switched off the radio himself, to draw attention to his expedition. From Norway, the loyal Balchen vehemently rejected the magazine's assertion while Admiral Byrd opined that the missing men were most probably safe and sound at Little America with a broken radio.

What Wilkins had not anticipated was Australia's response to the emergency. Sir Douglas Mawson, the country's foremost Antarctic authority, and Captain John King Davis, Commonwealth Director of Navigation and himself a veteran Antarctic mariner, told the government that a rescue vessel needed to be dispatched at once. Australia was best placed to reach the Antarctic coast, but if they delayed the Ross Sea would be impassable after early February and a ship could not gain access, or could be iced-in.[3]

The efforts of Mrs Ellsworth's group in New York to acquire an amphibian had failed. Next, in response to Wilkins' advice, they procured a similar Northrop Gamma 2 which reached as far as Atlanta where it crashed on take-off, though the crew emerged unhurt. The Texaco Oil Company immediately volunteered a replacement Gamma 2D which leading airline flyer Dick Merrill took the 12,800 kilometres (8,000 miles) to Argentina in a record time of 40 hours. *Wyatt Earp* reached Magallanes from Deception Island on 4 December. Lymburner picked up the aircraft from San Antonio (Argentina), flew it to Gallegos (Chile) where they fitted floats, and then continued onwards to Magallanes. Not until the 22nd was the loading of Texaco's machine complete; that same evening Wilkins headed *Wyatt Earp* out to sea on the first stage of its prearranged rescue mission to Charcot Island.

Despite continuous calls and listenings, *Polar Star*'s radio remained silent.

Sir Douglas Mawson led the initiative of the Australian rescue endeavours while his old skipper Captain Davis became officer-in-charge. Their effort would be focused on Ellsworth's ultimate destination at the Little America site on the Bay of Whales. Next they needed a ship — but what ship? 'Things are getting out of hand, could the British assist?' asked Davis in a cryptic memo which, supported by Mawson, went to the Prime Minister. The next link in the rescue chain reached to far-off London. From the Dominions Office to the Colonial Office in Whitehall, the question was put. The British government promptly offered the assistance of the Royal Research Society Ship, *Discovery II*.[4] On the icy edge of the Indian Ocean, far to Australia's south, *Discovery II* lay off the coast of Enderby Land pursuing oceanography and a whale count. The story goes that an officer came running along the deck as the scientists were about to lower the trawl net, waving a message and calling: 'Hey, just a moment. We're going to Melbourne. We have to find Lincoln Ellsworth'.

Prime Minister Joseph Lyons.

Crowds gathered at Williamstown dock to watch the Wapiti biplane, the larger of the two RAAF aircraft, swung aboard the ship.

But Australia's urgent interest in locating the missing pair and Britain's quick response with *Discovery II* and a New Zealand pledge of cooperation were touched by more than the quality of mercy. All three governments were wary of 'what the Americans are up to in Antarctica.' (Byrd had been politely reminded through British diplomatic channels that his Little America was on New Zealand territory.) Speed and effectiveness in dispatching a rescue mission were seen as an all-important underwriting of the validity of Britain's polar claims.

Wilkins, possibly unbeknown to Australia, had separately contacted the Discovery Committee asking that their ship in cruising along the coast listen for any wireless transmission from *Polar Star*. When he learned that Australia was taking over and intent on sailing *Discovery II* right into the Bay of Whales, he sent a signal to Davis expressing 'sincere appreciation' for the organisation but emphasised that, 'unless unlikely delays are experienced, the Ellsworth Expedition's own adequate arrangements will meet all requirements'. As a compromise he again suggested *Discovery II* should stand off the pack, monitoring the ether for a possible distress call while he would actually take *Wyatt Earp* into the bay, to effect whatever relief was needed. Despite

The men that Australia would go searching for:Hollick-Kenyon (left) and Lincoln Ellsworth wait beside *Polar Star* before the take-off from Dundee Island.

his professed Australianism, Wilkins' first and foremost loyalty lay with his American employer who specifically wanted the trans-Antarctic mission accomplished in its entirety by his own private American expedition. Hence the detailed contingency plan.

As a sidelight to the rapid exchange of messages, on 7 December Prime Minister Lyons received a cable signed 'Mary Louise Ellsworth' which said: 'Let me express my personal gratitude to the government and people of Australia'. Perhaps she did not share her husband's confidence that the expedition could go it alone.

At any rate, Australia was not for messing about. Not only would a ship be sent, but aircraft too. The Discovery Committee signed over their vessel to Australian management and by the time it docked in Melbourne on 13 December, after the 8,000-kilometre (5,000-mile) voyage across the Southern Ocean, workmen were waiting on the wharf to begin the task of clearing deck space so that two aircraft could be loaded.

The Royal Australian Air Force, now 14 years old, had a select few aviators experienced in Antarctic flying through secondment to the BANZARE voyage of 1929–31. Thus, when the government directed the Air Board to nominate a crew, the name of Flight Lieutenant G. E. (Eric) Douglas, one of Mawson's two pilots, was immediately submitted as leader. Davis joined in the recommendation of Douglas as a 'first-class man'; one in whom the government could be sure of 'not getting up to any stunts'. Second pilot and

navigator was the young Flying Officer Alister Murdoch; five other ranks were to be embarked for aircraft maintenance. The Board made two biplanes available — a de Havilland 60G Gipsy Moth and a Westland Wapiti.[5] Both machines were on floats and both were equipped with dual radio sets; the Moth was for short-range scouting, while the larger Wapiti had the task of dropping rations and a sledge to the missing aviators if the need arose. To save time it was arranged that the silver fuselages of the two aircraft would be painted yellow once the ship neared the Ross Sea.

Piloted by Eric Douglas, the RAAF Gipsy Moth lands beside *Discovery II* after locating the missing aviators.

The Gipsy Moth scout plane stowed on deck of *Discovery II* as the search party makes its way south.

Crowds assembled on the dockside each day to watch preparation for the Antarctic voyage. Among the tonnes of stores and equipment, Mawson provided his wooden sledge, taken from the Adelaide Museum. Newspapers covered the loading of the two RAAF machines. Two days short of Christmas, and a day later than *Wyatt Earp*'s setting out from Chile on the other side of the world, *Discovery II*, under the command of Lieutenant L. C. Hill, RN, sailed down Port Phillip Bay to a send-off of cheers, tug whistles and blazing sunshine.

After a call to rebunker at Dunedin, the summer cruise quickly faded as they ploughed through the roaring forties, furious fifties and screaming sixties; by the second week of January they had met the Ross Sea pack. *Discovery II*, successor to Scott's famous *Discovery* of 1901, was an ice strengthened vessel, but not an icebreaker. At times the crew had to line the rails, pushing out with long poles to deflect ice from vulnerable rudder and propeller as their ship went astern to prepare for another lunge at the white desert surrounding it. On 12 January 1936 Douglas and Murdoch took off in the Moth to search for a lead through the pack. A day later the ship broke into the open waters of the Ross Sea. Douglas recorded in his diary:

We are now about 74°S and should arrive at the Bay of Whales sometime tomorrow and shortly after this the mystery may be cleared up. If Ellsworth is not at the Bay of Whales we will then endeavour to carry out some flying with the Wapiti . . . the ice blink from the Barrier is now visible around the horizon ahead. Air temperature down to 21°F (–7°C).

They were 22 days out from Melbourne when, from the crow's nest, the watch called that the cliffs of the Great Ice Barrier were in view. Fortunately the Bay of Whales was open, allowing Lieutenant Hill to sail them into the harbour on the morning of 14 January. Shouts went up as the crew pointed to machines of some kind parked close by the cliff edge; through binoculars they proved to be the tractors left behind by Byrd in 1934. Next, back from the cliff they spied the dark triangle of a small tent with orange markers fluttering beside it; Ellsworth was known to be carrying orange coloured signal strips. *Discovery*'s hooter sounded and signal rockets went up. Nothing stirred from within the tent.

A week of negotiating the pack ice lay ahead of the rescue party before they would reach the Bay of Whales on 14 January 1936. Ellsworth had now been missing for seven weeks.

Returning from the flight to probe a passage through the Ross Sea on 12 January 1936. Eric Douglas, a BANZARE veteran, was at the controls of the Gipsy Moth, with Murdoch as his co-pilot.

Hurriedly the Moth was readied for take-off from open water beside the ship. Even on the short hop to Little America, Douglas and Murdoch suddenly found themselves enveloped in semi-whiteout conditions — 'like flying in a bowl of cream', Douglas put it, unable to detect the surface until they saw another flag and then the tips of radio masts protruding through the snow. They circled above the old camp site and saw a figure emerge from what appeared to be a trapdoor and wave his arms wildly at the plane. Murdoch dropped a small parachute attached to a metal canister containing provisions and a note. 'One of them is alive at any rate,' Douglas reported on their return to *Discovery*.

The Royal Research Ship *Discovery II* moored to the ice in the Bay of Whales. The Gipsy Moth (forward of mast) was launched to reconnoitre for a sign of life at Admiral Byrd's old Little America camp.

Ellsworth and Hollick-Kenyon had taken off for Little America in the early morning of 22 November 1935. Away from Dundee Island, they climbed *Polar Star* to around 2,130 metres (7,000 feet) and headed towards Ellsworth's first objective of 80° West longitude. Enjoying full sunshine, light winds and an unbelievable visibility, they were three hours in sight of the first immense range that intersected their path. Ellsworth, who took 31 pictures of the peaks and plateau with his expensive 35 mm Leica, called it 'the greatest hour of my life' and continued:

> In the clear air we could now see the mountains in all their sublimity. It falls to the lot of few men to view land not previously beheld by human eyes, and it was with a feeling of keen curiosity not unmingled with awe that we gazed ahead at the great range across which our route lay. Bold and rugged peaks rose sheer to an elevation of 12,000 feet above sea-level. Suddenly I felt supremely happy for my share in the opportunity to unveil the last continent in human history.

> We were indeed the first intruding mortals in this age-old region, and looking down on the mighty peaks, I thought of eternity and man's insignificance. So these first new mountains we saw will, I hope, in the future bear the name Eternity Range. (Ellsworth: 313)

Climbing to 3,000 metres (10,000 feet) and with outside temperature of –30°C (–22°F) they swung away at Hearst Land from the base of the peninsula and, on a steady south-westerly course, began the crossing of the unknown continent. Hollick-Kenyon, a man of few words and not given to frivolity, handed Ellsworth a message: 'So this is Antarctica! How do you like it?' Ellsworth wrote '100 per cent!' and passed the note back.

Eight hours out of Dundee Island, at an estimated 1,530 kilometres (950 miles) from Little America, the radio which had been carrying garbled transmissions to Lenz, the wireless operator on *Wyatt Earp*, though they did not realise it, suddenly went dead.[6] Hollick-Kenyon's note read, 'Transmitter out of action. What shall we do?' True to his resolve, Ellsworth replied 'Keep on to 80'.

Another mountain chain reared out of the plateau, shorter and more compact than the Eternities they had left behind, but possibly higher. Ellsworth named the most prominent peak, which he reckoned to be about 4,000 metres (13,000 feet), Mount Mary Louise Ulmer in honour of his wife. Sentinel Range he decided as the appropriate title for this giant stockade that stood guard over the ice desert that extended on all sides. The sighting of the new range meant that, in flying time, Ellsworth was well beyond his goal of 80° West. Before that magic line of where the unclaimed portion of Antarctica began, he did not wish to set foot on the plateau, not even to attempt a repair of the faulty radio. But 14 hours after take-off, with a deepening haze spreading over the horizon, he made a signal to his pilot: time had come for the explorer to leave his mark on this untouched crust of the ice continent.

Lacking a horizon or any feature on which to judge proximity, Hollick-Kenyon throttled back and with flaps extended waited for the bump that would tell him *Polar Star* had landed. Even with the pilot's expert care, they jarred so heavily against the smooth, hard surface that Ellsworth felt 'my teeth would go through my head'. They clambered stiffly out of the cockpit to find the fuselage 'crumpled' from the landing. This, however, did not prevent further flying; their position was fixed at 79°12' South and 104°10' West. Time had come to run up the Stars and Stripes, the flag his niece Clare Prentice had sewn and presented to him before leaving New York. Ellsworth's description continued:

> We stood in the heart of the only unclaimed land in the Antarctic—in the whole world. I felt a very meek and reverent person. To think that I, of all those who had dreamed this dream, should be permitted its realisation! For the moment I lost all sense of the troubled beginning, had no thought for the journey ahead. I was content, grateful . . . So here I raised the American flag. The area extending from Long. 80°W to 120°W I named James W. Ellsworth Land after my father. That part of the plateau above 6,000 feet I called Hollick-Kenyon Plateau. (324–5)

They dubbed it Camp I, or Desolation, at an altitude of 1,920 metres (6,300 feet) and an estimated distance of 1,040 kilometres (650 miles) short of the Bay of Whales, 'almost the most inaccessible point of the whole route'. Hollick-Kenyon cooked bacon and oatmeal on the primus stove while Ellsworth went for a stroll, but soon felt so overcome — intimidated, even —

by the endless monotony of the plateau that he returned to the aircraft. They took sextant readings, tried to operate the radio and then, with outside temperature around –26°C (–15°F) retired to sleep in the neat little weatherproof tent which had the silken sides sewn to a canvas floor.

After 19 hours they were refreshed and ready to go again. Warmed by Hollick-Kenyon's firepot, the Pratt and Whitney engine sprang back to life and from the granular hard-packed snow *Polar Star* lifted them into the air 'in a swift, breath-taking lunge of 50 yards or so' at noon on 24 November. The sky still showed bright and clear and, apart from the radio failure which they could not solve, there seemed no reason that Little America should not await them within another five hours.

It was as if the Antarctic weather watched the intruding pair and decided it had been too lenient, by far. Within 30 minutes they were forced to land in the face of an oncoming storm. With *Polar Star* dug into a snow pit, the tent at Camp II held them for three days, waiting for the sky to clear. They spent the time trying to check their position with the sextant, which seemed to be working erratically, and cranking a hand generator in the hope that someone in the world outside would hear the weak signal of their trail radio and could tell loved ones that Ellsworth and Hollick-Kenyon were still intact. They took off again on 27 November, to fly for a bare 50 minutes before failing visibility forced them down. No Little America today: for a whole week, a howling blizzard held them captive.

With Hollick-Kenyon's concurrence, Ellsworth had taken the hard-nosed decision to dispense with a meteorologist on the 1935 expedition, his reasoning being the impossiblity of forecasting distant Antarctic weather.[7] They would land Polar Star to ride out the elements and, when the weather cleared, fly on again. His logic stood solidly enough, provided a gale did not blow their tent away, that the fuel supply held out and they were not lost or disabled. At Camp III most of these hazards appeared ready to visit them.[8]

Upon *Polar Star's* third landing, Ellsworth and Hollick-Kenyon were blizzard-bound for a week on the Antarctic plateau. At times they feared the aircraft and their small tent — with them in it — would be blown into oblivion. Ellsworth spent a day in the tail section, bailing out drift snow with a pemmican mug.

For three days they remained in their sleeping bags as a matter of sheer survival from the intense cold and screaming wind which, but for iced-in anchor pegs, threatened to whip away their fragile tent and them inside it. They daily cooked two small meals and in the evening swigged from a bottle of grain alcohol Wilkins had slipped into their baggage. Fuel reserves were much lower than calculated; figures indicated the Wasp engine had been functioning at no more than two-thirds of its advertised speed and efficiency. Ellsworth began to lose the feeling in his left foot, due to a leather inner moccasin which contracted when moist, stopping the circulation. And he had to admit to Hollick-Kenyon that, because of the erratic performance of their sextant, he could not vouch for where they were. Nor, when it came to the time of leaving, would *Polar Star*'s motor start. This was their ultimate moment of terror.

Hollick-Kenyon was one of those silent men who contribute much yet leave a light footprint. He found the fault with Ellsworth's sextant in a loose index error adjustment screw and, having tightened it, worked out a compensating solution to restore accuracy. To get them off the ice, he connected the dead starter motor to the live batteries of their defunct radio and — presto! — the Wasp engine fired, ready to send *Polar Star* on the final 800 kilometres (500 miles) to the Bay of Whales.

Before they could leave, Ellsworth spent the whole of 4 December crouched within the aircraft, using bucket and pemmican mug to scoop out the hard-packed snow which drifted up every cranny of the fuselage. A storm returned next day, and the excavation had to be faced all over again. Weather soon improved on the flight from Camp III. They passed from Ellsworth's own 'Highland' to the continuing plateau of Marie Byrd Land (of Byrd's 1929 claimed territory), at which point their flight path reached above 80° South, the closest to the Pole that Ellsworth would ever come. Droning above the unbroken icesheet, they covered the penultimate leg in 175 minutes, noting an obvious downward sloping in surface elevation and the outbreak of huge crevasse fields, a sure indication of the approaching Ross Ice Shelf.

The landing at Camp IV was for a brief position fix, 79°15' South latitude and 153°16' West longitude. 'What an afternoon!' Ellsworth wrote, and continued: 'The snow sparkled like jewels. There was no wind. Once more it was good to be alive, for we were off the high plateau and on the Ross Barrier at last, 980 feet above sea level and only 125 miles from our destination, with fuel enough to reach it.' His reference to fuel reserves proved a trifle optimistic. And the distance to the Barrier was more like 256 kilometres (160 miles). Nevertheless, the final flight of 65 minutes brought them over the humped ice of Roosevelt Island, where a division in the Ross Shelf produces the Bay of Whales. Ellsworth's own description tells of the view that met their eyes when they gazed to the right:

> But at that moment something else was commanding our complete attention. All during this last hour of flight a great water sky had been building higher in the north. Then all at once, as we came past Roosevelt Island, we saw it — slate-coloured open water on the north horizon, looking almost black in contrast to the white expanse across which we gazed. The Ross Sea!
>
> There was a goal at which so much Antarctic exploration had aimed, and we had reached it. Behind this moment lay three years of planning, work, and travel, heartbreak and hardship, failure, discouragement, and renewed determination, and at last there it was. We had crossed the continent from the Weddell Sea to the Ross Sea.

> At such moments in the story-books men are supposed to make memorable remarks, but in actual life behaviour seems to be different. What happened was this: As soon as the open water appeared in the north, Hollick-Kenyon turned round and looked at me. I expected him to say something, but he did not. Nor could I think of anything to say. I stared back at him, that was all. Then we resumed our individual tasks. After all, what was there to say? (Ellsworth: 334–5)

A few minutes later the engine spluttered and went dead. The eerie sound of rushing wind filled the cockpit as the pilot guided them towards the glittering white of the ice shelf. 'Hollick-Kenyon picked his spot,' said Ellsworth. 'And at 10.03 a.m., local time, 5 December, the *Polar Star*, like a weary bird, came gently to earth.' They had covered 3,765 kilometres (2,340 miles) since leaving Dundee Island a fortnight earlier, and had flown across Antarctica for 20 hours and 15 minutes.[9]

The rescuers stand above the site of Little America camp where Ellsworth and his pilot sheltered for 31 days in a hut beneath the snow. Drift had reached almost to the top of the 21-metre (70-feet) radio towers erected by the first Byrd expedition in 1928.

At first reckoning, the pair believed Little America II to be but a half day's walk away. But in what direction amid this desolation of undulating ice? *Polar Star* was dug into the snow and a food cache piled on the wings. Rations disconcerted them. Should they carry a minimum pack or drag a heavy sledge-load of supplies? From the wing, Hollick-Kenyon spied what he thought to be a machine standing amid the snow and, beyond it, the outline of a camp; armed with pocket compass and sextant they set off on their snow shoes. This futile excursion fixed the pattern for the following 10 days — the most nightmarish of the whole trans-Antarctic epic. The 'machine' turned out to be one of Byrd's discarded oil drums and the 'camp' but a jumble of distant pressure ridges. Day after day through 24 hours of sunlight and fog they kept searching for Little America, pushing out from the stranded aircraft, stumbling back again, alternately dragging the laden sledge and abandoning it, utterly exhausted.

Relaxing aboard *Discovery II*, the explorers Ellsworth and Hollick-Kenyon seem none the worse for their exhausting flight across Antarctica and 10 days of tramping through the snow

Until the moment that a strange rushing noise drew them towards a steep ridge. At the very edge they halted, staring through the mist at the Ross Sea breakers dashing against the ice far below, where another step could have easily taken them. At least they had reached the Bay of Whales. But which way to turn to find Byrd's camp? Luckily they chose west.

Nothing could be seen of the buildings except for pipes, chimneys and masts protruding like dead men's fingers from the snow. They dug downwards beside a ventilator shaft, opened a hatch and scrambled into the quiet of Little America's radio shack, abandoned almost two years before. On 15 December, Ellsworth at last could say his trans-Antarctic crossing was complete. He dug into his rucksack and produced a small flask of Napoleon brandy, his wife's gift for celebrating the moment of triumph. He and Hollick-Kenyon shared the contents — 'the best brandy I ever tasted,' wrote Ellsworth, 'brown, fiery, yet smooth as velvet. Hollick-Kenyon took a sip and really smiled.' They had tramped over 160 kilometres (100 miles) to find Little America II; *Polar Star*, in fact, lay only 25 kilometres (16 miles) away, though in a direct line that was barred with crevasses.

Ellsworth and Hollick-Kenyon were never buddies. How they survived each other's company through the trials and tensions of those weary lost weeks stood as testimony to each man's self-control and to the respect they held for one another. In the hut five metres (16 feet) below the surface Hollick-Kenyon continued his fastidious dressing. Each day he shaved and bathed himself in melted snow water; somehow he kept his trousers and jacket looking as if they had just emerged from a well-kept wardrobe. On one occasion, irritated by Hollick-Kenyon's stolid silence, Ellsworth complained 'don't you ever talk?' Replied his pilot: 'I have a bad temper. I prefer not to'.

Rescued or 'Aided'?

Lincoln Ellsworth wrote,
in *Beyond Horizons* (351):

Grateful as I was to the Australian government and to the Discovery Committee in London for dispatching their expensive vessel to me — a steel ship, incidentally, and therefore one that ran a risk in butting through heavy ice — regretful as I was at having caused others all this trouble, nevertheless I have to state that the voyage of the *Discovery II* to the Bay of Whales was unnecessary.

For my own reputation as an explorer I must insist that my Antarctic expedition was self-sufficient. I allowed myself five weeks in which to cross Antarctica. We actually reached Little America in three weeks. The *Wyatt Earp* was instructed to pick us up at Little America on or after January 22, 1936. She actually arrived on the nineteenth.

At no time were we 'lost', in the sense that we did not have a general idea of where we were or were unable to proceed. At no time was Wilkins, on the *Wyatt Earp*, at a loss as to what to do next. At no time were Hollick-Kenyon and I in desperate straits. We experienced discomfort and even hardship, but we always had food, heat, shelter, and available transportation; and, though we encountered difficulties, we overcame them as best we could and pressed on steadily to a successful end. Our whole program went through as projected; and, if there were a few bumps in it, these had been anticipated and discounted.

Rendezvous at the Bay of Whales: moored against the ice edge, Ellsworth's vessel *Wyatt Earp* arrived on 19 January 1936, five days after the rescue. *Discovery II* stands out in open water. 'My Antarctic expedition was self-sufficient… at no time were we "lost",' claimed Ellsworth.

'A man scrambled out ... Started to wave his arms'

Lincoln Ellsworth (centre) with his rescuers at Little America. He had a severely infected left foot and had to be assisted on a sledge back to the ship.

At 8.30 p.m. the ship's officers reported they could see two orange-coloured flags and a tent some little distance in from the Barrier face...now as Ellsworth carried orange signal strips in his plane, it looked to me that they might possibly be living at Little America [situated about 5 miles south over the Barrier ice] and erected this outpost as a signal to observers at sea.

At 9.20 Al [Murdoch] and I were lowered over in the Moth and after a run of at least 800m I managed to get the machine in the air (air temperature 18°F) and then climbed steadily to 1,000 ft. I then nosed over carefully towards the Barrier face and set a course for Little America.

As we progressed on over the ice the flying conditions became extremely bad and it was all I could do to keep the machine at a uniform height and on course. This was entirely due to the glare from the ice merging with the reflected glare from the clouds and we could not see the surface of the ice until we picked up another flag about 2 miles in.

Shortly after this we saw what appeared to be a crevassed area, but as we approached it changed shape and we could then see that what appeared to be cracks in the ice were actually wireless masts and poles. As I circled this area we observed an orange-coloured ground strip placed near what appeared to be the top or roof of a hut. Then imagine our delight when a man scrambled out from this roof and started to wave his arms.

We continued to circle and after a few minutes I threw overboard a small bag of provisions attached to a parachute. This landed about 60 yards from the man who immediately walked across to it in his snow shoes...I turned east to look at an object that appeared to be a wing of an aeroplane. Sure enough it was the port wing of a monoplane and as I had heard that Admiral Byrd had taken home with him all his aircraft, I naturally came to the conclusion that this was Ellsworth's machine. I then headed away to the arc of water sky and in a few minutes could faintly pick out our ship. We cruised along the Barrier face observing this and the sea for a suitable place for men to walk over to Little America.

From the log of Wing Commander Douglas of 14 January 1936

Ellsworth had supreme confidence that Wilkins would adhere to their rescue plan. Apart from tramping to the Barrier edge, setting up the tent with orange markers and scanning the sea, they could do nothing much else but wait. Radio sets had been stripped from the hut. Hollick-Kenyon kept the coal stove alight and foraged for rations, of which he found plenty. Ellsworth lay in his bunk, wondering about his numb left foot, feeling feverish spasms of hot and chill and quietly fuming over his reading glasses, left in the aircraft cockpit. Hollick-Kenyon stretched himself on another bunk, absorbed in one of the library of detective magazines they had found on the shelves, contentedly sucking at his long pipe and dredging candy from a tin beside him — 'gurgle, swipe and crunch', as Ellsworth put it. Perhaps one of the bitterest moments between the two aviators arrived when Kenyon observed his millionaire leader had used three matches to light his pipe, then drily commented, 'You must be the president of a match factory'. To which Ellsworth retorted, 'You use a good many more matches than I do'.

So they existed through one week, and another, and another. Ellsworth was asleep when the sound of an aircraft brought Hollick-Kenyon scrambling from the hatchway on the morning of 14 January. To his surprise, the machine circling overhead displayed not the expected American markings but, to him, the familiar roundels of a British military plane. The note in the canister of food that fluttered down on a small parachute advised that a boat party would come ashore and, if able, he should go to meet it.

Captain Hill (in uniform) and the RAAF team aboard *Discovery II* with Lincoln Ellsworth. The American millionaire insisted on returning to Australia to tender his personal thanks to the Australian government — for a rescue, which he believed was 'unnecessary'.Eric Douglas is on Ellsworth's left, Alister Murdoch is on Captain Hill's right.

After the final flight, the RAAF Gipsy Moth was reloaded for the long voyage home; the larger Wapiti aircraft never flew.

Crew members of *Discovery II* confessed to being somewhat disappointed when, to their cheers and clapping, Herbert Hollick-Kenyon came alongside in the ship's motor launch. They had expected a bearded, emaciated and bedraggled explorer; instead, here was a beaming, ruddy-faced, clean-

Postscript at the Bay of Whales: beside *Wyatt Earp* at the fringe of the Great Ice Barrier stands Ellsworth's faithful *Polar Star*, and to the left the Gamma 2D which had been flown from the United States to assist Wilkins in a search for Ellsworth.

shaven and check-shirted Englishman who stepped on the deck — as a figure the nearest one could imagine to a well-dressed polar dummy. 'Well, well! The *Discovery*, eh?' Hollick-Kenyon exclaimed, accepting the offer of a whisky and soda. 'This *is* an affair! But I say, it's awfully decent of you fellows to drop in on us like this.'

His rescuers were so taken aback at the laconic greeting that the conversation seemed about to lapse until someone asked, 'Where's your aeroplane?' Hollick-Kenyon settled himself in a chair, deliberately filled his pipe and replied:

> 'The aeroplane? Oh, that's twenty miles away on the Barrier. You see, the old bus ran out of gas.'
>
> 'Did you crash?'
>
> 'Good Lord! No. We landed perfectly safely and walked in. The aeroplane's all right. We'll have to go and get it presently...Food? Oh, rather. Any amount at Little America. So much we hardly knew what to do with it. No, we weren't worrying. We knew the *Wyatt Earp* would come along sooner or later...Pity about the radio. The transmitter switch went wrong...Yes, we landed all over the countryside during the flight. Whenever the weather got a bit thick, you know...Ellsworth? Oh, he's all right. He's got a bad foot but he'll be along to-morrow.'
>
> 'So you had no hitches at all?'
>
> 'No, none at all. Oh, yes! One slight hitch. Ellsworth left his spectacles in the aeroplane twenty miles away so he can't read, poor old chap!' (Ommanney: 202–3)

Six men of the launch party, led by Hollick-Kenyon, returned to the Barrier and tramped across the icy path to Little America to meet the missing millionaire. Ellsworth preferred to spend the night hours resting before making the journey to *Discovery II.* They found the man to have a temperature of 104°F and his blistered left foot was in danger of turning septic when they carried him to the ship's sick bay next morning. On the same day, the signal went out on *Discovery*'s radio, to be picked up by the world press — 'Ellsworth Found!'[10]

Eric Douglas described the American as a man of slight build, face burnt brown by the Antarctic sun, quiet mannered and modest of speech. Except that Ellsworth did not want to regard the Australian airmen and the British crew as his rescuers. Despite his sincere appreciation of the doctor's treatment and the warm bed given over to him in the chief scientist's cabin (the doctor also had found a pair of spectacles that he could use), Ellsworth politely insisted that the whole Australian effort was really unnecessary; his own relief operation, true to its schedule, was close at hand.

On 19 January Ellsworth's faith in Wilkins' management was borne out when a small wooden ship, flying the Stars and Stripes, nosed around the headland into the Bay of Whales. Indeed, after an 8,800-kilometre (5,500-mile) voyage from the Antarctic Peninsula, probing the ice at various prearranged places to check for Ellsworth's presence, Wilkins had reached his leader three days ahead of schedule. A moment of humour came when Ellsworth chided Wilkins for flying *Wyatt Earp*'s flag at half mast with the comment that the report of his demise was somewhat exaggerated. 'You flatter yourself,' Wilkins replied. 'We heard on the radio that King George V has passed away.'

Wilkins came aboard *Discovery II* and sat next to Douglas at tea; their conversation led to another diary entry by the Australian airman:[11]

> I found him a charming man though I have no doubt he is a bit of a stunt merchant. He was a bit annoyed with the relief expedition (ours) and his reasoning appeared to be quite OK until I found that he had wired Washington asking the British Government to help with the *Discovery II* by this ship steaming south and listening for W/T signals. Well, he could hardly blame the Discovery committee and the Australian Government for wanting to carry it out properly or not at all.

LINCOLN ELLSWORTH

Welcomed in Melbourne

AUSTRALIA THANKED.

VIVID ACCOUNT OF ANTARCTIC RESCUE

MELBOURNE, Monday.

Mr. Lincoln Ellsworth, the American explorer and aviator, arrived in Melbourne to-day in the Royal research ship, Discovery II.

Simply and briefly he acknowledged the congratulations of Australia upon making the first flight across Antarctica, and voiced his thanks to the Commonwealth, the Royal Australian Air Force, and the officers and men of the Discovery II. for the rescue of himself and his pilot, Mr. Hollick Kenyon.

Smiling and deeply bronzed, Mr. Ellsworth showed no sign of the ordeal of a month spent with his companion in a hut in Antarctica after his aeroplane ran out of petrol.

Flight-Lieutenant Douglas, of the Royal Australian Air Force, gave a vivid description of the locating of Mr. Ellsworth and Mr. Kenyon from the Air Force Moth 'plane. Later, when the ice rescue party from the Discovery II. met Mr. Kenyon, his first words to them were, "I say, it is awfully decent of you fellows to drop in on us like this"—which was described as a laconic greeting which almost deserves a place in history with Stanley's, "Mr. Livingstone, I presume."

The scientific staff of the Discovery II. while in the Antarctic regions, were able to carry out valuable oceanographical research, principally into the three types of ocean currents found there.

CHEERS AS SHIP BERTHS.

MELBOURNE, Monday.

Several hundred enthusiastic spectators on the Williamstown pier cheered him again and again as the Discovery II. drew into the wharf.

The flags flown on the Discovery II., as she berthed, bespoke the international and inter-Imperial character of her mission. The Red Ensign flew from the masthead, the National Ensign of the United States from her truck, the flag of the Falkland Islands, the ship's base, from her stern, and lashed to the side of the training Moth 'plane of the R.A.A.F. was a short staff from which was flown the flag of the force. Both the Moth 'plane and the Wapiti had changed colour since leaving Melbourne. In Antarctica they were painted yellow in order to be more easily seen if forced down on the snow or ice.

Mr. Ellsworth was cheered as he came down the gangway to be welcomed officially by the Minister for Defence (Mr. Parkhill), the Mayor of Williamstown (Councillor J. T. Gray), representatives of the three defence services, the chairman of the British, Australian, and New Zealand Antarctic Research Committee, Sir David Orme Masson, and by two men who perhaps appreciated more than anybody else present the merits of Mr. Ellsworth's great flight, and the hazards of his experience —Sir Douglas Mawson and the Vice-Chancellor of the University of Melbourne, Dr. R. E. Priestley.

WELCOME AT SHIP'S SIDE.

Mr. Parkhill welcomed Mr. Ellsworth on the wharf by the ship's side. "Australians," he said, "are always delighted to welcome to the country people from other lands, who have displayed to a high degree the qualities they most admire—courage and determination. For three years you have stubbornly pursued your objective, and at length, having tired out hostile fortune, you have completed successfully the last major feat of exploration in the great South Land."

The voyage of the Discovery II. to the Bay of Whales, Mr. Parkhill said, had de- was two miles a day, but we walked more than 100 miles when we need only have covered 16 miles. The journey occupied 22 days."

At Byrd's camp their troubles were over if help came within two months. There was plenty of food for that period.

"Kenyon was cook, and I d[illegible] the cleaning out, which consisted of shovelling away the snowdrift and keeping the entry shaft to the dugout free," Ellsworth said. "The real hardship was the lack of exercise. It was 10 p.m. on December 15—two months after we made our forced landing—that Kenyon woke me from sleep and said that a letter had arrived for me. He spoke casually, as though a mail delivery in the Antarctic were a regular thing.

SOME LUXURIES.

"Kenyon set out on the table a tempting display of good things which had been dropped from the Australian Air Force machine. There was orange juice in tins, and also chocolates and raisins. In the message we were told to march toward the sea to meet a party from the Discovery II. Kenyon offered to go alone, as my foot was still bad.

"After he had been absent a long time, I became anxious and set out after him. A mile away from the camp I saw what appeared to be a huge army approaching through the thick fog. Actually, it was only five men, including Kenyon. A man from the Discovery spoke the first words between us, and asked, 'Have you got anything to eat?'

"We led them back to the camp, and were able to cook them a good meal, which included bully beef, and the Discovery men certainly enjoyed it, but not as much as I enjoyed the saltwater bath that I had as soon as I got aboard the ship. It was my first bath in three months, and, by Jove, it was good. I never wanted to come out of that bath. All the way back to Australia I have been enjoying baths."

To-night, Ellsworth and Lieutenant Hill shared a six minutes' broadcast which was relayed through the national network and by the British Broadcasting Commission and by the principal network in the United States.

The finding of Lincoln Ellsworth made world news. This story appeared in the *Sydney Morning Herald* of 23 January 1936.

Was it in the manner of a 'stunt merchant' to attempt a race with *Discovery II* to the Bay of Whales? Listening to radio transmissions from the other ship, Wilkins tried to arrive first but thick pack ice on his course from Charcot Island and the risk of burning out *Wyatt Earp*'s engine had slowed him.

The crew revived one of Byrd's abandoned tractors and loaded it with gasoline for the journey to where *Polar Star* lay buried. They dug out the aircraft and Hollick-Kenyon flew it the remaining distance to land on a floe beside Ellsworth's ship. Now it could be said the trans-Antarctic feat was really and truly accomplished. From the cockpit, Wyatt Earp's gun belt was restored to its owner who drily observed that *Polar Star,* rather like himself, had journeyed 104,000 kilometres (65,000 miles) by sea to spend but 20 hours making history in the sky. The machine, looking so small and fragile, was loaded on *Wyatt Earp*'s deck for the voyage home, eventually to find a place of honour in the Smithsonian Museum.

The RAAF team regretted Hollick-Kenyon had to accompany *Polar Star*. 'We are very sorry he cannot come,' wrote Douglas, 'he is such a fine chap, very modest and cheery.' Douglas also presented Ellsworth with the small parachute they had dropped on Little America. Sergeant Easterbrook, one of

The end of an epic journey: Hollick-Kenyon delivers *Polar Star* to the National Air Museum, Washington, D.C. Accepting Ellsworth's gift is the museum curator, Paul Gerber.

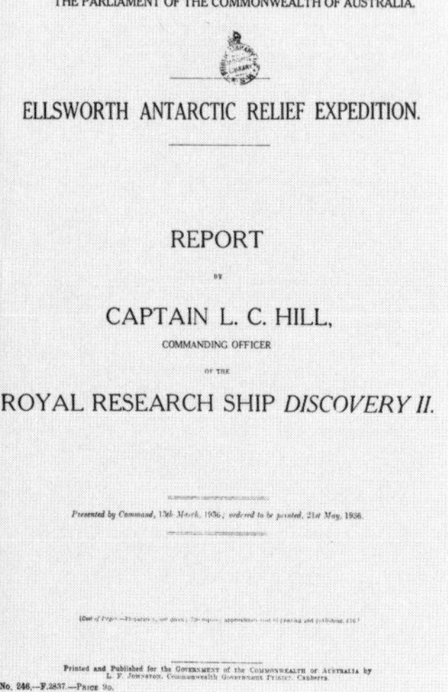

THE PARLIAMENT OF THE COMMONWEALTH OF AUSTRALIA.

ELLSWORTH ANTARCTIC RELIEF EXPEDITION.

REPORT

BY

CAPTAIN L. C. HILL,

COMMANDING OFFICER

OF THE

ROYAL RESEARCH SHIP *DISCOVERY II.*

Presented by Command, 13th March, 1936; ordered to be printed, 21st May, 1936.

Captain Hill's official report to the Australian government, giving the details of the voyage and the finding of the missing aviators.

the RAAF fitters, inscribed the fabric with the words: 'Compliments to Messrs Ellsworth and Kenyon from the personnel of the Royal Australian Air Force aboard the RRS *Discovery II* Bay of Whales, Ross Sea, Antarctica Jan. 15th 1936. Antarctic Parachute Co. Never-Failed-Yet.' At the bottom of the message, all the RAAF team added their signatures.[12]

Mawson and Davis were waiting to welcome this world famous American millionaire when the ship reached Melbourne on 16 February. Ellsworth was interviewed, photographed, feted, taken to Mount Buffalo resort and then flown to Canberra for lunch with Prime Minister Lyons and his Cabinet.[13] He joined the liner *Mariposa* in Sydney; at Honolulu his wife awaited him for the remainder of the voyage to Los Angeles where an honour guard of aircraft came out to escort the ship. At New York in April a celebrity's welcome greeted both Ellsworth and Hollick-Kenyon when *Wyatt Earp* docked in Manhattan with *Polar Star* proudly displayed on deck.[14]

On 16 June 1936, the United States Congress voted Lincoln Ellsworth a special gold medal — 'for claiming on behalf of the United States approximately three hundred and fifty thousand square miles of land in Antarctica between the eightieth and one hundred and twentieth meridians west of Greenwich, representing the last unclaimed territory in the world'.

Matters were rather more mundane in Australia where a totalling up of the rescue expenses showed that the RAAF effort had cost the taxpayer £2,696 4s 7d and after allowing for contributions to *Discovery II*'s expenses, an amount of £134 9s 8d was owed to the British government.

Mary Louise Ellsworth stands beside her husband as President Roosevelt presents him with the special gold medal voted by Congress — 'for claiming on behalf of the United States approximately 350,000 square miles of land in Antarctica... representing the last unclaimed territory in the world...'

Prime Minister Lyons and members of Federal Cabinet with Lincoln Ellsworth at Parliament House, Canberra, where a luncheon was given in his honour on 20 February 1936.

The stillness was almost uncanny. Only the rhythmic beat of the waves and the increasing soft chatter of the penguins broke the solemn silence.

Lars Christensen, at his first landing on the Antarctic continent

7

SCRAMBLE FOR THE ICE

Key to Germany's air exploration plan was the large seaplane 'mother ship' which could lift aircraft from the water and, after refuelling, catapult them on the next stage of the journey. *Schwabenland* served on Luft Hansa's Trans Atlantic run between West Africa and Brazil before being assigned to the Antarctic expedition.

Mrs Lars Christensen was the first woman to gaze on Antarctica from an aeroplane. The wife of a Norwegian whaling magnate, she made her flight on 27 January 1937 over the icebound coast of the land which now bears her name. Beneath the shadow of their Stinson float-plane lay Australian Antarctic Territory. Ingrid Christensen celebrated her feat by dropping the Norwegian flag.

Altogether four flights were made on this 'perfect day — with ice all around but dead calm and sunshine', to quote the whaling chief. The next flight took Christensen himself and another woman guest, Mrs Rachlew, aloft. 'It is always a strange feeling,' Christensen continued, 'to set eyes on an unknown land. But before long all other feelings give place to admiration of the wild magnificence of the landscape. The view of the Vestfold Mountains, in particular was thrilling in its loveliness.'

Four women joined the 1936-37 voyage of the tanker *Thorshavn*. They were Mrs Christensen, who was on her second Antarctic visit, and her youngest daughter, Sofie, together with Lillemor Rachlew and another friend, Solveig Wideroe. They spent four months cruising around Antarctica on a venture which was intended to clear up many of the blank spaces along the coast of the Indian Ocean sector. As Christensen put it: 'I intend this to be the final one of all my expeditions . . . and it appeared to me that, in order to wind up things satisfactorily, I ought to undertake the circumnavigation of the South Polar continent'.

The fact that in the all-male age of Wilkins, Ellsworth, Byrd and Mawson, four women could live in relative comfort aboard an 11,000-tonne motorship, most likely immune from the dangers of the encircling ice — and go sightseeing in the clear polar skies — pointed to one resounding truth: from the other end of the earth, the Norwegians had come to make Antarctica their happy hunting ground, complete with designs of territorial ownership.

Norway's earliest Antarctic probe had occurred 45 years earlier, when Captain C. A. Larsen sailed the sealer *Jason* to Graham Land. C. E. Borchgrevink, a Norwegian migrant living in Australia, claimed to be the first man to set foot on the Antarctic continent in a landing at Cape Adare from another Norwegian whaling vessel on 24 January 1895. Borchgrevink returned with his own *Southern Cross* expedition in 1899 and spent a year camped on the fringe of Victoria Land at Robertson Bay. At his conquest of the South Pole in 1911–12, that most famous Norwegian, Roald Amundsen, raised the flag over the bottom of the world and called the surrounding plateau after his sovereign, King Haakon VII, and to the great Antarctic mountains he gave the name of Queen Maud. For Norway, the word Antarctica smacked of pride, profit and possession.

From 1929, when Christensen began to carry aircraft on his whaling ships, the speed and range of Norway's penetration of the South Atlantic and Indian Ocean sectors significantly increased.[1] Thus, within 12 months of Wilkins' historic flight and with Byrd established at Little America, the Norwegians were quietly going about their own aerial exploits.[2] But finding new lands from an aeroplane was only half the story: fresh hunting grounds were also being identified, soon to draw the large mechanised whaling fleets.

Norvegia, a catcher of 290 tonnes equipped for exploration and research, came south with the fleet, loaded almost to the gunwales with two float planes — an F-18 Hansa-Brandenburg of a type used by the Norwegian navy and powered by a 185-horsepower BMW motor, and a Lockheed Vega similar to Wilkins' machine. Captain Hjalmar Riiser-Larsen, the well known Arctic pilot, and his navy observer, Commander Finn Lutzow-Holm, made the inaugural flight on 7 December 1929, to return with a thrilling account of white mountains and iceberg-studded seas. Before leaving Norway, the government had authorised Riiser-Larsen to annex new territory for the Crown.[3] He lost little time in doing so and on 22 December landed with his observer at Cape Ann on the tip of Enderby Land, taxied the plane over the ice edge, skied southwards for two hours and then raised the flag, leaving a deed of claim inside a sealed box. At the end of six and a half hours he reboarded the ship to announce their first territorial conquest.

However, Riiser-Larsen's exhilaration was short-lived. A radiogram from Christensen on 10 January advised him the Norwegian government had agreed to make no claim over areas where the British had prior rights. Cape Ann, indeed all of Enderby Land, was solidly 'British', being one of the first portions of the Antarctic mainland to be undisputedly recognised by man, in the person of the sealer John Biscoe who in 1831 named the region after his London employers, the Enderby Brothers.

Ingrid Christensen (*left*) and Mathilde Weger enjoying the Antarctic summer during a 1931 voyage on *Thorshavn* in the Norwegian whaling fleet. Mrs Christensen went on two exploration flights during her husband's 1936–37 cruise.

Between 7 and 16 January 1930 four more flights, completing 30 hours aloft, were made in observing new coastline, circling above hitherto unseen mountains and generously dispensing the Norwegian name, starting with Prince Olav Coast. On one of the flights, they reported the luminously blue ice-crystal slopes of a great range which Riiser-Larsen named Sor Rondane Mountains. The limit of his westwards exploration took Riiser-Larsen to the beginning of the Weddell Sea at Cape Norvegia on his Princess Martha Coast.

The day after Sir Douglas Mawson raised the British flag at Proclamation Island on 13 January 1930, the two tiny ships — BANZARE's *Discovery* and Christensen's *Norvegia* — held their unlikely meeting off the vast white dome of the Antarctic coast.[4] Like a pair of honest brokers, the commanders sat around *Discovery*'s chart table — Mawson, a world renowned explorer, and Riiser-Larsen, who had flown the Arctic routes with Amundsen and Ellsworth. Together they agreed (backed-up by the Norwegian government's decision) that the meagre resources of south polar exploration would be best served by regarding 45° East longitude as the dividing line for their exploits — Norway keeping to the west, Australia to the east.

Christensen's 1933 expedition, starting from Cape Town and with a planned near-circumnavigation of Antarctica, employed his *Thorshavn* as a depot ship for aviation. Sometimes the big motor-tanker operated alone, sometimes sending out the aeroplane on a modified catcher boat which could approach closer to the coast through leads in the pack ice. The expedition carried an Avro Avian aircraft, similar to a de Havilland Moth, powered by an 85-horsepower Mark III Cirrus engine. Because it was too small for the heavy radios of the day, pilot Lieutenant Gunnerstad was ordered not to fly beyond visual range of the ship. Christensen commanded the expedition and his wife, who accompanied him, made her debut in the record books as first woman known to sail beyond the Antarctic circle. (The 1933 expedition also put a sledge party ashore, led by Riiser-Larsen. Their ambitious plan called for a journey around the Antarctic coast. However, shortly after landing they lost dogs and sledges when an ice floe collapsed and they were fortunate to escape with their lives.)

The Avian flew its initial reconnaissance mission off the Lars Christensen Coast on 10 January 1934. A week later, having been transferred to the catcher *Ornen III*, it took off from open water in the lee of a large iceberg. With Gunnerstad at the controls and Nils Larsen, the mate of *Thorshavn* as observer, their course followed the West Barrier for 144 kilometres (90 miles) to the south and 80 kilometres (50 miles) to the east. As a result of the two flights, lasting three hours in all, Christensen gave the name of King Leopold and Queen Astrid Coast to the surface they had sighted.[5] They did not fly again until 10 February, when at 71°41' South and 134°11' West, eight sorties were made over a period of ten hours. Because of limitations the little Avian imposed on their exploration program, Christensen declared his next expedition would include an aircraft equipped with radio.

Roald Amundsen, leader of the first party to reach the South Pole on 14 December 1911. In their continuing exploration, the Norwegians took much inspiration from the deeds of the polar hero.

With Christensen's 1935 voyage, the international implications of Norway's exploration resurfaced. Captain Klarius Mikkelsen commanded the third *Thorshavn* expedition. On the score of papers contributed on geography, geology, oceanology and botanical and zoological subjects, the expeditions could not be faulted; the Norwegians were sound in their approach to exploration and science in Antarctica. Flights were made in early January and then in February of 1935. The Ingrid Christensen Coast, well beyond 70° East longitude where Mawson's BANZARE had proclaimed the area of Princess Elizabeth Land, was discovered and named by Captain Mikkelsen; this 'discovery', together with the adjoining King Leopold and Queen Astrid Coast, brought the Norwegians to almost a halfway point within the nearer Australian sector.

Did they intend to lodge a counter claim for part of Australian Antarctica? The Norwegians were intent on securing strongholds for their whaling operation[6]. And they continued to add to the record books. Caroline Mikkelsen accompanied her husband with the party of seven men who on 20 February 1935 landed the ship's launch at a small bay on the most northerly part of a strange ice-free coast which had been studied from *Thorshavn*'s aircraft.

They decided to name the remarkable area of bare rock and blue lakes after the province of Vestfold, the whalers' stronghold south of Oslo, which it closely resembled. To Caroline Mikkelsen, the landing at the Vestfold Hills meant that to her went the honour of being first woman ashore on the Antarctic continent.

Captain Riiser-Larsen in the cockpit of the F18 Hansa-Brandenburg which was taken south aboard *Norvegia* in 1929.

'Loaded almost to the gunwales', is how Sir Douglas Mawson described *Norvegia* which was sent on the hunt for new Antarctic territory. The Hansa-Brandenburg is on the stern and the Lockheed Vega secured forward of the bridge.

Christensen's crowning achievement, his expedition of 1936–37 would bring the potential international conflict to a head. *Thorshavn* came south carrying a leased 1936 model Stinson float plane, equipped with a 350-horsepower engine and extra fuel tanks to allow a 1,200-kilometre (750-mile) radius. The pilot was Viggo Wideroe, with Romnaes as his radio operator and photographer; two mechanics, Standrud and Fidjeland, and Erik Simensen a photo-survey expert made up the flight crew. Also included were the two seasoned ice mariners, Captains Mikkelsen and Larsen. Two radios were fitted to the aircraft, while *Thorshavn* had been equipped with the latest and most powerful sets to keep in contact with the flights over long distances. As the crew would say, they 'hung on' their engine and their radio.

Thorshavn met with the factory ship *Ole Wegger* to transfer oil on 14 January 1937. *Firern*, a catcher boat that had been modified with crane and cleared deck space aft to store the Stinson, then came alongside.[7] With Wideroe, Romnaes and Standrud aboard they set off along the Leopold and Astrid Coast to approach the Antarctic shores as closely as the pack permitted. In clear weather on 24 January using obliquely aimed cameras, they began the photo flight across the glistening white face of the West Barrier where cliffs up to 70 metres (230 feet) high rose from the sea. En route to rejoin the catcher, *Thorshavn*'s depth sounder revealed a shallowing of the sea floor from 900 to 150 metres. The underwater feature, off Olaf Prydz Bay, they named Four Ladies Bank in honour of the guests aboard the owner's ship.

Lars Christensen, the whaling magnate who directed the Norwegian Antarctic program. In 1929 his ships began carrying aircraft.

The voyage led to the discovery and naming of more coastline after the Norwegian royal family to the west of Enderby Land. A landing was made at Scullin Monolith on the Mac-Robertson Coast; the Stinson went on reconnaissance missions over the Ingrid and Lars Christensen Coasts, the Mac-Robertson coast, Kemp and Enderby Land coasts, all within the now proclaimed sector of Australian Antarctic Territory.

Mrs Christensen made her flag-dropping flight of 27 January 1937 over the Australian region. Three days later Christensen was able to say: 'At two in the morning, I experienced the unique pleasure of setting foot on the Antarctic mainland...where we made a depot. The stillness was almost uncanny. Only the rhythmic beat of the waves and the increasing soft chatter of the penguins broke the solemn silence'. His landing occurred off the Gustav Bull Islands, well within the Australian area. By 1 February, Wideroe and Romnaes returned from a seven-hour flight and reported photographing 400 kilometres (250 miles) of coastline, which meant they had covered the whole West Barrier through to Enderby Land.

In fact Christensen's 'perfect day' of 27 January had allowed four sorties in quick succession. First flight was another photo run of the West Barrier ice shelf. The next went south-west towards Sandfjord Bay, reporting thousands of drifting icebergs, more of the harsh rocky coastline and interior mountains (gunner Sjovold had described a 'volcanic peak' in the mountains which bore his name, but no telltale smoke could be seen); then came the historic flight of Mrs Christensen, followed by that of her husband and their guest above the Vestfold Hills, revealing a 'magnificent panorama of the rising icesheet and snow capped peaks'.

They photo-surveyed the Lars Christensen Coast, Gustav Bull Mountains and a jigsaw of bays and islands between Kemp Coast and Enderby Land. The whalers found a 'fine airport' in Thorshavn Bay, allowing the aerial exploration to continue, though on 1 February *Firern* had to return to the fleet. Mrs Christensen went back for her second flight with pilot Wideroe on 4 February and received her owner-husband's congratulations as 'a lucky and efficient observer', for she had seen a distant highland which they named Prince Harald Land after the recently born son of Norway's crown prince. Again the flag was dropped, but at 34° East, outside Australian territory. The last flight of 6 February revealed a new mountain range estimated to be 300 kilometres (190 miles) long and 2,900 metres (9,500 feet) high.

The second flight of 3 February had brought their closest shave with disaster when a heavy swell started to run beside *Thorshavn* while the aircraft was still aloft. From the deck they watched Wideroe trying to judge where to land amid the rising waves. The third mate in the lifeboat tender said he lost sight of the incoming aircraft in the deep troughs of the sea. Wideroe himself, pleased to have the Stinson attached safely to *Thorshavn*'s jib, said he would never have believed an aircraft could set down in such a wild sea if he had not been involved in it himself.

By 6 February with the flying season complete *Thorshavn* turned her bows northwards. Since 16 January the aeroplane had been aloft for 44 hours and 50 minutes; 30 hours and 50 minutes of it was spent in photo-surveying, 3 hours and 30 minutes on the ladies' 'passenger flights'. The aviators had covered 10,000 kilometres (6,250 miles), and made 2,200 exposures for the program of oblique survey mapping, as well as operating normal still and movie cameras.[8] They left behind an area of the Australian territorial coast with names like Aagaard, Thorgaut and Oygarden Islands, Bjerke Peninsula, Fram Bank, Framnes Mountains, Sorsdal Glacier, Thorshavn Bay and mountain peaks called Caroline Mikkelsen, Kjerke, Bortindane and Torlyn. All of these locations were between 46° and 90° East longitude, most of them in the region of Mawson's Princess Elizabeth Land.

Australia watched these developments with increasing apprehension. Australian Antarctic Territory was now *fait accompli*. By the Australian Antarctic Acceptance Act of 1933 and the promulgation of 1936, the Commonwealth had embraced a vast polar territory which it now had the responsibility to occupy, administer and protect. In reality it had precious little capacity to do any such thing.

Questions were asked about Norway's right to raise its flag on Australian ice. At the back of all the protests and posturing lay the conduct of whaling — and the wealth being extracted from the southern seas by foreign vessels.[9] Australia vacillated over what action to take; on one hand to participate in the whale hunt and its profits, on the other to protect the ocean resources of its territorial waters from the depredation of alien fleets. The Commonwealth passed the Whaling Act of 1935 and promulgated it the following year. Norway made its objection through challenging Australia's claim to the Leopold and Astrid Coast, and to the Ingrid Christensen Coast.

The Norwegian position was that they were responsible for naming and mapping these areas.[10] The Commonwealth was ambivalent about how to proceed; with government encouragement, a whaling venture was to be promoted to hunt the southern seas, partly to show that Australia was able to work its territory, and partly for the money.[11] Diplomatic moves by Canberra, and more importantly between London and Oslo, looked for a dignified settlement. But Adolf Hitler's interest in Antarctica and Germany's new resurgence as a world power possibly had as much influence as any action in solving the impasse.

King Haakon, by a formal proclamation of 14 January 1939, announced that Norway claimed all that portion of Eastern Antarctica lying between 20° West and 45° East longitude. To be known as Dronning (Queen) Maud Land, one extremity of it bordered the British claim at Coats Land; on the other boundary was Australian Antarctic Territory. Claims over other portions of the coast were forgotten. Territorial differences had been amicably and diplomatically laid to rest.

CHAPTER SEVEN

Hitler's Neu Schwabenland

Five days after King Haakon's announcement, a German expedition approached the Princess Martha Coast, on the Atlantic sector of Norwegian Antarctic Territory. Dr Alfred Ritscher, who had been in the Arctic 25 years earlier, led the Schwabenland expedition; he was now aged 60. Captain Kottas commanded the 8,500-tonne seaplane tender while two experienced aviators, Rudolf Wahr and Dicki Schirmacher led the flying group. Their aircraft, a pair of ten-tonne Dornier Super Wal flying boats — *Passat* (D-ALOX) and *Boreas* (D-AGAT) — were rugged long-range machines driven by push-pull motors mounted above the wing; the swastika emblem was prominent on the tail.[12] Each aircraft was attended by a radio operator and mechanic; all of the crew were Deutsche Luft Hansa men.

The German press announced that the target zone of Antarctica lay between 14° West and 20° East longitude in Queen Maud Land. They would photo-survey the interior and prepare for a coastal base to study meteorology and oceanography.

The Norwegians greeted the news from Berlin with deep resentment and suspicion. Despite the fact that Britain, Australia, France and New Zealand recognised the formal Norwegian territorial claim, the modern Germany of the late 1930s was not a nation to be trifled with. Earlier German expeditions had been Filchner in 1910–12 and Drygalski of 1901–02. Until 1939, these far-off exploits represented the extent of Germany's interest in the Great South Land.

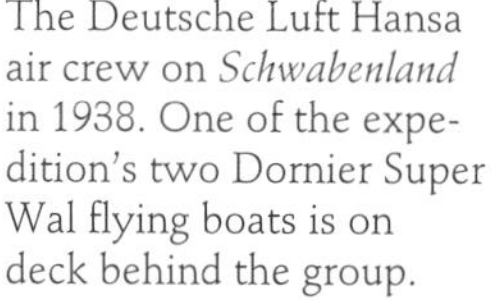

The Deutsche Luft Hansa air crew on *Schwabenland* in 1938. One of the expedition's two Dornier Super Wal flying boats is on deck behind the group.

Adolf Hitler had ruled that Germany should take part in the international scramble for Antarctica and its wealth. Resurgent German might demanded that the swastika should also fly at the bottom of the world; German whalers

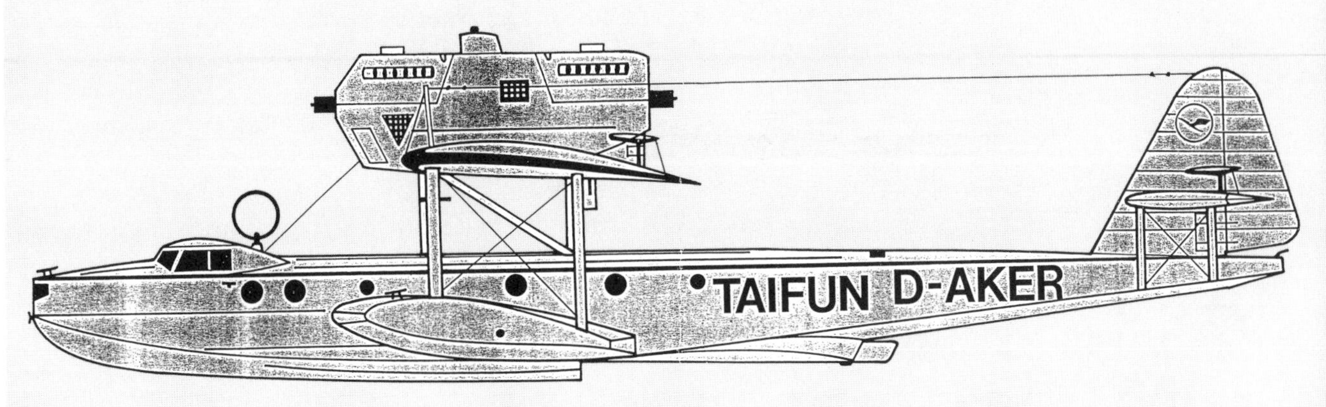

Diagram of the Super Wal (Whale) flying boat which had two push-pull motors mounted above the wing. The aluminium hull was supposed, under favourable conditions, to allow landings on the ice.

were to secure a greater share in the harvest of the seas. Hitler's regime also wanted fast answers. A surface expedition would be too complicated and time consuming and on 9 May 1938 Reichsfeldmarschall Hermann Goering announced that he would release a trans-Atlantic 'aeroplane mother-ship' for use in the South.[13] *Schwabenland,* the chosen vessel, measured 143 metres (468 feet) and was equipped with a powerful catapult that in seconds would accelerate a loaded flying boat to a take-off speed of 150 kph (93 mph).

As chief of the Luftwaffe, Goering directed that only the most experienced aviators and most tried aircraft should be picked for Antarctica. In a sense, the Schwabenland expedition was ready-made for the role entrusted to it. The Dornier flying boats and their crews and the large seaplane tender were an integral part of Luft Hansa's trans-Atlantic mail service between West Africa and Brazil. They were versed in long distances and stormy seas.[14]

Germany would show the world how to explore from the skies using the latest photo-surveying methods, incorporating colour stereo images. Navigation would be by sun compass and bubble sextant and without ground-fix parties. The essence of Schwabenland was 'in quickly and out again'. One item of stores differed from the usual polar supplies. Each aircraft would take on every flight 500 pounds (226 kilograms) of aluminium-and-steel-tipped javelins, bearing a swastika-engraved emblem on the hilt. Tests in the Alps proved that when dropped from 550 metres (1,800 feet) the rods would drive for about a third of a metre into the snow. The emblems were to dot the Antarctic surface about every 30 kilometres (18 miles). So Goering had directed.

Schwabenland made Antarctica's first catapult-launch on 19 January 1939.[15] Schirmacher, in command of *Boreas,* took the aircraft on an eight-hour mission which reached 600 kilometres (375 miles) to the south before being turned back by the rising face of the polar plateau. Next day, Wahr commanded *Passat* on another long-distance flight that attained 4,000 metres (13,000 feet) above the plateau seven hours out; on the same day, Ritscher went in *Boreas* to scout for a site where the seaplane could land on the interior ice, but without success. 'Always we see only ice, ice, ice,' said one of the pilots. 'Then suddenly, like needles sticking out of it, mountains and peaks become visible, showing in a strange rust-brown colour.'[16]

Captain Alfred Ritscher, leader of the Schwabenland expedition. Field Marshal Goering placed him in command.

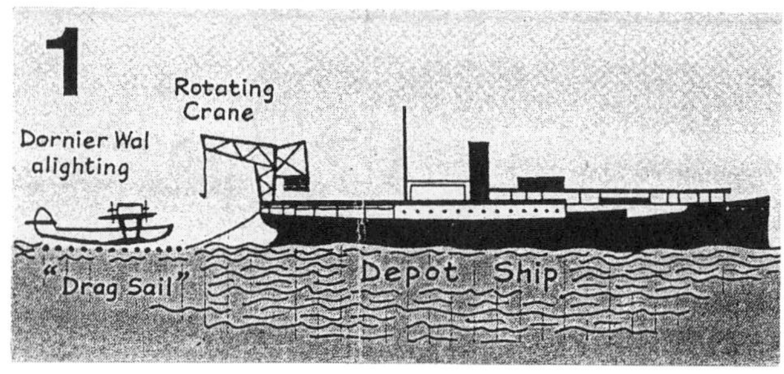

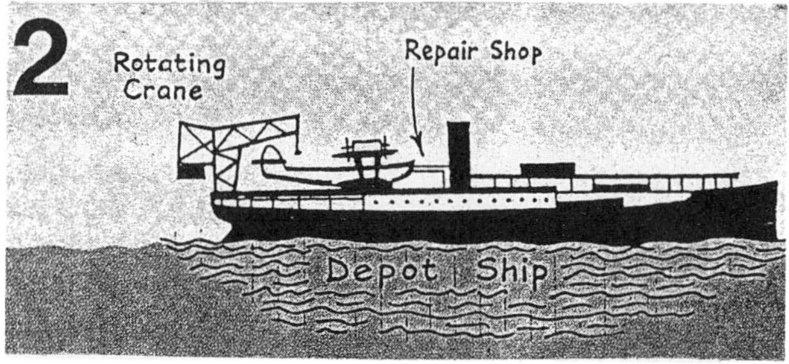

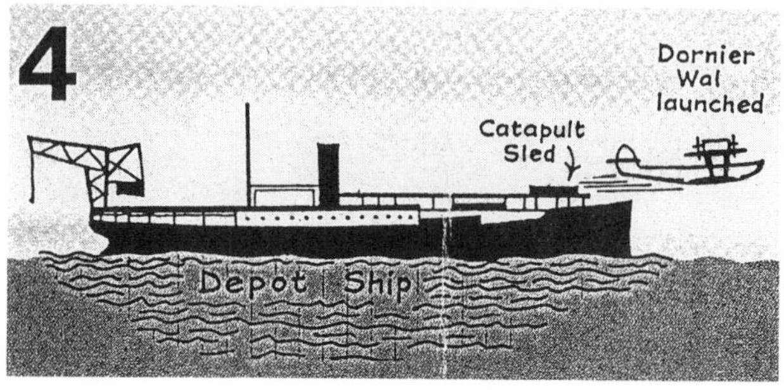

Stages in the landing and take-off procedure from the aircraft mother-ship. The catapult allowed launchings, regardless of sea conditions.

On 29 January, while *Boreas* flew south across the interior, Wahr took *Passat* along the coast to land on open water close to the ice edge. Having moored the flying boat, he and his crew walked a short distance across the snow where they ceremoniously planted and saluted the Nazi flag, the first occasion of a German surface claim. Another flag-planting ceremony came the following day, but a closing in of the floes abbreviated the ceremony and hurried their departure.

More flights were made on 31 January: *Boreas* on another photo survey while Wahr went in *Passat* to catch penguins. Landing at the ice edge and leaving a man on guard, they came upon a flock of emperors, resulting in five of the stately birds being collared for a German zoo. The ice was beginning to set and the weather turned bleaker. *Passat* developed a faulty tail elevator and did not fly again. *Boreas* went up on 3 February and two days later made the expedition's final photo survey.

With the two Dorniers aboard, *Schwabenland* headed north and after an absence of four months reached Cuxhaven on 11 April. They had achieved eight long flights in less than two weeks, a total of 86 hours aloft, of which 63 were concentrated on photo-surveying. Extreme cold weather performance of men and aircraft had been documented — knowledge stored away for Hitler's attack on the eastern front.

Behind it the expedition left 'Neu Schwabenland' written across part of Norway's Antarctic Territory; in the area of exploration they bestowed such names as Schirmacher Oasis, Kottas Mountains, Ritscher Flya, Aglman Ridge, Muhlig-Hoffman Mountains, Wohlthat Range. The German expedition lacked for nothing in modern equipment, nor in the professionalism of its aviators. They had viewed 595,000 square kilometres (230,000 square miles) of Eastern Antarctica; in photo-mapping more than half of the unknown region, they had exposed six reels of film, measuring 360 metres.

Despite brilliant colour-stereo aerial photographs of the icesheet, coast and mountains, the result of the 'quickie' expedition counted for very little in adding to the knowledge of interior Antarctica. Navigation by dead reckoning and the sun compass and radio reporting to the ship every 15 minutes without the correction of surface control proved insufficient to achieve a reliable map. Yet congratulatory messages from the Führer and Field Marshal Goering awaited them at home; a second expedition was planned.

Taxiing the Dornier flying boat towards the drag sail at the stern of the mother-ship. Once secured on the sail, the aircraft would be lifted on deck by a powerful crane. ▶

Crew of the flying boat *Passat* on 31 January 1939 gathered five emperor penguins to take back to the fatherland. The Schwabenland expedition embodied Adolf Hitler's plan to put part of Queen Maud Land under the German flag.

While Norway steeled itself to contest an oncoming German claim to its territory, and while the United States was sufficiently alerted to form the U.S. Antarctic Service and send its first government expedition south, other events were overtaking this Antarctic drama. Within another six months Nazi forces would march into Poland, to unleash World War II. The claim for Neu Schwabenland went on the shelf, lost beneath onslaught of bomb and bullet, never to be resurrected.[17] But for some, Hitler's adventure in Antarctica raised an uncomfortable question. Could those silent icy wastes also become a theatre of conflict?

Taken from one of the Dornier flights, rugged mountain territory spreads across what Nazi Germany would label 'Neu Schwabenland'.

The expedition reportedly viewed 595,000 square kilometres (230,000 square miles) of Eastern Antarctica, using 360 metres of film. Lack of surface control marred the value of Germany's ambitious photo-mapping program.

Flying boat *Boreas* moored to the ice edge on 29 January 1939 where the crew ceremoniously raised the German flag. Other territorial claims were made by dropping metal shafts bearing the Nazi emblem from the aircraft. Two days later, *Passat* returned for the capture of the five emperor penguins.

Preuschoff Ridge and Ruhnke Mountain in the Muehlig-Hofmann range, viewed from *Boreas* during a northern approach. Scenes of Neu Schwabenland between 14° West and 20° East longitude were recorded as colour-stereo aerial photographs.

Ellsworth's American Highland

Lincoln Ellsworth went back to Antarctica in 1938–39 for two good reasons. One was to confound those critics who dismissed his 1935 flight as not truly trans-Antarctic. The other was to lay claim to part of Australian Antarctic Territory for the United States government.

When details of his fourth expedition, aimed at exploring the almost unknown interior of the Indian Ocean sector, were released to the New York press, Ellsworth declared that a territorial claim was not on the agenda.[18] He gave a similar reply to a question from the *Sydney Morning Herald*: 'This area is already claimed by Australia. Consequently I will be unable to claim any new territory for the U.S.A.'. Sir Hubert Wilkins, once again appointed Ellsworth's manager and technical assistant, focused his attention on the opportunity to find a location for a meteorological station on the Antarctic coast.[19] To him, based on Ellsworth's undertaking, territorial rights were not an issue.

WEATHER BASE AT POLE.

EXPEDITION'S AIMS.

Sir H. Wilkins's Plans.

AUCKLAND, Friday.

Geographical reconnaisance of the hitherto unexplored areas of Antarctica and the collection of data that may lead to the establishment of a permanent meteorological station in the southern continent are the principal objects of the expedition to be led by the Australian explorer, Sir Hubert Wilkins, who arrived by the Monterey en route to Capetown to join Mr. Lincoln Ellsworth.

The party will leave South Africa in the Wyatt Earp on October 25 and will arrive at the Antarctic mainland about the middle of November, remaining until January.

On his return, which may be by way of New Zealand, Sir Hubert Wilkins intends to complete the building of a new submarine for carrying out important explorations at the North Pole.

FLIGHT POSSIBLE.

"I sent the Wyatt Earp out from Canada and Mr. Ellsworth and I will join it at Capetown," he said. "We will sail straight to Enderby Land or in an easterly direction to Lars Christensen Land. It is proposed to make a geographical reconnaisance to a distance of 500 miles inland, and possibly to make a flight to the Ross Sea. However, this will depend entirely upon the weather. If the flight is made it is likely we will return by way either of New Zealand or Australia.

"My work in the south will complete all of the programme for the Antarctic I set for myself in 1920. My submarine will enable me to carry out an expedition to the Arctic which will complete my programme in the north. I then hope to make every effort to encourage the Governments of the Southern Hemisphere to inaugurate an international meteorological bureau which would establish and maintain permanent stations in the Antarctic.

"The submarine is expected to be used as a base for scientists who will occupy a position at part of the Polar Sea where there are no islands and where it is impossible to maintain a base on top of the ice. We know, both from my own experience and from that of the Russian scientists who drifted about five or six miles a day last year, that the ice is always moving and that it is impossible to maintain a selected position while camped on top of the pack.

"However, in a submersible vessel underneath the ice, with access to the surface through a tube or funnel, scientists, after having drifted with the ice for one day, may retract the funnel and skid slowly beneath the ice back to their selected position and so maintain the base, that will be somewhere between the Behring Sea and the North Pole.

"This base, which will be permanent, can be provisioned by means of aircraft once it has been established, since the submarine can move at will to a good landing field at the time when the plane is expected. While the living accommodation will be in the vessel below the ice, all observations will be carried out on top of the ice. The equipment may include a wireless direction-finder as well as all meteorological requirements."

Ellsworth and Wilkins resumed their appointment with the world's press as the 1938 expedition took shape.

Wilkins went to Norway in May 1938 to recommission *Wyatt Earp*, which had been laid up at Aalesund since returning from the Bay of Whales in 1936. Norwegians were engaged for the 12-man crew, three of them Ellsworth's 'old hands'. The captain, Londer Johansen, had been gunner and catcher boat skipper in the Antarctic whaling fleet.

Ellsworth decided his expedition needed two aircraft. A two-seater Aeronca float plane would be used for scouting; Northrop's latest creation — the all-metal Delta, driven by a 750-horsepower Wright Cyclone engine was his choice for the major flights. Both planes were radio equipped.[20] As chief pilot he engaged J. H. (Jack) Lymburner who in 1935 had been second man to Hollick-Kenyon, who now had a permanent job with Canadian Airways. His reserve pilot and flight engineer was B. J. Trerice, a Quebec aviator; the doctor and radio operator were both Americans.

After six years together, Wilkins and his millionaire friend were well practised in the art of organising a polar voyage. Ellsworth's plan called for his ship to break through to the coast somewhere between Kemp Land and the Ingrid Christensen Coast, in the hope of catching optimum flying weather, well before late November. From here he intended to launch triangular-pattern photo-survey flights across the interior, in the area of Mac-Robertson and Princess Elizabeth Lands, discovered and named by Mawson during the 1930–31 BANZARE cruise.

Vale, Wyatt Earp

On his return from Antarctica, Lincoln Ellsworth sold his ship and aircraft in 1939 to the Commonwealth government for £4,400. Though Prime Minister Lyons announced *Wyatt Earp* would sail with a new Australian Antarctic expedition, the war in Europe intervened and the expedition never took place.

H.M.A.S. WYATT EARP
AUSTRALIAN NATIONAL ANTARCTIC RESEARCH EXPEDITION
Marcuse

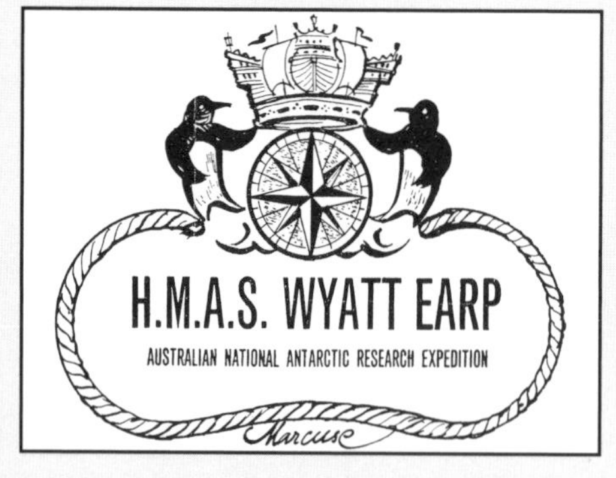

Wyatt Earp was inducted into the Royal Australian Navy, renamed HMAS *Wongala* (a Wild West sheriff apparently had no historical significance for the RAN) and spent the war patrolling Gulf St Vincent in South Australia. For two years following the war the old ship then served as a Sea Scout training vessel at Port Adelaide.

Once more, however, it was summoned to go south. Recommissioned on 17 November 1947 and again rejoicing in the name *Wyatt Earp*, it was to carry Australia's first postwar Antarctic expedition in December 1947, but owing to a breakdown, departure was delayed until February 1948. In the meantime it had been refitted in the navy dockyard with a new Crossley 450-horsepower diesel engine; accommodation was enlarged to house 30 men and cosmic-ray measuring equipment, magnetic observation equipment and radar were installed, while a RAAF Vought Sikorsky Kingfisher aircraft was fitted on deck.

However *Wyatt Earp* proved too small and slow for the growing needs of the Australian expedition. Once again the ship faced retirement. Sold into commercial service, it became *Wongala*, a name that severed the connection with its historic past. When sold again to other interests, it sailed under yet another name — *Natone* —

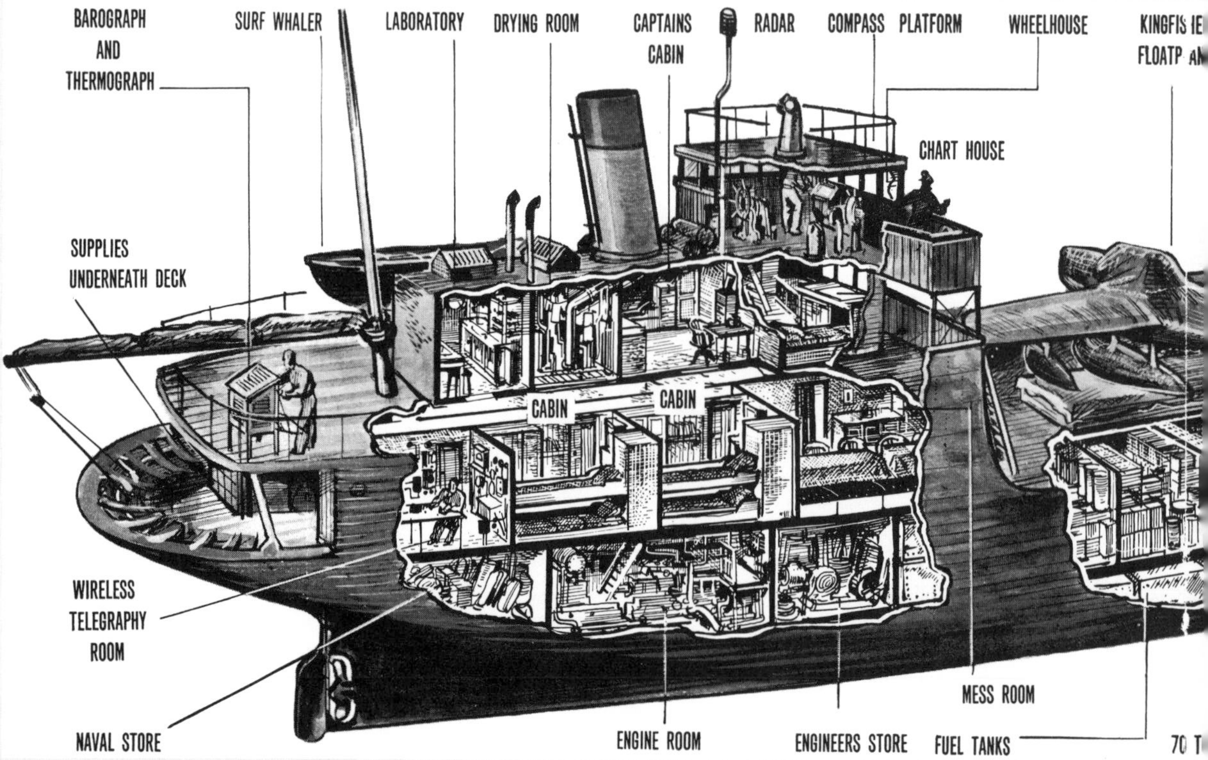

BAROGRAPH AND THERMOGRAPH
SURF WHALER
LABORATORY
DRYING ROOM
CAPTAINS CABIN
RADAR
COMPASS PLATFORM
WHEELHOUSE
CHART HOUSE
SUPPLIES UNDERNEATH DECK
CABIN
CABIN
WIRELESS TELEGRAPHY ROOM
NAVAL STORE
ENGINE ROOM
ENGINEERS STORE
FUEL TANKS
MESS ROOM

in the east coast potato trade. In January 1959 Ellsworth's ship struck a rock off Double Island Point, close to Queensland's Fraser Island, and that is where its rotting bones lie today. Few people would know that so much achievement and drama were locked within the ribs of that tough little wooden ship that bore the name of a two-gun Arizona marshal... as its owner once said, 'the bravest man I ever heard of'. *Wyatt Earp* the ship was just as brave.

Wyatt Earp crunches through the ice to reach her owner, Lincoln Ellsworth, at the Bay of Whales in 1936.

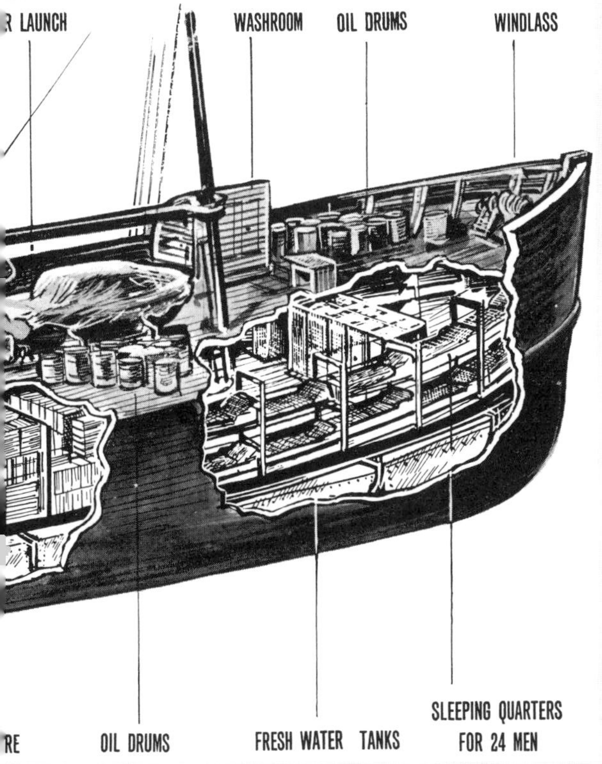

The little, wooden ship once a naval vessel,HMAS *Wyatt Earp,* began life as a Norwegian herring boat ended her days carrying potatoes and other produce on the Australian coast. The final name, *Natone*, disguised the fact that she was once called after a legendary U.S. sheriff, the fastest gun in the West.

The Lockheed Delta made only one major flight which fell far short of Ellsworth's cherished South Pole objective. However, his interior journey over Australian Territory of 11 January 1939, covering some 640 kilometres (400 miles), resulted in the controversial claim of 'American Highland'.

More speculative, yet rather more cherished, was his aim to take the big low-wing Delta which, with auxiliary tanks, had a range of 3,200 kilometres (2,000 miles) from the coast to the South Pole and onwards to the Great Barrier. As a repeat of the 1935 exploit, he and Lymburner would camp at the Bay of Whales until Wilkins on *Wyatt Earp* retrieved them. Could anyone argue against that as a trans-Antarctic epic?

TO WHOM IT MAY CONCERN.

RECOGNIZING THE RIGHTS OF THE COMMONWEALTH OF AUSTRALIA TO ADMINISTRATE THE AREA REFERRED TO IN AN ORDER IN COUNCIL DATED 7th FEBRUARY ,1933, WHEREIN IT IS ORDERED AS FOLLOWS:-

" THAT PART OF HIS MAJESTY'S DOMINIONS IN THE ANTARCTIC SEAS WHICH COMPRISES ALL THE ISLANDS AND TERRITORIES OTHER THAN ADELIE LAND WHICH ARE SITUATED SOUTH OF THE 60th DEGREE OF SOUTH LATITUDE AND LYING BETWEEN THE 160th DEGREE OF EAST LONGITUDE AND THE 45th DEGREE OF EAST LONGITUDE IS HEREBY PLACED UNDER THE AUTHORITY OF THE COMMONWEALTH OF AUSTRALIA."

I PLACE THIS DOCUMENT AS A RECORD OF HAVING PUT FOOT ON THE ANTARCTIC MAINLAND IN SEVERAL PLACES AND UPON SEVERAL OF THE ISLANDS IN THE VICINITY BETWEEN LATITUDES 68 South AND LATITUDE 69 SOUTH AND BETWEEN LONGITUDES 77 EAST AND 79 EAST AND HAVING FLOWN THE FLAG OF AUSTRALIA, LEAVE IT WITH THIS RECORD ON THE LAND BORDERING THE PRESENT CONTINENTAL GLACIER SURFACE AT APPROXIMATELY LATITUDE 68.30 SOUTH AND 79 DEGREES EAST LONGITUDE.

DATE JANUARY 11th, 1939. HUBERT WILKINS.

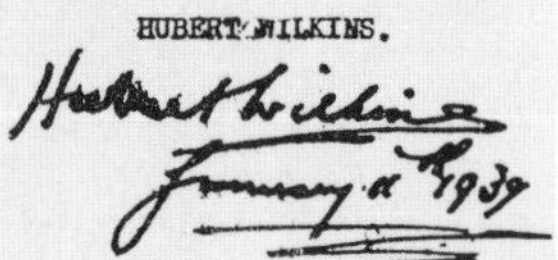

The many details fell into place. The New York *Times* and North American Newspaper Alliance signed up for exclusive press reports. Stores and gasoline were loaded and the aircraft prepared for embarkation from Floyd Bennett Field in New York. Ellsworth and his wife joined a big-game safari in Africa. Wilkins travelled via Australia to discuss the Antarctic coastline with Mawson and J. K. Davis. Crewed and loaded, *Wyatt Earp* sailed from Cape Town on 29 October 1938. So far it had all been smooth going…so far.

The southward voyage ran into unexpectedly severe storms. Furious seas overtook them at the Kerguelens and made a call at Heard Island impossible. With rigging and deck shrouded in ice and wallowing in a deep swell *Wyatt Earp* bumped the first floes at 55° South on the midnight of 21 November. Never had Ellsworth expected the summer ice to reach so far north. Here signalled the start of a most unfortunate journey.

Wyatt Earp was 65 days in sailing from Cape Town to the ice coast, 45 of which were spent struggling against a 1,350-kilometre (840-mile) band of thick, unyielding pack. Peril lay, not in the sky but on the seas where a cat and mouse game was played with huge icebergs that drifted silently out of the fog and only the Norwegians' expert seamanship saved them, sometimes literally by the skin of their timbers. Lymburner made two daring flights in search of open water. From a shrinking pool beside the ship three take-off attempts were required for his initial scouting run which then threatened to disappear into a blinding snowstorm. For the last 13 days of December, *Wyatt Earp* remained a prisoner of the slowly southward grinding pack.

At the height of their predicament — charging the ice, backing off again, floating helplessly when the encircling pack closed in — Ellsworth called Wilkins to his cabin. He held a letter bearing the State Department crest; he said the American consul had delivered it to him confidentially before they left Cape Town. The letter authorised Ellsworth, in the name of the United States, to claim whatever part of Antarctica he discovered. With it came a copper cylinder containing an American flag with a proclamation of possession for dropping on the Antarctic surface. The instruction said it would be advisable for Ellsworth, on behalf of his government, to make a claim for any territory that he explored, irrespective of whether it lay within an area already claimed. In support of the statement, the letter cited an extract from an article in the American *Geographical Review* — ironically one in which Wilkins quoted the wording of a proclamation which he, with the authority of the British Crown, had dropped on a previously unseen part of Graham Land (the Antarctic Peninsula) in 1928–29. To both Ellsworth and Wilkins it was obvious the only 'discovery' likely to be made lay inside Australian Antarctic Territory.

Sale of *Wyatt Earp* to the Australian government prompted an *Adelaide News* cartoonist to imagine a new trade in Antarctic real estate and tourism.

The battle to reach the coast had been uppermost in Wilkins' mind. Visibility fell, snow squalls blew, jagged pack tore a section of hardwood sheathing from the hull. A spark from the over-revving engine lodged in the fabric of the Aeronca's wing and only Lymburner's quick action in grabbing a fire extinguisher saved them from a disastrous wind-whipped blaze amid the 5,000 gallons (19,000 litres) of aviation fuel stored on deck.[21] And now, what was Ellsworth trying to tell him: that America intended to claim Australian territory?

Sir Hubert Wilkins: the 1938 venture with Ellsworth was his last Antarctic expedition.

At 3 a.m. on New Year's Day near the outer edge of the Amery Ice Shelf they at last glimpsed Antarctica. Impenetrable pack ice continued to deny them the coast. *Wyatt Earp* was headed eastwards across Prydz Bay, making for the Ingrid Christensen Coast, still battling ice floes and squalls of condition zero visibility. Such was to be the agonising pattern of their progress for the following two weeks. Lymburner made only three reconnaissance flights: the first, on 1 January, went across Prydz Bay and the Amery Ice Shelf; the second two days later traced the Ingrid Christensen Coast; the third in the same direction on 10 January reached as far as West Barrier. So far the unlucky fourth expedition had precious little aviation to show for all its pain.

By 5 January they were able to approach the Rauer group where *Wyatt Earp* was moored to level bay ice held fast between the islands and within shouting distance of a large, grounded berg. The Delta had been brought on deck and reassembled with wings and skis. Ellsworth hoped it was their first serious chance to fly. While waiting for a storm to pass he went ashore on one of the islands to collect rock samples, bearing iron, copper and nickel.[22] On 7 January they were ready to go. Fuel drums had been stacked on the bay ice when suddenly they realised the supposedly anchored iceberg was creeping towards them. The drums were rushed aboard and within minutes *Wyatt Earp* had cast off. Two days later while again trying to unload the aircraft, they sighted a large ice floe propelled towards them by several drifting icebergs. Again the ship had to flee; when they returned the bay ice had broken out and the Delta's ski strip disappeared with it.

ELLSWORTH TO SPEND WINTER AT SOUTH POLE

SYDNEY, Tuesday.—Lincoln Ellsworth, the American explorer, announced today a new expedition to the Antarctic for 1941, during which he will camp for the entire winter at the South Pole itself.

"I have two statements to make," said Ellsworth today. "Firstly, I propose to name the 81,000 square miles of highly elevated land south of Princess Elizabeth Land, over which I flew, and which I claimed for the United States this year, American Highland.

"Secondly, the year after next, in January, 1941, it is my intention to establish a camp at the South Pole itself, where, with a party of not more than two companions, I plan to winter and to carry on continuous observations of importance in several branches of scientific research pertaining to this interesting spot."

Ellsworth probably will use two planes on this expedition, and will dig them in at the Pole. He will fly from the Bay of Whales, from where it is 700 miles to the Pole.

"I should be the first man to live for more than a few days at one of the poles," said Ellsworth. "This vast continent is still full of mystery. There is 100 years of research to be done in every branch of science."

Plans for yet a fifth Ellsworth expedition failed with the outbreak of World War II.

During the spell at the Rauer Islands, Wilkins had time to ponder his situation. Once again he was in American pay, aboard an American-owned ship and pursuing the objectives of an American, though private, expedition. But this time the zone of Antarctica that lay off their bow was Australian-claimed territory, and he was an Australian. Wilkins made three shore visits in the ship's boat to show the Australian flag and read his 'home made' proclamation of territorial possession. On the highest island of the Rauer group, he buried the message in an enamelled canister beneath a cairn of rocks. He was, in fact, the first Australian to land on the Rauers — Mawson had only sighted the islands during BANZARE. Twice he visited the rocky Vestfold Hills coast where *Wyatt Earp* had moved through a break in the ice. On 9 January, at the western end of the Vestfolds, and two days later at the north, he repeated his proclamation to confirm the existence of Australian Antarctic Territory.[23] Jack Lymburner, himself a Canadian, witnessed one of Wilkins' landings. From his third reconnaissance flight, Lymburner reported a possible ski strip where West Barrier met the bare granite slope of the Vestfold Hills. *Wyatt Earp* took five hours to negotiate a course among capsized 'bergs, dodging around ice tongues and, using the ship's motor launch as a pilot, avoiding the many submerged and uncharted rocks. By 10 January they were at a new mooring north-east of the Vestfolds where conditions looked reasonable enough for a flight until an easterly gale drove another iceberg towards them. A small bight where the end of West Barrier joined the bare granite rocks offered them the next refuge. The snow-covered surface behind the mooring was short and not particularly inviting and rough seas chipped away at the ice edge. But by now Ellsworth was desperate. The crew managed to hoist the Delta ashore from a swaying deck; with the engine warmed, Lymburner took the machine on a brief test flight — since leaving New York it had been stowed in *Wyatt Earp's* hold.

Sir Hubert Wilkins stands against *Wyatt Earp's* funnel. He sailed on four out of her five Antarctic voyages.

Just after 6 o'clock on the evening of 11 January, carrying rations sufficient to keep two men alive for five weeks, Ellsworth and his pilot climbed into the cabin. Alas, no trans-Antarctic dash for the leader. The brevity of the remaining ski strip allowed enough fuel to be carried for only a three-hour flight.

Ellsworth directed Lymburner to follow 79° East longitude on a due southerly course. For the first 80 kilometres (50 miles) they flew above a wild crevasse field which, he noted, would promise sure disaster should an aircraft be forced down. Eventually they had to climb to 3,500 metres (11,500 feet) to surmount the steeply rising continental icesheet. Sastrugi ridges slashed the surface into 'a gigantic white ploughed field'. Ellsworth estimated visibility to be 180 kilometres (110 miles) on every side, with the view uninterrupted by a single distinguishing feature of mountain, rock or nunatak.

POLAR SECRETS.

WEATHER FORECASTS.

Sir Hubert Wilkins's Plans

FOR INTERNATIONAL BUREAU.

(FROM THE SPECIAL REPRESENTATIVE OF THE AUSTRALIAN PRESS ASSOCIATION.)

NEW YORK, Aug. 26.

The Australian explorer, Sir Hubert Wilkins, plans to make futther polar explorations by aeroplane and submarine.

In a special interview Sir Hubert Wilkins said the two projects would complete his polar investigations, for the supplying of remaining data on which to organise an international bureau for the purpose of establishing permanent meteorological bases in the Arctic and Antarctic zones to give the northern and southern hemispheres weather forecasts years in advance.

Sir Hubert Wilkins has already spent 11 years on this work. He is particularly interested in the Antarctic, and declares that this meteorological information would be of great value to Australia, New Zealand, South American countries, California, Florida, South Africa, India, Malaya, and China.

AUSTRALIAN CITIZENSHIP.

Sir Hubert Wilkins, although American finance has enabled him to earn fame, still cherishes Australian citizenship.

While attending the conference of trans-oceanic aviators in Rome last month, he saw the American flag stuck on the bonnet of a car. He would not enter the car until someone found an Australian flag, which he carried from then on. He understands the difficulty of obtaining Australian support for scientific enterprises. Conditions are very different in the United States, where many millionaires are eager to give substantial backing. Nevertheless, Sir Hubert Wilkins hopes to persuade the Australian and New Zealand Governments later to participate in the international bureau.

Between expeditions Sir Hubert Wilkins makes an income by lecturing and writing newspaper and magazine articles. He points out that his scheme for a chain f meteorological stations is important from the Australian and New Zealand standpoint, and promises that reasonably accurate seasonal forecasts will be possible many years in advance.

Sir Hubert Wilkins explains that the Antarctic mass of ice is a refrigerating unit, and that it is important to have details of the distribution of ice in the surrounding waters, also the surface conditions, and the influence ar 1 direction of low temperature currents from the Antarctic Complete international co-operation is necessary for success. Peru and Chile are delaying their projected meteorological programme in the hope of wider combined action. Sir Hubert Wilkins says that his work hitherto has een practically without Government assistance. It only remains for a little geographical investigation to determine the best sites for weather stations.

In Ellsworth's description, it was 'a vast and apparently limitless expanse of ice and snow. The horizon was, for 180 degrees and as far as we could see, straight edged and unmarked by colour or contour. Visibility was perfect in all directions except north, where, behind us the ominous storm clouds were thickening and banking higher'. At 320 kilometres (200 miles) from the coast and with fuel nearly half consumed, Ellsworth told Lymburner it was far enough. But before they turned he opened the hatch and let go the copper cylinder that enclosed the Stars and Stripes and his note of proclamation:[24]

> To whom it may concern: Having flown on a direct course from latitude 68:30 south, longitude 79:00 east, to latitude 72 degrees south, longitude 79 east, I drop this record, together with the flag of the United States of America, and claim for my country, so far as this act allows, the area south of latitude 70 to a distance of 150 miles east and 150 miles west of my line of flight and to a distance of 150 miles south of latitude 72 south, longitude 79 east which I claim to have explored dated Jan. 11, 1939. Lincoln Ellsworth.

They returned to find *Wyatt Earp* being rammed against the ice edge and their abbreviated landing strip fast disintegrating. With the Delta quickly reloaded, the ship turned into the pack, setting another easterly course. Their leader was still determined to find a better surface which would allow him to fly once more. Two days later misfortune struck again. First mate Liavaag and other crew were balanced on rocking 'bergy bits, hacking ice for the ship's snow melter, when a sudden jolt threw them into the freezing water; all were rescued but Liavaag's leg had been jammed between the colliding lumps of ice. Dr Rhoades, the ship's physician, told Ellsworth that a tossing *Wyatt Earp* was no place for an involved operation on a crushed knee and broken kneecap. Ellsworth took his last look at Antarctica and ordered the course set for Australia.[25] As they cleared the ice, Wilkins noted they received the salute of another vessel which emerged from among the 'bergs, heading

A monument to Ellsworth's exploration can be found in Western Antarctica, where on the flight of 22 November 1935 he sighted and named the Sentinel Range. In this region, known as the Ellsworth Highland, stands the Vinson Massif, at 4,897 metres (16,070 feet) the highest known peak in Antarctica.

south and flying the Nazi flag. With bridge stove in and stanchions torn away — scars of another 240 kilometres (150 miles) of threatening pack and the wild Southern Ocean beyond it — *Wyatt Earp* reached Hobart on 4 February 1939.[26]

If Ellsworth did not make the headlines with an epic flight, he achieved world news by another route. The New York *Times* of 13 January had already published the surprising announcement of his claim to a part of Australian Antarctica. In Hobart he said that his original estimated claim would be extended to 1,114,000 square kilometres (380,000 square miles) on the basis of territory 'sighted'. When he reached Sydney on 29 January he announced 'American Highland' was the name he had given to the section inside Australian Antarctic Territory.

The Australian government quickly dismissed Ellsworth's claim as the action of a private individual, devoid of official backing.[27] When Admiral Byrd insisted that the United States would claim Marie Byrd Land and 'the 75,000 square miles [*sic*] of Australian Antarctic Territory which was flown over by Lincoln Ellsworth', a councillor from the Australian Embassy in Washington called on the State Department to request clarification of the United States' position. He was told (in a message passed to the External Affairs Minister, and then to Cabinet) that 'America planned to confine itself to James W. Ellsworth Land, so far not claimed by any country and which has been an area of U.S. activities'.[28]

The Commonwealth government bought Ellsworth's ship and aircraft for £4,400, whereupon Prime Minister Lyons and Treasurer R. G. Casey on 13 February announced the raising of a new Australian expedition — as Sir Douglas Mawson had been urging since the end of BANZARE — to reinforce Australia's Antarctic claim.[29] Ellsworth and Wilkins went home to New York, proposing another aircraft expedition within a year or two, aimed at making a South Pole base. Ellsworth, 'with no intention of claiming any of the area seen for the United States', suggested a cooperative effort with Australia to establish weather bases, one possibly backed with the millionaire's money. Wilkins wrote to 'Dear Casey', urging him to support Ellsworth's initiative — 'he might endow an observatory there'. The only stipulation was that the base should be known as 'The Lincoln Ellsworth Observatory'.[30] (See

Appendix I.) In an article written for the *National Geographic* of July 1939, Ellsworth estimated the cost of his four expeditions at $400,000. Had it been worthwhile in the effort and money expended, he reflected. His answer was unreservedly 'Yes'.

Ellsworth's claim and the United States' official role in it were never quite explained. Not since the cruise of Lieutenant Wilkes' naval squadron of 1840 had America shown interest in the ice continent to Australia's south, although at one stage some citizens had urged the raising of the Stars and Stripes over Wilkes Land.[31] Had Ellsworth requested the State Department letter as a gesture of retaliation against the unwanted Australian 'rescue' of his 1935 expedition, an action which clearly expressed territorial undertones? The somewhat petty reason for such an action would not seem to accord with the nature of the man. More likely, Ellsworth's fourth expedition provided an opportunity for the United States to emphasise its non-recognition of all existing territorial claims.

In 'authorising' Ellsworth to launch his own counterclaim to a strictly interior region, perhaps the U.S. Government sought to display its challenge to the validity of the historic sector-based territories, established often for reasons of mere coastal observation. Perhaps, more subtly, it served as a message to others in the field, particularly the Germans, that the United States reserved its right to go peacefully abroad in Antarctica, where, when and how it pleased. Ellsworth's quasi-official standing was never resolved, nor followed up, except that American Highland to this day remains a name on maps of Australian Antarctic Territory.

Lieutenant Charles Wilkes who brought an American naval squadron to Antarctica in 1840.

SOUTH POLE CAMP.

MR. ELLSWORTH'S PLANS.

Scientific Research.

Mr. Lincoln Ellsworth announced yesterday that in 1941 he planned to establish a camp at the South Pole and with not more than two companions he would spend the winter there, carrying out continuous scientific observations.

Two planes would probably be used on the expedition, he added. They would be "dug in" at the Pole and would serve as comfortable living quarters.

"To my mind there are three men in exploration—the trail blazer, the mapmaker, and the man who looks out for the resources of the country," he said. "I have been a trail blazer since boyhood, and I always will be.

"This is not a stunt. It should be productive of discoveries of definite scientific value, particularly in meteorology and the ionisation of atmospheric layers. The Antarctic attracts me because of all the world it is the only place left where there is so much trail blazing still to be done—nearly a whole continent left where you can push out into the unknown, see land no man has seen before.

"When I was a boy I used to lie on the floor gazing at the blank spaces on the map. I was still a boy when I was taken to the memorial service for Scott in London. That was when I first decided I was going to be an Antarctic explorer."

His first act towards that end was to buy a compass, which he still possessed and which had guided him on his flight across the Antarctic Continent on the recent expedition.

"AMERICAN HIGHLAND."

Mr. Ellsworth said that he proposed to give the name of "American Highland" to the inland area of 81,000 square miles of highly elevated land south of Princess Elizabeth Land, over which he flew in January, and which no man had seen before. This he claimed for the United States.

Mr. Ellsworth, emphasising the need for an active interest in the Antarctic, particularly by Australia, said that there was 100 years of work to be done there in many different fields of research. As an example of the value of meteorological research he said that observations in the Weddell Sea by whalers and others had shown that a particularly cold winter in that sector of Antartica was invariably followed by droughts in the cereal areas of South America.

"When I am at the South Pole in 1941 I may be able to be of assistance," he added. "Our work on our last expedition had to be restricted because it took so long to get down there. The voyage from Capetown to the Barrier was one of the worst I have ever made. We fought our way through more than 750 miles of pack ice in 65 days, and at one period the propeller did not turn for 13 days.

"We were fortunate to make our flight as the bay ice was beginning to break up when we took off. I had planned to go much further and cross Little America."

Apart from talk about weather stations and interior exploratory flights, Lincoln Ellsworth also hoped to uncover mineral wealth, in keeping with the geological finds of the Mawson expeditions.

To Whaling: First Air Loss

On Christmas Day, 1929, the Norwegian aviator Leif Lier flew out from the whaling vessel *Kosmos* in the vicinity of the Balleny Islands, off the Oates Coast at the eastern end of Australian Antarctica. For a diversion, the ship's doctor, Ingveld Schreiner, went with him on the spotting excursion in the small float plane. Bad weather developed and the aircraft, unequipped with radio, was never seen or heard from again. Lier and his passenger were Antarctica's first aviation fatalities, lost in the hunt for the mammoths of the deep.

Whaling was the fundamental key to Antarctic politics in the decades that followed World War I. The maturing of the mechanical age, supplanting that of shore station, sail and brawn, meant a considerable income could be derived by those nations that embarked on the pelagic whaling expeditions. Huge self-contained factory ships, flotillas of fast catcher boats and tanker-supply ships, raised the stakes in the harvest of the southern seas. With the turn of the 1930s, the use of spotting aircraft together with radio communication enabled the catch and the resultant output of whale oil and other by-products to rise to multi-million-pound levels.

Two Norwegians pioneered the modern age of whaling, Svend Foyn, with the invention of the powerful harpoon gun in 1860, and Carl Larsen, who dispatched the first floating factory ship in 1905. Larsen was also the one who, after his voyages of the 1890s, fixed his country's eyes on the rich Antarctic feast. Despite World War I, by 1915–16 the southern seas were home to 11 factory ships, 57 catchers as well as 7 shore stations: a kill of 11,792 whales produced 558,806 barrels of oil. From 1910 to 1920 the whale oil taken from sub-Antarctic seas had an estimated value of £15,000,000.

After World War I, whaling gained a new impetus from peace on the world's oceans. Hunting grounds could widen, spreading to

Whaling is a bloody business: in the hunting of the giant prey by the swift harpoon-armed catcher boats, and in the flensing of the great whales which, on the factory ship deck, are quickly reduced to so much oil, meat and crushed bone.

hitherto little-touched Antarctic waters and approaching closer to the Antarctic coast. In July 1923 Britain proclaimed control over the Ross Sea area, based on the historical justification of Sir James Clark Ross's expedition 80 years earlier, together with the exploration of Scott and Shackleton from McMurdo Sound; administrative control over the Ross Dependency was given to the governor-general of New Zealand. Britain was able to extend its imposition of royalties to those who would whale the Ross Sea, principally the Norwegians. Christensen's 13,000-tonne factory vessel, *Sir James Clark Ross*, with five catcher boats in attendance, reached Discovery Inlet that same year, to embark on two months of summer whaling.

Leif Lier, pilot in the first Antarctic aviation tragedy. Sixteen catcher boats went out in search when he and his passenger disappeared in 1929.

But although the Norwegians negotiated a five-year monopoly in the Ross Sea, they were far from happy about the spreading British influence. In their eyes, questionable historical and governmental rights were being exercised, especially in the levy of royalties on the catch north of 60° South latitude. Might British dominion, which began with the Falklands region, eventually enclose the whole of Antarctica as each new whaling ground was opened up? To the government in Oslo it was clear that Norway must pursue its own territorial rights in Antarctica.

Norway's attention to exploration as an outgrowth of its whaling activities began to raise suspicion in Britain as well as Australia. Sir Douglas Mawson cautioned the federal government that the Norwegians intended to make a territorial claim to Australia's south. In a letter of 1929 to the Council for Scientific and Industrial Research, Mawson stated that the Norwegians were 'preparing for an expedition to seize Enderby Land' in the ensuing summer, and that their ships would continue 'year by year to explore the Antarctic and take possession of the lands visited'.

The Adelaide *Advertiser* of 8 April 1929 reflected the anxiety surrounding Norway's actions with an editorial: 'A Scramble for Antarctica'. By a presidential decree of 29 March 1924, the French had confirmed their right to Adelie Land as well as the sub-Antarctic islands of Kerguelen and Iles Crozets. Mawson and others believed that France's hold on Terre Adelie almost directly south of Tasmania represented an unwarranted intrusion into a region which, despite

Dumont d'Urville's discovery of 1840, had been ignored by France over the following 80 years. Mawson wanted Australian ownership over the entire 'Australian quadrant' of Antarctica, extending from 90° to 160° East longitude, which should allow no room for other claimants.

The Imperial Conference of 1926 in London ruled that Britain had rights, based on discovery, over wide sections of Antarctica. If circumstances required, formal territorial claims should be made over regions which included Enderby, Kemp and Queen Mary Lands and Mawson's King George V and Oates Lands.

News that Norway had annexed Bouvet Island in the 'South African sector' on 19 January 1928 further aroused British anxiety. Subsequently, through diplomatic channels, the governments of Britain and Norway reached an understanding that Norway would confine territorial ambitions to those Antarctic lands not included in the 1926 Imperial ruling. The two parties agreed that Norway would retain Bouvet Island (a French discovery), following which Norway annexed Peter I Island (a Russian discovery). Certain of the coasts of the Australian sector were not covered by the 1926 London conference, causing Mawson and his confreres to hold that these regions were under risk of annexation, in particular the future Mac-Robertson and Princess Elizabeth Lands.

Lars Christensen was a modern giant of the whaling industry. His nine expeditions, five of them aircraft equipped, sailed a grand total of some 105,000 kilometres (66,000 miles) in the southern seas, equivalent to three times around the equator. Christensen claimed that his ships and planes would plant Norwegian names on some 25 per cent of the Antarctic coast. Norwegians, not only those under Christensen's house flag, were active in many parts of the polar zone They provided the transportation for Sir Hubert Wilkins' aircraft and a floating base to accommodate him alongside their shore factory on Deception Island. Byrd drew on their services to bring the heavy equipment of his American expeditions back and forth through the Ross Sea pack. (In return, after Lier's disappearance, Byrd provided a doctor from one of his ships to serve on *Kosmos*.)

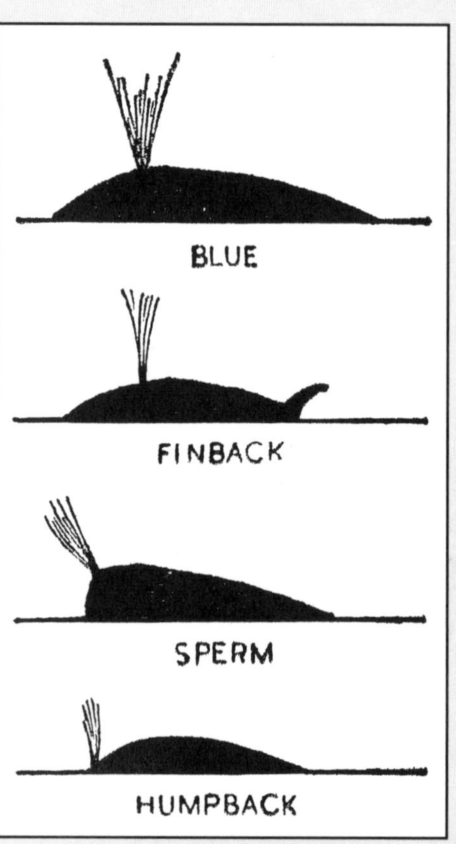

The whales of the Antarctic seas: from top, the blue, finback, sperm and humpback. The popular perception of the commercial value of the whale was different when Sir Douglas Mawson embarked on the BANZARE voyages of 1929–31. In one of his press dispatches appearing in the *Sydney Morning Herald* of 3 February 1930 headed 'Abundance of Whales' he went on to say, 'the defining of whale feeding areas has received attention. West of Enderby Land, whales were found to be exceptionally abundant, recalling the Ross Sea whaling grounds at their best'.

The largely unseen and unexplored coast of Eastern Antarctica, the region lying beneath the South Atlantic and Indian Oceans, attracted Christensen's fleet. His spotting planes, in between his sorties of discovery, reported rich new fields for harpoon gun and bomb. What of whaling itself? Through the 1920s the industry progressed with ever-enlarging fleets and international participation, bringing about a rising death toll among the great mammals of the oceans. In the 1928–29 season, 20,341 whales were caught in Antarctic waters and 30,167 the following season when 194 catchers, 38 factory ships and 6 shore stations produced 2.5 million barrels of oil. It shrugged off the temporary setback of the 1931–32 depression to recover with a renewed vigour for the kill.

A giant fin whale makes its final journey to the flensing deck of a factory ship. In a matter of hours, it will be reduced to a cargo of oil, meat and crushed bone.

1935–36: 175 catcher boats, 24 floating factories, 2 shore stations, a yield of 30,000 whales (42 per cent of them reckoned to be immature), producing 2.5 million barrels of oil, a return to the 1929–30 production level. In the 1936–37 season, whale oil reached a new high of £20 per ton. On the southern seas were 196 catchers, 30 factory ships, for a harvest of 34,579 whales and 2.7 million barrels of oil. The following year the figures continued to grow: 256 catchers, 31 factory ships, a kill of 46,000 whales for a yield of 3.3 million barrels of oil, an all-time record.

But the mechanised depredation of the whaling grounds eventually became obvious even to those whose only view of the giant mammal was as so many lucrative barrels of oil, crushed bone and shredded flesh. Nineteen nations signed the 1931 Convention for the restriction of whaling. When a new International Whaling Convention came up, only eight nations were prepared to put their names to it while eleven declined. Germany and Japan did not sign. Japan signalled its attitude by launching a fifth big factory ship that year. In the 1938–39 season Japan sent to Antarctic waters a fleet of 58 catchers, and 6 factory ships crewed by 2,650 men. Lieutenant Shirase, who had led Japan's 1912 expedition to the eastern end of the Ross Ice Shelf, close by the Bay of Whales, lamented that his nation had failed to follow-up with a territorial claim to provide a base for shore factory stations.

Four big factory ships flying the Norwegian flag reached New Zealand and Tasmanian ports in March 1930, carrying record cargoes of whale oil. *Kosmos* alone was loaded with 116,000 barrels worth £570,000. Ironically, an opportunity had been sought by Australian interests to combine with the Norwegians in a joint international whaling venture, equipped with Norwegian-crewed ships and aircraft.

As with Christensen's findings, the BANZARE voyage of *Discovery* reported immense whaling grounds off Enderby Land and stretching from Mac-Robertson Land to the Ross Sea; British fleets were among those which sailed the Enderby Land grounds. Mawson recommended that the Commonwealth government should assist in promoting an Australian-backed industry to share in the wealth of the Southern Ocean. Australian participation, coupled with an official Australian Antarctic claim, would also allow the government to impose scientifically based limits on the number and types of whales taken by the foreign fleets. But opportunity slipped away and the proposed sailing of the Australian pelagic whalers in October 1930 never took place.

Men who have sailed ships, flown planes, or carried out any sort of military operation south of the Antarctic Circle will find nothing to baffle them in the far north.

Admiral Richard E. Byrd at the planning of Operation Highjump

8

WAR, AND RUMOURS OF WAR

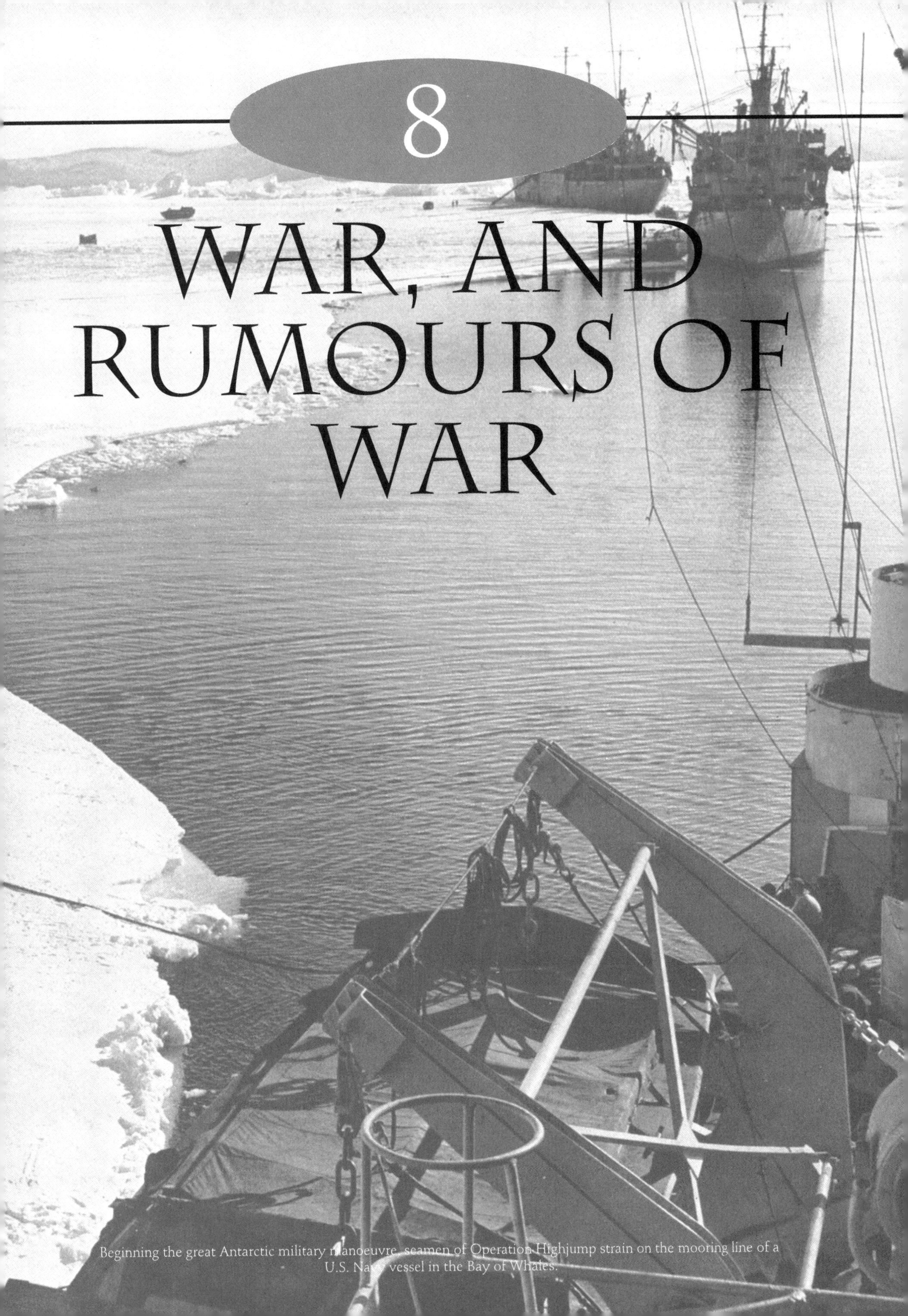

Beginning the great Antarctic military manoeuvre, seamen of Operation Highjump strain on the mooring line of a U.S. Navy vessel in the Bay of Whales.

Two years after the Schwabenland expedition sailed away, the Norwegian whaling fleet rode peacefully at anchor off the coast of the same Queen Maud Land that had attracted the German air explorers. Though war had been declared, the remoteness of the southern polar seas were reckoned to be safe enough to continue the hunt. The factory ships *Ole Wegger* and *Polglimt* lay serenely at anchor, whales yet to be processed secured between them, the catcher flotilla like a pack of exhausted hounds silently riding nearby. After a hard day's processing the catch, all on board were asleep, even the watch.

Blinking into the muzzle of an unfriendly revolver was Captain Andersen's first intimation that all was not well on *Ole Wegger*. From his bunk he groped for the pistol in his jacket pocket but the intruder to his cabin

Out of the silence of the Antarctic sea came a Nazi raider. 'It's war, you know,' said the voice.

kicked over the chair and told him not to be silly. 'Sorry to disturb you, captain, but it's war, you know,' said the voice.

Pulling on his greatcoat, Andersen went on deck to find a strange ship close by. Through the mist he could see it had guns — big guns — trained squarely on them. He needed no other advice. Their visitor was the armed raider *Pinguin*, officially HK33 and sometimes 'the ghost cruiser'. The Germans had returned to Antarctica.

Pinguin, under the command of Captain Ernst-Felix Kruder, sailed from Bremerhaven in June 1940. The 7,800-tonne ship, the former freighter

German raider HK33 — otherwise *Pinguin*, 'the ghost cruiser'. Her two Arado float planes carried machine gun and bomb racks. In her wake, before heading towards Antarctica, she mined the Australian south-east coast.

Kandelfels, carried six 5.9 inch guns, four torpedo tubes, an array of other weapons, including 250 mines, and a multitude of disguises. The hold sheltered two Arado float planes which, though intended for reconnaissance, also carried a machine gun and bomb racks.

The route to the southern seas led *Pinguin* through the Indian Ocean, where 65,000 tonnes of allied shipping were sunk within six months. Accompanied by her 'prize', a captured Norwegian tanker which the German crew had renamed *Passat* and transformed into a makeshift minelayer, *Pinguin* reached the Australian coast late in October 1940. Between Newcastle and Sydney the raider sailed so close to shore that the officer of the watch was able to note the lights of houses along the beaches and headlamps of cars moving on the highways; at one time, off Sydney Heads, they were caught in a searchlight's glare yet went unchallenged.

According to the official history of the Royal Australian Navy in 1939–42:

> During the night of 28th October [1940] *Pinguin* with her bridge officer plotting searchlights and navigation lights at Newcastle and Port Stephens, Norah Head, Barrenjoey and Sydney, laid mines between Newcastle and Sydney. The last four lays were completed at midnight, and shortly after *Pinguin* set course for Hobart and laid two fields off that port during the nights of 31st October–lst November . . . A few nights later *Pinguin* laid minefields in Spencer Gulf and off Adelaide . . . *Storstad* (proper name of the prize ship) on the nights of 29, 30, 31st October laid fields in Banks Strait and off Wilson's Promontory and Cape Otway (Gill: 231–7)

First news that an enemy vessel had stolen through Australia's home waters came on 8 November when the stern of the freighter *Cambridge* blew apart, her crew taking to the boats and landing on Wilsons Promontory. Next evening *City of Bayville* went down 'due to a mysterious underwater explosion' off Cape Otway; she was the first American ship lost to a belligerent action in World War II. And so it continued.

Australian naval units went hunting the mines and the ghost ship, but by the time the alarm had spread *Pinguin* and *Passat* were at full speed on a south-westerly course for sub-Antarctic waters. Nor was the ABC news of much help to the allied cause in broadcasting that HMAS *Canberra* had just been dispatched from Western Australia to find the enemy; it was a broadcast that Captain Kruder found most useful.

JATO (jet assisted take-off) was used for the first time in Antarctica to boost Highjump's fleet of six R4D aircraft on their missions of exploration. The take-off is from the compacted snow runway at Little America IV.

On 17 December *Pinguin*'s lookout called the first iceberg. Within days the sighting tally had risen to 150. Unguarded radio signals coming from the south told them they were closing on their quarry. Not only were *Ole Wegger* and *Polglimt* taken on the night of 13–14 January 1941, but *Pinguin,* leaving small prize crews behind, immediately went in pursuit of a third factory ship, *Pelagos,* which had 35 whales in tow. Using a faked Norwegian radio call, *Pinguin* then summoned all the remaining catcher boats home — into the German trap. All 42,000 gross registered tonnes of Norwegian shipping and 29,000 tonnes of highly valuable whale oil had been captured without a fight in one of the more audacious surprise actions of World War II.

Sub-Antarctic waters gave the German raiders a refuge that was unlikely to be visited by the hard pressed allied warships. Kerguelen Islands, the French possession to the west of Australia's Heard Island, was known to the

Highjump's command ship, USS *Mount Olympus,* is moored in the right background as a Norseman scout plane is towed across fissures in the bay ice, bridged with metal plating and packed snow.

German command as 'naval base Kerguelen'. At Port Couvreux's deserted sealing station, *Pinguin* dropped anchor on 12 March 1941 to rendezvous with Admiral Eyssen aboard the auxiliary cruiser *Komet* (HGK45) and the supply vessel *Alstertor*. While off-duty seamen went rabbit shooting around the island, *Pinguin* carried out urgent maintenance, loaded ammunition for the camouflaged guns, took on fresh water piped from a Kerguelen waterfall and changed her identity to that of the Norwegian freighter *Tamerlan*. *Pinguin*'s aircraft, flown by pilot officer Werner and observer-lieutenant Muller, made at least two flights while in the port. Kerguelen was known to have been used by three German Hilfskreuzers around this time while another raider, *Kormorant* (HK41) which sank HMAS *Sydney* off north-west Australia the following November, was also in the area.

First of the three Nazi gunboats to arrive was *Atlantis* on 14 December 1940. Disguised as civilians, an advance guard of her crew landed on another part of the island and crept around to Port Couvreux, to find a dilapidated settlement with a sleepy sea elephant as the only occupant. While moving to a more secure anchorage, *Atlantis* struck an uncharted rock in Basin de le Gazelle but managed to break free during a heavy swell three days later. A weathered cross stands above the grave of Seaman Hermann, a Silesian who was repainting the funnel (part of *Atlantis*'s new disguise as a Norwegian freighter) on Christmas Eve when he fell to his death. Beneath a cairn of rocks, his is the most southerly German grave of World War II.

Dr Paul Siple: from Eagle Scout with Byrd to one of America's foremost polar scientists.

Suspicious of the raiders' disappearance into the southern seas, HMAS *Australia* broke from Indian Ocean convoy patrol to make a surprise dash to Kerguelen on 1 November 1941[1] The shore party found telltale evidence (which German skippers were usually at pains to avoid) of worn scrubbing brushes, straw bottle containers and an empty bootpolish tin bearing a German label. The lesson was obvious. Antarctica was not necessarily a zone of peace.

CHAPTER EIGHT

America's Operation Highjump

The Americans came back to Antarctica in 1946 to prepare for the possibility of a polar war against the Russians. Organised and managed by the United States Navy, the expedition embodied the most massive military force ever sent to Antarctica; and so it remains.

Known as Operation Highjump, its principal purpose was to test ships, vehicles and aircraft in a savage polar environment that, as closely as possible, resembled Greenland's ice cap and the far Siberian wastes around the Arctic seas. Rear Admiral Richard E. Byrd (ret.), veteran leader of three American expeditions, was nominated officer-in-charge of the 'Antarctic Development Project 1947'. Describing the role of Operation Highjump he said:

> The object lesson of all this is obvious. The shortest distance between the new and old worlds is across the Arctic ocean and the north polar regions. It is freely predicted that here will be one of the great battle areas of future wars.[2]

Twenty-three military aircraft went to Antarctica for Operation Highjump, varying in size from the small Norseman scout, being unloaded from *Mount Olympus*, to the massive PBM Martin Mariners.

Until 1955 the directives of Highjump were marked 'Secret'. When released by Congressional order, one objective was shown to be a testing of the feasibility of building an ice air base, 'with particular attention to later application of such techniques to operations in interior Greenland'.[3] Again to quote from Byrd: 'From the war there was a heritage of powerful new weapons which could be adapted for exploration and turned from fighting men to overcoming the even more malevolent elements which guard the secrets of Antarctica.'

Among the assortment of wartime wonders brought to Antarctica was the modern helicopter, the airborne magnetometer, heavy tracked landing-assault vehicles (LVTs), the lifesaving immersion suit, the adaptation of radar-

Aviation history of another kind was written across Antarctic waters as six R4Ds one by one left the deck of USS *Philippine Sea* in a trail of JATO vapour. They were then the largest aircraft ever to attempt a carrier take-off.

equipped fire control directors to range-finding and trimetrogon photography; with the last named instrument (in reality, batteries of five synchronised cameras arranged at angles in the aircraft) some 130,000 square kilometres (50,000 square miles) of the surface could be photo-surveyed in a single six-hour flight.[4]

Admiral Byrd made his fourth visit to Antarctica as Highjump's Officer-in-Charge. He spoke of weapons of war overcoming 'the even more malevolent elements which guard the secrets of Antarctica'.

The Atlantic Fleet directed Operation Highjump and named it Task Force 68. To perform the expedition's southerly mission, the Task Force employed 13 ships and 23 aircraft including heavy seaplanes and ship-borne helicopters. All 4,700 members of the expedition (about 90 per cent of whom had never experienced a polar environment) were drawn from the United States Navy, Army and Marine Corps and associated Federal departments. No extensive surface expeditions were planned and purely civilian endeavours were out. 'It was the first [expedition] which was entirely naval,' said Admiral Byrd, 'with the exception of a few army and civilian observers and scientists.' He added: 'I recommend strongly that the next large polar expedition be made a joint Army-Navy project'.[5] Dr Paul Siple was chief scientist-observer for the U.S. Army. He had been on all Byrd's previous Antarctic expeditions; later he was to become science attache at the U.S. Embassy in Canberra.

President Eisenhower forwarded Navy Secretary James Forrestal and Fleet Admiral Chester Nimitz, Chief of Naval Operations, his official approval of the expedition on 26 August 1946. In just seven weeks from Atlantic Fleet authorising the raising of the Task Force, Operation Highjump was ready to go. Appointment of tactical commander went to another navy

Windmill and Whalers Return

The 70,000 aerial photographs taken by Highjump's battery of trimetrogon cameras were of minimal use for mapping without the establishment of fixed control points. In December 1947 the navy went back to Antarctica with a new and much smaller expedition known as Operation Windmill. Utilising two icebreakers, *Edisto* and *Burton Island*, they approached the polar coast in the Davis Sea region along the Wilkes Land rim of Australian territory. Helicopters ferried the surveyors ashore, to deposit them on prominent features which could be used as control points. In just over three weeks they worked along 960 kilometres (600 miles) of coast, making nine control point landings.

Plans for a Highjump II were frustrated. Paul Siple claimed that the expedition became a victim of President Truman's feud with Senator Harry Byrd of Virginia. 'There are too many birds [Byrds]' newspapers quoted the President. Said Siple:

> The administration took revenge on his [the Senator's] brother, the Admiral, even though he was in no way involved in the controversy ...a matter of great regret to Byrd and me.... a lost opportunity for the U.S. to gain the major voice in the Antarctic's future. (Siple: 81)

But, in Siple's view, more than just Uncle Sam's 'voice' was at stake, for he continued:

> Success [of Highjump II] would establish a pre-eminent American claim over the entire continent ... the U.S. could be in a unique position to claim Antarctica for its own should it so desire.

Admiral Byrd wrapped up the close of Highjump and Windmill with a thought for the future: 'One day it is quite possible, someone will make money out of the bottom of the

PBM Martin Mariners crowd the deck of USS *Pine Island*. Barely a year before, the big seaplanes had been flying over the Pacific searching for enemy submarines. Now they were assigned to long-range exploration of the Antarctic coast.

In searching for open water and transporting survey teams, the helicopter came of age during Highjump and in Operation Windmill which followed.

world. We know, for example, there are huge reserves of coal there...almost certainly oil will be found under the ice ...vast mineral wealth of many kinds may be buried in its rocks'.

World War II's returned aviators formed the aircrews of Britain's first postwar Antarctic whaling expedition. Indeed, if the Norwegians claimed to have pioneered the use of aircraft in the 1930s to assist in the discovery of new whaling grounds, the British could submit that they were now the first to actually hunt whales from the sky.

The 15,000-tonne factory ship *Balaena* which cruised along the coast of Australian Antarctic territory in the 1946–47 season carried two Walrus amphibians, one named *Snark* and the other *Boojum*.[6] These lumbering but well-tried aircraft had an endurance of about five and a half hours at a 145 kph (90 mph) speed and were powered by a single Bristol Pegasus pusher engine. They were usually launched by catapult and upon returning manoeuvred to a towed 'mat', from where they were lifted by crane to the hangar aboard ship.

United Whalers sent 410 men and 10 catcher boats to hunt the baleen and sperm whale; all but 85 of the complement (which included the airmen) were experienced Norwegian crew. The aircraft began flying off Enderby Land on 22 November 1946 and by the close of the voyage in the following March had accumulated 96 hours in spotting whales for the catchers.[7]

John Grierson, who was one of the pilots, records in his book *Air Whaler* that an aircraft radioed back the position of 27 sperm whales in a single day's flying on 1 December. Some of the Norwegians, however, regarded the aircraft with distrust, believing them to be omens of bad luck for the hunt after the disappearance of their flying countryman, Leif Lier, in 1929. After *Balaena* sailed, the Dutch factory ship *Willem Barendsz* soon followed, also carrying two Walrus amphibians, though without catapult or hangar.[8] So the air war against the whales was begun.

Skilled polar flyer, William 'Trigger' Hawkes (*left*), and fellow air crew of the Central Group at work in the operations room at Little America IV.

man with Antarctic experience, Rear Admiral Richard Cruzen; he, in fact, and not the 'retired' Admiral Byrd, was the operation's real leader.

Task Force 68 focused on three separate sectors of Antarctica. A central aircraft group was to be based on the Bay of Whales, while two subordinate groups were assigned to exploring and photo-surveying the vast continental coastline that fanned east and west from the boundaries of the Ross Sea. The eastern group would concentrate on the Pacific sector, the region of 'American influence' first entered by Byrd, and Ellsworth's expeditions. The western group would focus on the coast of Australian sector and the adjoining French and Norwegian territories. Instructions given to the eastern and western groups were not so much to prepare for a northern war, rather to fulfil another of Operation Highjump's confidential directives, essentially political in purpose. Reaffirming as quickly as possible a United States' presence in Antarctica was the objective: one of 'consolidating and extending U.S. sovereignty over the largest practicable area of the Antarctic continent'.[9]

World War II had ended barely a year earlier, but in the short time since, the world had changed and not for the better. An iron curtain was poised over the borders of eastern Europe. Stalin had nuclear weapons and marshalled an immense and hostile military machine. The shape of the new peace moved towards Cold War. In these grim circumstances America's mili-

The vast crater of the volcano Mount Erebus as it would have been seen by Commander Hawkes on his pioneering flight of 20 February 1947 from Little America IV to the eastern edge of Australian Antarctic Territory.

tary men believed in the wisdom of preparing, and as quickly as possible, for a global stand-off that might be staged amid ice and snow.

But the United States faced a practical difficulty in practising polar manouvres. Across the narrow waters of Bering Strait, should she choose to play war games in the northernmost state of Alaska, the Russian bear was watching. A miscalculation during a military exercise in this sensitive place could touch off shooting hostilities; what if an American ship or aircraft strayed into the Soviet Arctic region? Antarctica offered no such risks. Remote and uninhabited, it was an area in which war machines could be tried and tested without the chance of sparking a territorial incident. Britain, Australia, France, Norway and New Zealand had no reason to object, nor for that matter had they the muscle. All were equally apprehensive of the lengthening shadow of Soviet Communism. What if Russia decided to make a missile base in Antarctica? The American giant was free and welcome to trial its war machines. To quote from Admiral Byrd:

> It was an excellent opportunity to meet and learn how to overcome many situations which will certainly be encountered if ever it becomes necessary to carry on actual warfare in polar regions...
>
> Our Army and Navy must be trained to cope with the severest conditions they may be subjected to in any possible emergency...any severe natural conditions ever likely to be met in the Arctic are more than duplicated in the Antarctic. Life is far more difficult here. Men who have sailed ships, flown planes, or carried out any sort of military operation south of the Antarctic Circle will find nothing to baffle them in the far north.[9]

The aircraft carrier USS *Philippine Sea* was the major fighting ship assigned to Task Force 68. Standing 1,200 kilometres (750 miles) off the coast, safely above the limit of the pack ice, it awaited the signal to send its brood of six R4D transports, wheel- and ski-equipped, towards the snow runway prepared by an advance ship's party of Seabees — the Navy Construction Battalion — at Little America IV on the Bay of Whales. Ahead of the carrier, crunching its way among the floes, went the armed 10,000-horsepower Coastguard icebreaker *Northwind*, the first ship of its type to enter south polar waters. Following in its wake came the big command ship USS *Mount Olympus* which not long ago had served to direct the invasion of Leyte and Luzon in the Philippines; and behind it came the military transports *Merrick* and *Yancey*, and finally USS *Sennet*, the first submarine to dare Antarctic ice.[10]

No rehearsal had been possible for the flight of the R4Ds (navy nomenclature for the Dakota or DC-3) which idled their propellers on the deck of *Philippine Sea*. They were the heaviest aircraft ever to launch from a carrier. They would also be the first to attempt a take-off on wheels at one end, and at the other to make a landing on skis. Worse, only 120 metres (400 feet) of take-off space was available to them, otherwise their wide wingspan would come into collision with the carrier superstructure.

The captain of *Philippine Sea* ordered full ahead to 30 knots (56 kph). First to go was Commander William ('Trigger') Hawkes, one of the navy's most seasoned aviators, with Admiral Byrd among his passengers. To get airborne before running out of deck, Hawkes fired the four JATO (jet-assisted take-off) bottles strapped beneath the fuselage which literally shot them into the air with but a few lengths to spare.

With its powerful radio beacon *Mount Olympus* guided all six safely to the Bay of Whales on 29 January 1947. Due to the delayed passage of the ships through heavy pack, Highjump was now running seriously behind schedule. Flights of the central group began on 4 February but not until nine days later did clear weather allow a start on the concentrated aerial program. In the next eight days, the R4D transports flew twenty-nine camera missions to the east, south and north from the Great Ice Barrier, accumulating 220 hours of flying time and a route distance of 36,500 kilometres (22,800 miles). A flight by two aircraft on 16 February took Admiral Byrd for the second time to the South Pole.[11] On 20 February the first airborne magnetometer survey was made over Antarctica. On the same day, 'Trigger' Hawkes flew his R4D across the Ross Ice Shelf, skirted the smoking crater of Mount Erebus and went beyond the western mountains into the plateau of Victoria Land, making the first airborne exploration of the eastern Australian Antarctic Territory.[12]

The two sea groups probing east and west around the coast each comprised a destroyer escort, tanker and a seaplane tender. Secured to the tender's decks were three PBM Martin Mariner flying boats that not much more than a year before had been scouring the Pacific for enemy ships or submarines. The PBMs had a 33-metre (108-foot) wingspan, were 27 metres (90 feet) long, 5.5 metres (18 feet) high; powered by two 1,600-horsepower Wright engines they had a flying endurance of 18 hours. The eastern group, commanded by Captain George Dufek, who had been navigator on Byrd's previous expedition (and a future admiral of Operation Deep Freeze) began the aerial exploration of the coastal region, starting from the Amundsen Sea. Within a few days of launching the flying program, the seaplane *George I* disappeared in a whiteout, somewhere in the vicinity of the Thurston Peninsula. The loss was confirmed on New Year's eve; the shipboard turkey dinner was postponed.

Three men perished in the wreck when the big machine slammed into an ice slope. Six survivors huddled together for 12 days of fearful weather, hoping for rescue.[13] The disaster was headlined as 'the world's loneliest plane crash'. Eventually Dufek's storm-bound ship *Pine Island* was able to reach the peninsula and the exhausted survivors of Antarctica's first major air disaster were retrieved. Those who were buried in the ice were the first American air crew to die in the Antarctic.

The western task group, under the command of Captain Charles Bond, achieved spectacular discoveries. His three ships were the destroyer USS *Henderson*, the tanker *Capacon* and the seaplane tender *Currituck*, carrying the three 36-tonne Martin Mariners. Following a westerly course outside the pack, 33 flights were made between January 1947 and the following March. Bond could rightly claim that the survey pictures resulting from his group's long-range missions revealed more of Antarctica to the human eye than had been learned in the entire century beforehand.[14] Between Adelie Land and the Shackleton Ice Shelf they covered what he called 'the longest unexplored coast in the world', equivalent in distance to the west coast of the United States.

The long-range Mariners were the only means of finding the indistinct coastline and defining what lay beyond where thick pack ice, in places held fast by grounded icebergs, made a close approach to the continent impossible. Flights begun on 4 January at 720 kilometres (450 miles) off the Oates coast encountered rugged mountains rising to more than 2,750 metres (9,000 feet) in the vicinity of 160° East. Gradually the ships pushed westwards past Cape Freshfield, beyond the Ninnis and Mertz Glaciers in the region of the

When Highjump closed in 1947, the R4D arcraft were tied down amid the snows of Little America — hopefully to be used again. However, President Truman cancelled Highjump II and the planes were lost forever.

South Magnetic Pole. Mawson's old site at Commonwealth Bay lived up to its reputation as the 'home of the blizzard', so shrouded in wind-driven snow pouring off the ice cap as to make aerial photography impossible. Yet in the magnificent views sometimes available from the flight deck, crews estimated their vision could extend 160 kilometres (100 miles) in either way along the coast; at an altitude of 4,000 metres (13,000 feet) with the help of binoculars, they reported seeing mountains protruding through the ice sheet up to 480 kilometres (300 miles) off.

Storms interrupted flying until 21 January, when over the next five weeks the PBMs covered another 1,600 kilometres (1,000 miles) of coast. Off the Knox Coast, they reported a deep embayment that took an hour to fly across. On nine missions they went some 160 kilometres (100 miles) across the interior of Wilkes Land where they saw a limitless icesheet rising from 1,800 metres (6,000 feet) to 2,900 metres (9,500 feet) as it rolled towards the polar plateau. Across Adelie Land the flying program had reached its deepest interior penetration of 680 kilometres (425 miles), turning back at 72° 30' South and 135° East longitude.

Most newsworthy of the western flights were those within the first two weeks of February 1947. Expecting to see more of the endless ice-bound coast, the PBM pilots were amazed to find a dark shadow across the horizon, contrasting with the surrounding glare of the snow-capped continental sheet.

A flashback picture of a world emerging from an ice age of maybe 50,000 years ago could not have been more startling. The first sighting was on 2 February from the aircraft commanded by Lieutenant W. R. Kreitzer who had been assigned to photograph the coast between 105° and 114° East longitudes. Wholly unlike his anticipation of a continuation of floe and pack was his sighting within the crescent of Vincennes Bay of a huge area of naked rocky terrain, some on off-shore islands, some coastal, all of it interspersed with the silvery gleam of open water lakes rich in algae.

Captain Bond's log described the unexpected find:

> The new coast, never before sighted and up until today just a dotted line on the map, was very different from what had been expected. Four new glaciers were found. The most spectacular and largest one had a jagged ice tongue and a 1,000 ft sheer drop. It was on a large, open and glassy calm bay, with many skerries or rocky islets. The pilot also found new nunataks, and land outcroppings. Apparently this land formed dust that discoloured the glacier and icebergs in the vicinity. The pilot found what he considered to be an excellent landing field site on the shore of this open bay. He came down to 1,000 ft and thoroughly photographed the area. The results were some of our most spectacular and amazing photographs. He stated that this area could easily be available to ships once they were through the ice pack. I consider this one of our most successful flights.[15]

Nine days after Kreitzer's mission, a new and even more dramatic discovery lay in wait for the patrolling PBM piloted by Lieutenant David Eli Bunger. He had been tracing the eastern cliffs of the Shackleton Ice Shelf close to 100° East longitude when the world ahead of his cockpit view seemed to turn abruptly from white to darkish brown. Bunger estimated he was seeing an area of at least 260 square kilometres (100 square miles) of rocky ice-free terrain — cratered, hilly and pockmarked with lakes coloured deep blue, green and chocolate brown and enclosed by ice cliffs perhaps over 90 metres (300 feet) high. Two days later after sighting a range 480 kilometres (300 miles) from the coast, the most southerly mountains yet noted in the area, he landed his flying boat on one of the larger lakes in effect, intrusions of the sea walled-off by ice. He and his crew dipped their arms in the water and found it perceptibly warmer than the surrounding sea; when analysed later the samples indicated 66 per cent more salt than normal sea water.[16]

So far as public attention was concerned, Bunger's 'oasis' (later changed to Bunger Hills) overshadowed all other discoveries of the expedition. A navy news release referred to a polar 'Shangri-la', which immediately captured the headlines, with some of the more imaginative rewrite men speculating on the likelihood of finding palm trees in a forgotten Antarctic paradise and perhaps the resort of a beautiful race of South Sea Island natives. Subsequent investigation, including the navy's follow-up Operation Windmill, dismissed any similarity between Kreitzer's and Bunger's finds and the traditional notion of an oasis, much less the South Seas.

Exposed by retreating glacial fronts (similar to the condition of dry valleys found on the western side of McMurdo Sound), the oases were dry, barren and in the case of Bunger's discovery, lifeless and walled-off by the thickest of pack ice. Kreitzer's area, however, was rather more promising in being open to the sea in summer and consequently the haunt of seal and penguin; later it would be chosen as the locale for Wilkes Base in Operation Deep Freeze.

Beyond Australian territory, more gigantic mountains lay in wait for their cameras behind the Princess Ragnhild Coast of Queen Maud Land where they began flying on 22 February. 'Surrounded by high mountains, having a wonderful time', radioed one of the flying-boat pilots as they looked down in awe at the magnificent chain of mountains, some rising to 4,000 metres (13,000 feet) in the vicinity of 72° South and 25° East. These they believed to be an eastward extension of the same glittering blue crystal peaks sighted by Lars Christensen's expeditions ten years previously.

More flights of the western group were made in the vicinity of Gaussberg (Drygalski's 1902 discovery) where Bond reported seeing 100 newly calved icebergs 'in course of production'. Their photographs, taken in the vicinity of Mawson's 1912 western party's march, provoked amazement at the tortuous crevassed area through which the Australian expedition had fought its way. Last flight of all was a continuous photo mission from the Kemp to the Ingrid Christensen Coasts, which included the Mac-Robertson Coast discovered by Mawson. At 160 kilometres (100 miles) inside the Coast's western end they made the first sighting of what would later be called the Prince Charles Mountains.

The freezing of the sea around the ships at the start of March told Bond it was time to turn for Australia. But the furious fifties and the roaring forties lay in wait beyond the swell of the pack ice. In mountainous seas, *Currituck* lost one of its three Martin Mariners which tore from deck lashings and disappeared overboard in the space of 20 seconds. On their return to the United States, Admirals Byrd and Cruzen were able to report to Secretary Forrestal a major leap in America's knowledge of the white south.[17] They had sighted 3.9 million square kilometres (1.5 million square miles) of Antarctica and mapped one-third of the continent. Their photo-surveying had covered 8,700 kilometres (5,400 miles) of coast including 2,250 kilometres (1,400 miles) previously unknown, a total of 65,000 aerial trimetrogon negatives were exposed. Among their discoveries they listed 22 hitherto unknown mountain ranges, 26 islands, 20 glaciers, 9 bays and 5 capes. So was the Antarctic scorecard filled when Highjump came home. The command of preparing for 'consolidating and extending U.S. sovereignty over the largest practicable area of the Antarctic continent' had been well obeyed.

The navy's six R4D aircraft, the Douglas Skytrain covered 36,500 kilometres (22,800 miles) and were aloft for 220 hours during the Central Group's peak exploration month of February 1947. At the end of the total operation, Admiral Byrd claimed that one-third of the continent had been mapped. But Paul Siple criticised the program for lacking scientific emphasis.

Antarctic Honeymoon

Harry Darlington was the first aviator to take his wife to Antarctica. Jenny Darlington fell pregnant during the expedition, while her husband fell foul of their leader and was barred from flying. The Finn-Ronn expedition of 1947–48 represented, for Americans, the ultimate depth in economic organisation — a $50,000 cash budget, a volunteer crew, a small ship borrowed from the U.S. Navy, three aircraft loaned by the U.S. Air Force and, as a base, the derelict American station on Stonington Island.

Finn Ronne brought along his wife, Edith, after whom he named the icesheet behind the Weddell Sea. Jenny Darlington appears to have enjoyed no such recognition. The Ronnes lived in a small separate hut. The Darlingtons spent their honeymoon behind a partitioned end of the men's bunkhouse.

The inexperienced but gung-ho outlook among some of the men (there were a few Antarctic veterans, like Ike Schlossbach of the Byrd and USAS expeditions) and Ronne's idiosyncratic style of leadership soon divided the expedition into two opposing camps, those who at mealtime sat at Ronne's table and the rest polarised around the young Darlingtons. By way of further distraction, the British, who laid claim to Stonington Island, initially resented Ronne's intrusion; through diplomatic channels they tried to prevent his party landing at all. Ronne retaliated by flying a huge American flag, measuring 8 x 5 metres (430 square feet) at the base, raising the Stars and Stripes over the ice he discovered and having himself appointed as official U.S. postmaster of the peninsula.[18] However, the Chileans also had a say in the matter — because of their claim to this portion of Antarctica, they insisted on issuing Ronne and his party with visas before they sailed from South America.

Jenny Darlington.

Commander Finn Ronne.

Despite the wrangling of ill-assorted personalities and other miscellaneous disabilities, the emeritus president of Johns Hopkins University hailed Ronne's work as returning 'a harvest of scientific findings that would do credit to a far more costly expedition'. Ronne, an engineer and member of the U.S. Naval Reserve, was the son of Martin Ronne, a Norwegian sailmaker who voyaged to Antarctica with Amundsen and was in Byrd's 1929 expedition. Young Ronne's expertise as skier and dog sledge driver won him a place in Byrd's 1933 party. In the U.S. Antarctic Service expedition of 1940, as second in charge at Marguerite Bay he completed a 2,000-kilometre (1,250-mile) sledging journey that lasted for 84 days.[19]

The Ronne expedition of 23 people landed from *Port of Beaumont*, a converted navy harbour tender, on Stonington Island in March 1947. Ronne's captain was Ike Schlossbach who would go on to be a veteran of six Antarctic expeditions.

The ship's decks were crowded with three ski aircraft — the first two, a Stinson L5 and a Norseman, were single-engine while the third, a twin-engine Beechcraft, carried sufficient fuel for nine-hours endurance and was equipped with a trimetrogon camera rig. Apart from the lanky Harry Darlington who had worked with Ronne in 1940, his pilots were two air force men, Captain James Lassiter and Lieutenant Adams. The main goal of the flying program was penetration of the unknown ice region flanking the Weddell Sea.

Even before the flights proper were under way, Lassiter went out on 22 September in search of three men in a British Auster who had been missing for a week. He sighted the stumbling figures and landed his Norseman

Ronne's *Port of Beaumont* leaving harbour with the aircraft packed at the stern. The expedition carred a Norseman, a Stinson L5 and a twin-engine Beechcraft.

on the sea ice beside them as they attempted to march the 130 kilometres (80 miles) back to base. Starving and poorly clad, it is almost certain the three would have perished. During the same search, Adams climbed the small L5 reconnaissance plane to 2,750 metres (9,000 feet) to cross the mountain backbone that traverses the peninsula. Each time, in the words of an observer at the British base, he was 'tossed back like an autumn leaf'. The same watcher added, 'It was courage of the kind that knows what it is in for and still goes on, courage of the finest and highest type'.

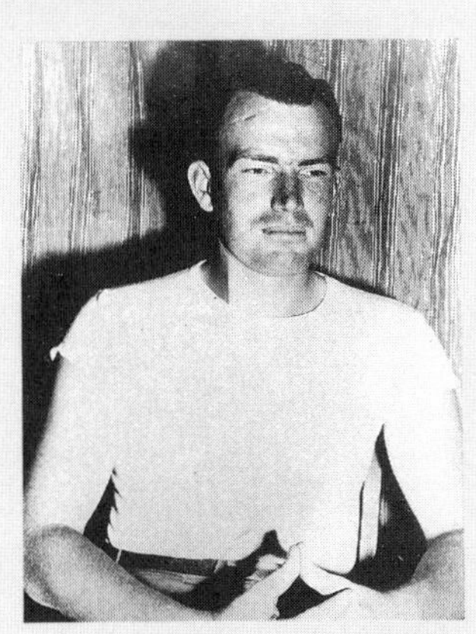

James Lassiter, who became a veteran Antarctica aviator.

Ike Schlossbach, an aviator with Byrd and captain of Ronne's ship.

From a temporary base at Cape Keeler on the Peninsula's eastern side, the first of Ronne's three major flights in the Beechcraft was made on 21 November. He went south into new territory along the Filchner Ice Shelf, his journey reaching its uttermost point at 77° 28' South and 71° 30' West, where he named Mount Hassage and dropped the American flag. The second flight, on 12 December, again followed the Filchner Shelf for about 720 kilometres (450 miles) to Gould Bay until beaten by approaching storm clouds, but not before 4,500 survey photographs were taken without a single prominent feature being seen on the enormous ice-sheet — the leader's Edith Ronne Land. The third flight, on 23 December, took a different tack in the direction of the Pacific sector, exploring the Ellsworth Highland and making the first ever landing on Charcot Island, which had been originally sighted from an aircraft by Sir Hubert Wilkins. All Ronne's flight plans allowed for surface sun-sights to verify the aircraft's course in relationship to the pictures taken, an action that would be a boon to the map-makers. In all, his crews made 86 field landings.

Lassiter well earned the coast named after him at the foot of the Antarctic Peninsula. Returning to base on the flight of two days before Christmas, poor visibility forced him to fly the Beechcraft at barely 90 metres (300 feet) altitude while dodging between icebergs and around the ice tongues protruding from the coastal cliffs. In Ronne's four and a half months of aviation, his three aircraft flew a total of 346 hours, surveyed 647,500 square kilometres (250,000 square miles) of hitherto unseen territory beyond the Antarctic Peninsula and returned in March 1948 with 14,000 aerial pictures covering both sides of the peninsula, Alexander I Island and the Weddell Sea ice shelf area — a most impressive record.[19]

In her book *My Antarctic Honeymoon,* Jenny Darlington describes an interesting yet not particularly happy year on Stonington Island as her husband, after feuding with Ronne, is demoted to the non-flying sidelines. Jenny missed her own grand opportunity to make history when the icebreakers *Burton Island* and *Edisto* freed Ronne's ship from the ice grip. With the expedition's departure for America went her chance of giving birth to the world's first native Antarctican.

I was waiting for the crunch.
I don't know how I got out of it.
The Lord must have guided my hand.

Squadron Leader Doug Leckie,
leader of the first RAAF wintering-over team

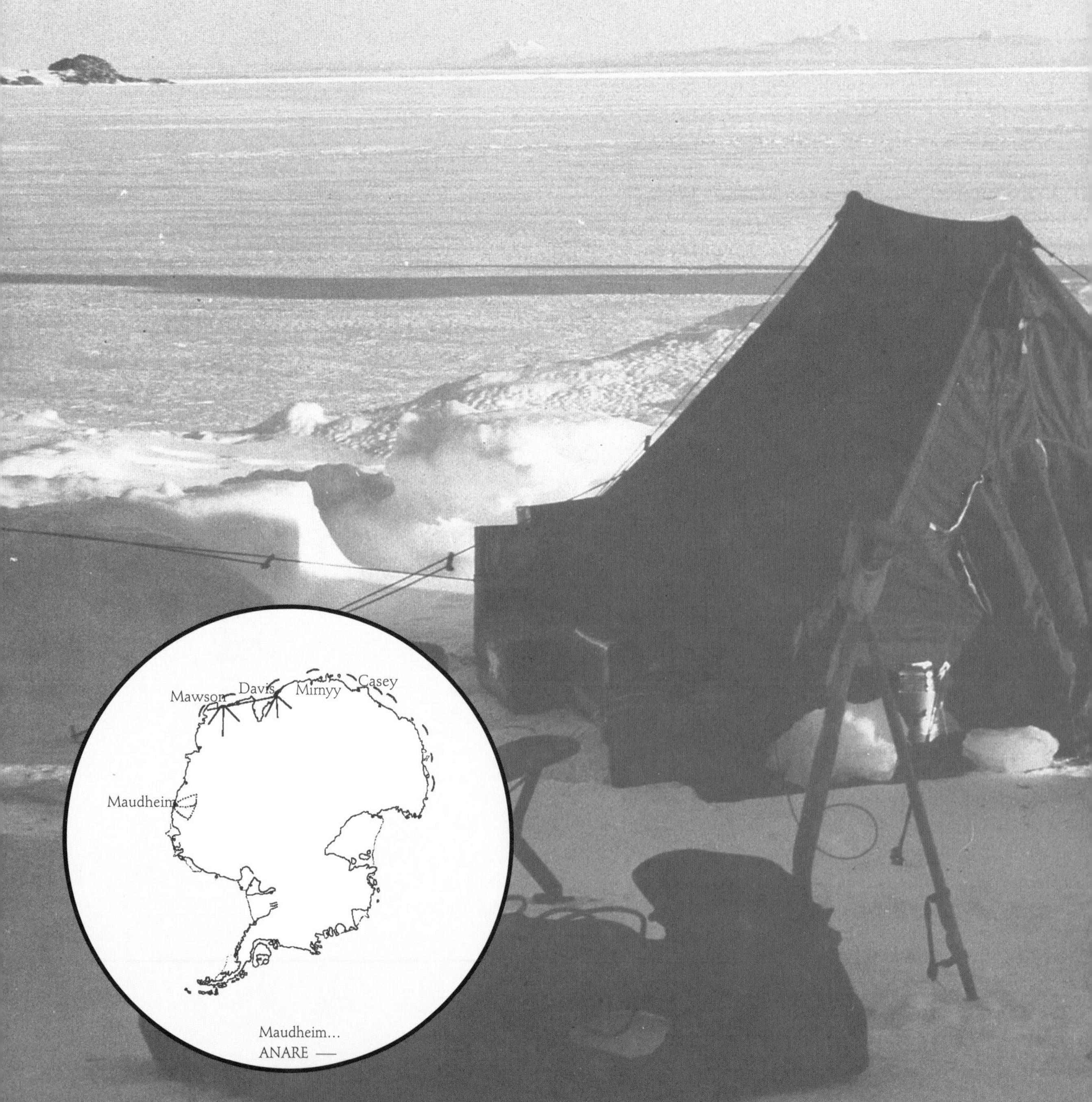

ANARE: YEARS OF LIVING DANGEROUSLY

Typical of the support given to the Australian expedition, a Beaver aircraft of the RAAF transfers a field party and supplies at King Edward Gulf.

Antarctic aviation almost began with an Australian venture. Douglas Mawson's 1911–14 Australasian Antarctic Expedition (AAE) pioneered the use of wireless communications with the outside world, but the aeroplane which the scientist-explorer took to Commonwealth Bay never left the ice. A fellow South Australian, Sir Hubert Wilkins, was to win the distinction of first Antarctic aviator.

In the year after Wilkins' inaugural flight, Mawson (now Sir Douglas) returned to Antarctica with the small de Havilland Moth on the BANZARE voyages of 1929–31. At the same time the Norwegian whalers had introduced aircraft aboard the vessels of Lars Christensen's fleet. Silence again enveloped Australia's polar skies until 1946 and the massive fly-in of the U.S. Navy's Operation Highjump, followed by the helicopter missions of Operation Windmill.

After World War II, aircraft of the Royal Australian Air Force began a cautious probe of southern high latitudes with reconnaissance flights by Lincoln and Liberator bombers reaching to 52° South and as far as Macquarie Island, though still above the Antarctic Circle.[1] Then in 1948, a Catalina flying boat was sent on a hazardous mission to Macquarie Island, with a replacement diesel mechanic for a man who had drowned. Closer approaches to the

The remains of Sir Douglas Mawson's 'air tractor' at Commonwealth Bay. Later reports said the tangled relic had been 'blown away'.

A *Sydney Morning Herald* editorial agreed that Australia faced an 'aviation headache in Antarctica'.

Southward Ho!

ANARE is a combination of initials standing for an enterprise of which this country should be increasingly proud. For year by year the Australian National Antarctic Research Expedition re-mans its four stations at Macquarie Island, Mawson, Davis and Wilkes, and further consolidates the work which, for half a generation, our explorers and scientists have carried out amidst the icy desolation of the White Continent.

This continuous occupation is not, admittedly, a wholly unselfish display of curiosity and energy; it is, in our eyes at least, a proof of the validity of our territorial rights in a huge area of Antarctica. And even if, under the terms of the Antarctic Treaty, all territorial claims in the Antarctic are "frozen," the preservation of a legal basis for our administration in the region is a proper precaution by this country

But the real international interest in our Antarctic participation derives from the effectiveness of the Australian scientific work and from the exploration which, courageously and skilfully carried out, has resulted—among other benefits—in the mapping of many thousands of square miles which once appeared to be beyond the resources of delineation. Fortunately the Antarctic is now one of the few areas of the world where groups of men from a number of nations can co-operate for the common gain without calculation of political advantage, and the consequent possibility of embitterment, and Australian teams have more than once been grateful for assistance from other national expeditions, including the Russians.

Indeed, Australians have been sharply reminded on several occasions that ANARE does not enjoy the facilities or amenities in its missions that the more richly endowed American and Soviet bases command. This is particularly true of air transport, although the chartering of helicopters —there will be two with the party which leaves on the Nella Dan for the Wilkes Base tomorrow—is now a regular palliative of Australia's aviation headache in the Antarctic. Too many of us still think of the ANARE bases as being "out of this world," but as an administrative reality they are part of Australia and the national gratitude is due to those who brave the icy wilderness to confirm this fact.

continent came in 1947– 48 when an RAAF crew went south with a Walrus amphibian on HMAS *Labuan,* a tank landing craft converted to relief ship for the Heard Island expedition. A Sikorsky Kingfisher float plane was aboard the *Wyatt Earp* (now HMAS *Wyatt Earp*) on the fault-plagued voyage to King George V Land. Neither aircraft did much to distinguish itself: the Walrus was wrecked in a storm; the Kingfisher made but two flights, to report an impenetrable pack which denied Ellsworth's old ship access to the coast.[2]

The Sikorsky Kingfisher sent south in 1948 is lowered overboard from *Wyatt Earp*. The late-running expedition permitted only two exploratory flights in the vicinity of the Ninnis Glacier.

Two Austers, under the charge of an air force crew, were on the supply vessel *Kista Dan* when Dr Phillip Law led the new Australian National Antarctic Research Expedition (ANARE) to Mac-Robertson Land in 1954.[3] The little high-wing monoplanes, purchased from the RAF, were already seasoned in the polar climate having come from the Norwegian-British-Swedish Expedition of two years earlier. Before the season was out, however, both were casualties, one lost overboard — a pointer to the aviation hardships that lay in wait. From this first year of continental settlement until 1963, the RAAF was to be an integral part of every wintering-over party. Soon equipped with the more powerful de Havilland of Canada DHC2 Beavers, they were in the forefront of ANARE's drive to map and understand the nature of Australia's sector of the huge frozen continent.

Doug Leckie, then with the rank of flight lieutenant, led the three men of the RAAF who went south on *Kista Dan* to establish Australia's first continental station since the AAE left Commonwealth Bay in 1914. Leckie and the leader went out to find a site for the base in a region which Law generally favoured from studying the coastal photographs taken by Operation Highjump seven years previously.

On one of his early flights, pilot John Seaton returned with this view of the western rim mountains and subsidiary glaciers, disclosing the vast Lambert Glacier on its march to the sea.

> I joined Leckie in the cockpit of the little Auster. This aircraft is underpowered for use with floats and we made two long runs without being able to leave the water. As the calm conditions were adding to our difficulties by preventing the floats from breaking clear of the water ('getting up on the step' is the technical jargon) we arranged for the motor boat to make two transverse runs across our take-off path to break up the smooth surface of the sea and, following this procedure, we were able to lift off the water. (Law: 81–2)

The flight of 95 minutes led to the decision to place the base at the head of a rocky harbour, shaped like a horseshoe. Law hoped that their ship would be able to move into the harbour through the gap between the headlands to anchor with protection from wind and drifting ice. Behind the harbour he noted a 'terribly forbidding' surface of blue, polished, glacier ice that rose steeply towards the interior, riven in many places with crevasses and scarred with ice falls overhanging the edge of the plateau. To the south he and Leckie could see the blue and rocky face of Mount Henderson and, to the west, the striking black outcrops of the Masson, David and Casey Ranges, lying almost at right angles to the coast.

On 13 February 1954 on the shore of Horseshoe Harbour on the MacRobertson Land coast, Law raised the Australian flag and gave the base the fitting name of Mawson.[4]

Promoted to squadron leader, Doug Leckie led the first RAAF wintering-over team back to Mawson in 1956, with John Seaton as second pilot. Augmenting their Auster came the de Havilland DHC2, a Canadian machine well tested in cold and frontier environments. The Beaver was able to operate on wheels, skis or floats while the Auster went only on skis (made of hickory). As if to demonstrate the contribution that aviation could make to Australia's exploration of its Antarctic Territory, the aircraft that year achieved 598 flying hours despite whiteouts, blizzards and the eternal drifting snow, reaching along the coast from Enderby to Princess Elizabeth Land. The same year saw the building of an aircraft hangar at Mawson, reputedly the then largest structure in Antarctica. For the RAAF crew and base personnel, construction of the metal building involved struggling against freezing gale-force winds to provide safe accommodation for the aircraft before winter closed in.[5]

For the RAAF crew, discovery came almost without pause from the cockpit of the bright yellow aircraft (in later years, the colour was changed to 'survival orange'). On the first flight of the season, 20 April 1956, Leckie reported a massive range of mountain peaks protruding through the ice cap some 260 kilometres (160 miles) south of Mawson. He and his surveyor-observer Syd Kirkby estimated the mountains extended for 200 kilometres (125 miles) in a south-westerly line. Such a sighting in the white unknown would touch the aviation program with the excitement of pioneer exploration. In a more prosaic achievement, the tiny winged fleet of that first full year in Antarctica airlifted 11 tonnes of rations, fuel and equipment in depot-laying flights, as well carrying 150 passengers, mostly field parties to be put down on the ice. Some 18,000 photo exposures were made with the trimetrogon cameras, in all embracing an area of 777,000 square kilometres (300,000 square miles); coastline recorded on the cameras amounted to close on 3,200 kilometres (2,000 miles); the most distant interior missions reached 800 kilometres (500 miles) from the base.

Group Captain Stuart Campbell (left) was a pioneer Antarctic aviator, and later became leader of the Australian expedition. With Chief Petty Officer Liddell he visited a penguin rookery on Macquarie Island during the 1948 voyage.

Wyatt Earp, the ship made famous by the Ellsworth expeditions, completed its fifth and final voyage to Antarctica in 1948. On returning with a frustrated Australian party, it was sold by the government into cargo service.

Leckie, who began his flying on a seaplane in Singapore in 1934, was awarded the OBE, AFC and a Polar Medal for his notable contribution to Antarctic aviation. In all, he would join five expeditions to Antarctica and accumulate more than 2,000 flying hours while spending the equivalent of two and a half years based at Mawson or aboard the supply ships. Seaton, his companion, received an MBE and Polar Medal. ANARE reports spoke almost

casually of the dangers that faced these daring young air force men. Leckie recalled a radio altimeter malfunction when flying the Beaver. He found himself trapped in a narrow ravine among the coastal mountains instead of in clear space over the sea ice. 'I was carrying 44 gallon drums of fuel in the Beaver and I had to climb in a tight circle to get out of there; it was very close. I was waiting for the crunch. I lost my nerve and flew back. I don't know how I got out of it. The Lord must have guided my hand.'[6]

With the resumption of the summer program, the Beaver and Auster were taken out on more exploratory sweeps over widely separated regions of the Australian territory — Enderby Land, to the west, and the Prince Charles Mountains to the south-south-east. In a flight of 12 October, reaching almost 500 kilometres (310 miles) south-east of Mawson, Pilot Officer Seaton sighted further evidence that a vast drainage system originated in this segment of the plateau when he reported the presence of a huge glacier estimated to be almost 40 kilometres (25 miles) wide and at least 400 kilometres (250 miles) in length. Confined in a valley between newly discovered mountain ranges, the glacier swept north-north-east to Prydz Bay where it emptied into the immense Amery Ice Shelf. Seaton had come upon the flank of what would be named the Lambert Glacier, after the Director of Commonwealth's Division of National Mapping. The Lambert is one of the major features of Antarctic topography, larger than the famous Beardmore which had been Captain Scott's path to and from the South Pole, indeed it proved to be the world's largest glacier.[7]

In his flight to Enderby Land the day before, Leckie's discovery included a great ice shelf enclosed within a gulf that measured 160 kilometres (100 miles) inwards from the coastline. First aviation contact at Mirnyy occurred on 4 September when the RAAF aircraft was lowered to the sea ice for a flight during *Kista Dan*'s visit to the new Russian base. In this first of many friendly meetings between the Australian and Soviet expeditions, the visitors to Mirnyy found an encampment of 160 scientists, technicians and aviators, with a fleet of 14 aircraft, including three helicopters.[8]

The following month was marked by one of the hair-raising incidents that were to punctuate ANARE's aviation program. On a flight of 28 October in the Auster, returning the 300 kilometres (190 miles) back to Mawson from King Edward VIII Gulf, John Seaton found his elevator controls jammed:

> I was at about 4,000 feet heading towards Mawson along the edge of the continental ice but at times over the sea ice. Sea ice is normally pretty unreliable for landing, unless previously inspected but in this case the winds were calm below whilst at Mawson there was a known 40 knot katabatic blowing. With the elevator problem I was experiencing, to reduce power caused the nose to drop which in turn had an unacceptable effect on the landing attitude of the aircraft. To keep the nose up I had to power at cruising r.p.m. which in turn kept the speed high.
>
> My only solution was to approach and land at cruising speed, touch down 'hot', but then get the power off and attempt to stop the landing run as soon as possible. On the very smooth blue ice where I set down, and in the calm conditions prevailing, the aircraft slid on and on for what seemed ages — no brakes — until finally I had to ground loop the ship through 180 degrees and apply power again to prevent sliding backwards into a substantial tidal opening, or into the looming face of the ice cliff

Seaton traced the fault to an instrument box bracket which had broken loose, jamming the elevator controls. He disconnected the bracket, took off again and returned safely to Mawson.[9]

◄ Austers were the original aircraft taken to Mawson base by ANARE (the Australian National Antarctic Research Expedition) in 1954. Though the first two aircraft were wrecked, small machines of the type provided reliable support in the early years.

◄ Unloaded from the tank landing ship, HMAS *Labuan*, the Walrus amphibian made a photo flight over the volcano Big Ben on Heard Island, Australia's sub-Antarctic possession.

Inset: Members of the 1956 RAAF Antarctic flight (from left): Doug Leckie, John Seaton, Gerry Sundberg, Geoff Johanson.

On these flights the aviator could be looking at clear blue sky above the glistering white ice cap and next instant have ice crystals cascading into the cabin, temperatures dropping instantly from –30°C to –70°C and struggling to save the engine from cutting out. He could be in a ski landing on blue ice, rushing helter-skelter towards a cliff or crevasse, as John Seaton had, desperately trying to brake the suicidal advance of his aircraft, or he could be pitted against the 'vague-out' of wind driven snow, not to speak of the deadly confusion of an impenetrable whiteout. Courage, enterprise and sound navigation were the order of the day in the first decade of ANARE's push to unlock secrets of an ice-bound territory close to the size of the Commonwealth itself. Nineteen Polar Medals were awarded to these RAAF airmen.

'The largest structure in Antarctica' was the description given to the steel-framed hangar erected at Mawson in 1956. The building could hold two aircraft and in the summer thaw had open water almost to the front door.

Three major exploratory flights were achieved by the first wintering-over RAAF team. Leckie and Kirkby flying south-west from Mawson had discovered a new range of high mountains in Enderby Land. Seaton and geologist Peter Crohn made a southerly flight which explored the western fringe of the mighty Prince Charles Mountains and sighted a fresh cluster of peaks stretching further to the south.

Leckie completed 19 missions and logged 80 flying hours in laying a new depot on the King Edward VIII Gulf. The flights transported heavy loads of fuel, rations and equipment and landed expeditionaries at various surface control camps to coordinate with the aerial photo missions. In describing flying through the winds of up to 112 kph (70 mph) they sometimes encountered, Leckie said it was only necessary to 'gun' the engine and release the aircraft's brakes to have it spring off the ground like a kite. When coming in to land he flew over a selected spot and reduced flying speed until his machine 'went down like a lift'.[10]

Availability of the hangar at Mawson helped to extend the flying season in allowing maintenance to be performed under cover, and in adequate lighting. While aircraft of an Antarctic expedition were normally expected to be immobilised by the onslaught of winter, the RAAF crew at Mawson made flights to check on the extent of the spreading sea ice even during mid-year darkness.

Photo-mapping an uncertain coastline, finding a path for the supply vessel through the stubborn pack, carrying field parties to remote interior sites on floats or skis, all were part of their mission. Many a journey chanced the likelihood of sighting something new. According to Seaton:

> It was on these flights that one had the opportunity to really 'explore' the coastal areas and much of the immediate interior fringes — penguin rookeries, ice movements, small glaciers and a host of other interesting phenomena.

Dr P. G. Law, director of the Antarctic Division and Leader of ANARE, 1949–1966.

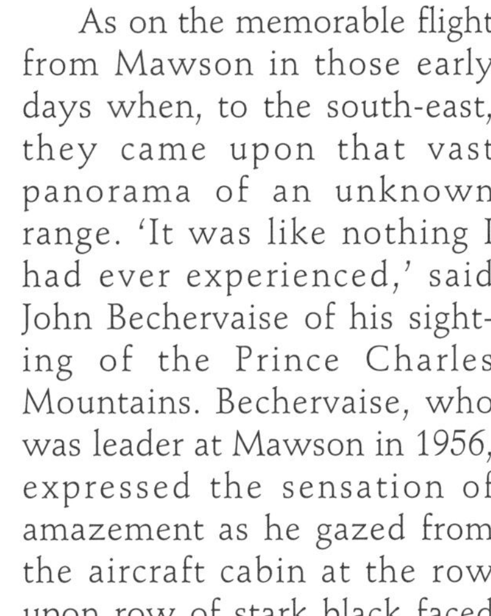

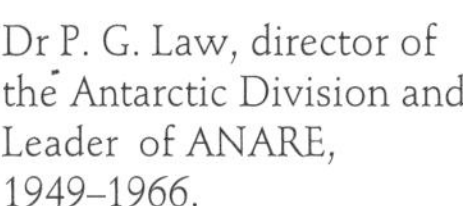

◀ Flying above Prince Charles Mountains, one of the memorable features of Australian Antarctic Territory.

As on the memorable flight from Mawson in those early days when, to the south-east, they came upon that vast panorama of an unknown range. 'It was like nothing I had ever experienced,' said John Bechervaise of his sighting of the Prince Charles Mountains. Bechervaise, who was leader at Mawson in 1956, expressed the sensation of amazement as he gazed from the aircraft cabin at the row upon row of stark black faced peaks rearing above the plateau. 'A vast range of mountains loomed ahead in the clear air.' Trying to describe the unreality of it all, he added, 'It was as though we had created these mountains within our own minds.'[11]

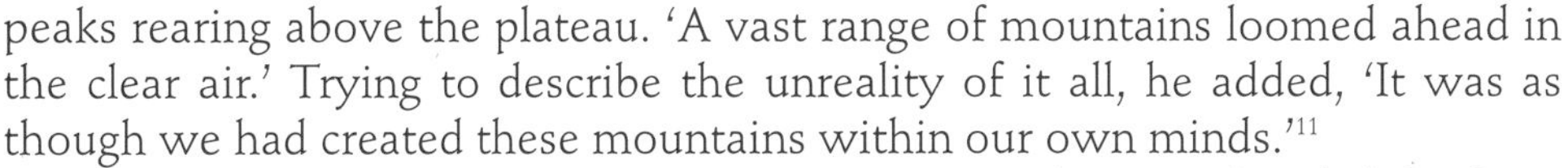

In the next expedition, Flight Lieutenant Peter Clemence headed the four-man air force contingent. His fellow aviator was Pilot Officer D. Johnston. This was the first year that ANARE could field two Beavers, allowing a big expansion of the aviation effort. 'Australian airmen risked their lives time and time again in long flights over the rugged terrain in single-engine aircraft,' said Phil Law in his report of the year's flying program. With *Kista Dan* again the chartered relief ship, the aim was exploration of the little known

The Maudheim Partnership

The air forces of three nations uniquely combined in assisting the Norwegian-British-Swedish expedition of 1949–52 to discover what lay beneath the icesheet of Queen Maud Land.

Like Rymill's operation of 15 years before, the three-nation study into the glaciology and geology of Norwegian Antarctic territory was relatively modest in scope, yet undertaken with painstaking attention to detail. In personnel, skills and equipment, each of the three countries made a carefully defined contribution to the Maudheim expedition–the name given to their principal base located on

the ice shelf of the Princess Martha Coast, near Cape Norvegia.

In aviation, Britain supplied the two Auster cabin aircraft together with RAF crews to be used in the first year's flying.[12] Norway supplied the air support in the second year while in the third year the Swedes were responsible for the aerial program.

The Norwegian air unit of the second year (1951) chartered two aircraft from the Wideroe Aviation Company. Captain Kare Friis-Baastad was in command with Andreas Jocobsen as first pilot. One aircraft was a C.5 modified for polar flying and fitted with aerial camera equipment; the other was a K.Z.111 short range machine. Bad weather frustrated much of the flying program. The C5 was wrecked in a landing at Cape Norvegia on 29 January but the crew escaped serious injury. The Swedish air unit of 1952 was under the command of Captain R. von Essen of the Swedish Air Force. Their Beechcraft aircraft flew to the mountains south-east of Maudheim and produced a 260,000-square kilometre (100,000-square mile) photo survey.

Much of the expedition's surface exploration, under the leadership of John Giaever, administrative head of the Norwegian Polar Institute, retraced Schwabenland's hurried airborne path of 1939.[13] Dog sledges were used to find a secure route to the advance interior depot. Travelling by Weasel tracked vehicles, which towed a sledge 'caboose' to provide accommodation and shelter, surface parties reached 600 kilometres (375 miles) from Maudheim, until halted among the towering peaks of Queen Maud Land.

The seismic team which was in the field late in 1951 measured the icesheet beneath them at a maximum depth of around 2,600 metres (7,800 feet). On an exposed rocky slope the explorers also made quite a different and unexpected type of discovery in the primitive life forms of tiny scurrying spider-like creatures amid a brightly coloured field of lichen. When their vessel *Norsel* came home with the expedition in February 1952, beneath the enormous mantle of snow and ice they had mapped a hidden face of Antarctica that much resembled the fjord coastline of Norway itself.

Inset: Goal of the Maudheim parties – the rugged interior of Queen Maud land.

The Norwegian-British-Swedish expedition of 1949–52 flew the aircraft of all three nations, beginning with RAF Austers. Australia bought the two Austers at the close of the expedition from the Maudheim group and began the ANARE aerial program with the seasoned little planes.

Wilkes Land coast and to find a site for ANARE's second continental base in the Vestfold Hills area, 550 kilometres (340 miles) east of Mawson.

Law was anxious to determine a place to put the station before another nation (possibly the Russians, but not necessarily so) moved in. On the morning of 5 January 1957 he set out, with Peter Clemence flying the Beaver, to examine the rocky Vestfold area, named by the Norwegian skipper Klarius Mikkelsen who had landed there in 1935. The valuable flight lasted seven hours but nearly ended in the dreaded signal 'one of our aircraft is missing', as Law subsequently described:

> We had some concern after passing Cape Darnley, for we had to cross Prydz Bay, which was mainly open water with a 40-knot wind whipping the sea into white-crested waves. Over the centre it would have been half-an-hour, either way, to reach safe landing areas in pools sheltered by pack ice.
>
> During the reconnaissance I made a bad mistake. We arrived over the Larsemann Hills, which I erroneously thought to be the Vestfolds, and this gave rise to later confusion . . .
>
> On our return flight we flew over the Amery Ice Shelf just as clouds moved in beneath us. I suggested to Clemence that we should turn to starboard and move to intersect the coast but he said he was on the right course for the ship. However, I continued to worry and finally asked him to veer to starboard, arguing that if we could see the coastline we would be quite sure where we were. He finally agreed and altered course 30° to starboard. Shortly after that the cloud cleared away from beneath us and we crossed the coast to fly over the sea. It turned out that we had been well off course and, if we had continued, would have run out of fuel inland over the continent somewhere south of the Scullin Monolith! No-one would have had the faintest idea where we were.[14]

On 13 January the new base was opened, bearing the name of Davis, after Australia's distinguished polar mariner; on 1 May, Clemence completed the first flight across from Mawson, to commence a regular service between the two ANARE outposts. Memories of BANZARE were recalled on 3 July when Doug Johnston landed close to a cairn in the Taylor Glacier region. The pilot and his companions found a plaque with an inscription 'sovereignty asserted' and a handwritten message of 1931 in a copper cylinder, bearing the signature of Sir Douglas Mawson. Again on 6 August, Johnston was making a return trip from the Scullin Monolith east of Mawson when he and his passenger Jim Goodspeed noticed a 'deep brown stain' covering the coastal ice near the Douglas Islands. Bringing the aircraft lower to circle the area, Johnston found that he and Goodspeed were staring at what was believed to be the largest penguin rookery so far discovered in Antarctica, later investigation estimated a population of 23,000 birds. The RAAF's tally for August was 37 flights, indicative of the intensity of the aviation program; 40 missions were completed in October, with 150 hours aloft.[15] The two aircraft flew a total of 548 hours for the year, of which 106 were on reconnaissance, covering altogether a distance of over 160,000 square kilometres (62,000 square miles).

The year was also marked by the announcement that ANARE had been allocated government funds to purchase a third DHC2, allowing two Beavers always to be available in the south, while the third came back to Australia for overhaul at the de Havilland plant in Sydney.

The following year was notable in that the new chartered supply vessel *Thala Dan* sailed along the entire coastline of Australian Antarctica during the summer relief and exploration season. Squadron Leader Ivan Grove headed the RAAF contingent; a new problem confronted them when a melt-water pool in front of the Mawson hangar made it difficult to extricate the aircraft.

On one of the flights, a combined man-dog-sledge supply mission into the recently sighted Enderby Land mountains 560 kilometres (350 miles) west of Mawson, casual mention was made that 'dog fight occurred . . . King was bitten on the arm while trying to separate dogs'. The prospect of a battle between husky dogs in the confined cabin of a Beaver beggars the imagination.

Then on 15 August, a routine mission to Davis base suddenly dealt ANARE the year's first serious air emergency. Falling oil pressure forced Grove, with his two passengers Manning and McLeod, to land the Beaver on the desolate icesheet about an hour away from Mawson. According to ANARE's official statement:

> The pilot wisely decided to land on land-based ice rather than on sea ice, which can break up or be blown out to sea in a storm. But thick cloud and severe air turbulence along the coast made the operation most dangerous. Moreover, the area where the plane touched down was surrounded by a mass of small crevasses, and in the gale force winds the men had difficulty in tying down the aircraft on the icy slopes. They spent the night in their survival equipment.
>
> The following day Flight-Lieutenant Wilson took off in the second Beaver aircraft from Davis. Wilson flew first to Mawson where he picked up Sergeant Richardson [the engine mechanic] and all necessary tools and spares for repairing the Beaver's engine. Then he flew to the stranded plane, landing Richardson and picking up Manning and McLeod, who were flown back to Mawson. For the next two days Richardson and Grove worked unceasingly on the disabled engine. In the low winter temperatures, manual work in Antarctica is uncomfortable even with gloves on, yet Richardson went for long periods without gloves. In an icy gale, he then had to stand in the freezing slipstream to check for leaking oil from the repaired engine.[16]

Remains of the Walrus amphibian at Heard Island after it had been savaged on the ground by a severe storm on 21 December 1947.

Solar activity conveniently blacked out all radio communications between Mawson and the men working on the plane, whereupon Flight Lieutenant Wilson made a second relief flight from base, bringing the officer-in-charge to find out how repairs were proceeding. Although bearings were damaged, the cockpit gauges indicated the engine could produce sufficient power for flight. The aircraft was made as light as practicable and successfully took off at reduced power. The second Beaver accompanied the disabled aircraft in case of a second forced landing. Engine oil pressure and temperature showed steady deterioration during the flight and 24 kilometres (15 miles) from Mawson it appeared necessary to land. However, by descending very slowly and using the minimum engine power, Grove managed to bring the aircraft back to Mawson safely.

Two aviation parties went south for 1958–59 summer operations. Squadron Leader J. C. Sandercock, leading his five-man RAAF wintering-over team, reached Mawson aboard *Thala Dan*; an additional team member was Squadron Leader J. Kitchenside, who would command the RAAF flight in the following year. Under air force policy the next season's commander came south as a 'round-tripper' to be introduced to polar aviation; also aboard ship was one of the Beavers on return from overhaul at the de Havilland plant. A second chartered vessel, *Magga Dan,* carried Antarctic Division Director Phil Law and pilot Doug Leckie as part of a three-man RAAF crew on a summer attempt at the exploration of Oates Land, that most forbidding sector far to the eastern corner of Australian territory. Raising the Australian flag to signal the handing over of Wilkes base to the Commonwealth by the Americans of Operation Deep Freeze also occurred during the cruise on 4 February.[17]

Raising the American flag at Wilkes Base on 16 February 1957. Two years later the Deep Freeze outpost was transferred to Australian ownership. In recent years, a new ANARE base has taken its place, named after the late R. G. Casey, a friend of Mawson and Wilkins and the Australian politician most active in Antarctic affairs.

During the voyage from Wilkes, the *Magga Dan* party encountered an iceberg measuring 40 kilometres (25 miles) in length and 12 kilometres ($7\frac{1}{2}$ miles) wide and with a height above water level of 40 metres (130 feet). The Oates Land Coast — named after Scott's 'gallant gentleman' — greeted them with awesome coastal scenery of snow shrouded peaks rising from the icesheet and in places plunging their flanks almost vertically into the sea. From deep valleys between the mountains issued the glaciers, one of which thrust its crevassed and icy tongue some 32 kilometres (20 miles) out to sea.

In this grim region, after taking off from an open pool beside the ship, Leckie and Law on a photo-reconnaissance flight of 20 February in the Auster float plane suddenly lost direction in trying to regain the ship above a jumble of icebergs and the glitter of the pack. Continual radio contact with *Magga Dan* and visual position descriptions from the ship failed to bring them home. Worse, the captain informed them that drifting ice had covered the pool. Without radio compass aid and with fuel running low, they were in danger of being forced to attempt a landing amid the drifting floes; with no clue as to their location, it was the sort of scenario in which men are never found again. Law rapped out a command — 'Collect all binoculars, issue them to individuals. Divide the sky into sectors and have each man scan one sector!'

The ship's crew and expedition members scrambled on deck in response to the Captain's orders. 'We were spotted as a speck in the sky,' Phil Law recalled. 'With engines churning, the ship's wash produced a 40-metre (130-foot) stretch of open water astern into which Leckie skilfully landed the Auster. We had five minutes of fuel remaining.' So ended a tense 30 minutes which Law vowed he never wished to repeat.

On 21 February, changing to skis, they flew the Auster over a viciously rough coast until sighting Hom Bluff, 130 kilometres (80 miles) away, indicating that the entire Australian Antarctic coastline had now been witnessed.[18]

At Mawson a new airstrip on the plateau was scheduled for completion in April. Typical matter-of-fact references were made to Squadron Leader Sandercock's Davis visit of 22 May: 'the runways had been clogged with the snow accumulated on the Davis sea ice and had to be dug by night-long work. The westward return eked out sufficient light by chasing the moon but the home landing [at Mawson] on the sea ice in 50 gusty knots crowned the flight.'

In the following October, when 72 hours of flying were achieved, a report described the return from King Edward VIII Gulf with two machines 'caught in a sudden white-out, both planes made a prudent landing on the sea ice at Crooked Island and waited for an improvement in the weather . . . the incident fully and successfully tested the emergency gear and rations provided for such occasions.' John Bechervaise, the station leader, reported: 'The RAAF Antarctic flight continued to give fine support to the expedition flying, almost daily, on twilight "milk runs" to Taylor Glacier, carrying out surveys over the Plateau, making landings on sea ice for coastal triangulation and, until very recently, for astro-determinations at Mount Elliott and Baillieu Peak.'

During the year they had safely flown 169 sorties for 371 hours airborne. All ANARE's safeguards were not sufficient to avert disaster on the ground, however, when three days after Christmas, with both Beavers securely tied down at the skiway known as Gwamm, a short distance south of Mawson, a wind gusting to 185 kph (115 mph) roared down from the plateau.[19] To quote from the ANARE report of 28 December 1959:

> The vivid story from the Leader at Mawson, Mr J. M. Bechervaise, indicates that this polar hurricane, which reached an estimated 115 m.p.h. with erratic gusts far in excess of that speed, developed without warning. Parties had left Mawson Station during the morning to make routine inspections of the aircraft on the plateau strip. When these parties reached the airfield the wind had already reached 80 m.p.h. and one Beaver aircraft had snapped a tie wire, despite its three-ton breaking strain. The second Beaver seemed secure.[20]

The de Havilland of Canada Beaver — the DHC2, later became the mainstay of Australia's polar aviation. The capable cabin aircraft could be used on wheels, skis or floats. All three flying for ANARE were finally destroyed in blizzards.

The Unlucky Twelfth

Final blow to the early use of fixed wing aircraft came during the exploration of the Kemp Land coast 400 kilometres (250 miles) west of Mawson in 1963. It was unlucky 12 January — or, rather, 'lucky' for Captain John Whiting and his passengers — when as he readied for take-off from beside *Nella Dan*, the Beaver VH-PGL, under charter, speared its skis through a weakened patch of sea ice.

A report from Phil Law continued:

On Sunday night at 8.30 pm the Beaver aircraft of the Australian Antarctic Expedition broke through a weak patch of sea ice while taxiing from near the ship to its take-off strip. On board were the pilot, Captain John Whiting and passengers Maxwell Corry, surveyor, and Leslie Miller, radio operator, who were to have been landed on Rayner Peak for surveying. They barely managed to scramble out of the cabin before the aircraft settled beneath the sea.

The high level wing resting on the surrounding ice prevented the plane from plunging to the bottom. Men pushed inflatable sausage sections from the Expedition's rubber pontoons beneath the wings and inflated them by a pneumatic line from the ship. When the aircraft was thus safeguarded from sinking, Captain Petersen carefully manoeuvred the *Nella Dan* to break through the fast ice until it was level with the stranded plane. The ship's derrick then hoisted the Beaver out of the jumbled ice onto the deck of the ship. Dr Law said that the expedition's program of survey and geology would be curtailed by the loss of use of the Beaver but that it would continue on a reduced scale, using three helicopters.

No place for a forced landing: a view from an Auster flight of Mt Rivett and the crevassed icesheet to the south of Mawson. 'Terribly forbidding', was Phil Law's description.

The hero of the day was Jim Sandercock, who acted quickly and without thought of personal safety in climbing into the sliding aircraft, starting its engine and holding its nose into the prevailing wind during the increasing storm for two hours before assistance arrived in the form of a weasel tractor. Further cables were attached to the aircraft and for a short time the situation seemed to be under control. However, further gusts reaching 190 kph (120 mph) quickly wrote-off both planes. A wing, wrenched off the first Beaver, was thrown through the air. The other wing broke in the middle. The second Beaver tore loose from its securing cables and disintegrated, despite strenuous efforts to secure it. (See full report in Appendix II.)

Australia's aircraft appeared to be much safer in the Antarctic skies than on the surface. Two Austers and two Beavers had been lost while secured to the ice or aboard ship. 'It is difficult to see how the aeroplane can be anchored to withstand the blizzards,' wrote Professor Griffith Taylor in an article as long ago as 1928, for the London *Times*. Part of the hazard lay in the somewhat fragile nature of the aircraft themselves — small, lightweight and in that sense an easy prey to a savage wind.

When weather seemed to be forgotten there came a major advance in Australia's air exploration of Antarctica with the government announcement that a Dakota twin-engine transport had been purchased from the RAAF by ANARE's parent body, the Department of External Affairs. With an air force crew of 12 the aircraft would be sent south next summer season to commence flying in 1960. As a back-up, another Beaver in civilian registration VH-PGL came on *Magga Dan* flown by the distinguished fighter pilot of World War II and the Korean War, Wing Commander R. C. (Dick) Cresswell, now an employee of the de Havilland company. Cresswell completed nine sorties totalling 18 hours before it was decided to induct the Beaver back into the RAAF flight to replace one of the lost machines.

The Douglas-built Dakota originally served in the U.S. Army Air Corps but had been part of the RAAF fleet since 1945 when, with 64.5 hours in the log book, it was received almost new. Part of its polar modification included ski landing gear, a provision for JATO (jet-assisted take-off) cylinders and the installation of a housing for the trimetrogon camera equipment which would be operated on long range photo-survey flights.[21] Keith Mather, who had been leader at Mawson in 1957, described the decision to ship the Dakota from Melbourne with the next ANARE party as a transformation 'in one stroke, of the entire concept of Australian Antarctic operations. Equipped with skis and JATO bottles, the plane will be able to land and take off again from surfaces up to 10,000 feet in altitude. With some modifications it could operate a thousand miles from its base, compared with the 400 miles which is the extreme range of the Beaver presently in use'.

With Dakota support, Mather declared, Australia would be able to stage a full-scale exploring venture into the Prince Charles Mountains to the south-east of Mawson. He continued:

> With a weasel for scouting in possibly heavily crevassed areas ahead of the air-fuel supplied tractor train, these trains could then push on to the 'zone of inaccessibility' at 82 degrees South, linking up with the Russian probings from Mirnyy into the same area, and then filling in a vast unmapped region between the Prince Charles Mountains and the Sor Rondane Mountains inland from the Princess Ragnhild Coast.[22]

Squadron Leader J. Kitchenside was in command of the RAAF flight that sailed on *Thala Dan* with the partly dismantled Dakota A65-81 stowed on deck. At Mawson the machine was hauled ashore in early February and the reassembly procedure started, though in the open air, always to be dogged by the problem of drifting snow. Introduction of the bigger aircraft brought plenty of technical difficulties and showed the need for careful handling of heavier equipment. While being taken on 12 May to the sea ice to allow a flight to the plateau strip (close to Mount Twintop) known as Rumdoodle, the 'Dak' began to slide forward and despite frantic efforts to avoid a collision, the impact with the tractor towing it resulted in a damaged wing. The RAAF ground crew worked non-stop to repair the wing with the happy outcome that history was made at midday on 14 June when, with the sun just beneath the horizon, A65-81 took off and made circuits above the sea ice of Mawson harbour. Considerable celebration followed the successful first flight, even overshadowing the traditional midwinter's day feast.

To prepare for a busy summer schedule, electrical fitter John Arthur connected the JATO bottles allowing the first jet-assisted take-off by the RAAF in Antarctica to be placed in the records. Watching the flight, a group of expeditionaries who were man-hauling a sledge unanimously agreed that 'Scott really did it the hard way'.

A flight of 16 August gave an indication of what great things ANARE could expect from the employment of the new aircraft. At the request of National Mapping, the Dakota set out on a lengthy photo-survey south-west from Mawson; in a flying time of 7 hours and 20 minutes it covered a distance of 1,770 kilometres (1,100 miles), reaching 72°30'South and 40° 30'East. Later in the month the Dakota left for Davis to accomplish part of the year's survey program in the Vestfold region and to lay depot fuel for surface exploration among the Prince Charles Mountains. The aircraft had to return to Mawson for an engine change, which was assembled and fitted in quick time. In the third week of November, it made a brief return visit to Davis.

Experience and a smoother performance were being chalked up — the outlook for long range flying indeed appeared inviting, with full use to be made of the Plateau airstrip when the sea ice showed signs of breaking-up.

Then in early December the Dakota and its promising airborne program came to an abrupt and catastrophic end. Storm clouds and a howling wind descended upon Mawson and within less than an hour the Dakota, and the Beaver anchored beside it at Rumdoodle, were torn apart and wrenched away while the men who laboured to fly and maintain them watched helplessly, themselves lucky to escape from being whirled into eternity by the force of the mother of all blizzards. An Antarctic Division message of 13 December, transmitted from Mawson over makeshift aerials erected after the permanent radio masts had been destroyed by the force of the storm, recounted part of the grim story:[23]

> The blizzard was one of the worst ever experienced at Mawson, and was associated with a deep depression in the Southern Ocean. The barometer fell to 27.9 inches. Hurricane force winds bore down on Mawson and the ice plateau behind the station. Gusts at Mawson were as high as 116 mph, with the wind blowing for hours at about 80 mph. Up on the ice plateau nearby, at the airfield, they were estimated to be even higher. Some idea of the force of the hurricane is given by the fact that during the attempted rescue operations, men were lifted bodily into the air and thrown yards away to slide helplessly over the ice until rescued. Only the prompt action of men in holding on to each other prevented others being blown away with the wrecked parts of the Beaver aircraft which they were trying to save. Nothing further could be done without clearly jeopardising the lives of the men.

The Dakota earlier in the year had weathered winds of 110 mph. The most thorough methods of tie-down were devised and were still operating this week when the blizzard struck. The front tie-down cable of the Dakota broke inside the ice where it was secured. The fifteen-ton cable sheared at the junction to the undercarriage, and both seven-ton wing tie-down cables failed. The Dakota disappeared and has not yet been found. The Beaver was not large enough to break its cables; the tiedown lugs on the aircraft broke and the men then had the painful experience of watching helplessly whilst the plane itself disintegrated. The wings pulled out from the wing roots and the rear fuselage fractured. Back broken and wings torn apart, this plane rapidly broke up. The workshop caravan on the airfield broke its guys and was blown away. (See full report in Appendix III.)

An Auster on floats prepares for the take-off run. Locating the ship if adverse weather closed in was one of the hazards confronting the RAAF crews.

Down at the base, expedition members had to take shelter when lumps of ice amid the driving snow bombarded the huts. Fuel drum stacks collapsed, the drums careering down to the rocks at the edge of the harbour. Sleet transformed the surrounding rocks into an ice rink so slippery that crampons were needed to let the men move safely from hut to hut. A D4 tractor set out from the plateau to search for the Dakota, but on nearing a crevasse belt the journey had to be abandoned. Dog teams were then readied to resume the search as soon as the wind dropped. However, it was a base member riding his motorcycle along the sea ice who finally located the missing plane. The Dakota lay wedged nose-down in a large crevasse at the top of a 106-metre (350-foot) cliff above the sea. The blizzard had blown it a distance of 16 kilometres (10 miles) west of Mawson, leaving a trail of damage, the engines wrecked, the undercarriage and starboard wing smashed. Valuable navigation and other instruments were removed and taken back to base on the dog sledge; the aircraft itself was never recovered and as time went on only the top of the tail fin remained protruding above the drifting snow.

The ANARE emblem, designed by the late Nel Law.

For ANARE, the wrecking of the Beavers had been a bitter blow. Losing the Dakota and a third Beaver was the worst of all anti-climaxes, a ruinous stroke to a well-planned program of research and exploration. Yet, thankfully, no lives had been lost. The ANARE aviation program bravely continued for the next few years, but the writing was on the wall: the RAAF Antarctic flight no longer wintered-over; the government had obviously lost its enthusiasm for investing in expensive fixed-wing aircraft that fell victim to the raging blizzards.

The approach of 1960 had seen what could be termed the first air link between Australia and its Antarctic Territory when a seriously ill member of the wintering-over party at Wilkes had to be evacuated. The Russians had flown in to treat the same man seven months previously, making the first ever aircraft landing at Wilkes.[24] The only available transportation now lay with Operation Deep Freeze. From McMurdo the U.S. Navy sent in a P2V Neptune which spent just 2 hours and 18 minutes on a makeshift icecap strip while loading the patient and refuelling. During the rescue a second American aircraft, the R7V Constellation, circled the station with survival gear in case of a mishap. From McMurdo, a C-130 completed the mercy mission to Christchurch; a commercial flight was then used to reach Melbourne.[25]

The ill-fated Dakota, as prepared by the RAAF for a major aerial program over Australian Territory in 1960. It was ski-equipped and able to use JATO equipment; a furious storm cut short its active life.

In 1961 hopes were raised that Australia's polar force was in for a new deal when the *Financial Review* of 8 June reported that ANARE might be equipped with ski-fitted C-130BL Hercules, similar to the American transports. The big four-engine aircraft had the range to fly direct between Australia and, once reaching the coast, its three continental bases of Wilkes (Casey), Davis and Mawson. The newspaper continued: 'Polar experts claim the Hercules would effect great savings in the Australian Antarctic budget which is currently running at about £800,000 a year. The aircraft would reduce to a matter of hours the present weary weeks-long sea journey from Melbourne to the bases.'

Wreckage of the RAAF Beaver after the hurricane near Mawson in 1959.

About the same time, Dr Law, after one of many voyages through rough seas and hostile ice he endured each year, expressed a cautious hope that it would soon be possible for him and his expeditionaries to reach Antarctica in a matter of hours by aeroplane. All of it amounted to an idle hope. Over 30 years later Australia would still have no air link with its icy territory. If emergencies arose, if Australian lives were at stake, the government remained content to rely on the goodwill of the Russians and Americans. 'Let them spend the money and take the risks,' as one Antarctic cynic would say.[26] (Ironically, this same year saw the combined Russian–U.S. rescue of a sick Australian from Mawson; see Chapter 10.)

Then began another year of living dangerously. As the new expedition aboard *Thala Dan* approached the forbidding coast of Oates Land, Pilot Officer G. C. Cooper went out to photograph the King George V coast eastwards to Cape Freshfield. When close to the limit of the Beaver's range he was called back, advised that weather around the ship had closed in with fog and snow showers. Guided by radio compass, he managed to find the vessel, landing on a patch of open water where visibility was down to 100 metres (300 feet). But Phil Law, though forever a stickler for safety, was not one to let bad weather deter his plans to survey the Oates coast when good weather soon followed. 'Then our luck changed,' he said, 'and we had two full days and two half days of fine weather. My impatient men needed no urging...the Beaver float plane with the RAAF pilots made flight after flight for aerial photography and determination of the Plateau height up to 100 miles inland.'[27]

On 19 January the Beaver, with Gary Cooper again at the controls, had a closer brush with disaster. Two geologists were observing ice movements of the great John Quincy Adams Glacier, out from Wilkes base, when the engine failed. The alert came at 6.20 p.m. when a helicopter flying close to Wilkes received a radio message from the base flight control operator: 'We are losing contact with the Beaver...it may crash into the ice cliffs 60 miles to the south-east.'

Captain Hans Nielsen, who was in the harbour with *Thala Dan*, immediately ceased cargo operations and sailed towards Ivanoff Head, 80 kilometres (50 miles) away. Two helicopters, loaded with fuel and survival gear, went with the ship, then flew ahead to search the coastline. After about 30 minutes one of the helicopter pilots picked up Cooper on the radio. He was telling them, with the engine stopped, that he had barely managed to clear the ice cliffs by about 18 metres (60 feet) to land on open water.

Approaching the supply vessel *Nella Dan* off the Oates Land coast. Finding that ice had closed in around the ship was another hazard awaiting the crew, if the exploratory mission was made on floats.

The helicopter pilots soon after saw a Verey light signal, and turned to find the Beaver tied up in a tiny cove between the steep rocks of Ivanoff Head and the glacier tongue. The redoubtable Flight Sergeant Richardson and a helicopter mechanic were flown in to check the downed machine while *Thala Dan*, having negotiated ice-littered waters around the glacier outfall, reached the scene at 11.20 p.m., when the Beaver came taxiing out to meet it. With the aircraft lifted aboard, the ship returned to Wilkes base in the early hours of the morning. Once again the RAAF had brought back crew and aircraft intact. Living dangerously, yes — but more significantly, living to tell the tale.

The Vietnam war placed new demands on RAAF resources, and after 1963 the air force flight ceased to be a part of annual ANARE operations. Flying passed to non-military hands with a lone Beaver in civilian colours, augmented by chartered helicopters. The years that followed were marked by ANARE's lack of success in persuading the Federal government to spend money in enlarging and modernising a fixed-wing fleet, though a turbo Beaver and a Pilatus Porter were both employed under private contract as time went on.

In three decades of Antarctic aviation, Australia lost a total of 10 fixed-wing aircraft, mostly due to the relentless force of the blizzards.[28] Probably ANARE's worst reversal was the destructive storm of 1960 which swept away its only twin-engine machine, the RAAF-operated Dakota. It had held the promise of great things in helping to push back the unknown frontiers of the frozen south. In a sense, this was a loss from which the Australian expedition has not recovered.

Flightless Bird

Sir Douglas Mawson's 1911–14 Australasian Antarctic Expedition (AAE) pioneered the use of wireless communications with the outside world; but the aeroplane the scientist-explorer took to Commonwealth Bay never left the ice. Another Australian, Sir Hubert Wilkins, was to win the distinction of first Antarctic aviator, but on the far side of the continent with the backing of American money.

Mawson was an immensely resourceful and forward-looking leader. The Wright Brothers' flight with a heavier-than-air machine had been made less than eight years earlier when he elected to spend 1,200 guineas of AAE's funds on purchasing an aeroplane. Kathleen Scott, wife of the British explorer who was Antarctica-bound on his final and fatal expedition, possibly played some part in Mawson's decision. The bohemian Kathleen had flown in the aeroplane herself and claimed to have been instrumental in AAE's recruitment of a pilot — Lieutenant Hugh Watkins, of the Essex Regiment. However, Mawson's manner annoyed Mrs Scott when, during a display at Hendon aerodrome, he deserted her to speak with Shackleton. She recorded his action as ill-mannered and ungrateful and added 'the man is an ass'.

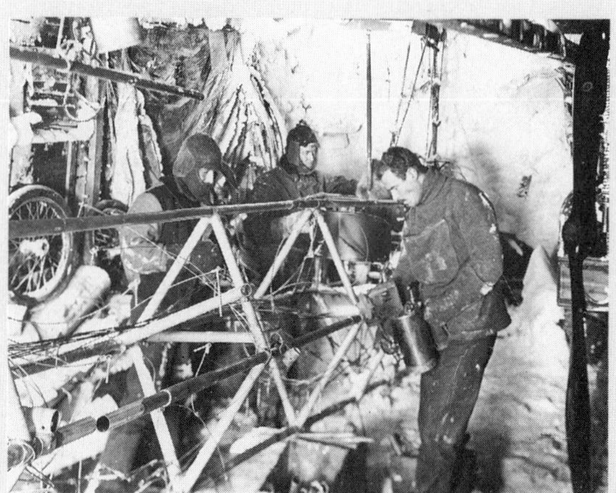

Empty packing cases provided the hangar for Sir Douglas Mawson's aircraft at Commonwealth Bay in 1912. Despite Frank Bickerton's attention, it proved fairly useless as a wingless bird.

Vickers supplied the monoplane from its works at Brooklands in Surrey. The spindle-shaped machine had a 15-metre (45-foot) wingspan, space for a pilot and one passenger and an 88-kph (56-mph) top speed. It was only the second REP type (taken from the initials of the French designer) that the company had built. 'It was intended,' wrote Mawson, 'that so far as its role as a flier was concerned, it would be chiefly exercised for the purpose of drawing public attention to the Expedition in Australia, where aviation then was almost unknown.'

However the demonstration program, when the aircraft was shipped to Adelaide late in 1911, proved to be short-lived. Early on the morning of 5 October Lieutenant Watkins took off with Frank Wild in the passenger seat. The crowd which had gathered at Cheltenham Racecourse, drawn by the sound of the engine, saw it swoop low, swerve and smash one wing into the ground. Luckily neither Watkins nor his passenger was injured — Frank Wild survived to lead AAE's Western Party and become one of the memorable figures in polar exploration.

A sorry Watkins returned to London, his chance of being an Antarctic 'first' denied. Undismayed, Mawson had both wings removed and the machine loaded on SY *Aurora* for Commonwealth Bay. 'Shackelton had tried a motor car,' he continued, 'and Scott had set out with caterpillar-tractor sledges. Though both useful to a certain degree, both had failed to be of any great service. We had decided to try an air tractor.'

Would Mawson have flown the aeroplane if it had remained intact? The question goes unanswered; certainly, the ferocity of the wind at Commonwealth Bay would have made aviation a very risky pursuit, if not downright impossible. As it was, the wingless machine, once in Antarctica, met with a sudden and ill-starred end.

Frank Bickerton, the expedition's mechanical 'wiz' seemed to spend much of 1912 tinkering with the air tractor. To the long skis (intended to protect it from falling into crevasses) which augmented the four-wheel landing gear, he added home-made brakes fashioned from a pair of rock drills. A speed of 30 kph (20mph) was attained on 15 November to the depot they called Aladdin's Cave. On 3 December three men, with Bickerton driving the spluttering machine which had four sledges in tow, set out to examine the coastal ice slope west of Commonwealth Bay. Speed did not reach much above a crawl and, 16 kilometres (10 miles) south of the base a horrible noise came from the motor, which stopped so suddenly that the propeller shattered.

Technology was not in step with Mawson's ambitions. 'Had Adelie Land been favoured with a normal Antarctic climate,' he said, 'or a surface to travel over comparable with the Ross Barrier, where its rivals had been put to the test, there would have been a very different tale to tell.' In a continuing extract from *Home of the Blizzard*, he then recounts the abrupt demise of Antarctica's first 'aeroplane':

> An hour after leaving the camp Aladdin's Cave was passed. The three men with the air-tractor towing a chain of four loaded sledges continued on towards Cathedral Grotto. Very soon the engine developed an internal disorder which Bickerton was at a loss to diagnose or remedy. This necessitated pitching camp for the night before the Grotto was reached. At 4 p.m. next day, after drifting snow had subsided, the engine was started once more. Its behaviour, however, indicated that something was the matter with one or more of the cylinders. Bickerton was on the point of deciding to take the engine to pieces, when his thoughts were brought to a sudden close by the engine, without any warning, pulling up with such a jerk that the propeller was smashed. A moment's examination showed that even more irremediable damage had occurred inside the engine, so there was nothing left but to abandon the air-tractor and continue on the journey man-hauling their sledge. At a later date Bickerton succeeded in bringing the air-tractor back to the Hut where it was opened up and examined. It appeared that several of the pistons had seized and were broken. (Mawson 1930: 241–4)

The flightless bird remained at Commonwealth Bay until achieving its only real flight in Antarctica — it was finally blown away.

Wreckage of a more recent era lies outside Mawson, where wind and shifting ice have claimed a Russian Li-2 transport which was disabled in a rough landing.

Your heroic, honourable work in the name of science, in the rigorous conditions of the Antarctic, move the honest admiration of all mankind.

Chairman Khrushchev's greeting to Americans in Antarctica

10

RED WINGS

Original 'workhorse' aircraft of the Soviet Antarctic Expedition, an Li-2 is posed at Mirnyy for the Moscow media.

'At last they were there, fourteen smiling Russians in their leather trousers and jerkins and long black boots,' wrote Mike Lucas, recalling stormy weather that brought Russian aircraft to Mawson in January 1962. 'The planes were fuelled and tied down. At 11.30 p.m., the six Australians and the Russians all climbed into the Weasel and sledge and set out, up along the moraine line that leads to Rumdoodle (the airstrip where a caravan served as an "air terminal").' The description by the Australian expeditionary continued:

> Somehow all twenty-one of us crammed into the one small fourteen by seven foot caravan, sitting on the top bunks, bottom bunks and on each other's knees. In this remote place, where the silence of the great rock mountains rising sheer from the surrounding ice is only broken by the audible swish of snow petrels as they dive and bank around the buttresses high above, there followed the most extraordinary party I have ever witnessed.
>
> The chicken was passed round, the 'plonk' and 'clubbers' uncorked, and much linking of arms, clinking of glasses and cries of 'friendship' ensued.

The adventure was not quite over. The pair of An-2 aircraft had already been forced down on the plateau before the Russians found a safe haven at Mawson. Next came a hair-raising sledge trip from the caravan to reach the parked aircraft:

> We piled out into the cold Antarctic twilight. Mattresses were laid on the sledge and the passengers wrapped up in blankets. Off we go: Cheers — this is splendid! I look back from the driver's seat—on the sledge thumbs up, bottles waving and cheers! It's a glorious 'night'. One a.m. and the sun just hidden, the ice shining, the motor humming and the sleds singing.
>
> Suddenly the sledge starts to side slip, faster, faster. I can't hold the Weasel straight; round we all go in a jerking tail flip. When the mattresses, bodies, bottles and blankets were all sorted out . . . on we go — a little slower now and soon reach the parked aircraft. It is 1.30 in the morning, temperature below zero. The Russians collect their luggage and we set off again. The Weasel feels funny; I stop and look back. There is our right-hand track neatly laid out on the ice behind us. There are no alternatives. We must walk the nine miles home.
>
> Each evening while the visitors were at Mawson we had a party where they entertained us with Russian dancing and singing to the accompaniment of a splendid guitar player. We returned with hakas, jive and Australian bush songs. Presents were exchanged. Two ballet films, vodka and cigarettes for us. Australian wine, cigarettes, records and a set of stamps and photographs for them. Monday saw their reluctant departure. Goodbye, Russkies — see you in Moscow.

Mike Lucas's episode illustrates one of the many visits which the friendly Soviet expeditionaries made to the Australian National Antarctic Research Expedition (ANARE) bases and to those of other nations operating in Antarctica.[1] Hardly had the Soviet team settled in for the International Geophysical Year of 1957–58 than the goodwill calls began. Sometimes they radioed ahead. Sometimes they just 'dropped in'. On other occasions, hostile weather drove them to seek shelter. Early occupants of Australia's tiny Davis base beside the Vestfold Hills fondly remembered an unexpected IL-12 aircraft which landed on its way from Mawson to Mirnyy to await a weather clearance. The Russian crew and the Australians spent a memorable night 'films, Russian cigarettes, vodka and general goodwill making it a very happy meeting. An almost unwelcome favourable weather report next morning brought the visit to an early close'.

One could never be sure what contingent of VIPs might step from the Russian plane. Among the five scientists and crew of six who landed at Mawson for a four-hour stay during the IGY were Messrs Tolstikov, leader of the Soviet expedition and a veteran of the North Pole drift stations, Ostrekin the chief scientist and Bugaev chief meteorologist at Mirnyy. Dr Alexander Dralkin, chief of the Arctic and Antarctic Institute, Leningrad (St Petersburg), and expedition leader called at Davis on an overnight stop. Dralkin, a noted oceanographer, asked to be taken to the open water lakes of the ice-free rocky region surrounding Davis where he wandered around Long Fjord and Club Lake taking samples of water for analysis at Mirnyy laboratory.

The main Australian base, with its bay ice strip and later a skiway on the plateau at Rumdoodle, frequently proved an invaluable emergency landing place. Dralkin led the IL-12 team which left Mirnyy on 12 October 1959 to make the longest Antarctic flight yet attempted by a Russian aircraft, across the 3,600 kilometres (2,250 miles) separating Mirnyy and the New Lazarev base on the Princess Astrid Coast of Queen Maud Land. They left Mirnyy in blowing drift and, on the first leg of their westbound route received regular reports of conditions ahead from Mawson. With the storm worsening, they homed on the Mawson radio beacon and advised that they needed refuge. Meanwhile an Australian party had marked a 1,160-metre (3,800-foot) landing place on the sea ice to the west of the base, and stood by with a Weasel transport and tie-down equipment. Directional flares were lit and out of the overcast came the twin-engine machine, to set down safely on the ready made strip. Dralkin and his five-man team spent a week at Mawson waiting for clear weather, during which time they joined in the normal activities of the base, including a short tractor journey to the interior.[2]

The 'happy hour' at Mirnyy, first main base of the Soviet expedition. Some 160 men and women lived at Mirnyy in the early years of the base's establishment.

Sometimes an arrival could really tax ANARE's accommodation facilities. Sixteen Russians were on the aircraft piloted by the veteran A. Pimenov, and including their leader Dr Korotkevitch. Their brief refuelling stop in late 1960 became a three-day stay when a blizzard locked them in — however 'a very pleasant visit was enjoyed by everyone'.

Not every Soviet aircraft landing was the signal for one big party. Sometimes the mission was a matter of life and death. The case of Alan Newman remains a prime example of international help and cooperation from the 'big two' of Antarctic exploration. The sixth Russian expedition was in residence at Mirnyy when it received an urgent request to pick up a member of the Mawson base team who had fallen desperately ill. Both Russian and American assistance would be needed to get the sick man out. What followed in the words of the then Commonwealth Minister for External Affairs was 'a reflection on the manner in which exploration and scientific research are being conducted in Antarctica, and of the spirit of the 12-power Antarctic Treaty'.

Alan Newman, a 41-year-old diesel mechanic, suddenly collapsed with a cerebral haemorrhage on 2 November 1961. The Mawson medical officer, Dr

Russell Pardoe, radioed for the guidance of a Melbourne surgeon in preparing the two delicate operations to save Newman's life, one on 30 November and the second on 3 December. Dr Pardoe had not performed this type of surgery before; his assistants were a geophysicist who gave the anaesthetic and the cook as general nurse. The patient improved briefly, then suffered a relapse. The Australian base had no aircraft and the next supply ship was two months off.[3] Melbourne received another radio message: survival depended on full-scale hospital attention.

Calling briefly into Sydney was the IL-18D long-range airliner, en route to Mirnyy via Christchurch and McMurdo Sound. Dr Phil Law, head of the Antarctic Division, flew from Melbourne on 22 December to intercept the expedition leaders. In Canberra, the External Affairs people made a formal approach to the Soviet ambassador. Without hesitation, the Russians agreed to help.

Meanwhile at Mawson, the patient's condition continued to deteriorate. In Dr Pardoe's opinion, they needed to get to Mirnyy which had three doctors and more extensive hospital facilities to keep him alive until evacuation might be possible. The Australians did not have a 'wheel' airstrip; nor, since a disastrous blizzard, did they have an aircraft. Over again to the Russians who had a ski-equipped Li-2 transport on its way. By 30 December they were at Mirnyy at the close of a four hour journey — but only the start of a long haul home. Then the patient suffered an allergic shock. 'I thought I was going to lose him,' Dr Pardoe said. 'His blood pressure went down and mine went up.' Reaching a hospital in the outside world became ever more urgent.

The Ilyushin airliner reached Mirnyy on the first direct flight from Moscow (which is another story) on 27 December. By 4 January, Newman's condition had stabilised sufficiently to permit a start on the exit flight. Bad weather frustrated the first take-off but by next day they were flying the 2,700 kilometres (1,700 miles) which separated the Russians from the American base on McMurdo Sound. The Australians received the full attention of the U.S. Navy sick bay, allowing Dr Pardoe who had hardly left his patient's bedside for two months to win some rest. The Russians said goodbye, leaving Rear Admiral David Tyree, commander of Operation Deep Freeze, to organise the next step in a remarkable feat of international cooperation. The navy's LC-130 Hercules stood by to fly the next 3,800-kilometre (2,400-mile) leg from McMurdo to New Zealand, still with Dr Pardoe in attendance for fear that an emergency might arise.

They reached Christchurch on the morning of 8 January, where a commercial flight was waiting for the final trip to Australia. Alan Newman awoke in February and wondered about the year that was missing from his life. He recalled sailing from Melbourne in January 1961 and that was all; Antarctica remained a blank in his memory. To reporters who visited him in St Vincent's Hospital, Sydney, he said, 'When I woke up I couldn't remember a thing. I recognised my mother but I could not recognise my wife. In fact I was yelling out that I wasn't married. It was pretty embarrassing'. His weight had almost halved from his 16 stone.

The Newman story was but one of numerous emergency missions to the credit of Russian aviators — they had already made a dash to Wilkes at the onset of winter in 1959.[4] Except for the Americans, the resources at Mirnyy of Polyarnaya Aviatsiya far outstripped those of every other aviation endeavour — certainly those of ANARE's slender wing. From the first year, callers at Mirnyy airstrip would see the line-up of one or two IL-12 passenger planes, four or more Li-2 transports, several An 2 light cabin machines as well as a covey of Mi-4 helicopters. Several of the aircraft were equipped for photo-reconnaissance, with a supporting corps of photo interpreters. The An-2 and the Li-2, the latter a DC-3 look-alike, were mounted on skis; beginning with the fourth expedition (1958–60) the heavier IL-12, similar to the American twin-engine Convair, was given skis.[5]

A force of about 100 men came to winter-over with the early Soviet expeditions, about 20 of them being members of the aviation detachment. The veteran Arctic aviator, I. I. Cherevichny, led the pioneer air group which reached the site of Mirnyy on 6 January 1956. Within little more than a month, non-stop reconnaissance flights had reached the South Magnetic Pole and on 3 March probed to 78° South in the zone of the lofty Pole of Inaccessibility. An urgent task for the aviators was finding a path for surface transport through the 48-kilometre (30-mile) crevasse belt which lay behind the base. Fixed-wing machines of the first expedition made 253 'first time landings' in different parts of the continent and on supply runs delivered some 200 tonnes of goods from ship to shore. Little time was lost in sending aircraft on exploratory missions, far south above the polar plateau and east and west from Mirnyy along the coast. The first IL-12 flew across the South Pole on 25 October 1958 after a round trip of nearly 14 hours from Mirnyy; a call was made at McMurdo Sound on the return leg. Surveying a route for the epic seismic traverse planned for the following year was one purpose of the aerial marathon. Another South Pole flight was then planned for 1960 to complete the work of the tractor team.[6]

In 1957, Russian aviators noted a mammoth iceberg, estimated to measure several thousand square kilometres, apparently aground on a shoal to the north-east of the Shackleton Ice Shelf, about 320 kilometres (200 miles) from Mirnyy. Within a couple of years, they planned to set-up a temporary observatory on the 'berg, landing transports on the surface to discharge men and equipment. The journal *Water Transport* of 19 May 1960, described the making of the unusual camp:

> Beneath the wing of the aeroplane there lies a colossal iceberg. The edges are heavily snowed under, and in a number of places smooth slopes descend to the sea ice. Obviously, many years ago this giant tore itself away from the Shackleton Ice Shelf and, drifting off, struck a submerged elevation. Here it remained grounded. Choosing a suitable place, pilot A. Pimenov landed the heavy transport plane. The gangway was lowered and the first people descended to the surface of the ice giant. Swiftly we unloaded stores, and then welcome A. Barbanov's aircrew. Within an hour a sturdy winter tent has been set up and all stores collected around it. When the aircraft departed for Mirnyy, it left behind on the iceberg three scientists and a radio operator . . . they have before them nearly two months of scientific observations at the station which we have named 'Pobeda'.

To reach the site of Lazarev base when thick ice blocked the passage of the supply vessel *Ob*, again the Russians chose a handy 'large iceberg' as a take-off point for the aircraft ferrying men and materials the 350 kilometres (220 miles) to shore. Pilot A. Pimenov, who headed the aviation detachment of the fifth expedition, made a memorable 11½ hour flight in his IL-14, following the coastline at an altitude of 4,900 metres (16,000 feet).[7] His fellow airmen took an Li-2 for the first time across the same route in the face of heavy weather during the 1960 expedition.

Australia Had No Aircraft

From Dr R.. Pardoe's account of illness and treatment of Mr A. Newman at Mawson in 1961–62:

Throughout the illness, advice was given by a Melbourne neurosurgeon by means of radio-telegrams. Neither the medical officer nor anyone else at Mawson had any previous experience in neuro surgery. Two men had attended Royal Melbourne Hospital for 2 weeks before sailing for Antarctica.

With aid of some illustrations from an instrument catalogue, a brain cannula was fashioned from a dental dry-air bulb syringe. In order to test these and other instruments a Weddell Seal was shot with a .38 revolver and the resultant cerebral haematoma was aspirated by the technique to be used on the patient. The medical officer recruited four assistants — the cook as theatre sister, the geophysicist to administer the anaesthetic, the ionospheric physicist to monitor cardiovascular function and the weather observer as 'dirty nurse'.

Surgery in the makeshift operating theatre began at 10.15 p.m. on the 28th day after the detection of symptoms, and concluded four hours later. A burr-hole was made over the left frontal lobe, 1 inch from the midline. The brain bulged through the incised dura.

The cannula was introduced downwards and slightly backwards, and aspiration was attempted at 1 cm. intervals. At a depth of 4 cm., 20 ml of old dark blood, blood clot, and necrotic brain tissue were aspirated. Another operation followed. Three of the attendants assisted in providing 24-hour care.

On Day 51...patient's prognosis extremely poor. Condition deteriorating...facilities for adequate investigation unavailable. No way of evacuating him. Relief ship not due Mawson until late January and back in Melbourne late March after rough voyage. From the onset of the illness, it had been apparent that aerial evacuation from Antarctica was desirable. Australia had no aircraft based in Antarctica, its four aircraft having been destroyed by blizzards in 1959 and 1960. All American and Soviet aircraft had heavy resupply commitments. Moreover the long flight from Mawson to McMurdo Sound (2,000 miles) was a serious undertaking for a medium-sized twin-engine Soviet aircraft based at Mirnyy, a fact emphasised in November by the crash of an American aircraft at Wilkes (en route Mirnyy-McMurdo) with loss of five lives.

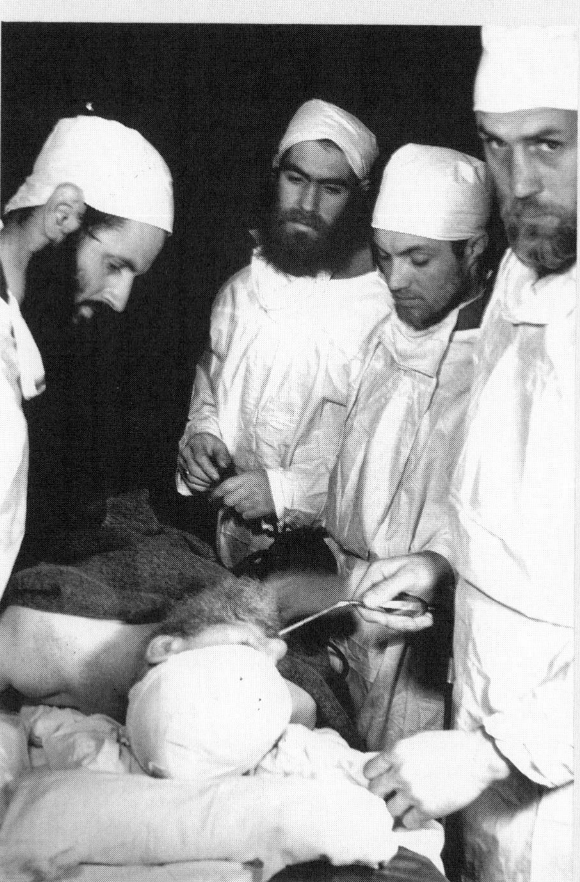

The makeshift operating theatre at Mawson where Dr Russell Pardoe is about to commence delicate surgery on a patient suffering a cerebral haemorrhage.

Then it was learned that two long range Soviet aircraft were making the inaugural flight from Moscow to Mirnyy...requested Soviet aid which was willingly given. December...Day 58: Li-2, en route NovoLaz–Mirnyy, landed to refuel at Rumdoodle, on plateau 11 miles from Mawson. December 30, the Li-2 flew the 720 miles to Mirnyy at altitude from 600–2,000 feet because unpressurised. Patient on stretcher on long range fuel tank. Two soviet

'Condition deteriorating . . . no way of evacuating him ...Australia had no aircraft.' The patient, Alan Newman, is lifted into a Russian Li-2 which will make the mercy flight to Mirnyy.

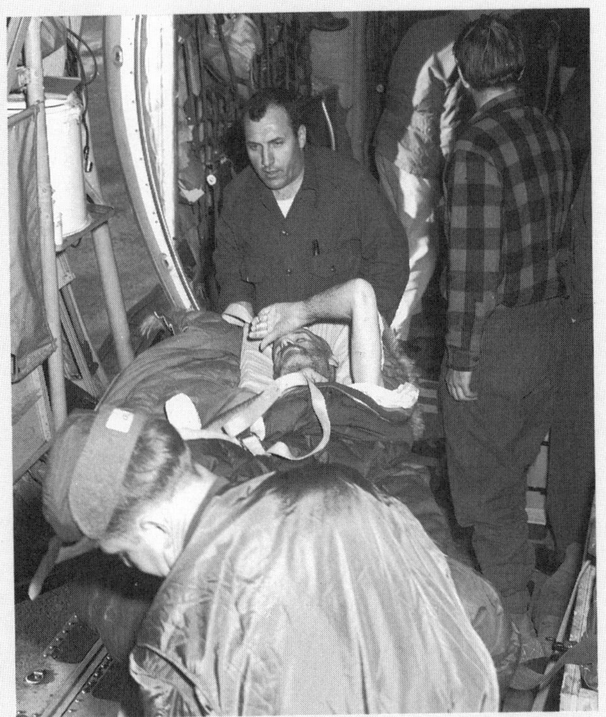

A Russian IL-18D has carried the patient to McMurdo Sound. In the third stage of the multi-nation evacuation, Mr Newman is settled in an American LC-130 for the next leg to Christchurch, New Zealand.

medical officers helped [at Mirnyy]. Milk feeds every 2 hours in snow covered sick bay.

Day 62 [2 January, 1962] Soviet decided to make special evacuation to McMurdo in IL-18. However McMurdo advised turboprop fuel contaminated by water, and one day delay until filtered. Then another day's delay because of blizzard at Mirnyy. In early hours of day 66, took off for McMurdo. After one hour's flying at 27,000 ft patient became cyanosed and thereafter given continuous oxygen from aircraft emergency portable bottles. Arrived McMurdo after 1,600 miles and 4 hours. Taken by helicopter to USN sick bay where for 36 hours nursed by USN medical corps.

Then $7\frac{1}{2}$ hours in LC-130 to Christchurch, then to TEAL [commercial airline] to Sydney. On evening of day 69 arrived St Vincents Hospital 10 days after departing Mawson. By late April patient had recovered memory up to time of illness.

(Extracts by kind permission of *Medical Journal of Australia* from 6 March 1965 issue.)

In the early years of Soviet Antarctic exploration, an An-2 scout aircraft is lowered from the supply vessel *Lena*.

On the sixth expedition (1961–62), which reported 2,000 flying hours in making the supply runs, pilots N. Sytepanov and S. Tarasov flew their Li-2 from the Pravda Coast to Queen Maud Land — Mirnyy to Novolazarevskaya — calling for fuel at Mawson where, according to a Tass news item, 'the Australians joyfully greeted the Soviet explorers and thanked them for the aid rendered to Alan Newman'.[8] They also called at the Japanese expedition's Syowa base on Ongul Island in Lutzow-Holm Bay, where another fuel dump existed, and then onwards to Novolazarevskaya.

Trained in Arctic skies, the Russians were no strangers to the hazards of polar aviation, nor to damage that could be sustained in ice and blizzard, except that in Antarctica they would be far more remote and face a new intensity of storm and cold that belonged to nowhere else but this other end of the earth.[9] During one frightening journey, an Li-2 with six crew aboard, caught in wild windcurrents while crossing the enormous breadth of the Lambert Glacier, dropped 550 metres (1,800 feet) in the space of seconds. 'With some relief,' they made it to Mawson. Ferocious gales tore at moored aircraft, lifted them against the heavy tie-down cables, tossing them like toys from side to side. The Russian public read of the devastating hurricane which broke upon Mirnyy on the night of 3 July 1961 with wind velocity reaching 160 kph (52 m/sec). Driving snow blanketed the searchlight beacon, so that with visibility down to three paces it was suicide to venture outside. The radio operations building, secured to an ice-free area, swayed under the blizzardly onslaught, as if in a storm at sea. From the airstrip, an Li-2 was wrenched from its steel hawsers, hurled over a 25-metre (80-foot) drop to the sea ice and wrecked.

The (Antonov) An -2, a sturdy cabin biplane widely used by Russian explorers in moving field parties.

The explorers who reached Mawson in March 1957 told of sheltering helplessly for five days while a raging blizzard gradually tore the camp apart around them. The party of 16 men were at a geological field outpost 220 kilometres (140 miles) from Molodezh on Alasheev Bay, close to the base of Mount Riiser-Larsen on Vernadasky Peninsula. They set up camp and had their two aircraft anchored nearby when the storm struck. In wind raging up to 200 kph (125 mph) one plane was wrecked, their tents shredded, the field kitchen was carried away and equipment, rations and belongings were scattered. They managed to save the second aircraft and, during a lull in the storm, eight of them took off for Mawson. Those remaining had to shelter against the rocks of the mountainside when the wind returned. The rescue plane from Mirnyy was forced to land and had to shelter at Mawson until the weather calmed. After five days the men could count themselves fortunate that the loss was in equipment and not in lives.

Sometimes aircraft were safer in the sky — on the surface the record of destruction was high. Nothing could be done to save the eight men who perished at Mirnyy in the fire which destroyed the meteorological building during a blizzard in the term of the fifth expedition in 1960.

Medical emergencies challenged the Russians to new feats of polar flying. Late in July 1964, Molodezhnaya in Enderby Land signalled the main base: 'Urgent transport required for sick man. Surgical treatment necessary'. The ice coast lay shrouded in the gloom of the south polar night.[10] From Mirnyy to Molodezh and back meant a journey of 4,000 kilometres (2,500 miles). On the morning of 26 July the plane set out, buffeted by strong wind, following a course through darkness along the Antarctic coast. Seven hours out from Mirnyy, a row of bonfires on the ice indicated that Molodezh was waiting. The crew spent less than half an hour on the surface, the aircraft was refuelled and checked, the patient and his doctor brought aboard. A green flare went up to signal a clear runway, and in the face of gusting winds they were airborne again. Hours later the radio operator turned to the pilot and shouted, 'Receiving Mirnyy. Wishing us a good landing'. The sick man was taken to the base hospital for a successful operation; the first long-distance winter flight was placed on the record of Russian aviation in Antarctica.

Establishing Vostok station at the South Geomagnetic Pole and reaching the Pole of Inaccessibility were major achievements of the Soviet expeditions.[11] Vostok lies 1,400 kilometres (870 miles) south of Mirnyy at an elevation of 3,500 metres (11,500 feet) on the polar plateau. By tractor train and aircraft the Russians set up a remote outpost at the coldest inhabited place on earth. Aerial reconnaissance found the site for the base at 78°27'South and 106°52'East, then brought in equipment and supplies as the tractor train progressed. Vostok experiences total darkness from 24 April to 18 August. A world-record low temperature fell to –88°C (–127°F) on 24 August 1960 — even lower readings would follow. The first tractor train with building materials and equipment from Mirnyy, under the command of A. F. Treshnikov, reached the site on 16 December 1957. Supplies at first were parachuted in a technique perfected by the Russians in the Arctic in 1937 until a 2,450-metre (8,000-foot) skiway was completed across the plateau. During the second half of October 1957, the Li-2 brought in 40 tonnes of fuel and supplies by parachute drop. The first Li-2 landed three days before Christmas of 1958. The first twin engine IL-12 came in on 8 December 1959.

Air drops over Vostok were made as early as September and as late as 22 March. In August the team reported an average daily temperature of –71°C (–96°F). Forty supply flights were reported reaching the base in the 1961 season at the sixth–seventh expedition changeover. Other supply flights came to Komsomolskaya, an intermediate depot and observatory for the tractor trains high on the icesheet and 850 kilometres (530 miles) from the coast. Landing strips were prepared for the flights from Mirnyy; on 14 November 1960 an Li-2 landed near the tractor train to pick up an expedition member who was taken back to base for an appendectomy. Said Yuri Arshenevsky, Chief Engineer, Northern Sea Route Administration, USSR Ministry of the Merchant Marine: 'Aviation serves as eyes of the Soviet expeditions. Both the landing on the ice continent and the organisation of inland research stations was always preceded by air reconnaissance'.

The formidable Soviet program of the IGY covered three major thrusts — exploration, mapping and the pursuit of many scientific disciplines, both at base observatories and in the field.[11] At the major stations of Mirnyy, Vostok, Molodezh and Novolazarevskaya the scientific program included studies related to geomagnetism, ionosphere, aurora, cosmic rays, glaciology, geology, meteorology, seismology, earth currents and medicine. Oceanography was conducted from the supply ships.

At the start of the IGY, the Soviet Academy announced an ambitious plan related to creating a geographic map of the whole Antarctic continent. The announcement said 'the Soviets intend to map one third of Antarctica in the next five years'. Cameras of 36 mm focal length would be mounted in high flying aircraft traversing 100 kilometres (62 miles) apart, to produce a new map covering from 46° East to the boundary of the Ross Sea. The process of discovery added many new mountains, glaciers, ice shelves, islands and capes that went into the drawing of 50 detailed maps on which some 300 new topographical features appeared.

As wings spread across the ice in the early years of the expedition, the Soviet media continued to report a series of dramatic finds in 'unknown Antarctica'. Boris Osipov's 1959 round trip of 6,700 kilometres (4,160 miles) from Mirnyy to Lazarev included stops at the Belgian station of Roi Baudouin, Japan's Syowa base as well as Australia's Mawson and Davis. Along the way, Osipov and expedition leader Alexander Dralkin reported locating two new mountain ranges over 3,000 metres (10,000 feet) above sea level at 72°South and 16°East. Another of Osipov's flights brought the first aircraft to land at Wilkes where a member of the recently installed Australian party needed medical assistance; immobilised by a 60-knot blizzard, the Russians stayed for three days.

To the last drop of oil! The graphic signal sent to Viktor Perov, pilot of an aircraft searching for lost Belgian explorers in Eastern Antarctica, characterised the dedication of yet another Russian mercy mission. From Roi Baudouin base on the Princess Ragnhild Coast of Queen Maud Land, an Auster had flown towards the 'Crystal' (Sor Rondane) Mountains on 5 January 1959, but failed to keep a field party rendezvous.[12]

Four men were aboard the missing plane, their leader being Adrian de Gerlache, son of the Belgian polar pioneer of 50 years before. A tractor and two sledges nosed into a crevasse as a rescue party pushed out, knowing that the missing men had rations sufficient for only ten days. Pilot Perov, with a team of six fellow Russians including an interpreter flew the 2,500 kilometres (1,550 miles) from Mirnyy to reach the search area in response to the Belgians' call for help. On 14 January the Li-2 crew landed close to the damaged and abandoned Auster, where a note from de Gerlache told them the four were making for an emergency depot on foot.

Testimony to the cooperating U.S.-Russian relationship in Antarctica, a large crate lettered 'Vostok' is delivered by a U.S. Navy LC-130 to the coldest inhabited base on earth.

For five hours Perov flew a zigzag pattern above the trail in the snow, but without result. Next day they landed beside another deserted camp and though the Li-2's fuel reserve was running low, the signal from Mirnyy relayed through Mawson base, told Perov to continue the search. The Russian command meanwhile sent the freighter *Ob* to break through to King Leopold Bay with a fresh load of fuel. On 15 January, the day when rations should have been exhausted, Perov sighted the little orange dot of a tent on the icesheet, with four figures standing beside it. The Belgians, all alive and well, were returned to base; in the two days of an almost non-stop rescue bid, the Russians had flown 3,970 kilometres (2,466 miles) in a span of 20 hours.

Reaching the position known to the Russians as the 'Pole of Inaccessibility' at 2,200 kilometres (1,367 miles) from the coast on the polar plateau was another feat of Russian aviation. The third expedition's leader, E. Y. Tolstikov, and chief pilot V. M. Perov achieved the first landing at the remote Pole which, at an elevation of 4,100 metres (13,450 ft), is identified as the most remote and, as the name suggests, most inaccessible point of the Antarctic continent.

Andrei Kapitza made the surface seismic traverse to the South Pole in 1959 and then led his Kharkovchanka tractor group from Vostok to the 'Pole of Inaccessibility'. The marathon journey then took them northwards to the new coastal base of Molodezhnaya — 16 men journeying over 2,700 kilometres (1,680 miles). Pilots reported the extreme difficulty in visually locating these interior traverses amid the white immensity of the plateau, a task compounded by low cloud cover, strong winds and an utter lack of surface features. But the minuscule dark spot that indicated the slowly crawling tractor trains would inevitably be found and parachute supply drops made, including on at least one occasion with 'luscious watermelon from Tashkent'.[13]

It was while on an IL-12 supply drop to a tractor train that pilot Valentin Melnikov reported from the traverse leader's message that they had reached a point known as the Pole of Cold at 81° South and 80° East on the Sovietsky Plateau, approximately halfway between Vostok and the Pole of Inaccessibility.[14] Here the estimated average temperature stood at –60°C (–76°F) with a low point of around –100°C (–148°F).

On V. M. Perov's supply flight of 8 December 1958 from Mirnyy to the tractor train making for the Pole of Inaccessibility, he reported during the return trip of flying above a previously unexplored region and discovering a range of 17 peaks that appeared to be part of an extension to the Prince Charles Mountains; one pyramid-shaped peak, half covered in snow, he estimated at 3,000 metres (10,000 ft) above sea level. Flights out of Lazarev in the 1959–60 season among the Wohlthat and Sor Rondane Mountains came upon two new groups of peaks of the same elevation in the vicinity of 72° South and 16° East.

Chairman Khrushchev beat the table on behalf of Communism and declared to the capitalist world, 'We will bury you'. And while the iron curtain grew more solid and impassable, and ICBMs were poised to bring mutual destruction to the West and East, something remarkably different was happening in Antarctica. The deep seated antagonism between the Communist and non-Communist worlds seemed singularly lacking. In a sense, the cold, white ice cap stripped ideologies of their stupidity in the struggle to study, live and survive; or was it that the peacefulness of remote Antarctica inspired men to behave like brothers. For all its roaring blizzards, stormy oceans and deep crevasses, they lived together in a continent of goodwill and peace: no cold war.

Said Dr Mikhael Somov, leader of two Antarctic expeditions and a Hero of the Soviet Union: 'Everywhere the Soviet people receive a warm welcome, enjoy friendly relations and find others ready to help — at the Japanese base; at the Belgian base of King Baudouin; at the American base of McMurdo, reminiscent of a big transit airport...McMurdo extended thoughtful hospitality, fuelling the aircraft, putting their aerodrome at our disposal for landings and take-offs'.[15] The Japanese extended a refuelling service to Russian aircraft which might have to land at Syowa. During the fifth expedition, an Li 2 set out from Lazarev to find a path for the Belgian supply ship, *Erika Dan,* to Roi Baudouin station. The tractor party which reached Pole station in December 1959 was met with a warm welcome and spent three days relaxing and enjoying American hospitality at Amundsen-Scott. Two days later Chairman Khrushchev sent a message of goodwill to American scientists and sailors serving with Operation Deep Freeze. 'Your heroic, honourable work in the name of science, in the rigorous conditions of the Antarctic, move the honest admiration of all mankind'. In praising the role of the Antarctic Treaty, he added: 'I wish you good health great happiness and further success in the scientific investigations'.[16]

Rear Admiral Jim Reedy paid a seven-hour visit to Mirnyy in November 1965 and on alighting from his U.S. Navy LC-130 Hercules found lunch waiting on a laden table. A Russian crew who landed at the South Pole had their IL-14 refuelled from U.S. Navy supplies and were given continuous weather briefings for the continuation of their flight. Russian reciprocation was evident when a Hercules, caught in bad weather which closed McMurdo and Pole stations, was forced to divert to Vostok.[17]

Russia's Rights in Antarctica

Russia links its historic right of Antarctic participation to the voyage of Admiral F. F. Bellingshausen and his deputy, M. P. Lazarev, in 1815. In July of that year, according to Russian historians, the two explorers in their ships *Mirnyy* and *Vostok* were the first to sight and chart the hitherto unknown southland. In a paper given by Evengi Tolstikov, leader of the third expedition, Bellingshausen's mission was, 'do all in his power and make great efforts to approach as closely as possible to the Pole ... seeking unknown lands and giving up the undertaking only in case of insurmountable handicaps. Following these instructions the Russian seamen, overcoming the elements, were the first in history to approach the ice continent of Antarctica ... then they made a cruise around it.'

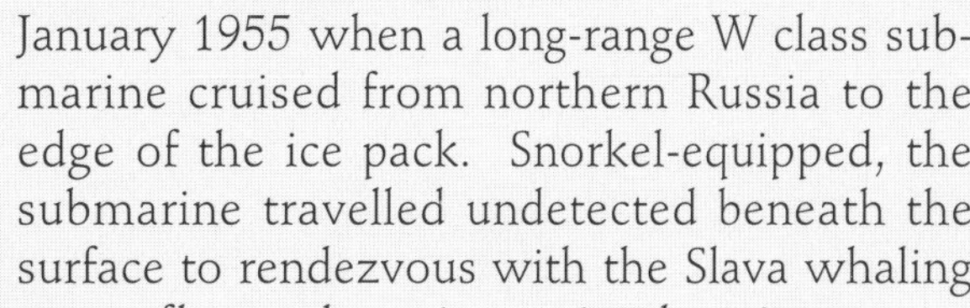

Admiral Bellingshausen: his exploration is the historic key to Russia's Antarctica presence.

The Soviet government alarmed the non-Communist world, and most certainly those nations with Antarctic territories, when prior to the International Geophysical Year (IGY) it announced a firm intention of taking a seat at any conference relating to the future of the south polar continent. Speculation about the Soviet's true intentions towards Antarctica was raised in January 1955 when a long-range W class submarine cruised from northern Russia to the edge of the ice pack. Snorkel-equipped, the submarine travelled undetected beneath the surface to rendezvous with the Slava whaling fleet where it received maintenance and refuelling. On returning to the home port of Murmansk, the captain and crew were congratulated and awarded decorations by the Commander in Chief of the Northern Fleet, Admiral Chobanenko.[18]

Reflecting the uneasy mood of the times, Rear Admiral Byrd told a New York audience during a speech in 1949 that the Russians were looking for uranium deposits in Antarctica. Soviet scientists were known to be aboard the Slava fleet, using ships as a base to prospect on ice-free portions of the polar coast. (The whaling ships which sailed from Odessa in 1949 and 1950 carried a team of scientists.)

Prior to the IGY, comments in the press sometimes raised the likelihood of the Soviet bases being used for military purposes, such as missile launch sites, to tighten the threat on the Southern Hemisphere and its shipping lanes.

Militaristic eventualities were shown to be without foundation as nationals of the various IGY countries, notably the United States, took up residence at Mirnyy and elsewhere, while Russian scientists went on exchange postings to Deep Freeze bases.[19]

Heading for a waiting IL-14, members of the expedition tramp across the bay ice from a moored supply vessel. The larger Ilyushin machine, when equipped with skis, took over the major interior flights and was the first Russian aircraft type to reach the South Pole.

Eyes of the Soviet Expedition

Said Yuri Arshenevsky, Chief Engineer, Northern Sea Route Administration of the USSR Merchant Marine:

Aviation serves as eyes of the Soviet expeditions. Both the landing on the ice continent and the organisation of inland research stations was always preceded by air reconnaissance. Every time when journeys of ground transport inland were being planned, aircraft flights were planned too. In these cases the pilots' work was organised so that the tractor and sledge trains could be reached by air at any point on their route, so as to ensure absolute safety of the party. There were many cases when the pilots warned the participants of an expedition of predatory crevasses on their route.

Russians serenade Admiral Jim Reedy, the Deep Freeze commander, on an American good-will visit to Mirnyy.

Some of the scientific parties could not have done any of their work without the aid of aviation. This goes for the geological team, for instance; not to speak of the work involved in aerial photography, aerometeorology etc. Of course aviation also rendered aid to those who were taken ill, delivering them quickly to the place necessary.

As a rule the aircraft groups of the Soviet Antarctic expeditions consisted of one or two IL-12 planes, four to six Li-2 planes, several An-2 planes and Mi-4 helicopters. The Li-2 planes were fitted either with wheels or with skis. The heavier IL-12 aircraft were put on skis later, beginning with the fourth expedition of 1958–1960. Some of the marine expeditions were given YK-12 planes that carried out coastal reconnaissance and aerial photography. All the planes were fitted with additional equipment, particularly with air navigation instruments.

What were the conditions aviation had to work under in the Antarctic? There is always much trouble with the minute snow particles that penetrate everywhere. They get into the motor, the wing tips, central plane. Immense snowdrifts accumulate at the planes on their parking spaces. The strong winds that frequently reached the velocity of 30–40 m/sec called for the planes being secured fast when standing on the ground. But even a secured An-2 aircraft which has a small weight and considerable wing area would get shifted from its place at wind velocities of up to 35 m/sec. Greater velocities even elevated it into the air, where it would soar held by its mooring ropes.

There were very different take-off conditions at the locations at altitudes of 3,000 metres above sea level. The periods from January to March and from September to January were the most favourable ones for the work of aviation in Antarctica. The winter months, from April to August, are distinguished for most adverse meteorological conditions. There were usually less flights during this period. But, nevertheless, there was not a single month in the year that airplanes would not be flying, even during the first expedition of 1955–57. There was not a single case of icing and very rare cases of corrosion, this being due to the quite low air humidity in Antarctica.

The pilots and navigators of Antarctic aviation have been accumulating experience and improving their skill from year to year. The equipment and machinery were also getting ever better and better. From the second expedition on, the aircraft were provided with turbo-compressors. Ways and means were found to reduce friction between the ski surface and the snow, which proved to be especially useful in areas with dry granular snow.

The world's coldest outpost received the American crew 'like long-lost cousins' and sat them down to a Christmas Eve dinner of caviar and shashlik, washed down with vodka. An American trail party which reached the closed Pole of Inaccessibility base found a note telling them where food was kept and how to cook it — and a PS that added, 'don't forget to close the door'.[20]

Sometimes the nations enjoyed a forced togetherness, as on the occasion that an IL-12 with 11 men aboard landed at Rumdoodle skiway above Mawson base, only to be trapped in a raging blizzard. Three Australians who had gone out to assist with landing facilities also had to take refuge with the Russians while for two days the big plane bumped and swayed in a screaming 150-kph (95-mph) gale that tore against the tie-down cables. Dr Alexi Treshnikov, director of USSR Soviet Arctic and Antarctic Scientific Research Institute, was one of those who sheltered from the storm.[21] He later wrote:

> Regardless of the weather and the time of day, members of the Australian expedition always take the trouble to meet our planes [at Mawson], bring up fuel using their own transport and, if the flight stays overnight, hospitably invite the pilots to rest at the base. Such visits often give the hosts much trouble.
>
> The author of this article once was delayed on that icy dome on account of stormy weather. For two days, the IL-12 transport aircraft, although firmly attached with steel cables to an ice anchor, was buffeted about by a hurricane force wind. Inside its cold fuselage, lacking the minimum passenger comforts, fourteen men huddled together, including three Australian expedition members who had gone up to the top of the glacier to meet us and help us to supply, and had become involuntary prisoners. The parting on the third day with these manly, modest persons was most touching.

Russian expeditionaries and their American summer visitors conversing at Vostok. The base, located at 3,500 metres (11,500 feet) elevation, annually reports the coldest winter temperatures on earth, with readings down to −89.6°C (−129.3°F).

The IL-18D four-engine turbo-prop airliner, together with the An-12 transport, made it possible to establish an air link from Moscow. The first flight reached Mirnyy in December 1961.

Russia alarmed the non-Communist world, and most certainly those nations with Antarctic claims, when prior to the IGY it announced a firm intention of participating in any conference relating to the future of the south polar continent. In a diplomatic memorandum of 7 June 1950 sent to the governments of Argentina, Australia, Chile, France, New Zealand, Norway, the United Kingdom and United States it stated 'the government of the USSR cannot agree that such a question as the question of the regime of the Antarctic should be decided without their participation'.[22] Three grounds were listed to justify Russia's right of participation: historical through the work of early explorers; commercial, specifically involvement in the whaling industry; and scientific studies. The memorandum added: 'the Soviet government cannot recognise as legal any decision on the regime of the Antarctic taken without their participation'.

Frank Illingworth, writing in *Flight* magazine of December 1956 reflected a mood of the times:

> Speaking in Canberra recently, Mr Richard Casey, Australian Minister for External Affairs, emphasised the strategic importance of Antarctica to Australia. Sir Douglas Mawson, veteran Australian explorer, has said it was 'disturbing' from a defence point of view to see so many countries setting up scientific bases in the Antarctic under the overall plan of the IGY. He put forward the view that Australia could be bombed from these bases and that the Dominion should herself build a base in Antarctica, by airlift from Hobart, Tasmania. He said it would be interesting to see if countries that established themselves in Antarctica during the IGY would withdraw from it when the year ended.

The Australian government opened the Commonwealth's Antarctic Territory to all nations intending to set up polar bases for the term of the IGY. The invitation was contained in a ministerial statement of 17 December 1956 wherein, 'as the host country in the Australian Antarctic Territory, Australia welcomes the efforts of any and all countries to help expand the frontiers of human knowledge in the Antarctic for the advantage of the world'. Russia took Australia at its word and announced the setting up of bases in the Australian sector, eventually six in all, for IGY purposes.[23] Australia's invitation was somewhat an exercise in diplomatic tiptoeing, for Russia, like America, recognised no territorial claims. Australia's action, in the view of one commentator, was rather like having a big black bear thump into your living room, and then you tell it what chair to sit on. In effect, the area of the Knox coast which had originally been assigned for the placement of the main Russian base could not be occupied, owing to the impassability of the pack ice. Thus when the first Soviet Antarctic Expedition under the leadership of Dr M. M. Somov arrived at the start of 1956, a new location on the Davis Sea coast became their goal.

From the lead vessel *Ob*, an aerial search by An-2 aircraft was made over a period of nine days along the 'blank spot' of Eastern Antarctica until a suitable site for the main base was selected west of Farr (or Depot) Bay, behind the Helen Glacier in the Haswell Islets area at 66° 37'South and 92° 57'East.

One of the spectacular feats of Soviet aviation came at the turn of the 1960s with the decision to bring the wintering-over scientists and technicians from Moscow to Antarctica by air. In two days' flying time, the journey would carry seventh expedition members across four continents and two oceans to reach their base at the bottom of the world. Two large turboprop aircraft were allocated to the flight, an IL-18D four-motor passenger machine and a four-motor Antonov-12 for freight. Each aircraft weighed about 63 tonnes, the An-12 landing gear also being convertible to skis. The An-12 would be the heaviest Russian aircraft to land in Antarctica. The flight plan called for a 7,600-metre (25,000-foot) average altitude and a cruising speed of 550 kph (340 mph).

Sighting the shifting folds of Aurora Australis is one of Antarctica's awesome rewards for those who 'winter-over'. At the Russian observatories, atmospheric studies are related to geomagnetism, the ionosphere aurora, and cosmic rays.

The first airborne party departed Moscow on 15 December 1961 (the shipboard portion of the seventh expedition had left a month earlier) on a route through Tashkent, Delhi, Rangoon, Jakarta, Darwin, Sydney, Christchurch, McMurdo Sound and then to Mirnyy. Alex Afanasyev, head of the Northern Sea Route administration, commanded the flight; with him was Mark Sheveler, chief of the Polar Aviation Board. The pilots, all senior men with polar experience, were Alex Polyakov, one of Russia's outstanding aviators, and Boris Osipov, Mikhael Stupishin and Pyotr Rogor. Polyakov and Osipov were both Heroes of the Soviet Union; all were decorated upon return to Moscow.[24]

American and New Zealand cooperation had been promised and at Christchurch on 23 December U.S. Navy navigators of the VX-6 squadron were added to the flight crew for the next 3,800-kilometre (2,400-mile) leg to Williams Field, McMurdo Sound. The flight was routine, except for a radio blackout which continued until 17 minutes out of McMurdo. In the meantime, communication had been passed to Mirnyy and then re-transmitted to Williams Field control tower. A welcoming crowd of navy and New Zealand expeditioners lined the ice runway, watching the first long-range Soviet aircraft make their approach. 'Our precision landing astonished everyone on the ground,' wrote the Tass reporter. Christmas Eve was spent in the McMurdo mess in a big celebration, a pleasant interlude of international goodwill assisted by the fact that Mirnyy and Oasis both signalled bad weather.

Seven thousand gallons of aviation fuel were pumped from the navy tank farm in preparing the Soviet machines for the next long leg. Meanwhile at Mirnyy, expedition members worked non-stop to clear the ice runway which had been covered for days by violent snowstorms. The blizzards abated, allowing repairs to be made, and then with renewed force returned again. At eight o'clock on Christmas Day the An-12, which had shorter landing requirements, took off for Mirnyy. Additionally, the crew aboard the big freighter could assist in the final preparations for the IL-18D, taking the runway up to full length of 2,300 metres (7,500 feet) and a width of 50 metres (160 feet). By midnight on 27 December the work was done and at 5.15 a.m. the second aircraft began the final leg. At the completion of the mammoth journey, the aircraft had covered 24,000 kilometres (15,000 miles). Flying time for the An-12 was 48 hours 27 minutes; for the IL-18D it was 44 hours 46 minutes. Describing the scene at the main base after the arrival of the IL-18D, Captain Polyakov said:

> At the aerodrome of Mirnyy, alongside the polar veterans, the piston-engined aircraft, stands the turboprop liners IL 18 and An 12 which had flown in from Moscow. The members of the sixth Antarctic expedition experienced much difficulty in accommodating these huge machines. Time and time again snow storms had reduced to nothing all work put in on constructing the airstrips. Recently, when a huge blizzard broke over the Pravda Coast, a group of men, worried about the state of the Antonov, travelled out to the aerodrome in a cross-country vehicle. Visibility was no more than five to seven metres and the driver of the vehicle was compelled to stop halfway between the base and the aerodrome. They spent the whole night amid the chaos of the storm. Anxious about their comrades, men from the base roped together set out to their aid but could not locate them. At Mirnyy anxiety was only allayed towards dawn when the storm abated and the search party returned to base.

Two weeks after arriving, the An-12 put on its 'winter footwear', which was the first time a Russian aircraft of the Antonov's size had transferred to ski-landing gear in Antarctica. Pilot Osipov made several test flights, using a new ski-field at the base. On 13 January they flew to Vostok in 3 hours 15 minutes, about half the time of a piston-engine Li-2. Next day Osipov brought the big transport back to the coldest base on earth with a cargo of four tonnes of diesel oil. By the third week of January cargo assignments were complete, and on 19 January the An-12 was back on wheels. On 24 January both aircraft were farewelled, the An-12 at 4 p.m. and the IL 18D 20 minutes later on the first 4,950-kilometre (3,075-mile) leg that would take them, direct, to Christchurch. Both aircraft reached Moscow on 2 February. The Russians used the McMurdo route for a few years more, but then changed their flying pattern.

The 'across the world to Antarctica' mission had been a complete success and demonstrated the practicability of a regular air connection between Russia and its Antarctic bases. Describing the significance of the flight, Dr Somov, the expedition leader, said: 'A large and decisive role has been played by the flight into Antarctica . . . as a result of the fly-in, new men at the bases had been able to start their work much earlier'.

International co-operation continued unabated into the next decade. When an Australian collapsed at Davis early in 1978, the Russians were again called upon — this time because Davis had no landing strip, sending a helicopter to carry the sick man 700 kilometres (435 miles) to Mirnyy where they awaited the arrival of a Hercules from McMurdo. Fourteen hours and some 6,370 kilometres (3,960 miles) later the patient reached hospital in Christchurch.

One year later the Americans were summoned to aid the Russians when an IL-14 suffered a port engine failure and crashed a short distance beyond the runway at Molodezhnaya. The pilot and two others died in the impact and 11 were injured, five of them seriously, including one with suspected brain damage. An LC–130 immediately set out on another mammoth Antarctic crossing in answer to the Russians' call for help; on both legs of the journey, landings were made at the Pole to take on extra fuel. Dr Caroline Deegan, a navy surgeon, treated the injured men aboard the Hercules as they began the return to McMurdo. To reach New Zealand, the American aircraft covered 11,200 kilometres (7,000 miles). As one Deep Freeze aviator said later: 'No big deal. The comrades would do the same for us.'[25]

Discarded Russian aircraft lie alongside the Mirnyy airfield. The Li-2 type in the foreground has served the expedition well.

Russia Covers the Poles

The Soviet Antarctic Expedition (SAE) moved into Australian Antarctic Territory on the following schedule:

First expedition

1955 The expedition of 92 men led by Dr M. Somov reaches ice coast in December; three ships are employed, the new 12,700-tonne freighter-icebreakers *Ob* and *Lena* and refrigerator-supply vessel *Number 7*. Air reconnaissance locates site of main base on Queen Mary Coast of Australian Antarctic Territory.

1956 *13 February:* Mirnyy base (named after one of Bellingshausen's ships — meaning 'peaceful') officially opened.

March: Trail party, led by Dr Somov, builds first interior station of Pionerskaya, 370 kilometres (230 miles) south of Mirnyy, at 2,700 metres (8,850 feet) altitude. Five men settle in for first full winter spent in Antarctic interior; in August, temperature falls to –67°C (–88°F).

The Polar vessel *Ob* which carried the first Russian aviators and their aircraft to Mirnyy in January 1956. The ship's An-2 searched for nine days to find a suitable base location.

October: following aerial reconnaissance, small coastal base of Oazis placed in Bunger Hills, 360 kilometres (225 miles) east of Mirnyy.

Second Expedition

1957 January: Led by A. F. Treshnikov, 150 men arrive aboard *Ob, Lena* and passenger freighter *Kooperatsiya* for activities of the International Geophysical Year, commencing July.

February: Tractor train strikes towards South Geomagnetic Pole, where station named Vostok (after Bellingshausen's flagship, meaning 'east') is to be built at 1,440 kilometres (900 miles) south of Mirnyy. Second interior station is intended at the Pole of Inaccessibility, 2,200 kilometres (1,375 miles) from coast.

March: Tractor train reaches a point on plateau at 830 kilometres (520 miles) for an advance supply depot and airstrip named Komsomolskaya (after the Communist youth movement). Main Vostok party halted by bad weather 620 kilometres (390 miles) from Mirnyy; they dig in for winter, naming the temporary station Vostok-1. Temperature drops to –73°C (–100°F) but American South Pole base is two degrees colder.

1 July: At start of IGY, Soviet has manned bases at Mirnyy, Pionerskaya and Vostok 1.

November: Tractor party, led by Treshnikov, reaches Komsomolskaya which is to be continuously manned until 1959.

16 December: Vostok established at South Geomagnetic Pole, elevation 3,500 metres (11,500 feet) above sea level. With Vasily Sidokov as station leader, 11 men are to winter-over at coldest inhabited place on earth. Tractor supply train returns to Mirnyy. Meanwhile another tractor party, travelling via Vostok and Komsomolskaya, heads towards Pole of Inaccessibility.

Third Expedition

1958 16 February: An intermediate depot known as Sovietskaya is opened at 3,566 metres (11,700 feet) elevation during difficult traverse towards the Pole of Inaccessibility.

14 August: Vostok reports new world record low temperature of –87.2°C (–125°F). Second phase of IGY now has six bases occupied — Mirnyy, Oazis, Pionerskaya, Komsomolskaya, Vostok, Sovietskaya.

14 December: Tractor party led by Y. I. Tolstikov reaches Pole of Inaccessibility at 4,270 metres (14,000 feet), the most interior geographic point in Antarctica. The station is occupied for two weeks, through to the end of the IGY on 31 December, and then evacuated.

Fourth Expedition

1959 January: Led by A. G. Dralkin, the first post-IGY expedition is reduced from 185 to 113 men. Sovietskaya, Pionerskaya and Oazis are closed while Komsomolskaya is converted to seasonal occupation.

February: *Ob* carries a landing party to establish the new base of Lazarev (after Bellingshausen's second in command) on the Queen Maud coast in Norwegian Antarctic Territory (this is the first SAE expansion outside of Australian Antarctica). Lazarev is to specialise in exploration of the surrounding ice shelf and geological probes into nearby mountains. Tractor team, driving three heavy Kharkovchanka vehicles, meanwhile leaves Mirnyy on the first Soviet attempt to reach the Geographic South Pole.

September: Second tractor party leaves Mirnyy for Komsomolskaya where first team has wintered-over.

October: More men and equipment directed to Komsomolskaya to support Pole Traverse.

6 November: South Pole traverse departs Komsomolskaya with Kharkovchankas and two smaller Pinguin tractors. Expedition leader Dralkin flies from Mirnyy to join Pole traverse.

6 December: Tractor party of 16 men leaves Vostok on final 1,280-kilometre (800-mile) leg to the South Pole.

26 December: South Pole is reached. Tractor team remains three days at Amundsen-Scott base as guests of the Americans, then returns to Vostok.

By the close of 1959, the Soviet Antarctic Expeditions had realised their goal of achieving a presence at all three 'South Poles'.

Jolly Good, Bloody Good, First Class.

Sir Vivian Fuchs' message to his chief pilot, John Lewis, on completion of first single-engine trans-polar flight

11

LONG FLIGHTS, LONELY MEN

Digging out the Otter's skis at Scott base. The Trans-Antarctic Expedition's aircraft had completed the first single-engine crossing of Antarctica, by way of the South Pole.

The first flight over Antarctica from the world outside came not from an aircraft with American or Soviet Russian markings, but from Argentina. Nor was that historic flight precisely for the purpose of science or support; more likely it was to see 'what the British were up to'.

The Avro Lincoln bomber which took off from a southern Argentine Air Force station of Rio Gallegos in Patagonia on 13 December 1947 swept over the northern coast of the Antarctic Peninsula and, at the finish of the long reconnaissance mission, returned non-stop to base. Four years later the Argentine Navy flew a force of 12 officers and 30 enlisted men in seaplanes from Buenos Aires to a military exercise at Hope Bay on the northern tip of the peninsula. Additional Avro supply drops were made in these years to army groups who were isolated by thick pack ice at Barry Island and Marguerite Bay.[1]

The Antarctic Peninsula — Graham Land to the British, the Palmer Peninsula to the Americans — is the one area of the 'continent of peace' that has not been entirely peaceful. The flags of Argentina, Britain and Chile fly above rival and overlapping claims. Only through the Antarctic Treaty of 1959 have these territorial imperatives been placed on the shelf, which is just as well for the Falkland Islands conflict would not have assisted the cause of Pax Antarcticus.

The peninsula figures as an area of strategic significance, especially as shipping in the event of the closure of the Suez and Panama canals would have to follow a far southerly course via the capes. During World War II the Royal Navy's highly secret Operation Tabarin occupied positions on the peninsula to deny enemy raiders a haven amid the maze of islands and channels along the majestic mountain-backed coastline.

An Avion Kingfisher float plane, operated by the Chilean Air Force in exploration of the Antarctic Peninsula.

On 2 February 1952 the peninsula heard Antarctica's only hostile gunshots when Argentine troops fired a machine-gun burst over the heads of British 'intruders' who were intending to disembark at Hope Bay. Four days later Britain sent the frigate HMS *Burghead Bay* to protect the scientific party's landing. The crisis of the early 1950s occurred when Argentina and Chile had both established a number of peninsula bases. A particular source of British irritation occurred at Deception Island where an Argentine military detachment placed their camp on Wilkins' old airstrip of 1928, within sight of the fluttering Union Jack. Retaliation again followed in February 1953, with the surprise arrival at Deception Island of a Royal Naval party consisting of a magistrate, two constables and 15 marines who dismantled the offending Argentine huts and, under the Falkland Islands Aliens Ordinance, 'deported' the two Argentinians found in residence.

At Lt. Rudolfo Marsh Martin airstrip, a Chilean C-130 awaits take-off clearance. Argentina and Chile both maintain regular air links with their Antarctica claims.

By 1955 the British had seven bases occupied by 50 members of FIDS (the Falkland Islands Dependencies Survey authority). The Chileans had four bases with 29 men; Argentina had six bases with 68 men; both relied on military personnel to provide the core of their Antarctic contingents. The Argentine Air Force said its planes were making almost daily sweeps over the claimed territory in a demonstration of sovereignty. Chile announced the completion of a 1,100-metre (3,600-foot) airstrip at Foster Bay.

All three nations used sea and air transport to support their claims. FIDS equipped its force with Auster, Beaver and Otter aircraft (and helicopters later) which flew internal missions over the peninsula and were stored for the winter.[2] In 1955, the British also used the commercial contractor Hunting Aerosurveys, equipped with two Canso flying boats to assist with mapping. Because of their proximity to the peninsula, San Martin Land to the Argentines, O'Higgins to the Chileans, the Latin American nations were able to fly in with larger machines. Argentina, in particular, introduced a variety of aircraft including Beaver, Otter, Neptune, Albatross, DC-3 and DC-4 transports. The naval aeronautical unit's PBY Catalina and PBM Mariner flying boats have landed on the harbour which in 1928 was denied to Wilkins at Deception Island, as well as numerous other open water locations. At General Belgrano base, an Argentine officer made the first parachute jump to the ice from a helicopter in 1958. In the same year they flew a Beechcraft to the peninsula. About the same time, by ship and aircraft both countries began to take tourists to photograph the wildlife and view the peninsula's awesome panorama of snowy peaks, glaciers and ice falls.[3]

The first Chilean aircraft reached Deception Island on 28 December 1955; the Catalina flying boat, commanded by Squadron Leader Humberto Tenorio and with a five-man crew went from Punta Arenas to Aguirre Ceda base. In the year following, a DC-6B of the Chilean National Airline carrying 66 paying passengers left Santiago on 22 December to complete an 8,000-kilometre (5,000-mile) sweep across the Antarctic coast, but not landing.

With two DC-3 naval transports, Argentina joined the elite of those few nations which have landed aircraft at the South Pole. Taking off from

Wreckage of a Cessna 180, lost during an Argentine reconnaissance of mountains lying beyond the Filchner Ice Shelf at 83°10' South latitude.

Ellsworth (an IGY base on the Filchner Ice Shelf which the United States transferred to Argentine occupation) they reached the Pole on 6 January 1962. During the eight-hour stay, the flight commander, Captain Quijada, presented the American base leader with a plaque honouring the memory of Roald Amundsen and Robert Falcon Scott; 13 men made the Pole flight.[4]

At the Argentine Air Force's first attempt to duplicate the navy feat and reach the South Pole, their DC-3 caught fire on take-off at Ellsworth; no lives were lost. The second and successful attempt was made by a DC-3 fitted with DC-4 engines and a jet propulsion unit located in the tail. After landing at the Pole on 3 November 1965 the DC-3 flew to McMurdo, achieving Argentina's first trans-Antarctic mission. On returning, it was joined by two Beavers which had accompanied it as far as the South Pole where they had been immobilised in the prevailing extreme cold of –51°C (–60°F).

On 4 December 1973, a C-130 commanded by Brigadier General Hector Fautario, chief of the Argentine Air Force, undertook a 24,000-kilometre (15,000-mile) round trip from Buenos Aires to Canberra, stopping en route at Marambio base on the Antarctic Peninsula to refuel. The aircraft, with a crew of 14, battled 100-knot headwinds along part of the 18-hour proving flight to Australia, to determine the path for a commercial air route.[5] A year later, two C-130s again made trans-Antarctic proving flights, with one of the Hercules landing at the Pole. Thereafter, regular C-130 supply flights became part of Argentine operations in the Antarctic zone.

Vicecomodoro Marambio station, on Seymour Island, prepares for departure of the Argentine C-130 aircraft on the historic journey of 24,000 kilometres (15,000 miles) that will join Buenos Aires with Australia's national capital.

'Nine Great Flights': Deep Freeze I

As Captain Scott once remarked: 'great things are being achieved in the South'. Rear Admiral George Dufek might have repeated that same phrase but with better prospects.[6] The first Operation Deep Freeze began with a feat never before attempted,a long distance fly-in to Antarctica from the world outside. On the airfields of the South Island of New Zealand in the summer of 1955, six aircraft waited for the word to launch across the 3,860 kilometres (2,400 miles) of empty ocean and dense pack ice to reach McMurdo Sound.

Vanguard of the expedition, a force of icebreakers and freighters had ploughed through the Ross Sea to moor at McMurdo close by historic Hut Point of Scott and Shackleton's exploits.[7] Between New Zealand and 'the ice' (as the Americans called it), six warships took up weather reporting stations and prepared for search and rescue duty in the event of the unspeakable — an aircraft forced down. Other weather reports were being collected from merchantmen, whaling fleets and the distant Australian base.

Dufek recalled the tense moments ticking away as his aircraft awaited the clearance to go.

A U.S. Navy Otter is parked on the bay-ice strip, outside Scott base. A Deep Freeze aircraft of this UC-1 type went to the aid of New Zealanders from Scott who had plunged into a crevasse.

Preparing for take-off, an R4D (later LC-47) known as 'Ahab's Clyde' was one of the pioneer aircraft to reach McMurdo Sound.

> They had the word of their skipper that the bay ice at McMurdo Sound was eight feet thick and that it was safe for wheeled aircraft landings. They had the knowledge that red trail flags were flying from bamboo sticks along the runway.
>
> They each pinched a rabbit's foot to ensure a white-out would not obstruct their vision. No one would dare to admit to himself that the Ground Control Approach equipment couldn't possibly have been unloaded from the ships' cargo holds and installed on the bay ice by then.
>
> They had their commander's word that all ships were on station in the South Pacific and in the ice pack to send out radio homing signals to guide the flights. Each forced himself to remember these same ships had a secondary mission — to act as rescue ship if their planes had to ditch along the way.[8]

On 19 December 1955 came the signal: weather okay, ice airfield ready. Dufek's plane, an R5D Skymaster, made the blessedly uneventful journey that 14 hours later saw them safely on the bay-ice runway of Naval Air Facility, McMurdo. The other aircraft, the four-engine Skymaster and two P2V Neptunes, followed at spaced intervals.[9] But not so the two R4D Skytrains which, with their limited fuel capacity, needed fair weather and a following wind to reach McMurdo. They were nearing the point of no return when the weather reports abruptly warned of a front which would turn tail wind into 30-knot head wind. 'Return to New Zealand', flashed the message from headquarters at Christchurch airport. They did so reluctantly, especially the over-zealous pilot of the second machine. Fired more with enthusiasm than good judgment, he proposed making a ski landing on unprepared snow at Cape Hallett, 700 kilometres (435 miles) north of McMurdo rather than turn back. After repeated commands from Christchurch he finally swung his Skytrain around but had the last say — 'am returning to base under protest!'

The supply fleet of an early Operation Deep Freeze assembled in Winter Quarters Bay. The tanker, USNS *Altana* (right) has carried fuel and aviation gasoline to McMurdo base.

Captain Scott's first expedition waits at Hut Point, on Winter Quarters Bay, in 1903; behind SY *Discovery* rises the landmark they named 'Observation Hill'.

Close to the same historic location, a company of Seabees built the runway of Deep Freeze I across the bay ice of McMurdo Sound; Observation Hill appears at the left.

Within days of landing, preparation began at the temporary flight command on McMurdo Sound for some of the world's most extraordinary feats of aerial exploration.[10] The pilots, living in tents and aboard the ships secured at the ice edge, were impatient to take off from the 1,830-metre (6,000-foot) strip that the Seabees had scraped from the ice crust of the Sound.

'Nine great flights', as Dufek called them, went out within a space of two weeks to probe the mysteries of unseen and unknown Antarctica. In total 36,800 kilometres (23,000 miles) were covered between 3 and 13 January 1956, reaching far to the east, south and west of McMurdo Sound.

Except for a few tiny coastal encampments, a vast, uninhabited and utterly hostile continent lay beneath their wings. From the air, the scene was one of unbelievable colour and stark grandeur; but to touch it, to be forced down meant coming face to face with the savage reality of a most unforgiving terrain, of crevasses, cliffs, tearing winds and paralytic temperatures. Nevertheless, the Skymaster and Neptune flights achieved their goal without loss or accident. Something more than a rabbit's foot must have favoured them, for on many occasions treacherous weather or failing engines narrowed the margin of survival.[11]

One of Deep Freeze I's most spectacular achievements was the 19-hour flight on 13 January of a P2V which went from McMurdo across the South Pole to view the far side of the continent at the coast of the Weddell Sea, covering a distance of 5,470 kilometres (3,400 miles). Another had crossed Wilkes Land to check out the Davis Sea where the first Soviet expedition would locate.[12] Admiral Byrd was a guest on the R5D which headed for the Pole of Inaccessibility until bad weather forced a detour to the geographic South Pole; for the third time the 'Admiral of the Ends of the Earth' gazed upon that single point in a lifeless white desert that had won him fame a quarter century before.[13]

By the end of January the long-range aircraft were back in the United States, leaving the first wintering-over force to button up through the oncoming months of blizzard and darkness in preparation for the major scientific assault of Deep Freeze II in the following summer season.

But a pattern was established. With favourable weather conditions and all regard for safety, it had been shown that aircraft could fly into Antarctica from the world beyond. The frozen continent no longer stood wholly isolated; by plane it was now a matter of 10 hours, not 10 days or 10 weeks away. Ships would still toil southwards, breaking ice and bringing in the bulk cargo. But in Antarctica itself, the aeroplane was the unrivalled winged chariot in mankind's new age of exploration.

New Zealand's neighbourhood

Scott base, nestling at the eastern edge of Ross Island close by Pram Point is New Zealand's toehold on its Antarctic territory. Scott himself, Shackleton and Mawson laboured on these very shores which, as the Ross Dependency, was proclaimed a British possession in 1923 and placed under the authority of the governor-general in Wellington. It was here, gazing across wondrous McMurdo Sound, that Operation Deep Freeze came to dwell in 1955 and has remained ever since. Authorities in New Zealand were then in two minds about the implications of the U.S presence; strong fears were expressed in 1955 that the right to the Ross Dependency might be in jeopardy. A letter to the Government stressed 'the ease with which any country could establish a valid claim to the territory'.[14]

Provisions arriving by John Lewis's Otter bring an ice-encrusted grin from dog sledger, Dr George Marsh, out on the Great Barrier.

Much mutual assistance is gained by being a neighbour of the large Naval Air Facility on the other side of Hut Point peninsula. Established with the building of Scott base in 1957 to support the Commonwealth Trans-Antarctic Expedition and the forthcoming IGY, the New Zealand air contingent consisted of one Beaver and one Auster aircraft, while out on McMurdo's great ice runways, the Americans sported their Globemasters, Skymasters, Neptunes and Dakotas.

In flying supply and reconnaissance missions, the small Royal New Zealand Air Force team, under Squadron Leader John Claydon, contributed important assistance to the success of the Commonwealth party's crossing from the Weddell Sea to the Ross Sea. At the conclusion of the IGY, the RNZAF team was withdrawn, but returned for the 1960 season with three pilots and five ground crew to participate in exploration and mapping of the rugged area in the vicinity of the Beardmore Glacier.

Among the rescue precautions of early Deep Freeze was the Navy's parachute team trained in polar survival. They are loading for a jump to the Ross Ice Shelf.

The value of the powerful friends located across the other side of Observation Hill, where stands Scott's memorial cross, was evidenced a few weeks ahead of the air force arrival when a Sno-cat from Scott base travelling across the Ross Ice Shelf near Barne Inlet suddenly plunged backwards into a hidden crevasse. Two occupants lay trapped and injured beside the body of a third crew member who had died as the vehicle fell some 33 metres (108 feet) into the chasm.[15] News of the disaster, radioed from the tiny New Zealand field camp nearby, reached an American exploring party in Victoria Land. Their relayed message was heard on a U.S. aircraft carrying Rear Admiral David Tyree on a polar flight, from where it was flashed to McMurdo Sound. Though tended by companions who courageously descended into the crevasse, the survivors lay trapped inside the crushed Sno-cat for 29 hours before a U.S. Navy Otter and helicopter brought additional help from McMurdo.

Ice-bound Ross Island, backed by Mt Erebus. McMurdo base lies to the left of Observation Hill (centre-left). Scott base is close by Pram Point on the opposite side of the Hill. Airfield huts are visable at the bottom of the picture.

Two weeks after the RNZAF unit began operations at Scott Base, the Beaver went on a supply and airlift mission to a survey team travelling by dog sledge in the rugged Mount Hope area, west of the Beardmore Glacier. While flying through a narrow valley, a whiteout closed in and the aircraft crashed into the ice. The wings were torn off, the fuselage twisted and the engine partially wrenched from its mounting. The commander, Squadron Leader Jeffs, and his co-pilot, Flight Lieutenant Rule, were hurled from the cockpit; they later attributed their survival to the precaution of wearing 'bone dome' helmets. Marooned in a fogged-in valley for six days, but receiving a food drop from a Navy R4D, they were finally rescued by their third pilot, Bill Cranfield (who had served with the TAE flight) in the little Auster, ferrying them out one-by-one to a temporary American weather station near the foot of the Beardmore. Jeffs was the first of the pair taken back to Scott Base, but when an unrelenting blizzard closed in, his co-pilot had to wait another two weeks before the rescue plane arrived.[16]

Weather balloon launching from McMurdo bay ice – the American and New Zealand bases are able to share in such observations and jointly use Williams Field.

Disaster of a different aviation kind almost befell three New Zealanders a few years later when they thought it was safe to drive their Weasel across the McMurdo ice runway to reach the control tower. They were nearing the centre of the strip when a four-engine Navy R7V appeared over a snow bank, bearing down on them at full take-off power. A split second decision of throwing the Weasel into reverse saved their lives — and possibly those of a lot of others, as well. The Super Constellation roared past, taking to the air just beyond the very spot where they had been driving. Said the Scott Base leader, Athol Roberts, who was a passenger in the vehicle: 'I had not believed the saying "my heart popped into my mouth", but I do now. I bit mine as it popped in, and it almost stopped!'

From 1965, the RNZAF began sending its own C-130 Hercules from Christchurch to assist in supply deliveries to the American and New Zealand bases; later RAAF Hercules briefly joined in. Two RAF Hercules appeared at McMurdo in the 1972–73 summer season, to gain polar experience through contributing to the 'milk run' from Christchurch. On 8 December, one of the Hercules followed Captain Scott's trail in achieving the first RAF flight to the South Pole. The aircraft 'flew around the world three times in 12 minutes' before returning for a wheel landing at McMurdo.

Squadron Leader John Lewis of the RAF: 'Viva trans-polar ...downhill all the way', he signalled as the memorable single-engine flight across Antarctica reached beyond the South Pole.

Bloody Good ... First Class!

Britain holds the distinction of accomplishing the first single-engine flight across the Antarctic by way of the South Pole. It was one of the many unsung achievements of the International Geophysical Year when the explorer (Sir) Vivian Fuchs set out with his Commonwealth Trans-Antarctic Expedition (TAE) to complete Sir Ernest Shackleton's failed attempt of 44 years before of journeying across the continent from the Weddell Sea to the Ross Sea.

Shackleton was the name given to TAE's first base and starting point, established on the Weddell Sea coast. From here, Fuchs and his Commonwealth party would begin their march, using Sno-cats, Weasels and dog sledges. Meanwhile on the other side of Antarctica, the hero of Mount Everest, Sir Edmund Hillary, undertook the laying of fuel caches from New Zealand's Scott Base on the Ross Sea coast, to the edge of the Polar plateau. Having completed his TAE task Hillary, ever the individualist, decided to push on to the Pole itself with his procession of tiny Fordson tractors, an action which was portrayed in some press reports as rather stealing Fuchs' thunder.

Amid the attention focused on science, discovery and personalities at the height of the IGY, the flight of TAE's bright orange Otter almost went unnoticed. Yet the four men in that small crowded aeroplane, with no surface support crews, achieved the dream of Lincoln Ellsworth: a non-stop single engine flight right across the Antarctic continent.

TAE's chief pilot was John Lewis, an expert at 'iceberg hopping'. He had been with Fuchs in the 1949–50 FIDS season. He was large, ruddy faced and forever cheerful; aged 35, married and with the rank of squadron leader, he came to TAE on secondment from the RAF. Three other air force men were his companions: Gordon Haslop, second pilot; Peter Weston, engineer; Taffy Williams, radioman. The Otter's assignment had been reconnaissance, transport and depot laying.[17] As the Fuchs' surface expedition progressed, air operations moved from Shackleton to the chillingly named South Ice, next staging point 435 kilometres (270 miles) to the south and at an elevation of 1,480 metres (4,850 feet) on the shoulder of the Polar Plateau.

Once the TAE party had pushed onwards to the Pole, the need to keep the Otter at South Ice also vanished. Major Jim Lassiter obligingly flew up from Ellsworth, the American IGY base, to Shackleton where he picked up nine drums of fuel to top-up their supply.[18] Lewis had the option of a trans-Antarctic flight or, if the weather proved impossible, of departing Antarctica via Ellsworth and the other Graham Land bases to the north — a somewhat uninspiring retracing of steps. Lewis was not of the stuff to relish the second option. His aim was firmly focused on crossing the Pole, though the first attempt nearly led them into oblivion.

To the Pole from South Ice measured about 900 kilometres (560 miles) while the rising face of the plateau reached to 3,050 metres (10,000 feet). The RAF crew realised that their Otter, heavily laden with fuel, survival gear and rations, would be hard pressed to better an altitude of 3,660 metres (12,000 feet).

They left for South Ice at 10.27 p.m. on 29 December 1957 needing a half mile run to get the Otter airborne. Encouraging reports had been received on the daily weather transmissions from the meteorologists at Pole station and New Zealand's Scott base. Four hours out, conditions turned sour. A dense cloud bank reaching high above the plateau loomed ahead. Sticky rime ice

Inside the cabin of the TAE Otter, taken during a supply flight across the Ross Ice Shelf. On their second attempt at the 11-hour journey from South Ice to Scott Base, the small aircraft carried a crew of four and was packed with extra fuel, survival gear and emergency provisions.

began to form on the wing leading edges, causing them to lose height dangerously. Lewis turned the aircraft to retrace their course to now deserted South Ice, hoping he could locate that minuscule dot in the white wilderness.

Another thick cloud bank closed in from the north. Visibility gradually reduced to 90 metres (300 feet) and navigating became near impossible. To land on the desolate plateau was a choice which none of them relished, would they ever get off again? Instead, Lewis elected to return to the early days of 'flying by Bradshaw' (referring to the well-known British railway timetable). He brought the Otter close to the surface and, sometimes at nothing but 9 metres (30 feet) above the sastrugi ridges, picked up the caterpillar tracks of Fuchs' surface vehicles. These he followed in reverse order back to base, as surely as if they were a railway leading to South Ice.

A wild storm locked them up at South Ice for almost a week. A dinner of tinned soup, fishcakes, stew and fruit, and a toast to Her Majesty marked New Year's Eve. In the extreme cold they found it impossible even to venture outside to inspect the tied-down Otter. On 6 January the Pole and Scott bases both radioed the weather had now cleared sufficiently to make the outlook as good as it ever might be. Hurriedly Lewis and his team prepared the Otter for a second trans-Antarctic attempt. Take-off time was 11.48 p.m. on 6 January 1958. Several hours later in clear weather they looked down on the TAE vehicles in snail-like procession across the white snow. A deluge of ice crystals poured from the unknown skies, hampering visibility, but by 4.30 a.m they could see the flags of the South Pole Base. 'Downhill all the way,' Lewis radioed to headquarters. 'Viva Trans-Polar!'[19]

At 7 a.m. they turned from the vast glittering bosom of the polar plateau and, via the mighty Beardmore, entered their final leg across the Ross Ice Shelf. Almost 11 hours to the minute from take-off, the 2,300-kilometre (1,430-mile) journey was an entry for the record books. As they approached the runway at McMurdo Sound, a brace of U.S. Navy Otters and R4Ds circled in a salute and on the skiway, cheers of a welcoming group of New Zealanders and Americans awaited as they scrambled from the cabin.[20]

Lewis' favourite phrase when he found something to please him would be, 'Jolly good, bloody good, first class'. From his leader still plodding across the polar plateau, the same message hailed the success of that historic first trans-Antarctic flight: 'JOLLY GOOD, BLOODY GOOD, FIRST CLASS'.

Let's get the hell out of here.

Admiral George Dufek after the first aircraft landing at the South Pole on 31 October 1956

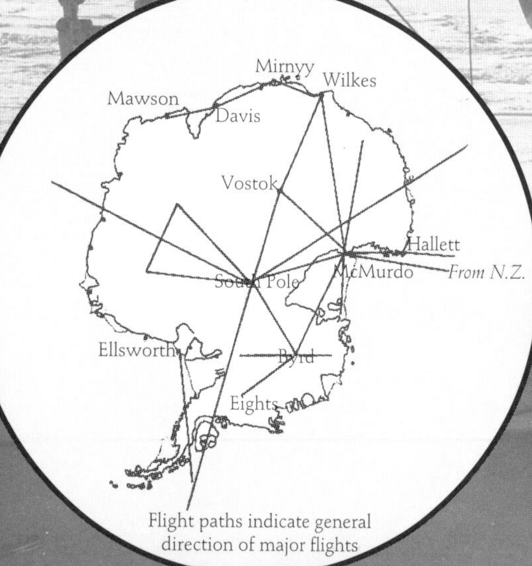

Flight paths indicate general direction of major flights

Que Sera Sera

First aircraft to land at the South Pole, *Que Sera Sera* waits beside the runway at Williams Field for its place in the hall of fame. After four years over Antarctica, the veteran R4D was shipped from McMurdo to the Smithsonian Museum in Washington, D.C.

They stood unusually quiet, the navy men who sheltered from the bitter wind, watching two aircraft rise from the ice airfield on McMurdo Sound. One was an 80-tonne Globemaster transport; four-engine, noisy, silvery fat fuselage and high orange tail. The other an R4D (U.S. navy terminology for a DC-3 or Dakota), twin-engine and looking as small and slender as the Air Force C-124 was huge.

When both aircraft vanished into the glitter of a bright polar sky that day in 1956, the navy workers turned away, some certainly with a whispered prayer. All Antarctic flying was dangerous, and this mission was dangerous in the extreme. Across its nose, the R4D bore the legend *Que Sera Sera* — 'What is to be, will be'; well named. The destination of both aircraft lay at the bottom of the world. The mission of the R4D was to be first aircraft to land at the geographic South Pole.

Rear Admiral George Dufek, commander of the Deep Freeze Task Force, stood watching from behind the R4D's flight deck. The survivor of two brushes with Antarctic death, Dufek had carefully chosen his crew. Captain William 'Trigger' Hawkes as chief pilot and with him another experienced aviator, Lieutenant Conrad Shinn, except that Hawkes had deferred to his friend who sometimes doubled as barber at the camp and put 'Gus' Shinn in the right hand seat.[1] The rest of the elite seven were all highly experienced in flying skills: John Swadener, the navigator who bore the responsibility of pinpointing the Pole; John Strider, the mechanic; Bill Cumbie, radio and electronics technician. Captain Douglas Cordiner, commander of the Deep Freeze aviation detachment (VX-6), came as observer. Like Dufek, he must share the risk.

Heading down the Beardmore Glacier, a U.S. Air Force C-124 has completed yet another 12-tonne load drop at the bottom of the world.

AIRDEVRON SIX
FLIGHT LINE AND READY ROOM

WILLIAMS TERMINAL
WELCOME TO MCMURDO
PARADISE OF THE ANTARCTIC

The faster Globemaster flew on ahead. Its commander, Major Cicero J. Ellen, could not attempt a wheels-down landing at the Pole, that was only for the ski aircraft — the lighter *Que Sera Sera*. In the event of a mishap to the smaller machine, Ellen's crew would lay down a parachute salvo of supplies, tents and sledges, enough to keep seven men alive until they could trudge back to a place where wings might safely reach them. The two aircraft chased each other across the flat white

surface of the Ross Ice Shelf, keeping the Antarctic mountains always on their right. Four days previously the Globemaster had made a supply drop to a midway camp set up near the foot of the Beardmore Glacier. If all went well, they would land here on their return to refuel for the final leg back to McMurdo. If *Que Sera Sera* failed them at the Pole, Dufek and his team would have to march the 650 kilometres (400 miles) to reach this tiny dot.

No man can fly the glacier route through the Antarctic mountains without being overwhelmed by the wonder of it all. Dufek recorded his emotions as Shinn turned the R4D towards the mouth of the mighty Beardmore:

> Gus poured on the power and we started to climb. We were heading towards the polar plateau. We were in a valley with hard blue ice beneath us. Snow-covered mountains were to the right and left of us. We had to climb to ten thousand feet to get above the plateau, then streak for the Pole.
>
> What a strange and weird land — all snow and ice, with the exposed part of the mountains coloured a chocolate brown. There was not a tree or bush, no human, animal or bird habitation. Everything motionless, and no sound except the drone of our motors and the voices in our plane. (Dufek 1957: 198–203)

Remaking Williams Field is a never-ending task as Antarctica's summer flying season approaches. Tractor-hauled snow levellers, bulldozers and heavy rollers are brought in to compact the surface of the airfield that floats above the waters of the Ross Sea. The main runways have been lengthened to 3,050 metres (10,000 feet).

They began to cross the plateau, leaving the stark Antarctic peaks to fall beneath the horizon that rimmed the white desert. Even at this moment Dufek had to admit to the mundane, observing one of his colleagues 'at the hot plate, brewing some coffee and making me a toasted-cheese sandwich'.

First to reach the Pole, Major Ellen flew his Globemaster in wide circles, leaving a vapour trail in the unbelievably blue sky around the position, as called out by his navigator, of the geographic South Pole. The R4D came in at lower altitude, searching for a place to put down. Neither Hawkes nor Shinn nor anyone else aboard knew quite what to expect when the skis touched the surface. One doomsday theory held that the plateau was so covered with soft snow it would immediately swallow them; another held quite the opposite view, that an aircraft would spin wildly out of control on the slippery hard or ridged ice, tear off its undercarriage and probably cartwheel to destruction. But Trigger Hawkes was of a more optimistic view; the navy's most experienced polar aviator had been planning this landing for almost two years. He had enlarged photographs taken 44 years earlier of Captain Scott standing at the South Pole, researched Scott's weight and from studying the depth that the Britisher's boots sank into the surface, estimated that a plane could land and survive.

Shinn flew a square of mile-long legs to enable navigator Swadener to check their position against the sun. This was surely the South Pole! Dufek recalled those final moments of no turning back:

> We strap ourselves in tightly with our seat belts. We will soon come in for the approach. It is up to Shinn and Hawkes now — and the snow surface. Hawkes calls over the intercom: 'Admiral, should we land now, or should we have the Globemaster drop some gear to mark the surface?'
>
> 'Use your own judgment,' I replied.
>
> 'I'll make three passes,' answered Shinn. 'One at four hundred feet, one at two hundred and then drag the surface at one hundred. If it looks all right, I'll come in.'

During the final approach, the gauge pressure fell and oil was seen streaming from the engines. Shinn reported his instrument panel 'lighting up like a Christmas tree'. From above, the Globemaster radio crackled with the casual voice of Major Ellen, wishing them a happy landing. They had now come 1,250 kilometres (780 miles) from McMurdo Sound and on that encouraging note, Shinn pointed them down. 'Coming in for keeps this time,' he announced. They felt the skis touch the surface. The aircraft jarred a little, but they knew *Que Sera Sera* was under control. They slowed to a halt. It was 8.34 p.m. on 31 October 1956 and at the South Pole, at an altitude of 2,804 metres (9,200 feet), the first aircraft had landed.

A blast of air at –50°C (–58°F) struck Dufek as he came down the stairs. 'Like stepping out into a new world,' the Admiral described the chilling sensation. To Hawkes it was 'like getting slammed in the face with a slab of ice'. Looking around, Dufek saw, beyond the presence of their R4D, nothing but the C-124 cruising overhead and an immense white plain encircling them from horizon to horizon. None of them could quite grapple with the truth that earlier men had actually reached 'this awful place' on foot: Amundsen with his hurrying dog teams, Scott wearily marching to his death. Hawkes felt the humility of knowing he was first man to stand at the Pole since the explorer heroes of his boyhood years. The rest of the seven came gingerly down the steps, except that one pilot always remained in the cockpit for they dare not let the engines stop. Being first Americans ever to stand at the Pole, in Dufek's view, only added to their feeling of insignificance.

In the intense cold of a wind blowing 10 to 15 knots, they were drilled to watch one another's faces for the telltale patches of yellowy-grey skin as they hurried about their tasks. Radar reflectors had to be positioned to aid the navigation of future flights. The Stars and Stripes had to be raised. Even planting the flag was a lesson in the hardness of the surface underfoot — an alpine axe had to be used to chip a small hole for the bamboo stake into which Dufek pushed a piece of paper proclaiming America's conquest. Cameras were taken out to photograph these events, but most of the gear quickly froze, making their triumph probably the worst recorded event in modern Antarctic history.

After 40 minutes at the Pole, each movement made them more breathless and they felt numbness striking into their limbs. 'Cover up, Doug, you have frostbite on your face,' Dufek said to Cordiner. 'You have, too,' replied Cordiner. They tried rubbing their cheeks with the fur-lined gloves. Bill Cumbie, who had been digging a footing for the radar reflectors, found he couldn't take his hands from the shovel. With his boot he kicked the handle free and scrambled for the plane. Trigger Hawkes said to Dufek 'Boss, I can't move the fingers on this hand. I think they're frozen. We've done everything we can. What about we leave?'

Said Dufek: 'Let's get to hell out of here'.

The R4D had been stripped to the minimum for the flight to the Pole, loaded mainly with fuel, with survival equipment to last them 14 days and with 15 JATO (jet-assisted take-off) bottles, each cluster of four bottles in a thirty-second burn giving them the equivalent power of a third engine. Dufek well knew their lives could depend on the fire-spitting JATOs slung beneath the fuselage, as he continued:

> The engines were up full for the take-off. The plane did not move forward but shook as if it would fall apart. The skis were frozen to the hard snow and ice. Gus fired off four of the bottles attached to her underside, the plane shook some more but remained frozen to the ice. He exploded four more JATOs. The plane moved forward slowly. Four more were fired, and then the last three. The plane staggered along the snow surface and lifted herself into the thin air at sixty knots.

Major Ellen added a touch of levity as he watched the R4D's struggle to break free. 'If you guys can't get off,' he radioed, 'I'll come and crash land alongside you and there'll be a house to live in.' The remark, Dufek added, was 'mighty comforting'. But humour from the Globemaster was short-lived, for in the burst of flame and cloud of vapour that enveloped *Que Sera Sera*, the watchers were momentarily sure that the Deep Freeze warrior had exploded on take-off and splattered itself across the bottom of the world. With much relief, they saw it emerge from the almost whiteout fog of its own creation and slowly — agonisingly slowly claw a path above the Pole.[2]

'Jettison all JATOs,' ordered Shinn, and the 15 empty bottles tumbled away, lightening the R4D's load by 2,500 pounds (1,135 kilos), allowing them to lift and accelerate. The drama was not yet finished. Another terse message from the cockpit: 'Port engine losing oil pressure rapidly. We may have a forced landing.' 'Oh, no!' gasped Dufek. 'We waited in silence, then came the reassuring voice from up forward. "Oil pressure building up. We're all right." I leaned back and closed my eyes.'

How the South Pole was won — 1956: parachutes bearing timber, gasoline and equipment float towards the waiting group of navy Seabees who have reached the Pole by the smaller ski-fitted R4D.

Dufek then ordered a wait of almost three weeks for the weather to 'warm up', if such a condition can be contemplated in deepest Antarctica. Then, on 20 November, America returned to the Pole, this time to stay. The R4D Skytrains, reassured that the surface was willing to accept them, came in with men and supplies. First to disembark was Lieutenant R. A. Bowers, aged 26, with a team of seven Seabees who would pioneer the building of Pole station. During the past winter, Bowers and six groups of four men each had trained to live and work together under the worst Antarctic weather. With them came a team of 11 husky dogs as emergency sledging transport in the event they had to evacuate, or fetch survivors if an aircraft went down. By theodolite, Bowers determined their landing point to be some 13 kilometres (8 miles) short of the actual geographic South Pole. The whole entourage moved itself across the freezing plateau until by sun observations their instruments told them they had reached the place where Amundsen-Scott, the name America had fittingly chosen for its base would be built.

Returning to McMurdo Sound, a C-124 at the end of a Pole supply flight.

A C-124 Globemaster approaches the Pole on an air-drop run after the 1,250-kilometre (780-mile) climb from McMurdo Sound.

Then began one of the great airlifts of modern history as air force Globemasters commenced the parachuting and 'free dropping' of some 750 tonnes of materials and machines in the remaining summer season.[3] Three times daily the labouring C-124s made the six-hour round trip between McMurdo and the Pole. A Weasel and a tractor were dropped, within minutes to be untied and driven away to assist the construction task. 'Free dropped' baulks of timber speared into the snowcap. Sometimes a parachute failed to open, and on one occasion a tractor buried itself 9 metres (30 feet) down. To check on air-drop failures, one of the Marine Corps' most experienced parachutists made the first ever man-jump at the Pole.

Bowers and a team now numbering 30 men spent 45 days living in metal and fabric Jamesway huts and building Pole station in temperatures that ranged around –37°C (–35°F) and worse. Then they boarded the Skytrains for McMurdo, turning Amundsen-Scott over to the new scientific and support crew led by Dr Paul Siple. By the end of January the air drop had ceased, leaving 17 men to spend a year in lofty and lonely isolation, much of it in total darkness, where men had not lived before.

Bowers' huskies were never needed for an aviation emergency. Landings on the plateau became part of each summer season's regular schedule — routine yet never devoid of risk. The P2V Neptunes ferried men and some materials to Pole station in the seasons of 1957–59, sometimes with difficulty — one turning back with an engine on fire, another grounded at the Pole. After the Neptunes came the powerful C-130 Hercules which changed the face of polar flying. On 4 February 1963 the U.S. Army's UH-1B Iroquois turbine-driven helicopters became the first rotary-wing machines to touch down at the Pole. Dufek was able to report all seven Deep Freeze bases ready and occupied for the start of the IGY on 1 July 1957. For the 12 nations engaged in research, an estimate of a billion dollars was put against the cost of their Antarctic effort. Setting up the United States' presence through the IGY called for an investment of US$245,000,000, only 2 per cent of it expended on science — such was the price of Antarctic logistics. Each of the men now living at the Pole had cost an estimated one million dollars to put him there.[4]

Commander 'Trigger' Hawkes (left) and Admiral George Dufek plant the flag and position a beacon at the first South Pole landing. Cameras froze in the bitter cold, making this moment of aviation history an ill-recorded event.

Photographed from the escorting C-124, *Que Sera Sera* has landed on the polar plateau.

And what of *Que Sera Sera*? The most famous of all the Antarctic R4D Skytrains (13 were lost in Operation Deep Freeze) was shipped to honourable retirement in the Smithsonian Museum, Washington, D.C. — where its ice-scarred fuselage and faded 'survival orange' colours can be seen today as it awaits the homage of all those whose hearts are stirred by man's air conquest of Antarctica.

Deep Freeze is Launched

Late in 1954 the United States government sent the icebreaker USS *Atka* to Antarctica on a scouting mission to prepare for the scientific assault of the International Geophysical Year. To find a site for the main American base, *Atka* sailed eastwards along the Great Ice Barrier towards the Bay of Whales, where all U.S. expeditions had been located since Admiral Byrd's first visit of 1929. But the bay had disappeared; in a huge break-out of the Barrier front it was now so many icebergs floating out to sea.[5] The *Atka* mission identified Kainan Bay, about 50 kilometres (30 miles) to the east as the alternative site for Little America V, but prudence suggested more solid terrain should be selected as logistic headquarters for the men, equipment and money that America intended to inject into Antarctica under the banner of Operation Deep Freeze.[6]

Emblem of VX-6, otherwise the 'penguin airline'; later the group was reclassified 'VXE-6'.

Time was of the essence. The IGY was scheduled to begin on 1 July 1957, with 12 nations participating in a massive scientific investigation of south polar phenomena through to 31 December 1958. McMurdo Sound at the western end of the Ross Sea had first been sighted by the British naval commander, Sir James Clark Ross, in 1841. The Britisher endowed his discovery with his own name, and those of his ships and seamen. The partly ice-bound Ross Island, crowned by the smoking crater of the active volcano Erebus, stood guard over the sound. On the far shore, magnificent peaks and glaciers of the Great Antarctic Horst lined the western horizon.[7] In summer ships could break through to the volcanic slopes of Ross Island. Here was the optimum site for Naval Air Facility, McMurdo Sound, the main American supply and aviation centre and the jumping-off point, just as it had been for the old explorers, to reach the South Pole. Deep Freeze I erected the first Jamesway huts and built the airfield on bay ice that would be thick enough to hold a C-124. In America the navy had commenced assembling the force of scientists, sailors and technicians who, for the first year, would live at the two interior and four coastal bases that Deep Freeze was making around the continent.[8]

A UH-ID turbo-motor helicopter, operated by the U.S. Army, is stowed inside the Globemaster at Christchurch airport for the 12-hour haul to McMurdo Sound.

Many a traveller in the early days of Operation Deep Freeze met the first chill blast of Antarctica through the opening clamshell cargo doors in the nose of a C-124.

Deep Freeze II and III brought a massive armada of men and materials, ships and aircraft to Antarctica for the IGY.[9] The air detachment known in the navy as VX-6 comprised

Antarctica's air transportation: an R4D 'somewhere on the ice' alongside a Hercules LC-130.

four P2V Neptunes, two R5D Skymasters, six R4D Skytrains and nine UC-1 single-engine Otters; all with the exception of the R5D were rigged for landing on skis.[10] To accomplish the airlift for the building of bases at the South Pole and Byrd Station, the U.S. Air Force contributed eight C-124 Globemasters to drop thousands of tonnes of supplies to the interior settlements.

The mighty Beardmore glacier, the historic 'highway' for man and aircraft to reach the South Pole.

Urgently moving an R4D at McMurdo as cracks appear in the taxi-way of the bay ice.

The bottom of the world, marked by a barber's pole, topped with a reflector globe. The navy publicity picture has an LC-130F waiting to begin a JATO departure from the South Pole's airstrip.

The first commercial flight to Antarctica reached McMurdo Sound on 15 October 1957, bringing with it two women who could claim the distinction of 'furtherest south'. The Pan American Stratocruiser *Clipper America*, on a military airlift charter, carried numerous VIPs, including the U.S. Ambassador to New Zealand and a New Zealand cabinet minister. Far more attention, however, seems to have been accorded to Pan Am hostesses Patricia Hepinstall and Ruth Kelly by the men who had not seen a woman for 12 months past, and would not for the 12 months to come. Their three and a half hours on the ice were spent as passengers on a U.S.–New Zealand husky dog-sledge race, judging a beard competition, touring the camp, signing autographs and eating a midnight supper.

Crew members of VXE-6 practise a crevasse rescue; for airmen forced down, the crevasse represents an ever-present hazard.

Many scary moments awaited those who flew to or across Antarctica in 'Old Shaky', the fond name for the Douglas 124. Never was it routine flying and far from the pampered comfort of an airline. The big Globemasters, until they were retired in 1963, seemed frequently to enrol their passengers in the 'rapid-rise blood pressure club'! One with 8 men aboard, northbound from McMurdo, reached Christchurch with an engine dead and a second spitting sparks. Another came back from the Pole with one engine dead and the generator of another streaming fire. A third returned from a parachute run to Byrd Station to find McMurdo totally socked in by bad weather. With half its engines shut down, the plane spent two hours searching for the runway; only by watching his radar did the ground controller know it had made a safe touch-down in zero visibility.

Loading an R4D for a flight to Cape Hallett in the so-called 'banana belt' of Antarctica.

Trigger Hawkes likened his early arrivals at McMurdo ice airfield to 'landing on a bowling alley in somebody's basement'. Parachute drops were also tricky. Nearing the South Pole, a consignment of 12 drums of fuel oil weighing two and a half tonnes suddenly broke loose and hurtled through the unopened hatch, damaging the locking mechanism. The Globemaster crew balanced on a narrow catwalk in a –51°C (–60°F) gale and the plateau 230 metres (750 feet) below as they struggled to hook the drop doors and drag them shut. In the 1958–59 season, the C-124 made 37 crossings of the wild Southern Ocean between Christchurch and McMurdo.

Weather dominates the brief Antarctic aviation season. Meteorologists in the old air operations building at McMurdo check the read-outs from an upper atmosphere balloon.

With the turn of the '60s came the new era of the Lockhead C-130 Hercules — powerful, high-flying ski-equipped aircraft that revolutionised Antarctric supply missions, landing on the surface and eliminating the expensive and sometimes wasteful parachute drops.[11] A typical Deep Freeze detachment in those years would be 4 Hercules, 3 Neptunes, 4 Skytrains, a Skymaster and 5 Otters, plus 4 helicopters, the last-named gradually taking over the Otters' role.

In one summer season, the Deep Freeze VX-6 air detachment made 1,646

▲ Three American icebreakers combine to shift an iceberg which threatened to drift across the channel leading to McMurdo Sound.

▶ Dr Paul Siple, first scientific leader of Amundsen Scott Station at the South Pole in 1957.

▼ An early edition of McMurdo Sound's own newspaper.

separate flights, logged 5,450 flying hours, carried 5,277 passengers and 4,050 tonnes of cargo (much of it fuel oil) to the interior. Photo-surveys recorded 106,000 square miles (275,000 square kilometres) of the Antarctic surface. A Project Magnet hydrographic survey aircraft in 1962 reached Punta Arenas, Chile, on the first flight from McMurdo Sound to the South American continent. The navy's Super Constellation R7V passenger planes plying between Christchurch and McMurdo completed 100 round trips from 1958 to 1964, equivalent to circling the globe 20 times. For *Phoenix Firebird*, the fastest time between New Zealand and the ice was 8 hours and 18 minutes.

On 22–23 February 1963 came one of the then longest flights in modern Antarctic history when Rear Admiral Jim Reedy, who had succeeded to the Deep Freeze task force command, took a C-130 on a gigantic triangular course from McMurdo to the South Pole and onwards to the Pole of Inaccessibility. By the time his pilot, Commander William Everett, returned them to McMurdo, the Hercules which was fitted with an internal auxiliary fuel tank had been airborne for 10 hours and 40 minutes in covering 5,790 kilometres (3,600 miles). Reedy's first big flight was followed by another epic journey in September of the same year from Cape Town to McMurdo — 6,600-kilometres (4,100 miles) lasting 14 hours 31 minutes.

To fill in the final missing link between Antarctica and the world out-

Preparing for the summer flights at McMurdo — thawing out the ground control radar units. Overhauling an aircraft engine. Checking the weather office's field recorders.

side finally came the marathon 15 hour and 39 minute first crossing between Australia, the South Pole and Byrd (see Chapter 1). Still looking for more records before he retired from the Deep Freeze command, Jim Reedy took his crew on an 8,000-kilometre (5,000-mile) scouting trip to the Sor Rondane mountains in distant Queen Maud Land where unexplained radar echoes had been picked up on the earlier flight from Cape Town. Commander Marion E. Morris stopped their C-130 at Pole station to refuel before continuing the aerial trek — now the longest exploratory flight in Antarctic history — which achieved the western edge of the Shackleton Range before turning back. Trimetrogon photography was operated throughout the journey, while two specially made flag poles bearing the Stars and Stripes and the Admiral's

Admiral Jim Reedy, USN. He completed Antarctica's grand fly-in program.

With the appearance of a frontier settlement, McMurdo Sound NAF (Naval Air Facility) emerges from the winter snows at the start of the International Geophysical Year (IGY). A much larger and more permanent base now occupies the site.

Inset: Disembarking passengers face an unpleasant welcome as a swirling snowstorm bears down on Williams Field.

personal 'two-star' standard were dropped above the peaks. 'They were last seen with flags streaming in the wind,' Commander Morris reported.

Sometimes it was not science but the demands of mercy that summoned the aviators on the most distant and dangerous flights. Deep Freeze was in its fourth year when the message came of a desperately ill Australian at Wilkes base on the Budd Coast. A P2V Neptune set out on the 1,900-kilometre (1,200-mile) journey, piloted by the aptly named Commander Lloyd Newcomer, and escorted by an R7V Super Constellation.

No American aircraft had landed at Wilkes before, but Newcomer put his machine down safely, took the patient aboard and headed back to McMurdo where a transfer flight to New Zealand awaited. The Super Constellation circled Wilkes base for two hours while the evacuation was in progress, ready to drop survival equipment in the event of an emergency.[12]

The labours of the Hercules helped to build New Byrd Station, located in Marie Byrd Land, 1,380 kilometres (860 miles) east of McMurdo.

Rescue generated a controversy two years later when Leonid Kuperov, a Russian exchange scientist, collapsed at Byrd Station with a serious stomach ailment. In early April of 1961 all long-range aircraft were home in America and the last outgoing ice-breaker had moved away to escape the thickening pack. But rescue it had to be. Two C-130s made the 19,000-kilometre (12,000-mile) return from their U.S. base. From Christchurch, one aircraft was assigned for the dash into the polar winter, landing at McMurdo and then forging deeper across 1,200 kilometres (750 miles) of darkness to reach Byrd Station on the blizzardly heights of Marie Byrd Land. If the journey had not been sufficiently risky thus far, the same Lloyd Newcomer soon had to grapple with an additional peril. On finding that thick snow would not let the aircraft lift from Byrd's skiway — even with JATO assist — he turned his C-130 into a steamroller, taxiing up and down until the surface was sufficiently compressed to permit a take-off. Kuperov eventually reached Moscow, but outside Antarctica the Cold War was alive and kicking. In America criticism was directed from some vocal quarters at putting the navy aviators and their aircraft to considerable risk for 'bringing out a Russkie'.[13] Absence of any formal thanks from the Soviet government did not help to reduce the hostility. But the fliers who had safely and skilfully covered the 10,000 kilometres (6,300 miles) from New Zealand to Antarctica and back saw the lesson differently. 'Perhaps we are a step closer to breaking the midwinter ice-curtain,' said Newcomer, when interviewed at Christchurch. His fellow pilot, Commander Bill Munson, had fewer reservations: 'We proved we can fly to Antarctica at any time of the year,' he announced.

A Navy helicopter hovers at the end of Williams Field, with the temporary Jamesway huts of the early aviation headquarters below.

◀ The R7V Super Constellation, *Phoenix Firebird*, which had completed 100 passenger trips across the Southern Ocean between New Zealand and Antarctica. Later the aircraft was designated C121-J.

From the early 1960s, the LC-130F (formerly 'C-130 BL') took over the role of Antarctica's workhorse, eliminating parachute drops from the ageing Globemasters, by then known to crews as 'Old Shakey'.
Inset: Battling the cold to refuel a C-130 aircraft.

Among the many other mercy flights — missions which would continue as long as men endured the hazards of Antarctic living — was an even riskier feat of penetrating the very depth of the polar winter. When in 1964 a sailor broke his back in a rooftop fall, two Hercules again were dispatched from the United States, one going on from New Zealand reached McMurdo in total darkness. Other winter rescues were performed twice in 1966, the second bringing out a scientist from Byrd Station who suffered acute appendicitis which required immediate hospital treatment.

Yet another mid-winter flight went to McMurdo in June 1967 by when a routine for the mercy missions had surely been set. The New Zealand government placed a frigate on station for weather reporting and search and rescue stand-by in the southern seas. Before leaving Christchurch the pilot, Commander 'Bull' Mayer, declared: 'I'll just be talking to the man upstairs and let Him guide me'. Minutes before the plane departed Harewood airport, a telegram arrived from the school children of Hawera which read 'May God

In the darkness at distant McMurdo, fuel drums are lit to illuminate the runway for the approaching plane.

The drama of a midwinter medical emergency flight: Commander Mayer receives a gift from Salvation Army well-wishers in Christchurch.

go with you, gallant gentlemen'.[14]

The flight reached McMurdo in forty degrees below zero where for eight days navy teams had worked around the clock in searing cold to clear the runway. As the Hercules approached every lamp at the base went on and barrels of oil were set afire at intervals along the skiway. 'It was fantastic,' Commander Mayer said afterwards, 'the most illuminated runway I have ever seen.' After a two-hour turnaround, the C-130 with the patient went heading back to civilisation. Proof indeed that if men must fly, the cold Antarctic night would not stop them. Then the first scheduled midwinter flights took place, carrying scientists, together with the mail and fresh milk and vegetables to McMurdo Sound. Another emergency evacuation was made from Byrd Station on 1 September 1969. Flown at the edge of the winter darkness, it was the third such mission across that frozen wilderness since 1960.

The ever-trusty Hercules (now classified LC-130F) had transported mountaineers to the remote Sentinel Range, 2,100 kilometres (1,300 miles) from McMurdo where they would climb Vinson Massif, at 4,897 metres (16,067 feet) the highest known peak in Antarctica. To establish Eights Station in Ellsworth Highland 75°14' South, 77°10' West, the C-130s completed 45

A rapid air-lift by Hercules transports added Siple Station to the list of Deep Freeze bases.
Inset: Dodging a freezing slipstream to welcome an incoming LC-130.

supply trips, each measuring a return distance from McMurdo of 4,345 kilometres (2,700 miles). They took the remains of Alfred Larkman an old Antarctican who, before his death in New Zealand, asked that his ashes be scattered above the nunatak named after him on the fringe of the polar plateau. They provided the transport to carry Weddell seals back to an American zoo for scientific observation. And they were the 'kidnapper vehicle' of the bewildered penguins lifted from Wilkes to McMurdo and again from McMurdo to Byrd Station, in a study of the birds' uncanny sun navigation internal clocks. They also flew a group of banded skua gulls to the South Pole, from where 10 days later the birds were back at their coastal nests. No job too small or too strange might well be the VX-6 motto.

With a favourable tail wind, a C-130 on 3 September 1967 took a record 6 hours and 2 minutes to complete the Christchurch–McMurdo journey of usually eight hours. But these times were soon to be eclipsed in 1968 with the arrival of the giant C-141 Starlifter, reducing the Christchurch–McMurdo journey to around five hours with a 40,000-pound (18,000-kilogram) cargo load.[15] So into the jet age, Antarctic aviation moved ahead. Piece by piece, the great flights had painted their vapour trails above Antarctica's unknown. But while the mysteries might be rolled back, the Great White Terror would never be subdued, always extracting its price.

Moments of Terror

Operation Deep Freeze was but a few days old when a single-engine Otter crashed on take-off at McMurdo runway. One passenger suffered a back injury, another broke a leg but otherwise the crew and four people aboard emerged relatively intact. They were luckier than many of the accident victims in the years ahead. Six weeks later another Otter came down 'somewhere on the Ross Ice Shelf' during a flight from Little America to Marie Byrd Land. Nothing went right for the rescue attempts. Another Otter, brought on USS *Glacier* to search for the missing plane, was dropped during unloading operations at Kainan Bay. A P2V Neptune rushed from the United States with a parachutist trained in remote rescue operations crashed in the Venezuelan jungle, fortunately without fatalities. The crew of the lost Otter was finally located by a third Otter as they trudged across the Ross Ice Shelf, having covered 60 kilometres (37 miles) and with twice as far still to go.

By Deep Freeze's first full year of establishment, the navy command hoped that operations would be sufficiently shaken down to make flying conditions more predictable and safer — relatively safer, that is. It was not to be. On 16 October 1956 Deep Freeze II began when Rear Admiral Dufek landed on the ice in his R5D Skymaster after a 13½ hour flight from Christchurch, New Zealand.

A P2V Neptune on launching with JATO-assist. A similar event which malfunctioned brought disaster at Wilkes Station. 'A burst of flame appeared to come from the aircraft,' said an observer of the tragic take-off.

The weather at McMurdo was fine. Dufek gave the word for the rest of the six aircraft of VX-6's summer detachment to depart New Zealand the following day. The lead aircraft of the flight, a P2V Neptune piloted by Lieutenant David Carey, had passed the point of no return when a furious blizzard hit the base, followed by a whiteout. Ceiling was 90 metres (300 feet) when his Neptune emerged from the overcast, having been talked down to 400 metres (1,300 feet) by the airfield's ground control. Carey radioed that he planned to make a visual landing and guided his aircraft downwind, to fly parallel with the runway. As he turned for the final approach, one wing clipped a snow bank — the aircraft cartwheeled, slammed into the ice and broke apart.

When rescue teams reached the wreck, Carey and two others were dead and a fourth man died soon afterwards. The final victim, Captain Rayburn Hudman, was the rescue specialist who had survived the previous year's Neptune crash in Venezuela. The P2V's smoking wreckage littered the airfield perimeter when the capricious weather lifted and ground control was able to talk down the rest of the detachment as they flew in at intervals of an hour apart. The orange tail section of the shattered Neptune remained beside McMurdo runway as a useful beacon, and a grim reminder of the hazards of Antarctic flying.

Three days after the Neptune crash, the big C-124 Globemasters ran into trouble. One, named the *State of Washington*, at the end of the long flight from Christchurch had a nose wheel collapse and slid halfway down the frozen runway on its clam-shell nose doors. The *State of Tennessee*, on return from a South Pole airdrop, undershot the runway, ploughed into a snow bank and

Monument to Seaman Richard Williams, first American to die in McMurdo Sound; this airfield now bears his name.

▲ Digging out an R4D at the end of winter. Thirteen of the navy's Dakota-type Skytrains were written-off during their flying years with Deep Freeze.
▼ Wreckage of the unfortunate Super Constellation *El Paisano* litters the side of Williams Field.

slithered 460 metres (1,500 feet) on its nose with flames issuing from ruptured fuel tanks. One aircraft was damaged but repairable, but the hulk of the other lay by the strip's rubbish dump for years to come, being the sort of sight that newcomers stepping from a plane at McMurdo preferred not to notice.[16]

The worst Globemaster accident came at the start of Deep Freeze IV when heavy 'milk run' traffic winged south from New Zealand. By early October 1958 the small U.S.–New Zealand joint station of Cape Hallett located on the northern tip of Victoria Land regarded itself as being 'back on the map' with the arrival of the first Adelie penguin to the rookery alongside the base, and then the sudden influx of five aircraft — four of them C-124s. All had been diverted by bad weather at McMurdo and, though Cape Hallett had no ground control installation, all were talked down safely to the recently installed standby strip beside Moubray Bay by the captain of an R4D which was the first to land. With good reason, the men of the base felt the occasion was deserving of congratulations all round for a happy end to a risky situation.

Ten days later the scene would tragically change. Coming in on the morning of 16 October to make a mail drop at Hallett, a Globemaster loaded with eight tonnes of heavy timber for the polar building program lost its way and slammed into a mountain slope. The aircraft ploughed for 270 metres (900 feet) across the snow-capped hillside, breaking into three sections. The seven men on the flight deck survived but six who were in the laden cargo area died instantly.

Three tracked vehicles, one driven by the base medical officer, Doctor Bornmann, immediately left Hallett for the crash site which was estimated to be some 50 kilometres (30 miles) to the north, in the vicinity of Cape Roget. But the rescuers entered 'cruel and hostile territory' crisscrossed with crevasses; when two of the Weasels nosedived into the chasms, they were forced to retreat. The six survivors, three of them seriously injured, were found huddled in the tail section of the wreck when a helicopter from McMurdo was able to reach them in clearing weather a day later. In freezing temperatures, they had lit a fire in the casing of the aircraft toilet but found it impossible even to warm their hands. No survival tents or stores were aboard, which must have been a lesson to the air force command.

Project Magnet was one of the major scientific studies which the McMurdo runway once again brought to an unfortunate end. The big R7V Super Constellation *El Paisano*, operated by the navy's Hydrographic Office, had completed a number of spectacular missions in the study of magnetic forces within the Southern Ocean. On 24 October 1960 it completed the first nonstop flight from Antarctica to Australia, on a route from McMurdo via the South Magnetic Pole to Hobart, a distance of almost 6,000 kilometres (3,700 miles) in 16 hours. A week later, the $6 million flying laboratory lay in pieces on McMurdo's Williams Field. All 16 crew and four geophysicists survived, though two were seriously injured and six others suffered slight injuries. *El Paisano*'s next flight would have been another record-breaker from McMurdo to Perth and then via the Pole to South America.

A second Super Constellation, the navy's *Pegasus*, also came to grief while attempting a 'wheel' landing on inner Williams Field in a blinding snowstorm and with only 40 minutes' fuel left after the crossing from Christchurch. All 68 passengers and crew escaped, but the loss in 1970 of a second valuable aircraft (the right wing was torn away as the plane veered off the runway)

Shattered wing and fuselage of the R7V *El Paisano* which crashed on landing in bad weather at McMurdo on 31 October 1960. For Project Magnet, the big Constellation was in the process of completing long-range flights between Antarctica and surrounding continents of the Southern Hemisphere.
Inset: Reminder of an earlier peril at McMurdo Sound is the cross in memory of Seaman Vince, a member of Captain Scott's 1901 expedition who fell from an icy cliffside.

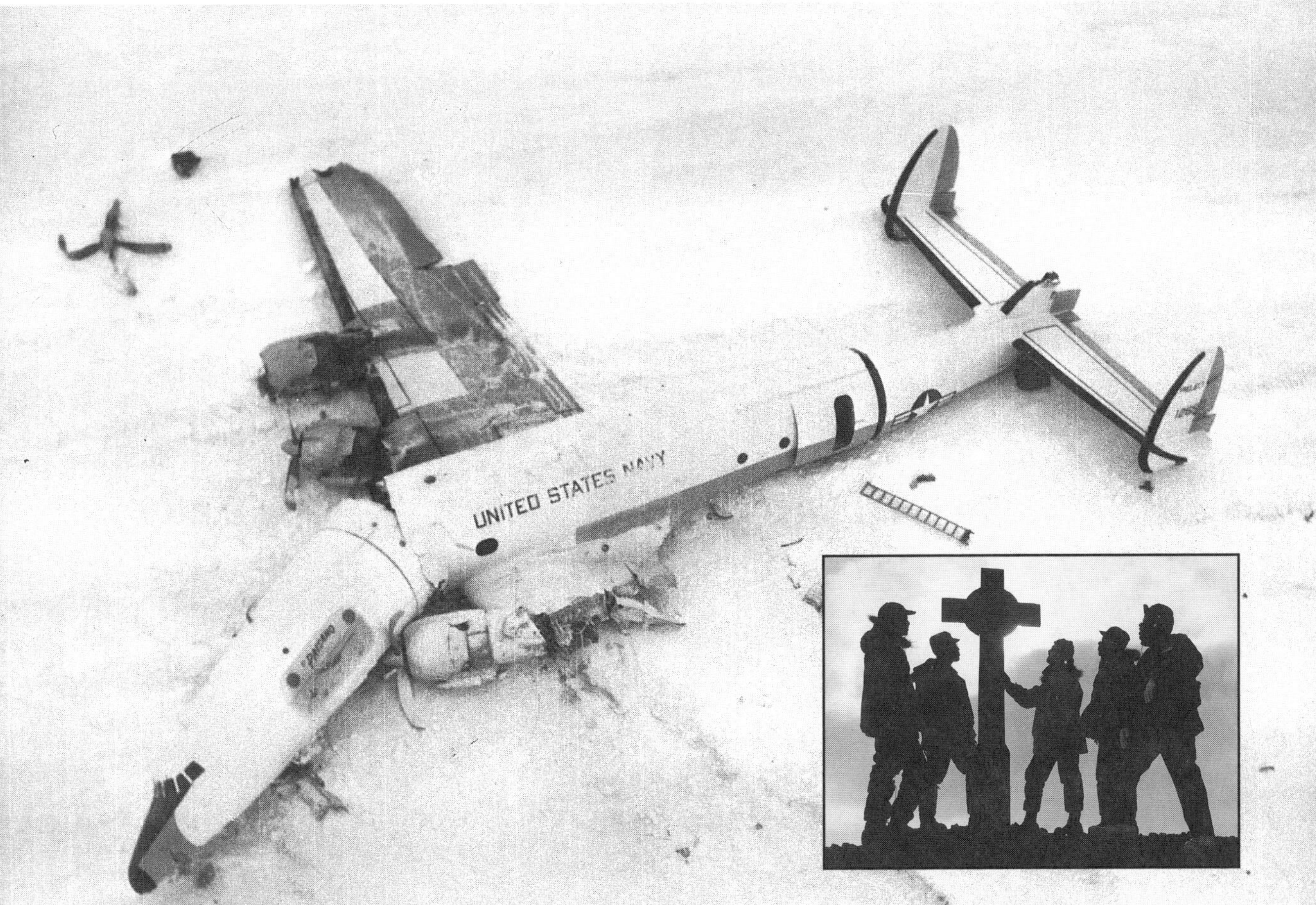

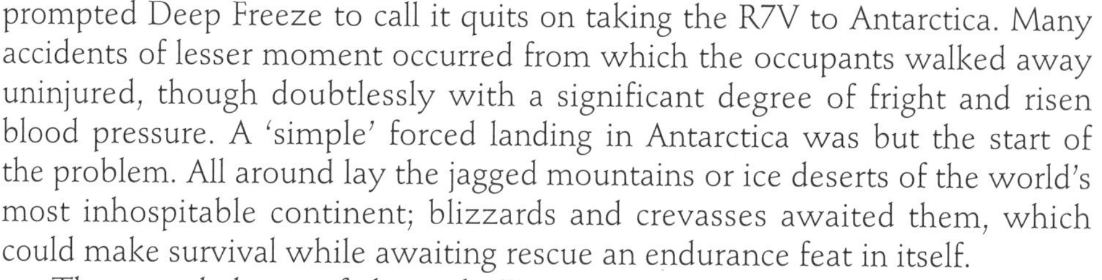

prompted Deep Freeze to call it quits on taking the R7V to Antarctica. Many accidents of lesser moment occurred from which the occupants walked away uninjured, though doubtlessly with a significant degree of fright and risen blood pressure. A 'simple' forced landing in Antarctica was but the start of the problem. All around lay the jagged mountains or ice deserts of the world's most inhospitable continent; blizzards and crevasses awaited them, which could make survival while awaiting rescue an endurance feat in itself.

An LC-130 prepares to unload its freight for the building of Plateau Station at an elevation of 3,660 metres (12,000 feet); summer temperature was –43°C (–45°F).

The record sheets of the early Deep Freeze years are stacked with accident entries, some of which in their recurrence are reduced almost to the status of passing interest...an R4D disabled with port landing gear in the Horlick Mountains...an R4D with sheared tail ski in the Ellsworth Highland...JATO breaks loose of R4D on take-off and shoots through propeller, causing engine to break apart — pilot pancakes the plane...sastrugi disables R4D ski gear at landing in the Sentinel Mountains, plane belly flops and occupants evacuate aircraft.

At Cape Hallett an R4D crash-lands while bringing in a doctor and medical corpsman to perform appendectomy; no personnel injured, but Skytrain is a write-off. Three days after the 1962's Thanksgiving celebration, an R4D stalls on take-off after picking up a polar plateau trail party, falls back to surface, port wing digs furrow in snow...only split-second power shut-off by Lieutenant D. R. Miller saves aircraft from cartwheeling...crew and passengers scramble out while petrol trickles on the snow...fortunately 30 degrees of frost prevent explosion; if aircraft had swung in other direction wing would have sheared through trail party's tents.

Gus Shinn told of a heart-stopping moment when, banking his R4D (believing he was at a respectable altitude) while scouting for a landing place beneath the Beardmore Glacier, he suddenly found a wing scraping the snow. He gunned the motors and returned to base, with nothing more than a crum-

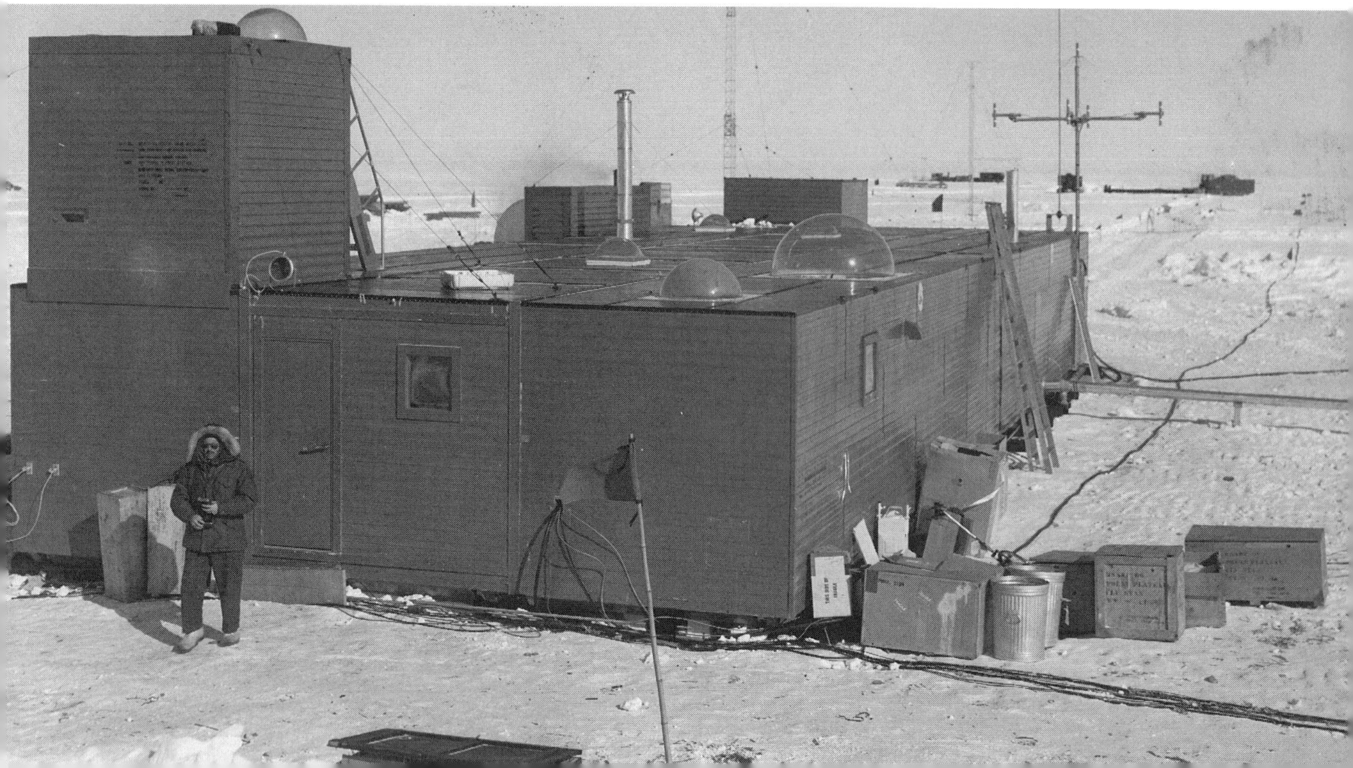

Ready for instant occupation, the prefabricated huts are all designed to fit within a C-130 fuselage and to be rapidly discharged through the rear cargo door. Plateau Station's location was 79°15' South latitude, 40°30' East longitude; at a distance of 2,240 kilometres (1,400 miles) from McMurdo, it was labelled the most remote of the American scientific outposts and, after Vostok, the 'second coldest place on earth'.

pled wing tip to show. Gus could console himself that one more aviator had escaped the deadly whiteout.

But if the rugged old Skytrain sometimes seemed to bear a charmed life, a tragic exception awaited those who joined the flight of 2 February 1966 to pick up a scientific party on the trail to the original Byrd Station. In a crash and explosion of the fuel tanks, all six of the crew perished. The occasions of narrowly averted disaster are almost too numerous to list. Sometimes the survivors could reflect on the comic aspect of their adventure, as when an Otter suffered structural damage in a rough landing on sastrugi and taxied for 50 kilometres (30 miles) to reach base. Passengers told of seeing the tail section actually 'hinge', letting in the freezing air as the disabled Otter limped home across the ice.

Christmas and New Year seem to figure as a most accident prone time in Antarctic aviation. Two days before Christmas, 1959, an R4D attempted to land at Byrd Station in a near whiteout. It stalled close to landing, the starboard wing dragged the snow, landing gear collapsed, the starboard engine mount snapped, part of the wing sheared off and the fuselage buckled. For those who lived through those heart-stopping moments, it was another miraculous escape. On Christmas Day of the following year, McMurdo crews unbelievingly watched an Otter overshoot the skiway, collide with a snow bank, bounce into the air, contact the skiway again, catapult into the air for a second time and then thump back on the ice. The aircraft survived and no one was injured.

Nothing comic — only stark fear for another Otter crew which went out on Christmas Eve, taking with them the Scott Base leader and a replacement husky dog and supplies for a New Zealand traverse party who were located, of all places, close to Mount Christmas about 500 kilometres (310 miles) south of McMurdo.[17] Two hours out from base, the single engine began to stutter and misfire, splashing a fine coating of engine oil across pilot Tim Morrow's windscreen and blotting out his starboard vision. A quick turn was made for home but the aircraft lost altitude and with speed reduced to 40 knots they broke through the cloud layer to see the surface of the Ross Ice Shelf rapidly closing up. Worse, they were above the shelf's horror stretch where the outflows of Byrd Glacier and Barne Inlet collide in a chaos of tumbled ice and gigantic crevasses.

'Mayday, mayday!' Captain Morrow shouted into the radio as they came down. The Otter struck the surface, bounced over a 20-metre (60-foot) crevasse, struck the ice again, slithered across three more crevasses and halted against a snowbank. All four men tumbled out, to find another gaping crevasse awaiting them on the far side of the bank into which the Otter would almost certainly have plunged. The engine was dead and the right ski assembly broken — no way for a take-off, even if they could reach a level patch of snow. Yet they had survived, thanks to pilot Morrow's masterly handling of the stricken machine. Even the Greenland husky seemed impervious to their plight, curled up in a tight ball at the rear of the cabin. Using the cabin stepladder as a probe, Morrow searched for a safe place among the crevasses which they could mark for their rescuers. But going aboard a helicopter a few hours later was not the end of their adventure. Against a strong westerly drift, the helicopter pilot lost direction and emerged from broken cloud to find they were flying amid mountain peaks rearing far above their maximum altitude. A break in the cloud cover let them see a gap leading to the Ross Ice Shelf. Christmas Eve, 1960, in McMurdo was one to remember.

Frozen to the Ice

Sergeant Charles Greer observing the first South Pole landing, 31 October 1956:

I watched as the pilot of the R4D fired four JATO bottles, but the aircraft didn't budge. It had frozen to the terrain within three minutes of landing. Four more JATOs were fired and the plane picked up speed. The last of the JATOs was fired and the plane became airborne at about 75 miles an hour.

Firing of the JATOs caused a whiteout condition and in the C-124 we could not see the R4D for some time. We tried to reach it by radio, but the pilot was too busy trying to keep his aircraft in the air.

Major Ellen got through to the R4D pilot as he was trying to take off, telling him if he couldn't make it, that he would belly land the C-124 alongside him to make a warm house for the crews to live in.

Que Sera Sera at the South Pole, 31 October 1956: after 45 minutes on the plateau, the crew realised they were rapidly freezing-up; temperature was –50°C (–58°F).

An LC-130 at the Pole: in –57°C (–70°F) conditions a trail of condensation, normally seen in high flying, rolls across the ice. Lowest safe flying temperature was regarded as –54°C (–65°F).

Then there was the unlucky New Year. Three days into Deep Freeze IV, an Otter went on a photo mission to the experimental runway at Marble Point. The site on the far side of McMurdo Sound was under study for an all-weather airport which might one day serve long-distance commercial aircraft on international routes. At the completion of the assignment, the Otter commenced its take-off, only to fall out of the sky with engine failure, killing the pilot and co-pilot and critically injuring the other three aboard. Two other close shaves were ahead, when the era of the C-130 Hercules began in Operation Deep Freeze. One would see a Hercules almost lost over the Southern Ocean, another the forced landing of a C-130 with only a single engine functioning. But these dramas lay well ahead. More tragic and soon to come was the crash of a VX-6 Neptune while attempting one of Antarctica's longest missions.

A memorable flight was planned for the P2V *Bluebird* which lifted off under the command of Lieutenant Eli Stetz from McMurdo strip on 9 November 1961. In triangular pattern it would make a magnetic survey of little known eastern Antarctica, by way of Mirnyy, the Soviet Station, and Wilkes, lately handed over to the Australians. The projected course of 5,600 kilometres (3,500 miles) would set a new interior distance record. All went according to plan until, after the stop-over at Wilkes, they readied for the final 2,250 kilometre (1,400 mile) leg back to McMurdo. But on take-off from the ice strip 12 kilometres (8 miles) behind the coastal base, as the ski undergear bumped across the rough and ridged surface, something went dreadfully wrong.[18] In the words of a VX-6 report, based on an eye-witness account:

First loss of a Hercules at McMurdo Base occurred when this LC-130 caught fire while preparing for take-off. The crew escaped injury.

> The aircraft, after travelling the full length of the skiway, became airborne rising in a straight course to a height of approximately 500 feet. Some small fragments of solid material were seen to fall from the fuselage of the aircraft during this ascent.
>
> The aircraft changed its course by banking to the left, shortly after which a puff of flame and smoke followed by a muffled report occurred toward the rear of the fuselage. The aircraft continued on a banking turn to the left and then dipped slightly and, while still banking, disappeared partially behind a low rise in the plateau surface approximately one and three-quarter miles from the point of observation toward the take-off end of the strip. A burst of flame appeared to come from the aircraft, which continued for some distance trailing flame, before finally coming to rest.

Two theories were advanced for the crash. One blamed the jarring loose during take-off of an auxiliary fuel tank located in the Neptune's bomb bay, spilling the contents which ignited and caused an internal explosion. The other was that a JATO bottle stored at the rear of the plane had been shaken, impacted and ignited. In either event, an explosion ripped through the plane, filling it with flame and smoke. Blind and choking, Stetz and his co-pilot fought to bring *Bluebird* down, but they lost control and smashed into the plateau ice. Five passengers died in the fiery wreck, four of them navy men including the new commander of the Deep Freeze air detachment, Lieutenant Commander W. D. Counts, while the fifth was a geophysicist attached to the Antarctic Research Program, Dr Edward C. Thiel; a mountain range close to the South Pole now bears the name of that distinguished scientist from the

Wreckage of the Navy's *Pegasus* at Williams Field. All eighty aboard the big Super Constellation managed to run to safety.

In a single summer season, usually from October to February, Hercules carried 5,000 tonnes of supplies, much of it fuel, to the Antarctic bases. Landing on cruel sastrugi-ridged surfaces in extremely low temperatures, together with JATO operation on the rough terrain, all added to the hazards faced by VXE-6 crews.

Sharing in the 'milk run' from Christchurch to McMurdo Sound, a Royal New Zealand Air Force Hercules unloads its travellers at Williams Field.

University of Minnesota. Pilots Stetz and Hand survived but were badly injured, as were the other two survivors. A C-130 Hercules flew a rescue mission from McMurdo to bring back the dead and injured. No equipment could be salvaged from the Neptune wreck.

Navy authorities believed their Antarctic operation would conclude at the end of the IGY on 31 December 1958. By the 1959–60 summer, they expected Operation Deep Freeze would have folded its tents and stolen away, leaving Antarctica to the seals and penguins. But in Washington the politicians had other ideas. 'Because of the success of the IGY gathering of scientific data and the requirement to learn more of the continent and its effects on the world,' Congress authorised a year-by-year continuation of America's polar research program, under grants funnelled through the National Science Foundation. That was one side of the story. The other referred to the strategy of who would remain in Antarctica once the IGY concluded — in essence, a visiting of Cold War diplomacy upon south polar calm. The Soviets showed no intention of withdrawing their large expedition; indeed it was rumoured (as Dufek had feared) that immediately Uncle Sam went out one door of Amundsen-Scott station, the Russians would enter through the other one.[19]

So with the turn of the new decade, the U.S. Navy prepared to continue its massive effort of supporting an American presence in Antarctica. To represent the change, Deep Freeze itself took on a new numbering system in which the operation would be classified by the year, starting with Deep Freeze 60. The decade of the 1960s also saw the introduction of the C-130 Lockheed Hercules. Equipped with sturdy wheel-ski landing gear, the C-130 was able to set down just about anywhere in Antarctica where a relatively level stretch of snow could be found. The plane was fast, efficient and carried a big payload which could be discharged from a rear door at surface or vehicle level; the batch of Hercules allocated to Operation Deep Freeze were the first to be regularly flown within the U.S. Navy.[20]

JD 321 was one of the damaged aircraft rescued by a team from the navy, Lockheed and National Science Foundation.

Deep Freeze aviation now had five years' experience in learning about the capricious and treacherous nature of the polar weather: the hazards of landing on rough sastrugi surface, the danger that lurked within a whiteout, and the impact of the cold on men and machines. All that knowledge was never sufficient to give Antarctic flying a clean slate. The year began — on 13 January to be precise — with near disaster.

It concerned a new C-130, not the navy's but of the U.S. Air Force, on the supply run from New Zealand. Somewhere south of Christchurch, in the blackest of nights above the Southern Ocean, the Hercules lost its bearings in flying beneath a high overcast that prevented the taking of star sights (magnetic compasses being useless in the high latitudes). From McMurdo, a P2V went out to find the straying aircraft and escort it home; the experienced navy navigator concluded that his air force counterpart, fresh to the Antarctic

The tail of the damaged Hercules, protruding like a beacon from the snows of Eastern Antarctica, elevation 2,225 metres (7,300 feet).

zone, was applying Northern Hemisphere corrections to his grid system. On this hunch, he directed the P2V pilot to fly an erratic course that by radar and then radio finally led them to intercept the lost Hercules which landed at McMurdo with fuel for another 10 minutes remaining in its tanks.

The navy's new C-130s assumed the role of 'workhorse of Antarctica'. The C-124 air drop missions were gradually phased out and turbo-driven helicopters ousted the ageing R4D Skytrains. The C-130 with its ability to 'go anywhere — land anywhere' dominated the supply assignments. Nothing seemed beyond the scope of the powerful Hercules. They brought an unrivalled degree of safety and reliability to Deep Freeze aviation; to say they led a charmed life was in fact another way of expressing the professionalism of the navy crews who flew those big silver machines with the high orange painted tails.

Then early in Deep Freeze 62 an incident occurred which almost put paid to the accident-free record of the remarkable machines. The 'Darbyville Affair', as it was known in VX-6 lingo, reminded everyone of how a close brush with disaster could come out of a clear blue polar sky. On 1 January 1962 a C-130 piloted by Major Leslie L. Darbyshire, and with Lieutenant Don Moxley as his co-pilot, left McMurdo carrying a scientist, a Catholic chaplain and 10 tonnes of gasoline and diesel fuel across the 1,380 kilometres (860 miles) to the new Byrd Station. The priest, Father August Mendonza, was awaited at Byrd station to celebrate a New Year's Mass.

The flight droned routinely across the Ross Ice Shelf and above the rising slopes of Marie Byrd Land until, without warning, number one engine suddenly faltered and stopped, followed by the failure of number three engine. Then the unthinkable — number two engine began to splutter and die. With full power applied to number four to keep them aloft, Darbyshire and Moxley scanned the surface of sharp furrows of sastrugi that lay beyond their windscreen. 'Ditch the cargo!' came the order from the flight deck. The loadmaster pressed a button, the rear cargo doors opened, the restraining chains were knocked loose and drummed fuel went hurtling out. The cargo doors sealed shut and all of them strapped in, waiting for what would happen next.

Dragging JD321 from the ice at position 'D59' in Adelie Land.

Looking down on '129', damaged during take-off in 1975.

In the Air Operations Building at McMurdo, the squadron and base officers listened helplessly around the radio to the crackle of Darbyshire's voice as he told them they were trying to land. Silence and then groans of relief as his voice came back…'We made it!'

When an R4D finally reached the stranded Hercules, the rescuers found survival tents set up, men busily carving shelter breaks from the snow blocks and a sizzling evening meal cooking on a portable stove. They called the settlement 'Darbyshire' after the pilot whose coolness and competency had saved them. On a routine flight and free of weather problems they had encountered doomsday difficulties; now with the elation of men who walked away from a crippled aircraft, even the cold winds and endless ice at 82°34' South and 152°30' West tasted good. Fuel samples flown for analysis to McMurdo showed that water had contaminated the JP4, allowing ice to clog the engine strainers — fortunately not that of the fourth engine, otherwise there would be no telling of the tale. On 5 January the C-130 was healthily airborne once again, minuscule 'Darbyshire' ceased to exist and, once home at McMurdo, the first action of Father Mendonza was to celebrate a Mass of thanksgiving.

Official insignia of the elite Air Development Squadron Six.

The untarnished record of the Hercules came to a regrettable halt with the turn of the 1970s when, within a succession of summer seasons, no fewer than four of the big machines (and ultimately a fifth) were lost in flying accidents, particularly while supporting scientific parties on the blizzardly plateau of Eastern Antarctica. By this decade the C-130 transports belonged to the National Science Foundation but were still flown by the navy detachment, now renamed VXE-6. The downturn in Deep Freeze's fortunes started on 15 February 1971 when a Hercules caught fire while taxiing for take-off at Williams Field. Fortunately the crew of nine and one passenger had time to flee, before flames engulfed their machine.

On the blizzardly slopes of Terre Adelie, the Hercules JD 321 is slowly released from the embalming snows.

Disaster struck in a scene similar to this when a Hercules, inbound with replacement parts for JD321 clipped a snowbank and was wrecked. Two died and nine of the crew were injured.

Then, on 4 December 1971 an LC-130 on an Antarctic resupply mission prepared to take-off in the Dome C region of Wilkes Land after linking with a French glaciological party working on an 800-kilometre (500-mile) traverse between the small interior French post of Carrefour and Vostok station. Once again the JATO at the moment of firing turned into a deadly projectile. The Hercules was already airborne when two of the 165-pound bottles separated from the port (left) side of the rear fuselage. Travelling forward with rocket like speed, they smashed into the port inboard engine, causing shattered metal to penetrate both the outboard engine and the aircraft skin. With half its engine power suddenly lost, the Hercules swerved to the left, but the skilful flying of Lieutenant Commander E. M. Gabriel brought it back to the surface where it encountered sharp sastrugi. With its nose wheel-ski collapsed, the aircraft shuddered to a halt, leaving 10 shaken but uninjured crewmen to stumble out. They lived for three days in survival tents, close by the French traverse party in –31°C (–24°F) temperatures and 64 kph (40 mph) wind which increased the chill factor to around –73°C (–100°F). When weather conditions improved, a relief Hercules arrived to carry the crew back to McMurdo, leaving their wounded aircraft, JD321, to the mercy of the drifting snow.

Seventeen years after it last departed McMurdo, the restored JD321 sweeps back safely to the Williams Field skiway. Some $140 million was saved in the rescue of the four stranded Hercules.

Four years and 11 months later to the day, the mishap repeated on this dome of ill-omen. Hercules No. 320 suffered a JATO explosion on take-off and, with its crew safely evacuated, had to be abandoned with a punctured fuselage, severed wiring and a wrecked engine and propeller.

For the navy and National Science people, 15 January 1974 would mark a very black entry. On that day, two aircraft were lost, both on the high ice-sheet of Wilkes Land. The first aircraft had flown out to Dome C between Vostok and d'Urville stations to pick up a party of American, French and Russian scientists who were collecting shallow surface snow samples. The take-off began, using full JATO-boost to lift the laden aircraft above the rough surface as quickly as possible. But barely had the JATOs fired than one of the bottles exploded. With the fuselage punctured and the starboard (right hand) inboard engine in flames the Hercules skidded in a half circle but still remained upright. Fire then spread to the right hand outboard engine, destroying the wing. Remarkably, everyone was able to leave the plane without serious hurt.

Dufek, Twice Dunked

Rear Admiral George Dufek, first commander of the United States Navy's task force in Antarctica, twice escaped death from freezing polar waters.

A veteran of two Arctic and six Antarctic expeditions, he first went south with Admiral Byrd in 1939 and, like Byrd, became a legend in his own lifetime.

He was one of the few men who had fallen into icy Antarctic seas where death comes in four minutes, and survived. Once he was tipped into the water while being transferred in a bosun's chair between two ships. Once a helicopter in which he was flying crashed into the sea. 'I made it each time, before those vital minutes were up,' he said.

For the first four years of Operation Deep Freeze his tall, silvery haired figure encased in parka and snow hood led a force that totalled nearly 15,000 men to Antartica's frozen wastes. He asked President Eisenhower for $58 million to begin Deep Freeze I. Eisenhower cut his budget to $22 million.

He built the expedition around 80-tonne Globemasters, 21,000-horsepower icebreakers, huge tractor trains and ice bases fitted with washing machines and radiograms. Under his leadership Deep Freeze established: seven Antarctic bases, including 18 men at the South Pole; an 1,800-metre (6,000-foot) ice runway at the main base on McMurdo Sound, capable of holding Globemasters at the end of the supply flight from New Zealand; air routes crisscrossing Antarctica and new voyages of discovery and exploration, including measurement of the depth of the ice cap; and scientific research opening up new chapters of knowledge on the upper atmosphere, the earth's magnetism, the world's weather, ocean currents and radio communications.

One of the greatest single feats during Deep Freeze was putting down a plane at the South Pole, the first step towards seeing if men could live at the bottom of the world. Dufek told his fellow officers, 'The only way to find out is to go up there and see'. In his book, *Operation Deep Freeze*, he also revealed 'a haunting concern that the Russians will beat us to the South Pole'.

Dufek retired from Deep Freeze in 1959, aged 56. He died in 1977.

Admiral George Dufek, the first leader of Operation Deep Freeze. He was Admiral Byrd's navigator on the *Bear* in 1939. Beside him is the Deep Freeze emblem.

JD320 had to be left in the snow whan a JATO bottle exploded on take-off, damaging fuselage, wiring and propeller. While making an engine change in unprotected conditions, the repair team reported a –30°C (–22°F) average temperature with frequent windstorms. A National Science spokesman described the recovery of the four lost aircraft 'a major feat in aviation and Antarctic history'.

The second Hercules dispatched from McMurdo to rescue the stranded men began its take-off from the crash site with a decision not to use JATOs. But the long run across the wickedly rough plateau proved too much for the front ski undergear. As they gathered speed, the nose ski collapsed, tearing into the under fuselage, pitching the aircraft forward and driving snow into the cargo compartment . Once more, they all got out and walked away.

The lost aircraft were too valuable to be just written off. The very treacherous polar elements which vanquished them would serve to preserve the machines in moistureless air and embalming snows. After a fly-in by aircraft engineers and navy technicians, National Science authorities decided on a rescue operation — 'a major feat in aviation and Antarctic history', to quote the commendation of the National Science Board. In the United States, the Lockheed company fabricated a complete lower nose section together with ski landing gear, and an entire wing assembly.

Through two summer seasons — certainly a misnomer for temperatures down to minus fifty on the Wilkes Land plateau — a temporary camp was set up for the 25 engineers, mechanics, electronics technicians and metalworkers who faced the challenge of putting the aircraft together again. The gruelling effort was reckoned to be justified, for the Hercules carried a price tag of some $US17 million, while restoration to flying condition would cost but $6 million. At Christmas, 1976, the navy announced that 'the crashed Hercules on Dome C in Wilkes Land have been recovered'.[21]

And what of Julet Delta 321, stripped of its instruments and abandoned to the blizzards in 1971? Declared a total loss, it had gradually been smothered by the snow until only the tip of an orange tail showed above the surface.

UNITED STATES OF AMERICA
VXE-6

But as the seasons went by and new aircraft increased in price, and with the successful recovery of the 1974 victims, the navy gave second thoughts to the retrieval of 321. Once more the repair team camped on blizzardly Wilkes Land. Beginning on Christmas Day, 1986, they commenced to dig away 15 years of accumulated snow to free the aircraft over the two following summers at a cost of around $3 million, plus another $7 million once the aircraft was fully repaired in New Zealand.[22] Again the effort was considered to be worth the price — less than a third of purchasing a new C-130 from Lockheed — except that no one anticipated a disaster which ensued.[22]

On the morning of 9 December 1987 a C-130 loaded with a new engine, propeller and starter equipment came from McMurdo Sound on one of the many runs to resupply the repair team. The only Hercules configured by National Science for aerial photography and other scientific observations, it clipped a snow bank with a wing tip at touchdown. In seconds, the big plane had wheeled about, tumbled and strewn the ice with its smoking wreckage. Men from the recovery camp, lugging their limited fire-fighting equipment, rushed towards the crash site. Seven crew and four passengers had been aboard the Hercules.

Two were dead and the rest suffered varying degrees of injury, some serious. They had no doctor or adequate casualty facilities and help from McMurdo was hours off. In navy records, Corpsman Second Class Barney Card was the principal hero of the rescue that followed:

> Just after 8.30 a.m. he heard the shouts of 'crash!' in the camp. Together with others of the team, he jumped on a snowmobile to get to the ski-way. A scene of fire and twisted metal awaited them.
>
> With two other workers, Howard and Honeycutt, he ran to the wrecked nose section, trying to locate survivors. Howard shouted to the others that he could see crew members on one side of the flight deck struggling to free themselves. Fuel could be seen leaking across the cockpit and electrical power was still on. They located a hole torn in the nose fuselage, somehow managed to batter it open and one by one dragged out the crew.
>
> Card and the others loaded the survivors on the sledges and hurried them away. They were only five metres from the wreckage when the first of several explosions engulfed the stricken Hercules. When they reached camp, Card turned the living tent into a makeshift emergency room. His first task was to determine how badly each survivor was injured, and whose condition was the most serious. He allocated nine men to stretcher duty, each one to watch his patient and advise him of any change in their condition. For more than eight hours, Card was in sole control of medical treatment. Not until a break in the weather did a rescue Hercules get through from McMurdo. The navy report states while they awaited help, it was Barney Card's calm and organisation that kept the victims comfortable, and in at least one instance, kept a man alive.

That is part of the Antarctic aviation story — keeping your wits about you in moments of terror.

◀ Dog teams, transported by aircraft, were used in remote parts of Antarctica.

Antarctic Territorial Claims
1
2
1
3
8
7
4
6
5
1-Australia 2-France 3-N.Z.
4-Unclaimed 5-Chile 6-Britian
7-Argentina 8-Norway

EPILOGUE

FIFTY YEARS AFTER

The modern day Antarctic traveller: skiers carried from Chile by Adventure Network International leave the base at Patriot Hills. The Twin Otter is used by ANI to reach internal destinations.

In 1928 the American Geographical Society held a seminar on the future direction of exploration and research in the polar zones. Three honoured members of the society spoke at the seminar — Wilkins, Byrd and Ellsworth. All three had recently distinguished themselves in feats of Arctic aviation; all three agreed that the aircraft was the key to the new polar challenge, man's conquest of Antarctica.

Within the year Wilkins would make the first powered flight beyond the Antarctic Circle. In the following year Byrd reached the South Pole by aeroplane. Ellsworth within a few more years would be flying across Antarctica. Courage bordering on heroism, or maybe foolhardiness, was the badge of the men who, in the blossoming age of aviation, flew out in flimsy aircraft to explore the immense chilling void that covered the bottom of the world. Communication by wireless (if indeed they carried a radio) was usually touch and go; advanced weather forecasting mostly unavailable. No alternative or intermediate base awaited them in the event of bad weather or a failing engine; navigation depended on a high degree of personal expertise and confidence in elementary instruments.

Fifty years later the same treacherous weather and savage ice-scarred surface had relented not one iota. Otherwise, how the scheme had changed! Swift jet aircraft crossed Antarctica at high altitudes.[1] Landings at remote interior bases became routine. Despite the cold and darkness, mid-winter fly-ins arrived from the world outside. Navigation and communication enjoyed the sophisticated age of space and electronics.[2] In those same fifty years since Wilkins' first flight, man's regard for the Pole had changed, and changed

Despite many announcements and proposals, Australia (claimant to 42% of the Antarctic Continent) still has no regular direct air link with its vast icebound territory.

Direct flights planned to Antarctica

By ANDREW DARBY

HOBART: For the first time since Australia established a permanent presence in Antarctica 35 years ago, the RAAF has been asked to test out direct flights between the continents.

The C-130 Hercules flights are being planned for next summer, on the 1,846 nautical mile crossing of the Southern Ocean between Hobart and Casey station.

The plan was disclosed in a Senate estimates committee meeting on Thursday and confirmed yesterday by an adviser to the Minister for the Environment, Senator Richardson.

"The Minister has given the go-ahead to examine options we have of flying to Antarctica," he said.

"There will be a re-assessment after these tests."

On the iced continent, logistics are to be further enhanced by the first use of long-range helicopters between the country's three permanent stations and summer field bases.

Such an improvement in air transport would open a new era for Australia's program and bring the country up to pace with most other nations working there.

It would also enhance Australia's claim to 42 per cent of Antarctica at a time when several nations are increasing their presence on the continent in preparation for possible claims to areas for exploration and mining rights.

WHERE REGULAR ANTARCTIC FLIGHTS WILL GO

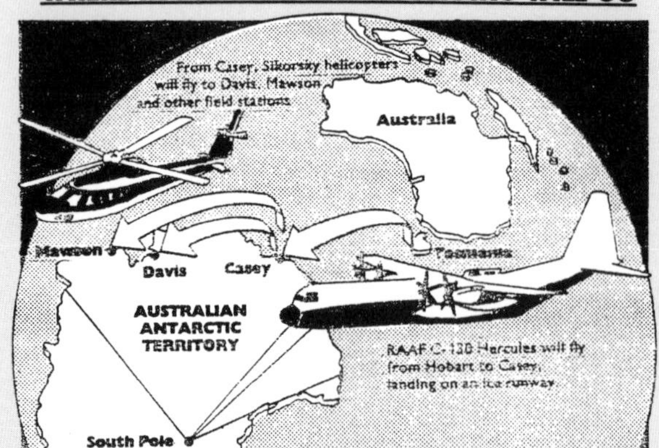

The chairman of the Antarctic Scientific Advisory Council, Professor John Lovering, said the link was very exciting news.

"This may be the beginning of an ability to get scientists onto the continent early and bring them out more quickly, with tremendous implications for the amount of work done there," he said.

A direct air-link would mean a break from long reliance on voyages of up to two weeks each way which, in addition to making access difficult for scientists with little time to spare, hampers medical evacuation.

Last season, two Australian men who were suffering from broken legs had to be evacuated from Davis station by Soviet aircraft via Argentina.

An inaugural proving flight between Hobart and Casey was completed by the millionaire adventurer, Mr Dick Smith, aboard a de Havilland Twin Otter last November. He said at the time he found it unbelievable that Australia had no air-link.

The C-130 would fly from Hobart to a wheeled landing on bulldozed ice near Casey. Subject to RAAF agreement, two flights are planned.

The use of long-range helicopters, likely to be leased by the Antarctic Division, would increase field program options and dramatically improve communications between stations.

Mr Smith advocated the Twin Otter for this job but Senator Richardson's adviser said helicopters had greater versatility and could be stored more easily against the hostile Antarctic weather.

Debate has grown recently about whether Australia should build a hard rock runway in Antarctica. The proposal is supported by tourism advocates but condemned by environmentalists such as Greenpeace.

But Senator Richardson's adviser signalled strongly that if Australia committed itself to an air capability, it would not be likely to construct a hard rock runway.

Australian businessman Dick Smith (centre), with his pilot, the late Giles Kershaw, after landing out from Davis Station to mark the 60th anniversary of Sir Hubert Wilkins' first flight of 16 November 1928. The Twin Otter, VH-SHW is named and registered in honour of the Australian-born explorer. A select few private aviators of the Smith ilk have entered the Antarctic skies.

again. Explorers of the early air age regarded the realisation of national ambitions bearing on territory and commerce as sufficient justification for the cost and risk of their expeditions.

Men like the great polar leader, Sir Douglas Mawson, in an article written for the Melbourne *Sun* in 1928, found it easy to talk of whaling in terms of:

> Here lie almost at the doors of Australia mighty stretches of sea teeming with wealth, and vast land areas of almost unknown possibilities. Can we, looking to the future, afford to neglect these regions? They can be made to yield in increasing quantities things of value to the world. It is for Australians to continue the work that has been begun and to preserve and develop this heritage for Australians yet to be.[3]

Other distinguished scientist-colleagues agreed with the need for a commercial foothold in the south. Professor Frank Debenham in an address given in 1935 said one day Antarctica might offer sites for sanatoria and tourist resorts; it was also possible that the polar winds could be harnessed to produce electric power.

Inevitably came the era of contemplating the mineral wealth contained in the coastline's rocky outcrops, or locked beneath the ice cap. Enormous bands of coal were recognised from Scott and Shackleton's time. Later the presence of exotic or precious metals was reported in geological probes around the coast; among those listed were gold, copper, molybdenum and uranium while, offshore, the possibility of oil and gas fields made news.[4]

Dr P. G. Law, while director of Australia's polar endeavours, delivered a paper describing a '1984' vision of a future Antarctica (not necessarily his personal view, but illustrating the 'possible'). In his Sir John Morris Memorial Lecture in Hobart he went on to forecast jet passenger services to the Antarctic from South Africa, South America, Australia and New Zealand, underground mining cities lit by simulated sunshine generated from nuclear power, small hovercraft used as taxis and massive harvests from the protein-rich ocean plankton to feed a starving world. He spoke of navigational and approach aids erected on stilts 30 feet above the snow, and of hangars and

The U.S. Air Force's Galaxy C-5, the largest aircraft to reach Antarctica, discharging cargo at Williams Field.

workshops buried beneath the snow. Heavy tractor trains were envisaged hauling mineral concentrates from underground treatment plants at mines unceasingly worked throughout the dark winter months, and experimental trials of giant hovercraft ore-carriers.[5]

The respected American polar scientist Dr T. O. Jones echoed similar views when he said: 'It is entirely possible . . . that within a decade or two the ingenuity of man may devise methods for exploiting the economic features of the Antarctic area'.

In each instance, the aircraft played a pivotal role as the machine which ferried the geologists who would define the mineral deposits, which would bring in the mining engineers, the highly paid workers and some of their machines — and perhaps in intercontinental jet transports carry out the exotic minerals, once refined.

Territorial rights were the unavoidable background to these scenarios. Seven nations had established claims to sectors of Antarctica, based on historic exploration and sometimes the maintenance of minuscule settlements. Other nations refused to recognise territorial ownership; yet even these, as in the instance of the United States, kept their own territorial options up the national sleeve for possible future proclamation.

In 1959, twelve nations which regarded the south polar continent as having a significant influence on the world's equilibrium signed an Antarctic Treaty.[6] They agreed to impose a strict order of conduct upon each country's presence in Antarctica, prohibiting militarism and nuclear materials, protecting wildlife and placing 'in abeyance' the existing and long-standing territorial claims. Any nation was free to set up a base (though possibly occupied or managed by military personnel) and, for peaceful purposes, travel anywhere its expeditionaries pleased.

Commander Mayer, USN, displays a poster which tells of his flight.

Within the lifespan of the Treaty and the various protective conventions that had followed it, the hands of the environmental clock have come about. Whaling is severely restricted.[7] Talk of extracting minerals or drilling the seabed is practically anathema. Through the efforts of the conservationists, especially those of the Greenpeace organisation, attempts are made to police the management of the bases and to force an improvement in the more odious habits related to the disposal of rubbish and sewage.

After 50 years of aviation, an age of private endeavour again reached Antarctica. Men follow Scott's trail to the South Pole. No less than five parties have trekked across the continent since Shackleton's failed attempt. Climbers scale rocky snow-clad peaks with seemingly the same routine acceptance they might display towards the Alps or Himalayas. Those who would evaluate the commercial attractions of Antarctica share an equal opportunity of access with the environmental watchdogs.

In mid-winter darkness, an injured American technician is evacuated to New Zealand from McMurdo Sound. Medical emergencies such as this led to the making of 'win-fly' supply missions by the U.S. Navy.

Grumman HU-1B Albatross aircraft employed by Chile in passenger service to the Antarctic Peninsula. The Chileans have been at the forefront of tourism in building a commercial airstrip at King George Island and a hotel to accommodate visitors.

Side by side with the amateur explorer-adventurer came the age of organised tourism for the masses. Proximity of the Antarctic Peninsula has brought boatloads of visitors from South American ports, as well as by air. Sobering is the thought that four ships, though only one specifically in the tourist trade, have been lost in Antarctic and sub-Antarctic waters since 1980.[8]

The Sydney businessman-entrepreneur Dick Smith began Australia's 'day tripper' trade in 1977 with a series of successful Qantas charter flights to the ice coast that, at the speed of a Boeing 747, lies little more than four hours south of Hobart. At the same time, Air New Zealand (whose evaluation team inspected McMurdo facilities back in 1965) claimed its share of this new international travel market with similar day excursion flights to the Ross Sea region.

Anyone with about $300 to spare could buy a ticket to sit in the warmth and safety of a wide-body jet, to gaze upon the frozen face of the Great White Terror where explorers of the heroic age had dragged their sledges and sometimes perished. In safety, that is, until that dreadful moment on 28 November 1979 when an Air New Zealand DC-10, enveloped in a whiteout and dogged by misleading coordinates entered in its inertial navigation system, crashed into the lower slopes of Mount Erebus. All 257 people aboard died in the impact. Tourist flights by the major airlines ceased.

Man is seldom persuaded to retreat. In the words of Fridtjof Nansen, 'when he does not want to know, he ceases to be a man'. A Canadian company, Adventure Network International, has spearheaded a new airborne trade, carrying a more dedicated (and higher priced) patron close to the heart of Antarctica. At a DC-6 landing field in the Ellsworth Highland, passengers from South America transfer to ski-equipped Twin Otters to reach the towering Vinson Massif, and fly onwards even to the Pole itself.[9]

Remains of the Air New Zealand 'day tripper' flight which crashed into Mount Erebus on 28 November 1979. All 257 people aboard the plane perished in Antarctica's worst air disaster.

The new era of private aviation has led to another type of international incident in which American bases in Antarctica refuse all but the most basic help to non-government travellers, be they on the surface or in the sky. As trans-Antarctic aviator Dick Smith found, a cup of coffee represented the sum total of American generosity for the tired flyer at the South Pole. Prompted, no doubt, by allegations of air traffic control negligence at McMurdo as a contributing factor to the DC-10 disaster on Ross Island, and the subsequent legal actions, the U.S. government formulated a deliberate policy in which all non-government travellers are regarded as being literally 'on their own'.

In the words of a statement made through the U.S. Antarctic Research Program (USARP), the National Security Council attitude towards the support of private expeditions is that 'the United States Government must limit assistance . . . in Antarctica to cooperative programs between US ARP and the Antarctic programs of other governments'. This means that in an emergency, the U.S. in Antarctica will help private expeditions but the government reserves the right to bill the survivors for all or any rescue costs.[10] The Russians, less fearful of litigation or recriminations, provided fuel for Dick Smith's aircraft which they had hauled across the icesheet from Mirnyy to Vostok, and at their bases were generous without reserve in their hospitality and assistance.

Yet American policy towards the lone aviator or the sledger stands in stark contrast to the many and continuing works of mercy performed by U.S. airmen in flying to the remotest corners of Antarctica when someone is in

Reaching McMurdo for the first time in 1968, the Lockheed C-141 Starlifter brought the fast and powerful jet transport age to the ice.

The Australian government spent abortive funds on investigating the making of an airfield at Casey Station, some five flying hours south of Hobart. 'Lanyon' was planned to have a 2,440-metre (8,000-foot) strip, capable of taking Hercules aircraft.

need. Such a mission was the flight of October 1985 from McMurdo Sound to Davis where an Australian expeditionary had suffered third-degree burns following an explosion of inflammatory material in the water tank he was trying to clean.[11]

The U.S. Navy crew in their ski-equipped LC-130 Hercules tested the recommended endurance of their aircraft in covering the 2,334 kilometres (1,460 miles) from the Ross Sea to the Ingrid Christensen Coast. At the small ANARE station, a makeshift landing strip was cleared on the sea ice. Transferring the injured expeditionary took but 20 minutes and then the aircraft was off again, on the seven-hour return leg. The end was unfortunate — but no one could say the navy crew had counted the dollars and cents or the

The airstrip complex at Williams Field, McMurdo Sound. The Deep Freeze force maintains 'wheel' and 'ski' runways, and emergency strips, as summer and ice conditions permit. The bay ice used for 'wheel' landings is about 2.4 metres (8 feet) thick; the soft snow skiway further south on the firmer Ross Ice Shelf has a thickness of some 18 metres (60 feet).

risk to their own lives in that hazardous attempt to save a single life. As the C-130 neared McMurdo, the 34-year-old patient, Stephen Bunning, died.[12]

The last decade of the twentieth century is one of increasing access to Antarctica. The Chileans installed a gravel airstrip on King George Island, alongside the Antarctic Peninsula. They have families in residence and have built a hotel to accommodate travellers arriving by charter flight. The Russians have a compacted snow runway at Molodezhnaya base which is now the main terminal station for airliners flying expedition members from Moscow, via Mocambique. America has studied making a hard rock airfield at Marble Point on the western side of McMurdo Sound but, for the time being at least, is satisfied that the various snow and ice strips at Williams Field (capable of taking a C-141 Starlifter or the even mightier Galaxy C-5) are adequate for the transport needs of the Antarctic Research Program.[13]

How the age of Antarctic tourism took hold.

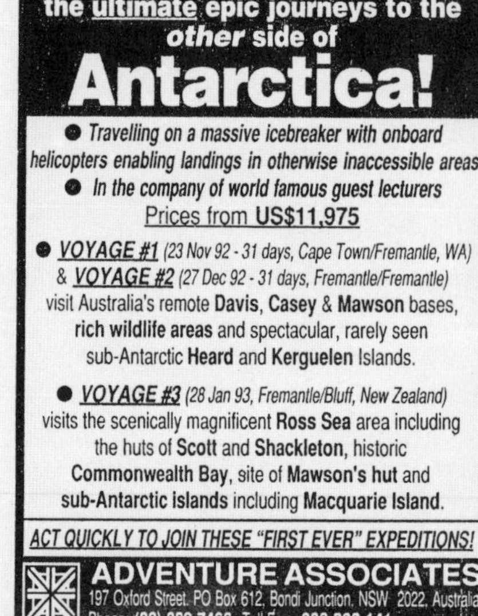

ANTARCTICA

THE LAST FRONTIER

Venturetreks

Antarctic Cruise December 1992

Even today, after so many years of exploration, Antarctica still remains a world apart - a majestic frontier surpassing even the early philosophers' wildest dreams. Due to modern technology and the availability of expedition ships, it is now possible to visit Antarctica - stand among thousands of chattering penguins and cruise through sparkling icebergs of all shapes and sizes. With a well planned itinerary we are now able to capture all the wonder and beauty of this wilderness as well as allowing ourselves an opportunity for adventure and discovery.

During this cruise you will visit unbelievably beautiful areas, as we aim to cover a wide cross-section of the many highlights of the Antarctic Peninsula. We will aim to make only one base visit during these days, as to us Antarctica is "nature" and not the less attractive human enterprises. We will certainly visit King George Island, Hope Bay, Deception Island, Melchior Islands, Paradise Bay, Port Lockroy, Trinity Island, Lemaire Channel, Peterman Island, Anvers Island and many other exciting locations. This will be a voyage of exploration and adventure!

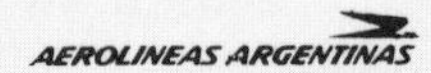

Flight 901, approaching Mt Erebus

From the report of the Royal Commissioner, the late Mr Justice Mahon, who investigated the crash in whiteout conditions of the Air New Zealand DC-10 on 28 November, 1979 with the loss of all 257 lives.

393 In my opinion therefore, the single dominant and effective cause of the disaster was the mistake made by those airline officials who programmed the aircraft (i.e. inertial navigation system) to fly directly at Mt Erebus and omitted to tell the aircrew. That mistake is directly attributable, not so much to the persons who made it, but to the incompetent administrative airline procedures which made the mistake possible.

394 In my opinion, neither Captain Collins nor First Officer Cassin nor the flight engineers made any error which contributed to the disaster, and were not responsible for its occurrence.

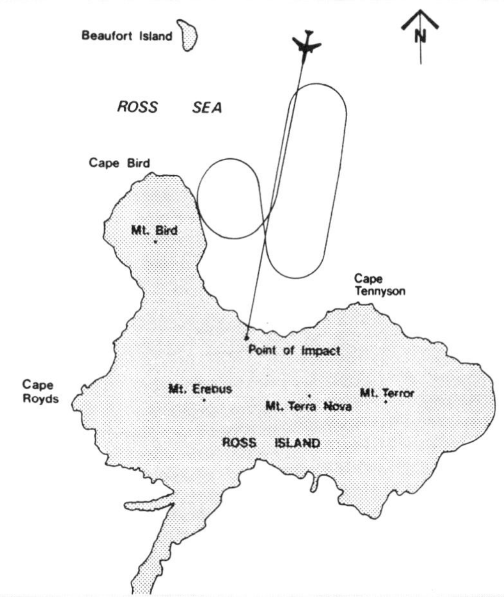

Flight path of the doomed DC-10

From the DC-10 flight recorder: 1, Captain. 2, First Officer. 3, Flight Engineer(s). 4, Commentator/guide. 5, Undefined voice. 6, Ground Proximity Warning system (and electronic voice).

5 Bit thick here, eh, Bert?
3 Yeah, my…oath! You're really a long while on instruments at this time, aren't you?
4 I reckon (Mt) Bird's through here and Ross Island there…and Erebus should be here
2 Terrain 1500
1 Capture
2 Alt hold
3 Hold on both, nav track
1 We didn't get that TACAN frequency, did we?
2 No
3 Have we got the latest Airad on the air craft?
5 What's the frequency… 1092?
2 Well, we think that's what it is, but it's channel 29
1 Actually those conditions don't look very good at all, do they?
4 No, they don't. You're down at 114 now, are you?
1 1500. Have we got them on the (McMurdo) Tower?
2 No, I'll try again
3 Only got them on HF, that's all
1 Try them again
4 That looks like the edge of Ross Island there
3 I don't like this
1 We're 26 miles north. We'll have to climb out of this
5 You can see Ross Island. Right. Fine!
2 Yes. You're clear to turn right. There's no high…
1 No. Negative!
2 No high ground if you do a 180
6 Whoop! Whoop! Pull up! Whoop! Whoop!
3 Five hundred feet (altitude)
6 Pull up!
3 Four hundred
5 Pull up!
6 Pull up! Whoop! Whoop! Pull up!
1 Go around power please
6 Whoop! Whoop! Pull…

The flight recording ceases. The impact with the slope of Mt Erebus came at 1.50 pm.

To the Ice in a Wheelchair

Miss Connie Ogden, a resident of Bowral, N.S.W. (until her death in 1990) made one of the Qantas B747 flights to Antarctica, organised by the businessman Mr Dick Smith. A precis of Miss Ogden's story "A Flight to the South Pole" follows:[14]

Thursday, 1st December, 1977, was the most adventurous day of my life! Conveyed to Mascot's International Airport and given VIP treatment with the checking of my ticket, I was taken in a wheelchair to the aircraft and helped on board to a window seat where I stayed for the whole flight.

Wilkins and Byrd pioneered the polar airways. Some fifty years later thousands of travellers, for the price of a few hundred dollars' day ticket, gazed down on the same wild and beautiful face of Antarctica.

After loading over 300 passengers and crew, our Jumbo Jet took off at 9.20 a.m. on its way to the South Pole. On board was Mr Eric Webb (88) from Wales who made the trip especially to see the hut he had built whilst with Sir Douglas Mawson's Expedition from 1911 to 1913. He told us that the Continent was 13.5 million square kilometres in area and divided into the Greater and Lesser Antarctica by mountains about 2,000 kilometres long and 2 to 4½ kilometres above sea level. It is the coldest and windiest continent in the world and is thought to be 300,000,000 years old.

At 1.10 p.m. we saw our first sight of pack ice, some 399 miles from the coast of the Continent and further north than expected. Shaped in a semi-circle, it looked crusty like stale cake icing as the thaw set in. One 'tiny' iceberg viewed from the plane was over one mile long.

Then Mr Webb donned the gear he had worn in 1912 and, with the long rope trailing with which he had pulled the sled, he paraded through the aircraft so that we could all see and appreciate the trials of his period of expedition and compare it with the comfort of ours.

My main memory will be the electric peacock-blue aura which circled the icebergs. The snowy whiteness of the bergs dotted about and this glorious blue circle around each one was caused by the reflection of the 'blue ice' from below.

We passed over Cape Freshfield where Mr Webb remembered that a Mr Ninnis had been lost down a crevasse with all dogs, sleigh and six weeks' provisions on the 4th December, 1912. Passing over the Ninnis Glacier named after this unfortunate man, we could see the 'blue ice' which is caused by the melting and refreezing process.

We then passed over the site where Mr Webb recalled the death of a Mr Mertz and where Mawson was left alone in the wilderness and had to eat his dogs to survive. We saw the Mertz Glacier which is the second largest in the world (sic) and Aurora Peak which was named by Mawson.

At 3.00 p.m. we found Mr Webb's hut which he had built, still in good condition after 64 years. At 3.30 p.m. we flew over and circled the French Base which comprised several red roofed huts on a rocky promontory. The Frenchmen were on the roofs waving. They spoke to us through the wireless and wished us a safe journey and a happy Christmas. We also saw about forty seals and flew lower to observe them more clearly.

Our return was aided by a tail wind and at 7.45 p.m. we had a glimpse of the Tasmanian coastline. From 5000 feet we saw the fantastic lights of Sydney after covering 5,228 miles of journey and we landed safely at about 8.30 p.m., one hour ahead of schedule because of the tail wind.

A Greenpeace team protesting the Dumont d'Urville airstrip in 1989. 'Opening up Antarctica' is a prospect of debatable merit; for better or worse, it is one in which air transport will have a critical role.

Greenpeace protested at the decision to build a hard surface airfield at Dumont d'Urville station in Adelie Land. Penguin and bird colonies were damaged or disturbed in the blasting and bulldozing of five small islands to join the strip together, but despite delays the French authorities pushed the project ahead and scheduled first flights to commence in 1993. Australia for over 30 years has studied locating a landing strip of various surface types at Casey and Davis Stations; successive Federal governments have been incapable of reaching a decision, despite the relative proximity of Antarctica to Australia and the fact that Australia's territorial claim represents 42 per cent of the Antarctic continent.[15] One might say that the Commonwealth prefers to leave the dirty work to the French; to turn to the Russians and Americans in times of emergency; and to let an individual flyer of the Dick Smith ilk bridge the gap.

While the international community debates a twenty-first century Antarctica — a world park, a moratorium on mining, international laboratory, zone of peace — who can tell what the future holds?[16] Big ships are already dredging the krill and plankton; the bottom step in the marine food chain is taking the place of the mighty whale in humankind's harvest of the seas. In far-away offices and laboratories, samples of Antarctic rock and profiles of the seabed are studied and filed for future reference. In a world where great empires crash within the space of months, it is a brave or foolish man or woman who will indulge in dogmatic forecasts of what lies ahead for the wild and uninhabited continent at the bottom of the globe. One thing is certain: in determining whatever that future is to be, air transport will continue to play a dominant role.[17]

Perhaps the cold face of Antarctica stands as the ultimate deterrent to the exercise of stupidity and greed. In a sense, that much of it has not altered since Wilkins, Byrd and Ellsworth and Mawson and Riiser-Larsen gazed from their little aircraft on a white continent that is at once so beautiful, so hostile and so unforgiving.

Map of the French expedition airstrip at Dumont d'Urville station.

BIBLIOGRAPHY

Books

Adams, H., *Beyond the Barrier with Byrd*, New York, M. A. Donohue & Co., 1932.

Auburn, F. M., *Antarctic Law and Politics*, Bloomington, Indiana University Press, 1982.

Balchen, B., *Come North With Me*, New York, E. P. Dutton & Co. Inc., 1958.

Barber, N., *The White Desert*, London, Hodder & Stoughton Ltd, 1958.

Bechervaise, J., *Blizzard and Fire — A Year at Mawson, Antarctica*, Sydney, Angus & Robertson, 1963.

Bechervaise, J., *The Far South*, Sydney, Angus & Robertson, 1961.

Bertrand, K. J., *Americans in Antarctica: 1775–1948*, New York, American Geographical Society, 1971.

Betts, M., *Australians in Antarctica*, Canberra, Commonwealth of Australia (Antarctic Division), 1981.

Bixby, W. *McMurdo Antarctica*, New York, David McKay, 1962.

Bowden, T., *To Antarctica and Back in Sixty Days*, Sydney, ABC Publications, 1990.

Brennecke, H., *Ghost Cruiser H.K. 33*, London, William Kimber, 1955.

Burkhanov, V. F., *K Beregan Antarktidy*, Moskva, Morskoi Transport, 1956.

Byrd, R, *Discovery: The story of the Second Byrd Antarctic Expedition*, New York, G. P. Putnam's Sons, 1935.

Byrd, R., *Little America: Aerial exploration in the Antarctic, the flight to the South Pole*, New York, G. P. Putnam's Sons, 1930.

Chester, J., *Going to Extremes: Project Blizzard and Australia's Antarctic Heritage*, Lane Cove, Doubleday Australia, 1986.

Christensen, L., *My Last Expedition to Antarctica*, Oslo, Johan Grundt Tanum, 1938.

Chipman, E., *Australians in the Frozen South: Living and Working in Antarctica*, Melbourne, Thomas Nelson Australia, 1978.

Cronin, P., *A Contribution to the Geology of the Western Part of Australian Antarctic Territory*, Canberra, AGPS, 1959.

Darlington, J., *My Antarctic Honeymoon*, London, Frederick Muller, 1957.

Debenham F., *Antarctic: The Story of a Continent*, London, Herbert Jenkins, 1959.

Dubrovin, L. I., *Navchnye Stantsii Antarktike*, Leningrad, Gidromet, 1967.

Dufek, G., *Operation Deepfreeze*, New York, Harcourt, Brace & Co., 1957.

Dufek, G., *Through the Frozen Frontier: The exploration of Antarctica*, Leicester, Brockhampton Press, 1960.

Ellsworth, L., *Beyond Horizons*, New York, The Book League of America Inc., 1938.

Fuchs V., and Hillary, E., *The Crossing of Antarctica: The Commonwealth Trans-Antarctic Expedition 1955–58*, London, Cassell, 1958.

Giaver, J., *The White Desert*, London, Chatto & Windus, 1954.

Gill, G., Hermon *The RAN 1939–42*, Canberra, Australian War Memorial 1957.

Grenfell Price, A., *Winning of Australian Antarctica: Mawson's B.A.N.Z.A.RE. Voyages 1929–31*, Sydney, Angus & Robertson, 1962.

Grierson, J., *Air Whaler*, London, Sampson Low, Marston & Co., 1949.

Grierson, J., *Challenge to the Poles*, London, Foulis, 1964.

Grierson, J., *Sir Hubert Wilkins–Enigma of Exploration*, London, Robert Hale Limited, 1960.

Halle, L. J., *The Sea and the Ice*, Boston, Houghton Mifflin, 1973.

Hatherton, T. (ed.), *Antarctica*, London, Methuen, 1965.

Headland, R. K., *Chronological List of Antarctic Expeditions and Related Historical Events*, Cambridge, Scott Polar Research Institute, Cambridge University Press, 1989.

Herr, R., Hall, H., Howard, M., *Antarctica's Future*, Hobart, Australian Institute of International Affairs 1990.

Hickson, K., *Flight 901 to Erebus*, Christchurch, Whiteoulls Publishers, 1980.

Hill, L. C., *Ellsworth Antarctic Relief Expedition*, Report to Commonwealth Parliament, Canberra Government Printer 1936.

Hudel'man, A. V., *Sovetskie Ekspeditsii Antarktiku*, Moskava, Nauka, 1965.

Jacka, F. and Jacka, E. (eds.), *Mawson's Antarctic Diaries*, Sydney, Allen & Unwin, 1988.

Joerg, W. L., *Brief History of Polar Exploration Since the Introduction of Flying*, New York, 1930.

Kearns, W., and Britton, B., *The Silent Continent*, London, Victor Gollancz, 1955.

Kingsford-Smith, C.E., *The Old Bus*, Melbourne, Herald Press, 1932.

Law, P. G. and Bechervaise, J., *ANARE*, Melbourne, Oxford University Press, 1957.

Law, P., *Antarctic Odyssey*, Melbourne, Heinemann Australia, 1983.

Lebeder, V., *Antarctica*, Moscow, Foreign Languages Publishing House, 1959.

Lewis, R. S., *A Continent for Science*, London, Secker & Warburg, 1965.

McKenzie, D., *Opposite Poles*, London, Robert Hale, 1963.

Mahon, P., *Verdict on Erebus*, Auckland, William Collins, 1984.

Mawson, D., *The Home of the Blizzard*, London, Hodder & Stoughton, 1930.

Mawson, P., *Mawson of the Antarctic: The life of Sir Douglas Mawson*, London, Longmans, Green & Co., 1964.

Montague, R., *Oceans, Poles and Airmen*, New York, Random House, 1971.

Muenchen, A., *Flying to the Midnight Sun*, New York, David McKay, 1972.

Murray-Smith, S., *Sitting on Penguins*, Sydney, Century Hutchinson Australia, 1988.

National Academy of Sciences, *Antarctica in the IGY*, Washington, D.C., U.S. National Committee for IGY (Symposium), 1956.

Ommanney, F., *South Latitude*, London, Longmans, Green & Co., 1947.

Peat, N., *Looking South: New Zealand Antarctic Society's First Fifty Years 1933–1983*, Wellington, New Zealand Antarctic Society, 1983.

Pound, R., *Scott of the Antarctic*, London, Cassell & Co, 1966.

Reader's Digest Services, *Antarctica: Great Stories from the Frozen Continent*, Surry Hills, Reader's Digest Services, 1985.

Rogers, E., *Beyond the Barrier with Byrd*, Annapolis, Naval

Institute Press, 1990.
Ronne, F., *Antarctic Conquest*, New York, G. P. Putnam's Sons, 1949.
Ronne, F., *Antarctic Command*, New York, The Bobbs Merrill Co., 1961.
Rymill, J., *Southern Lights: The Official Account of the British Graham Land Expedition 1934–37*, London, The Travel Book Club, 1939.
Scholes, A., *Seventh Continent: Saga of Australasian Exploration in Antarctica 1895–1950*, London, George Allen & Unwin, 1954.
Siple, P., *90° South: The Story of the American South Pole Conquest*, New York, G. P. Putnam's Sons, 1959.
Sullivan, W., *Quest for a Continent*, London, Secker & Warburg, 1957.
Swan, R. *Australia in the Antarctic: Interest, Activity, & Endeavour*, Parkville, Melbourne University Press, 1961.
Taylor, G., *Antarctic Adventure and Research*, New York, D. Appleton & Co., 1930.
Thomas, L., *Sir Hubert Wilkins: His World of Adventure*, New York, McGraw-Hill, 1961.
Treshnikov, A. E., *Vokug Antarktidy*, Leningrad, Gidromet, 1970.
Triggs, G., *International Law and Australian Sovereignty*, Sydney Legal Books Limited, 1989.
Wilkins, H. and Sherman, H., *Thoughts through Space*, London, Frederick Muller, 1971.
Wilson, D., *Alfresco Flight*, Point Cook, RAAF Museum, 1991.

Journals and Periodicals

Aircraft Magazine, Melbourne.
Antarctica, New Zealand Antarctic Society, Wellington, N.Z.
Antarctic Journal of the United States National Science Foundation, Washington, D.C.
Aurora, ANARE Club, Melbourne.
Australian Geographic, Australian Geographic Society, Sydney.
Geographical Review, American Geographical Society, New York.
Journal of the Royal Aeronautical Society, London.
National Geographic, National Geographic Society, Washington, D.C. (incl. issues August 1930; August, October 1932; October 1935; July 1936; July 1939; October 1947; August 1956; September 1957.)
Polar Record, Cambridge, U.K.
Walkabout, Melbourne.

Miscellaneous

Antarctic News Reports, Antarctic Division of the Australian Government.
Australian Archives, Access A705, 981, 989, 1066–8, 1838, Canberra A.C.T.
Commonwealth Gazette, Canberra.
Commonwealth Parliamentary Debates, Canberra.
Department of External Affairs Media Releases.
Ellsworth Antarctic Relief Expedition, report by Cdr. L. C. Hill. incl. aviation report by Flt. Lt. E. Douglas, Government Printer, Canberra, May 1936.
Historical Selections, Vol. 2, Penola, John Rymill, Mortlock Library, Adelaide.
Mawson diaries and pictorial collection, Barr Smith Library, Adelaide University; Mawson collection, National Library, Canberra; Mawson photographs, Mitchell Library, Sydney.
RAAF Antarctic Flight Reports, Department of Air, Canberra.
Recent Reconnaissance Flights in the Antarctic, Address by C. L. Christensen, London, Royal Geographical Society Proceedings, 1937.
Resources of Australian Antarctica, Address by P. G. Law, Melbourne P.O.A. Chronicle, 1963.

Publications of U.S. Department of Defence, Washington, D. C.

Report of U.S. Navy Antarctic Development Project, 1947.
The United States in the Antarctic, 1820–1961.
Aviation in the Antarctic, H. M. Dater, 1963.
Introduction to Antarctica 1964.
U.S. Navy Task Force 43, Reports of Operation (Misc. from 1955–56).
Chronology of Events During Deep Freeze 1954–8. History of Air Development Squadron Six (VX-6), 1955–62 .
Dakotas in the Antarctic, monograph No.1, 1970. Misc. news releases, from 1955–56.

Newspapers (1928–1978)

Examiner, San Francisco.
New York *Times*.
The Times, London.
Adelaide *Advertiser*.
The Age, Melbourne.
The Argus, Melbourne.
Daily Telegraph, Sydney.
Financial Review, Sydney.
Mercury, Hobart.
The Sun, Melbourne.
Sydney Morning Herald.
The Press, Christchurch.

APPENDICES

I Last Try for the Pole

Correspondence of Sir Hubert Wilkins and Lincoln Ellsworth with the Australian Government in 1939–1940, seeking to launch another Antarctic Expedition — one that never materalised.

Lincoln Ellsworth C/o Charles S. McVeigh, 60 Wall Street,
New York City.
11th November, 1939

The Prime Minister,
Australian Commonwealth,
CANBERRA, AUSTRALIA

Hon. Sir,
There is still much exploration to be done in the Princess Elizabeth Land sector of the Antarctic and I hope that the European situation will be such that it will be reasonably possible to go south for the season of 1940–41.

With no intention of claiming any of the area seen for the United States, I have in mind the possibility of making a flight from Princess Elizabeth Land to the Ross Sea. This will necessitate the establishment of a base and might mean wintering in order to start the trans-antarctic flight early the following season.

The base might be suitable for permanent occupation and I suggest that in the interest of science and international co-operation if it were possible for your government to make available to me, either under charter or other means, the M/S *Wyatt Earp* for transport, I would supply, establish and fully equip the base in a manner suitable for the observation, collection and transmission of meteorological data customarily supplied to government departments and provide a sum of not less than four thousand dollars U.S. currency per annum for its maintenance for a term of not less than ten years.

A proviso to such endowment would be that the base be officially known as the Lincoln Ellsworth Observatory.

I would be pleased to receive your reply in relation to your tentative reaction to such proposal, realising, of course, that any comment now made would be tentative and contingent upon future developments in Europe and elsewhere.

I remain, Sir,
Yours respectfully,
(Sgd) Lincoln Ellsworth

P.S. In the development of any such proposal I might mention that Sir Hubert Wilkins would be in charge of the details of my expedition.

COMMONWEALTH OF AUSTRALIA
Department of the Navy
Melbourne, S.C.1.
March 23, 1940

MEMORANDUM FOR:
The Secretary,
Prime Minister's Department,
CANBERRA, A.C.T

ANTARCTIC EXPLORATION — PROPOSALS OF SIR HUBERT WILKINS

With reference to your minute of 29th December, 1939, No.V.413/6, transmitting a copy of a communication from Sir Hubert Wilkins, enquiring whether the Polar Exploration Vessel (WYATT EARP) could be made available to Mr Lincoln Ellsworth for the 1940–41 season for an expedition to the Antarctic, either under charter or by other means, I desire to inform you that this vessel is to be used in the Examination Service. She will release a vessel now on hire, and thus will save the expenditure of Commonwealth funds.

2. As her services will be required by the Navy Department for the duration of the war, it is regretted that it will not be possible to make her available to Mr Lincoln Ellsworth.

(SGD) G. L. Macandie,
for Secretary.

CANBERRA, A.C. T .
2nd April, 1940.

Sir Hubert Wilkins,
The City Club of New York,
55 West 44th Street,
NEW YORK CITY. U.S.A.

Dear Sir,

With reference to your letter of 10th November, 1939, addressed to the Right Honourable R.G. Casey, I desire to inform you that the Commonwealth Government greatly appreciates your offer to provide, establish and maintain one meteorological base in the Antarctic.

The Commonwealth Government has given very careful consideration to your offer, but unfortunately it has been found necessary to employ the *Wyatt Earp* in the Naval Examination Service until the end of the war, and it cannot be released from this service without considerable cost to the Commonwealth Government.

The despatch of an expedition to the Antarctic would also involve the Commonwealth Government in other costs for which provision cannot be made at the present time. It is regretted therefore that your offer cannot be accepted at this juncture.

A letter has been sent to Mr. Ellsworth informing him that the Commonwealth Government will not be able to take advantage of his offer to establish another meteorological station.

Yours faithfully
(Sgd) J. McEwen, Minister for External Affairs

II *Path of a Polar Hurricane*

Destruction of the RAAF Beaver aircraft A95-201 and A95-203 at Mawson on 28 December 1959 as described in the report of John Béchervaise, the ANARE station Officer-in-Charge:

A midsummer polar hurricane, with steady wind-speeds reaching an estimated 115 mph and with erratic gusts far in excess of this speed suddenly developed on Monday, 28th December and struck the icefield airstrips 500 feet above Mawson with appalling destructive force. This hurricane gave no warning along the usual path of such disturbances — neither Syowa, the Japanese base 600 miles to the west, nor Roi Baudouin, 950 miles, experienced this blow. It appears to have suddenly veered directly towards Mawson with accelerated speed through the broad gap between Marion Island and the Kerguelen Archipelago, 1,500 miles north in the southern Indian Ocean.

In the morning of December 28, surface and upper winds at Mawson were moderate when a party started out by Weasel for routine inspection and maintenance of aircraft based on the plateau. Unfortunately this vehicle broke through an encrusted melt-water channel in the ice and was delayed. When it reached the airfield at 11.30, winds were 80 mph and Beaver Aircraft 201 had snapped its 3-ton tie wires and wing-tip fasteners and had broken loose. Beaver 203 was secure.

Sqn-Leader James Sandercock acted quickly and without thought of personal safety. He climbed into the glissading aircraft, started the engine and put its nose into the prevailing wind — in the increasing storm, a reaction that would be irreversible until help arrived. It saved the plane from complete loss. The wind increased and 203 broke loose by tearing out the heavy 'deadmen' railway sleepers sunk into the ice to a depth of two feet. Quick thinking set McIntyre and Bell charging after the aircraft in the D-4 tractor used for power generation. They dropped the dozer blade on the 'deadmen' and further secured the aircraft with 7-ton steel cables and wing-tip ropes. Help for Sandercock intermittently airborne above a steep ice slope leading down to 80-feet coastline ice cliffs was urgent, so Bell drove the Weasel down to the station. The second D-4, driven by Armstrong, broke through a bridged channel and was delayed. Béchervaise, Rippon and Bell reached the airstrip by Weasel, with heavy iron stakes, cables and mauls. The Weasel was now almost beyond control on the ice but was driven as close in front of the spinning propeller as possible and held there with track tension while the stakes were driven home by cramponed men leaning on the wind and wary of the propeller. Steel cables were made fast in the wind now approaching 110 mph. The tractor, having been extricated, arrived with Armstrong and Budd following on foot, and replaced the Weasel. Sandercock had been holding the plane for two hours. Further cables were attached to both aircraft and by 2.30 the situation seemed well in hand.

The seven men fought their way to the sledge caravan whose heavy iron runners had providentially sunk into the ice. Its 5-ton steel guys alone could not have held it through the next 20 hours. It was then that the wind reached a force unprecedented in this hurricane. It was erratic over a south-east quadrant in which wing-lift spoilers were ineffective, but it averaged at least 100 mph for many hours. The aircraft had on a previous occasion weathered 110 mph on sea ice. This tremendous buffetting tore the securing rings from the aircraft. 203 snapped 7.5 ton cables and slithered away down hill, bending both main planes at grotesque angles. By immense effort in the furious wind, charged now with heavy ice fragments and grit from Mount Henderson six miles distant, this was again secured, but it seemed intent on self-destruction. At times both aircraft dragged their 6-ton tractor anchors over the ice. 201, directly upwind from the caravan, started to break up. One wing collapsed in the middle, the other was wrenched off and hurled through the air for a hundred yards without touching the ice. It missed the port side of our shelter by five yards. A wheel-ski charged past to starboard. The aircraft lifted itself madly in the air, even on half a wing, and dashed itself repeatedly in an intermittent spray of ice fragments and petrol, destroying the undercarriage and tailplane. The propeller slowly revolved against engine compression. We feared fire for the battery of 201 could not be removed . . .

The disaster is a bitter blow. Since plateau operations commenced, more flying had been accomplished than from sea ice in any comparable period this year. In the three days preceding Christmas, Armstrong and Sandercock obtained three remote fixes in the Napier and Scott Mountains and at an unmapped group of nunataks at an elevation of 7,300 feet in lat. 68°31' South, long. 52°03' East. Everything was ready for an all-out effort for geology, survey and photo-mapping in the Prince Charles Mountains where all depots had been established. There are two faintly alleviating aspects of the disaster — firstly, we believe the lessons learned can make plateau-based flying safe, secondly, we are thankful that this calamity did not occur far south at Beaver Lake without such hardly gained knowledge.

III *Rum Doings*

Loss of the RAAF Dakota A65-81 and Beaver A95-202 at Rumdoodle Skiway, Mawson, on 9 December 1960, as taken from official ANARE reports:

Overcast skies, reduced visibility, falling snow prevailed during the late evening period on 8 December. Wind was gusting, but remained in the vicinity of 20–25 kts. There was no sign of the onset of a blizzard by 2400 hrs LMT. At approximately 0230 LMT the wind gusts increased suddenly and were of sufficient intensity to shake the caravans (at Rumdoodle strip). The wind strength increased in the next few hours and reguying of several caravans was necessary. The situation at 0600 hrs was that gale-force winds were lashing the camp area and the visibility over the plateau was down to a few yards. The wind could be heard roaring over the top of the mountain and outside movement was dangerous. Visibility lifted about 0800 hrs and while the intensity of the wind was much the same, the D-4 tractor (the only form of transport) was started up and five personnel were transported to the tiedown area by sledge. By following the old D-4 tracks a rather hazardous trip was made, with wind gusts still in excess of 100 kts (estimate only).

On arrival in the area, it was found that the Dakota had broken away from its tiedowns and disappeared, the Beaver had structurally broken up around the tiedowns and all pieces were still held. There was no weakening of any of the Beaver tiedowns and the separate pieces (i.e. wings were held, though they had been pulled straight off; the fuselage was broken in two and the front section turned over on its back). An effort was made to remove the battery and resecure the wings to the windfence, but after a couple of narrow escapes from injury, it was abandoned. In the period at the tiedown area the high winds maintained and all the high gusts (that were sufficient to blow men off their feet and slide helplessly across the ice) were into the direction the aircraft were parked, plus or minus 20 degrees.

Nothing could be done and the only safe recourse was to get all personnel back to the shelter of base camp until the blizzard ceased. Towards 1200 hrs the visibility improved considerably and while still of blizzard strength, the wind had lessened. Another trip was made out to the airfield area and it was found that in those few hours the only remaining part of the Beaver was the broken fuselage, and the starboard wing. The workshop caravan had broken its guys and disappeared. An attempt was made to carry out a recce for the Dakota but wind and reduced visibility made this impossible and the party again returned to base camp. The only thing that remained of the airfield installation was the Beaver windfence. It was not until 2100 hrs on 10 December that a search could be carried out for the Dakota.

The battered remains of the Beaver fuselage had finally broken away and was located approximately 200 yards behind the windfence. Following the plateau slope down towards the coast, the workshop caravan was found overturned where it had hit a melt stream. This distance was approx. 5–6 miles from the tiedown position. The recce was continued on to the coast, but no sign of the Dakota was found. On the 0830 hrs radio sked with Mawson, a request was made for a coastal search to be carried out from Mawson. Sqn. Ldr. Kitchenside, Flg. Off. Assender and Sgt Murphy walked down to Mawson that afternoon and shortly after arrival it was reported that the Dakota had been located by Mr Currie who had been along the coast riding a motor bike on the sea ice. A65-81 was wedged into a heavily crevassed and broken ice cliff about 400 feet above the sea-ice. It had been blown about 8nm down the average one in-38 slope.

It was a sad end to a hard year's work and occurred just when experience and confidence were returning dividends. Recovery of the Dakota was out of the question, so a salvage operation was begun. A base camp was set up at Ringoya, in case the sea-ice should break up. From here it was easy to get to the plateau where A65-81 was. Equipment worth salvaging was lowered down the cliff and taken to Ringoya. A dog team, a motor cycle, a sledge and 15 men were employed for two days. Salvagable items were also recovered from the Beaver. Bereft of its aircraft, the Flight could only wait for the little red relief ship to appear steaming down Kista Strait.

IV *Private Wings*

Pioneer flights to the Pole by private aircraft

1965	Rockwell 'Round the World Over Both Poles' flight on B707-349C of Flying Tigers Line, November 14-17. Total distance from California over North and South Poles, 57,784 km (32,990 miles).
1970	Max Conrad (US), dubbed at 67 'the flying grandfather' pilots his Piper Aztec aircraft *White Penguin* from McMurdo Sound to the South Pole on 19 January but crashes at Pole on take-off; aircraft abandoned.
1970	Norwegian duo Thor Tjinveit and Ennan Pedersen in Cessna Twin 4-21 *Roald Amundsen* reach South Pole from McMurdo, 20 January (12 hours after Mr Conrad).
1971	Captain Elgin Long (US), takes Piper Navajo on a 57,000-kilometre (36,000-mile) route across both Poles; crosses South Pole from Punta Arenas on 22 November.
1980–81	Sir Ranulph Fiennes' Trans–Globe Expedition crosses Antarctica — expedition's support aircraft is flown by Captain Giles Kershaw, making four landings at the Pole.
1983	Brooke Knapp, a 40-year-old member of the U.S. Congress, with 3 women companions (a journalist and 2 photographers) and 3 co-pilots and a mechanic flew her Gulfstream III business jet on a circumnavigation of north and south poles, 14–18 November. The aircraft crossed the South Pole on 16 November.
1987	Richard Norton (US) in Piper aircraft flies in January from Marambio Station on Antarctic Peninsula to South Pole and to King George Island.
1988	Dick Smith, an Australian businessman, with Giles Kershaw as his chief pilot flies Twin Otter *Sir Hubert Wilkins* from Australia to Antarctica; Smith's aircraft VH-SHW is only the second to make this Southern Ocean crossing since the U.S. Navy flight of 1964. First leg of journey is made on 6 November from Hobart to Casey Station 3,500 kilometres (2,200 miles) in 14 hours. While in Antarctica, aircraft is used to serve require-

ments of Australian National Antarctic Research Expedition, calling at all three ANARE coastal bases. Visits are also made to American, French, Greenpeace, Japanese and Russian bases, and two landings are accomplished at South Pole before Smith leaves via Antarctic Peninsula to complete 85,000-kilometre (53,000-mile) circumnavigation of the globe, including a crossing of North Pole.

1990 Giles Kershaw, acclaimed as Antarctica's most accomplished and experienced pilot, is killed on 6 March in the crash of a gyro-plane on the Jones Ice Shelf, off the west coast of the Antarctic Peninsula. Kershaw, aged 41, had been flying in the Antarctic since 1974. One of the first men to fly across both North and South Poles and a pioneer of blue ice 'wheel' landings, he was largely responsible for furthering independent (i.e., non-government) aviation on the polar continent. His immense ice record included flying for British Antarctic Survey, the British Trans-Globe Expedition and Adventure Network International (ANI) of which he was a founding director. His flying supported several major expeditions, including Seven Summits (for the climbing of Vinson Massif), the Footsteps of Scott and the Dick Smith trans-Antarctic exploit. He was responsible for several major rescue missions, including one across Antarctica in which he was at the controls of a Twin Otter for 32 hours. At the time of his tragic death, he was a holder of the Polar Medal, The Sword of Honour (British Guild of Air Pilots) and had been elected a Fellow of the Royal Geographical Society.

V ANTARCTICA – *the Cold Facts*

Antarctica is the world's coldest, highest, windiest, driest continent.

Δ It is the world's fifth largest continent, covering an area of some 14,000,000 square kilometres (5,400,000 square miles), while the permanent 'floating ice shelves' add another 1,300,000 square kilometres (500,000 square miles). The area is equivalent to that of the United States and Mexico combined, or almost double that of Australia. Less than 2 per cent of Antarctica is ice-free. The continental bedrock is, in places, displaced to lower than sea level by the overlay of some 30,000,000 cubic kilometres (7,700,000 cubic miles) of ice. Among Antarctica's many immense glaciers, the Lambert Glacier, in Australian Antarctic Territory, is the largest, measuring 400 kilometres (250 miles) long and averaging 40 kilometres (25 miles) wide.

Δ Coldest: Antarctica contains 90 per cent of the world's ice and some 70 per cent of the world's fresh water. Average ice thickness is 1.5 kilometres (almost 1 mile).

Δ Surface temperatures recorded at interior bases reach extremely low levels each winter; Vostok, regarded as the coldest manned base, has reported August temperatures down to –89.2°C (–128.6°F). At South Pole station, readings have fallen to –82.6°C (–116.8°F). Coastal temperatures range from zero (C) in summer to –30°C (–22°F) in winter. The South Pole average is –56.6°C (–70°F). In general, Antarctic temperatures are about 30 degrees lower than the minimum Arctic readings.

Δ The barrier-like ice cliffs which surround much of the Antarctic coast are between 23 metres (75 feet) and 45 metres (150 feet) high. The ice cap is plastic — it is continually on the move towards the sea, opening deep crevasses which are forever a danger to surface travellers. Huge tabular icebergs continually break away from the continental fringe, gradually moving out to sea or running aground on off-shore shoals. One iceberg reported by USS *Glacier* in November 1956 was 330 kilometres (205 miles) long and 95 kilometres (60 miles) wide — an area equal to the size of the state of Connecticut. The Ross Ice Shelf measures 720 kilometers (450 miles) in width and at its most southerly point some 960 kilometres (600 miles) in length, an area equivalent to the size of the state of California.

Δ Highest: The shape of Antarctica resembles that of a huge upturned saucer. Average continental elevation is 2,300 metres (7,500 feet). Average thickness of the ice cap is 1.5 kilo-metres (about 1 mile), but in places it has been measured to around 4.8 kilometres (3 miles). At the South Pole, elevation 2,800 metres (9,200 feet), the ice depth is 2,700 metres (8,850 feet). At the Pole of Inaccessibility it is even deeper — 4.8 kilometres (3 miles). The maximum plateau elevation is found in the vicinity of this Pole, rising to 4,100 metres (13,450 feet). The highest known mountain is the Vinson Massif in Ellsworth Highland, elevation 4,897 metres (16,070 feet). Antarctica's active volcano, Mt Erebus on Ross Island, McMurdo Sound, is 3,794 metres (12,447 feet) elevation.

Δ Windiest: Gusts of around 320 kph (200 mph) are recorded in the coastal regions where the cold and heavier katabatic winds sweep down from the plateau. At Commonwealth Bay (Mawson's Home of the Blizzard) wind blew at the rate of 150 kph (95 mph) for up to 10 hours continuously. Men and their equipment face an extreme danger of being 'swept away' if caught unprotected from the high wind, especially in slippery blue ice zones. Wind-whipped fire is the other great risk to Antarctic bases.

Δ Driest: Average annual precipitation is about 12 centimetres (5 inches), almost all of it in the form of dry snow. On the polar plateau the precipitation reduces to about 5 centimeters (2 inches) annually. Humidity is almost eliminated. The Antarctic is drier than Australia's desert area — in dryness it compares with the Sahara Desert.

Δ Antarctic territory is claimed by seven nations-Argentina, Australia, Britain, Chile, France, New Zealand and Norway. Australia claims the largest section sector of Antarctica, equivalent to 42 per cent of the continent, with an area of some 5,840,000 square kilometres (2,470,000 square miles) (Australia's area is 7,600,000 square kilometres.)

Δ Modern day Antarctica contains some 40 occupied scientific bases, with a summer population of around 2,000 men and women which reduces to about 800 in the wintering-over season. These figures are considerably less than the crews of 12,000 men who sailed to Antarctic and sub-Antarctic waters at the height of the whaling season from 1930 to 1950.

Δ Antarctica rests upon the world's deepest continental shelf and is washed by the world's richest waters. The Antarctic seas, swarming with plankton at the bottom of the marine food chain, are also home in summer to the greatest of mammals, the largest being the blue and sperm whales. The sea and ice harbour more than half the world's seals and in excess of 100 million birds, among them the stately emperor penguin, the only true 'permanent resident' of the Antarctic continent. The male emperor remains at its coastal rookeries, nursing the unhatched egg throughout the fierce winter cold and darkness.

Δ Distances (based on best available flight data, figures rounded to nearest zero) are kilometres (miles): From Mirnyy to: Lazarevskaya 3,360/2,082; Mawson 1,360/845; Molodezhnaya 3,680/2,286; Sovietskaya 1,280/795; Pole of Relative Inaccessibility 2,080/1,292; Vostok 1,400/870; Wilkes 777/485. Vostok–South Pole 1,278/794.

Δ From McMurdo to: Byrd 1,384/860; Casey (Wilkes) 2,183/1,357; Christchurch 3,862/2,400; Little America 711/442; Mirnyy 2,560/1,591; South Pole 1,356/843. Casey (Wilkes)–Mawson 2,033/1,263; Mawson–Davis 640/400; Casey–Hobart 3,539/2,199.

ENDNOTES

Abbreviations

Advertiser Adelaide Advertiser
Geogr. Rev. Geographical Review
Nat. Geo. National Geographic
NYT New York *Times*
SMH *Sydney Morning Herald*
Times The (London) *Times*

A full reference to the works listed hereunder is to be found in the bibliography.

Introduction

Reference to the first balloon ascent is contained in Scott, R. F.: *The Voyage of the Discovery*, Vol 1, London, Elder Smith 1905. Scott's first expedition took two balloons to Antarctica; to fill them they carried 50 hydrogen gas cylinders aboard *Discovery*, each containing 500 cubic feet of gas, in total 'sufficient for three fills,' according to Scott. However it appears that after the risky ascent at the Great Ice Barrier, no more ballooning was attempted.

The balloon ascent of the first German expedition is described in Drygalski, E. von, The *Southern Continent — The German South Polar Expedition Aboard the Gauss 1901–03* (transl.) Bluntisham Books, Erskine Press, U.K. 1989. The Vickers monoplane episode of the AAE is in Mawson, D., *The Home of the Blizzard*, London, Hodder & Stoughton 1930. The incident with Mawson at Hendon, taken from the diaries and unpublished letters of Lady Kennett (formerly Lady Scott), is mentioned in Pound, R., *Scott of the Antarctic*, London, Cassell & Company, 1966.

Chapter 1

References to the first Australia–South Pole flight are to be found in the author's news reports published during 30 September–7 October 1964 in the Adelaide *Advertiser*, *Canberra Times*, *Courier Mail*, *Sydney Morning Herald* etc.; and in his article 'First Flight to the South Pole' appearing in *Aircraft* Magazine, January 1965. Also in P. G. Law's, 'Australia/Antarctic — Last Intercontinental Air Link', appearing in *Walkabout*, March 1966. Also in Department of External Affairs (Canberra) press release of 30 September 1964; *Copy* Magazine of The Journalists' Club, Sydney, November 1964; *Newsletter* of The Institute of Navigation, August 1966; and in news releases of the U.S. Navy Antarctic Support Force McMurdo Sound, September–October 1966. Other details of the flight are taken from the author's personal notes compiled during the journey.

Chapter 2

1 *Argus*, 9 October 1920.
2 *Argus*, 5, 15 June, 6, 12, 14, 20 August, 21 October, 31 December 1925.
3 For his arctic exploit, C. B. Eielson received the Harmon Trophy from President Hoover. The honour for a nationally recognised feat of aviation had been previously awarded only to Charles Lindbergh and Richard E. Byrd.
4 *Argus*, 8 December 1928, SMH, 24 April, 2, 8, June,August 26 December 1928; *Times*, 21, 22 December 1928. Griffith Taylor, writing in the *American Geographical Review* of 1928 (Problems of Polar Research) supported Wilkins' theory and the need for weather reporting stations.
5 Mill, H. R., Geogr. Rev. pp. 377–86 July 1929.
6 *Geogr. Rev.*, July 1930; SMH, 6–11, 22, 23 May 1929; *Times*, 26 September 1929. Hearst Land subsequently became Hearst Island and the channels were recognised as glacial incursions.
7 Eielson, a native of North Dakota where he trained as a schoolteacher, enlisted in the U.S. Army Air Service in 1917 and served as a second lieutenant in World War I. While teaching at Fairbanks High School, Alaska, he purchased his own Curtiss JN4D and in February 1924 won the first Alaskan air mail contract. When the contract lapsed, he re-enlisted in the Army Air Service and then turned to commercial flying. After teaming with Wilkins, he returned to Alaska to organise Alaskan Airways Inc. He was lost in a snowstorm over Bering Strait on 9 November 1929.
8 Wilkins learned to fly at Hendon airfield in 1910.
9 Lowell Thomas reports this statement (pp. 1–2 in his Wilkins biography) from a conversation he held with General Monash, commander of the Australian Army Corps in France.
10 Charles Kingsford Smith and his crew, in the renamed *Southern Cross*, completed the first aerial crossing of the Pacific Ocean from the U.S. to Australia, reaching Brisbane on 9 June 1928 after a flying time of 3 days 10 hours and 42 minutes, at an average flying speed of 70 knots. The Melbourne emporium owner, Sir Sydney Myer, gave Kingsford Smith £1,500 towards the purchase of the tri-motor from Wilkins.
11 Wilkins and Ellsworth first met 'officially' in early 1930 when Wilkins visited Ellsworth at his Schloss Lenzburg castle in Switzerland. Wilkins outlined his planned submarine voyage to the North Pole which Ellsworth supported.
12 A year before his death, Wilkins made his last visit to Antarctica on 12 October 1957 as a guest of Admiral Dufek aboard an R5D Skymaster, flying to McMurdo Sound at the start of Deep Freeze III. Lady Wilkins willed to be buried the same way as her husband, her ashes were scattered at the North Pole in 1975 from the submarine *Bluefish*.

Chapter 3

1 Byrd 1930: 32–3. Byrd describes actions taken at the Ford factory to reduce the weight of the *Floyd Bennett*. Byrd had considered landing at the Pole, but became convinced the aircraft's ski gear might fail under the stress.
2 NYT, 21 December 1928. 'Hearty congratulations, don't forget you will find a warm welcome if you fly to our base,' wrote Byrd. Reports were published in the New York *Times* during the currency of the expeditions, commencing with Russell Owen's accounts of the 1928–30 expedition.

3 NYT, 21 February 1929, 12 January 1931. 'I have claimed, in the name of the United States, 125,000 square miles of land we discovered,' said Byrd. '[It] lies beyond the claims of Britain, being east of the 150th meridian.' He added 'Antarctica is big enough for all.' However Norway queried America's intentions, after Byrd's first expedition.

4 NYT, 19 March 1929. Montague: 259. Rogers: 72–3.

5 Bernt (Bert) Balchen, born 1900 in Norway, and later becoming an American citizen, served in Norway with the mounted artillery and as a flight lieutenant in the naval air service. He first gained prominence in polar aviation as a member of the Amundsen–Ellsworth–Nobile Arctic flight to Kings Bay in 1926. He first flew with Byrd in the 1927 Atlantic crossing which reached the coast of France. Balchen's impressive list of achievements included Middleweight Boxing Champion of Norway as well as being a noted ski racer. He was also known for his skills as a seaman, designer, mathematician, navigator, artist, cook and carpenter. (He built a wooden lightweight man-hauling sledge in case the South Pole flight failed.) During World War II he helped to establish the Greenland air base and flew many dangerous missions to supply the Norwegian underground and rescue crashed airmen. He was president of Norwegian Airlines (parent of Scandinavian Airlines); he died in 1973.

6 During his team's 2,400-kilometre (1,500-mile) sledging journey, Byrd's second-in-command, Laurence Gould, on 21 December 1929 raised the American flag on Supporting Party Mountain in Marie Byrd Land and within a rock cairn, deposited a note stating 'in the name of Commander Richard E. Byrd (we) claim this land as a part of Marie Byrd Land, a dependency or possession of the United States of America'.

7 On 24 February 1934, to a note from the British Foreign Office querying the claims made by the Byrd and Ellsworth expeditions, the U.S. Assistant Secretary of State replied that his government did not propose to discuss the question and added, 'However I reserve all rights which the U.S. and its citizens may have with respect to this matter'.

8 With a 267 kph (167 mph) cruising speed, the large Condor aircraft had a range of 2,080 kilometres (1300 miles) with a 2,600 lb payload. Alfred Sloan, the president of General Motors, loaned the Fokker, named *Blue Blade*, American Airways contributed the single-engine *Miss American Airways*.

9 SMH, 13 January, 10, 17 July 1939; 6 March 1940.

10 The letter of instructions, signed by President Roosevelt on 25 November 1939, stated, 'Members of the service may take appropriate steps such as dropping written claims from airplanes, depositing such writing in cairns et cetera, which might assist in supporting a sovereignty claim by the United States Government. Careful records shall be kept of the circumstances surrounding each act. No public announcement of such act shall, however, be made without specific authority in each case from the Secretary of State.' In compliance with the presidential authorisation, a U.S. seismic party on 12 December 1940 raised the American flag and left a statement of claim in a rock cairn at 78° 06' South and 154° 48' West which would appear to be within the border of the Ross Dependency .

11 Three important seaplane flights were made as the vessel *Bear* cruised eastwards from Little America These flights explored the Walgreen Coast, Thurston Peninsula and Seraph Bay. From West Base itself, flights visited the interior of Marie Byrd Land (four flights), the Ruppert Coast as well as extending to the Queen Maud Range by way of the Beardmore Glacier. From East Base (on Neny Island in Marguerite Bay), flights were made across the Antarctic Peninsula and Alexander I Island and along the length of George VI Sound and the Bowman Coast; to assist•flight operations, a weather reporting station was established on the plateau to the east of the base.

12 West Base officially closed on 1 February and East Base on 22 March 1941.

13 Rodgers cites Finn Ronne's 1979 biography *Antarctica My Destiny* (New York, Hastings House 1979) in which Ronne claimed that Byrd had confessed in secrecy to Isaiah Bowman (President of the American Geographical Society) in 1930 that his famous 1926 flight had missed the North Pole by 240 kilometres (150 miles).The Swedish meteorologist Professor Liljequist raised the same question in his 1959 paper. The account of the conversation with Floyd Bennett in Balchen's 1958 book *Come North With Me* was modified before final publication, reputedly under legal pressure from Byrd family interests. A feud which reputedly developed between Dean Smith, the expedition's second pilot, and Byrd after their return to America in 1930 was never resolved or properly explained.

Chapter 4

1 Built of oak and elm timbers for Scott's first expedition of 1901, *Discovery* was a steam-assisted sailing vessel; for BANZARE *Discovery* was rigged as a three-masted barquentine.

2 The Antarctic Committee of the Australian National Research Council, established on 10 June 1927 to assist the Commonwealth in implementing the (polar) decisions of the 1926 Imperial Conference.
In March 1929 it was given governmental status with Senator Sir George Pearce, who was responsible for CSIR, as chairman. On 12 March 1929 the Committee outlined the work of BANZARE.

3 SMH 3 May, 11 July 1929. (Sir) Macpherson Robertson (1859–1945) was founder of the largest Australian owned confectionery company, based at the Melbourne inner suburb of Fitzroy, near his humble origins as a maker of novelty sweets and candies in his parents' cottage bathroom. As a noted philanthropist, he provided £100,000 for public works to stimulate employment during the 1934 Melbourne centenary celebrations, as well as £15,000 prize money for a London to Melbourne air race. He was knighted in 1932.

4 *Cape Argus*, Cape Town, 8 October 1929, 'A New Race for Antarctica Starting¿'; *Cape Times*, 9 October 1929, 'Under Sealed Orders — Norway's intent in Antarctic annexation from the air¿'.

5 *Morgenblad*, Oslo, 14 October 1929.

6 Casey, R. G. (1890–1976) still stands as the Federal politi-

cian most identified with the encouragement of Australian endeavours in Antarctica. After distinguished service in World War I, Casey was appointed in 1924 as liaison officer at the Dominions Office in London. In 1931 he was elected to the Commonwealth Parliament and in 1935 became Federal Treasurer. He was Minister for External Affairs 1951–60. He was also the first Australian Minister to the United States, a member of the British War cabinet and as Lord Casey, Governor of Bengal and from 1965–69 Governor-General of Australia. Casey Station on Vincennes Bay in Wilkes Land is named after him.

7 SMH, 25 January 1930.

8 On 4 July 1929 the Norwegian government authorised Lars Christensen to take possession of any new lands which he might discover and which had not previously been occupied in due form by the government of any other country.

9 SMH, 29 January 1930.

10 SMH, 1 February 1930. The coastline between 45° East and 73° East was claimed on behalf of the Crown.

11 *Argus*, 20 June 1930.

12 Commonwealth Parliamentary Debates (1930) 2044; *Argus*, 14 April 1930; SMH, 11 April, 2 May, 3, 26 November 1930. On 13 April 1930 the Antarctic Committee met to discuss the charter of the second BANZARE voyage. The sailing orders directed Mawson to concentrate on the more easterly sector of coastline between Adelie Land and Queen Mary Land and Gaussberg and Mac-Robertson Land.

13 *Argus*, 28 March, 16, 18 April 1931.

14 SMH, 14 March 1931.

15 Commonwealth Parliamentary debates, pp. 1949–58, 26 May 1933; *Advertiser,* 15, 16, 24 February; *Argus* 15 February 1933.

16 *Commonwealth Gazette*, 24 August 1936; *Advertiser,* 17 June, 31 July, 1 August 1933.

17 *Argus,* 7 July, 11 September 1928.

18 This odd reference appears in *The Respectable Sydney Merchant:* A. B. Spark of Tempe. p. 92, Sydney University Press 1976.

19 SMH, 10 April, 22 October 1929.

20 SMH, 17 November 1928.

21 On 10 October 1929 the London *Daily News* quoted Mawson: 'Collaboration among scientists is usual in all truly scientific endeavours. The fact that they [Norway] have made no attempt to discuss with us such matters suggests they are not deeply interested in science'. However it was also suggested the Norwegians spent £100,000 a year on science in Antarctica.

22 *Commonwealth Parliamentary Debate* (1929) 461–3, 1747–9; SMH, 23 February 1929; *Canberra Times,* 22 February 1929.

23 SMH, 20 June 1930. Sir Macpherson Robertson, after his £6,000 donation to the second BANZARE later gave £4,000 to help reduce the expedition's indebtedness. He said, 'It was imperative that a most thorough scientific investigation of the Antarctic should be made with a view to the exploitation of any economic possibilities it offered... at all costs the great work which had been undertaken by Sir Douglas Mawson must be completed by sending another expedition to the Antarctic this year.'

Chapter 5

1 *Advertiser*, 3 February 1935; *Argus*, 6 April 1933, 16 July, 6 October 1934; *Nat.Geo.* July 1936.

2 The ship's library contained books on Wyatt Earp's life in the wild west. The 'hero' of the gunfight at O.K. Corral died peacefully, aged 90 in Los Angeles.

3 John Knudsen Northrop, a former Lockheed and Douglas employee, founded the Northrop Corporation in January 1932, with the Douglas Aircraft Corporation holding 51% of the stock. Northrop acquired 100% of the stock in 1937. According to Ellsworth, *Polar Star* was the first aircraft produced by Northrop. He said the enlarged 466 (U.S.) gallon (1,271 kg) fuel tanks made it the longest range aircraft yet built, having a cruising range of 8,000 kilometres (5,000 miles).

4 Ellsworth's run of adverse luck continued. Worn gears, caused through ice-breaking manoeuvres, made *Wyatt Earp* difficult to control at slow speed. As a result, the bow needed extensive repairs after the ship crashed against the wharf on reaching Dunedin.

5 *Argus,* 10 September 1934.

6 Wilkins spoke of a proposal to operate 12 weather stations around the Antarctic coast, observing the 11-year sunspot cycle. He suggested an unnamed society was willing to invest one million pounds in the project if Australia contributed £250,000; however the idea lapsed.

7 *Geogr. Rev.* No 26, pp. 454–62, 1936; No 27, pp. 430–44, 1937. Ellsworth stated that he was spending $5,000 a month to support his expedition. Ellsworth: 294–9.

8 Ellsworth's meteorologist on his second expedition held twice daily radio schedules with Byrd's weather team at Little America.

9 Ellsworth and Wilkins were both 'older men' when they began married life. Wilkins was 41 when in 1929 he wed Suzanne Bennett, the actress from Walhalla in Victoria. Ellsworth at 52 proposed to Mary Louise Ulmer, whom he met at a Zurich flying school. They were married in New York on 23 May 1933. Both brides were rather younger than their husbands. (Later in life, Lady Wilkins became a prominent portrait painter.)

10 Hollick-Kenyon was under age when he enlisted in the Canadian Expeditionary Force; he was twice wounded in France. Upon discharge, he joined the Royal Flying Corps. He did not get to fly in World War I but in 1923 re-enlisted in the RAF for 5 years as a commissioned officer. In 1928 he joined Canadian Airways. By 1935 his 6,000 hours of flying experience included much time in the Arctic zone. 'He was a fine fellow,' said Ellsworth, 'a grand pilot, and the quietest man I ever knew.'

11 On 25 November, two days after Ellsworth's departure, Wilkins received a message from Kenneth Rawson, navigating officer of the second Byrd expedition, advising of food caches located at Mt Grace McKinley and the Rockefeller Mountains, and at Little America where 'there is ample food and coal in the tunnels'.

12 A whiteout occurs when light is trapped between low overcast or cloud cover and the continuous surface of snow and ice beneath. As a result, horizon and shadow, and with them all perception of depth, altitude and distance are obliterated.

Chapter 6

1 *Age*, 19, 26 December; *Argus*, 20 December; SMH, 26 November, 3, 6, 10, 12, 27 December 1935; *Times*, 31 December 1935; *Walkabout*, May 1936.

2 Ellsworth: 298. Aviation was already in the headlines. Just over two weeks before Ellsworth's flight the Australian pioneer aviator, Sir Charles Kingsford Smith, on the night of 7–8 November 1935, disappeared in the *Lady Southern Cross* above the Bay of Bengal while en route from Allahabad to Singapore

3 Details of the Commonwealth Government's rescue mission, organised by Mawson and Davis, are held in the Antarctic file, Australian Archives, Canberra.

4 Ellsworth Antarctic Relief Expedition Report. *Discovery II*, successor to Captain Scott's original vessel, was a steel hulled motor ship of some 2,200 tonnes displacement.

5 The RAAF aircraft were A7-55, a DH 60G Gipsy Moth, fitted with a 100-hp Gipsy engine and extra fuel tank to allow 4 1/2 hours safe flying time; A5-37 was the Westland Wapiti, driven by a 550-hp Bristol Jupiter engine. Ski undercarriages were also taken.

6 *Polar Star* carried a 300-watt HF radio and a petrol generator to supply power when landed on the ice; an emergency manual HF set was also included. Morse key was to be the main communication link with *Wyatt Earp* as distance increased.

7 Ellsworth took a meteorologist on his first and second expeditions. Because Little America was now deserted, and thus no weather data could be exchanged, he excluded, with Hollick-Kenyon's agreement, a meteorologist from the third expedition. This vacancy also allowed space for the inclusion of the second pilot.

8 Ellsworth named the blizzardly Camp III after Hollick-Kenyon's home city of Winnipeg. Camp IV was called Tranquille, because of the prevailing windless conditions.

9 Ellsworth divided his great circle route into 14 sectors, each equal to one hour's flying. However he was dismayed to find that instead of 240 kph (150 mph), *Polar Star* averaged only 163 kph (102 mph) across the continent. The excessive weight of the heavily laden aircraft (3,630 kg) would have been partly responsible for the lower performance.

10 To those who questioned his radio silence, Ellsworth replied: 'Had our radio not failed, the world of the streets would have hailed the crossing of Antarctica as a most intricate and difficult undertaking in exploration carried through without a hitch. As to the charge that I suppressed the radio for the sake of publicity, I would have had more publicity and the newspapers a more dramatic story than our mere "disappearance" gave them, had I been able to send a daily account of our fortunes — how we fared during the long blizzard on Hollick-Kenyon Plateau, for example, or in our blind wanderings through the fog at the Bay of Whales.'

11 Ellsworth Antarctic Relief Expedition report. Also diary of Flt Lt. G. E. Douglas, *Aircraft*, February 1986.

12 Other members of the RAAF detachment Sergeants S. F. Spooner (engine fitter and emergency pilot), J. Easterbrook (metal rigger), J. W. Reddrop (wireless operator-mechanic); Corporal N. E. Cottee (metal rigger); ACI C. W. Gibbs (engine fitter).

13 *Age*, 17 February; SMH 18 February 1936.

14 Hollick-Kenyon returned to Canada where he became general manager of Trans Canada Air Lines, Toronto, in 1938. He died in July 1975, aged 78; his name is entered in the Canadian Aviation Hall of Fame. At the rank of Group Captain, Eric Douglas retired from the RAAF after World War II and died on 4 August 1970, aged 67. His co-pilot became Sir Alister Murdoch, Chief of the Air Staff 1965–70; he died on 23 October, 1984. Douglas's son, lan, led an ANARE party to Davis station in 1960.

Chapter 7

1 Christensen 1935: 32; 1938: 9. 'Norway has as much right as anyone to go anywhere in Antarctica,' Christensen was reported in the Oslo newspaper *Morgenblad* on 14 October 1929. He was replying to questions raised over his expedition's intentions in two Cape Town dailies, the *Cape Argus* of 8 October and *Cape Times* of 9 October 1929.

2 In the *Cape Times*, Mawson was quoted: 'apparently they are out to race and are working in secret, as Amundsen did when he beat Scott to the South Pole'. Mawson however claimed there was a certain amount of misreporting of his words.

3 On 31 August 1927 the Norwegian government authorised Lars Christensen and his captains to occupy on behalf of Norway all discovered territory not previously under the dominion of other powers. Christensen was originally intent on claiming from 60°East to 20°West. Riiser-Larsen set off with a silken flag from the King and Queen of Norway to raise above their discoveries.

4 SMH, 29 January 1930.

5 They received permission from the Norwegian government to name Princess Astrid Land (or 'Coast') on 17 January 1934. The Norwegians accepted that they were in BANZARE's Princess Elizabeth Land and no claim resulted.

6 Mikkelsen's naming of the Ingrid Christensen Coast on 3 February 1935 aroused fresh anxiety in British-Australian circles over Norway's intentions. In 1931, Mikkelsen had named Lars Christensen Land, between Mac-Robertson and Princess Elizabeth Land, only a few days after Mawson had visited the same region aboard *Discovery*.

7 Christensen 1938: 7. Christensen records the entanglement of the aircraft in *Firern*'s rigging, resulting in a buckled elevator and twisted tail. 'Some of us got cold feet,' he wrote. However the damage was repaired in the welding shop of the factory ship *Ole Wegger*, providing an example of the resources of the Norwegian whaling fleet.

8 The 80,000–square kilometre (30,000–square mile) coastal strip photography went to the Norwegian Geographical Society and also ultimately appeared in 12 maps compiled by Christensen's associate, Captain H. E. Hansen (*Atlas of Parts of the Antarctic Coastal Lands*, Oslo, 1946).

9 Norway was estimated from 1905 to 1937 to have caught 430,935 whales in Antarctic waters. However the largest Antarctic whaling fleet was being closely pressed by the

growing size of the Japanese pelagic industry.

10 Norway opposed the 1933 British Order-in-Council which resulted in the Australian Antarctic Territory Acceptance Act, just as it had earlier signalled opposition to the claiming of the Ross Dependency in 1924; in 1931 the United States government had also been queried over the intention of Byrd's flights, with a reminder of Norway's prior rights in eastern Antarctica. Christensen (in *Such is the Antarctic)* wrote in defence of 'those natural rights which we have won for ourselves through the whaling industry'. They were particularly dissatisfied over the British/Australian claim to Princess Elizabeth Land which contained the King Leopold and Queen Astrid and Ingrid Christensen discoveries.

11 SMH, 22 April 1929, *Argus*, 3 June 1931; SMH, 1, 10 June 1937.

12 The latest 10-tonne version of the famous Domier flying boat ('hydro-plane') entered production in 1934; it was the first Dornier to have an enclosed cockpit. The new model was powered by push-pull BMW 690 hp motors, allowing a range of 3,200 kilometres (2,000 miles).

13 The Deutsche Luft Hansa regular trans-Atlantic service began in 1933 with two catapult ships stationed in the Atlantic Ocean between North Africa and South America. The airline advertised a 4-day Berlin to Rio airmail service.

14 Aviators assigned to the trans-Atlantic service were qualified in high seas navigation. For much of the ocean crossing they flew at an elevation of only 10 metres (30 feet) above the sea to gain 'surface effect' acceleration. Crews said the aircraft needed 'double-refuelling' en route — 'a strong drink for the pilot as well as the aircraft'.

15 *Schwabenland*'s 38,000-hp Heinkel catapult had the advertised capacity to launch a 10-tonne Domier to flying speed in two seconds. After landing on the water, the aircraft taxied up to a 'drag sail' towed behind the ship. It was then hoisted aboard for refuelling and placement on the catapult.

16 In reports published in the German press, Captain Ritscher said that each flight, allowing for favourable weather, could photograph an area of 'roughly 200,000 square kilometres (77,200 square miles).' In effect, the average daily coverage was considerably smaller. Maps resulting from the expedition covered some 350,000 square kilometres (140,000 square miles) of previously unexplored regions.

17 German aviation ultimately returned to Antarctica in the 1983–84 season with ski-equipped Dornier 128-6 and 228-100 aircraft, known as *Polar 4* and *Polar 2*. They flew from Bremen to the third German expedition, landing at the Georg-von-Neumeyer station in Queen Maud Land, in the general area of the Schwabenland expedition of 45 years before. Tragically, the Dormier 228 was shot down by guerrilla forces over the western Sahara during its homeward flight on 24 February 1985. The two pilots and engineer were killed. Theirs had been the first German aircraft to reach the South Pole.

18 SMH, 3 September 1938; NYT, 6, 19 May, 25 July 1938; Commonwealth Parliamentary Debate, 28 June 1938. Ellsworth told the New York *Times* he planned to find a site for a weather reporting station.

19 SMH, 7 May 1938; NYI, 6 May 1938.

20 The Delta had its cabin cleared, except for the two crew seats, to accommodate auxiliary fuel tanks.

21 NYT, 14 December 1938

22 On 3 January, two days before reaching the Rauer group, Ellsworth landed on one of the Svenner Islands and collected garnets from among the rocks.

23 On one of his landings, Wilkins buried a copy of *Walkabout* magazine with his proclamation at a place later known on Prydz Bay as Walkabout Rocks. In 1957 an ANARE party uncovered Wilkins' cairn of 11 January 1939; it contained an Australian flag and Wilkins' message.

24 NYT, 12, 13 January 1939. A letter of 30 August 1938 from the Secretary of State to the American Consul in Cape Town authorised Ellsworth to act on territorial claims as he felt appropriate, mindful that he would do so as a private U.S. citizen.

25 NYT, 8 December to 31 January 1939.

26 SMH, 13 January, 2 March 1939; *Nat. Geo.*, July 1939.

27 SMH, 7, 17, 18 February 1939.

28 SMH, 14 February 1939. Ellsworth also said 'claims to all areas in Antarctica on behalf of various nations are very vague and I would like to see an international commission explore the whole question and define the claim'.

29 *Argus*, 9 March; SMH, 2 March 1939. At the 1937 Imperial Conference in London, R G. Casey, Australian Federal Treasurer, had chaired a Polar Committee which recommended adopting Wilkins' plan to establish one or more weather stations along the Antarctic coast. Casey frequently spoke of the potential value to Australia of Antarctica's evident mineral resources and the significance of future trans-polar air routes. In 1951 he noted that whaling was a £60 million international industry.

30 Australian Archives file; Ellsworth atempted to repurchase *Wyatt Earp* for his proposed 1940–41 expedition but on advice from the navy, the government advised Ellsworth and Wilkins in a letter of 2 April 1940 that the ship was now in war service.

31 In his cruise of 1938–42, Wilkes reported tracing some 2,400 kilometres (1,500 miles) of Antarctic coastline from 166° East to 106° East. Though his sightings were originally disputed, later evidence showed much of his work to be accurate. The area of Antarctica to Australia's south, now bears his name — ironically bestowed through the work of Mawson during BANZARE.

Chapter 8

1 In February 1941 the raider *Komet* (HK45) also cruised off the pack ice between Cape Adare and the Shackleton Ice Shelf in search of whaling vessels.

2 *Nat.Geo.*, October 1947.

3 Ibid.

4 The United States in the Antarctic 1820–1961, p.4.

5 *Nat. Geo.* October 1947.

6 *Balaena,* launched at Harland and Wolf, Belfast, in 1946 was the first factory ship to be specifically designed to carry aircraft, incorporating hangar, flight-deck, catapult and a crane

at the stem.

7 Grierson says the aviators' principal task was finding a passage through the ice, though whale spotting became an important secondary role. The aircraft marked the position of a whale by dropping a smoke marker which would be visible to the catchers. As the whale swam away, the pilot flew low over the spot in an endeavour to indicate the track of the whale.

8 *Balaena*, with 2135 whales killed, reported the second largest catch of the 1946–47 season; oil and by-products were worth about £2½ million.

9 Sullivan: 173–4. Reports of U.S. Navy Antarctic Development Project, 1947. Questions of consolidating United States sovereignty and preparing for polar warfare are mentioned by Walter Sullivan, who was New York *Times* correspondent on Highjump.

10 Because of the danger of serious damage from ice floes, the submarine *Sennett* was withdrawn from the convoy and towed to safety by *Northwind*.

11 On his flight to the South Pole on 16 February 1947, Byrd commented that the outlook had not changed. 'The pole lay in the centre of a limitless plain — no mountains were visible,' he said in 1929; on the second occasion 'only the rolling white desert from horizon to horizon.'

12 Trigger Hawkes said he considered photographing the interior of the volcano but pulled his aircraft away at the sight of smoke and dust billowing from the crater.

13 Kearns & Britton: 184–203. William H. Kearns, a navy lieutenant, was flying the PBM at the time of the crash. Though his right arm was fractured, he helped to free his commander, Lieut. LeBlanc, from the burning cockpit.

14 Narrative of Captain Bond, Report of U.S. Navy Antarctic Development Project.

15 Ibid

16 Siple criticizes the lack of emphasis on science in Highjump; he instances the navy crew 'popping their arms in the water' at Bunger Oasis as an example of the unscientific approach. He alleged Admiral Cruzen considered scientists superfluous to Highjump's exploratory mission . . . 'many vowed never to return with the navy to Antarctica' (Siple: 79).

17 *The United States in the Antarctic*, p.23. Plans for a Highjump 11 were cancelled by President Truman in 1949, ostensibly for reasons of economy. Siple says, had the operation proceeded, the United States 'would have gained the major voice over Antarctica's future.' On 28 August 1948 the Department of State announced it had informally proposed an 'internationalisation' of Antarctica to the claimant governments; only Britain and New Zealand showed some interest.

18 *The United States in the Antarctic*, p.22. Before leaving to reoccupy the East Base site, Ronne sought the advice regarding territorial sensitivities from the Department of State. Under-Secretary Dean Acheson replied in part: 'As you are no doubt aware, the proposed base for the expedition at Marguerite Bay is within an area to which several countries have advanced territorial claims. The United States Government, however, has not recognised any claims of any other nations in the area and has reserved all right which it may have in the area'.

19 Ronne's third Antarctic command came during the International Geophysical Year when he was leader at Ellsworth Station on the Filchner Ice Shelf. He later joined Lindblad Travel as Antarctic tour leader; in all, he participated in 5 Antarctic expeditions. He died in January 1980, aged 80.

Chapter 9

1 SMH, 24 February, 11 March 1947; *Argus*, 7, 8, 17 March 1947. A modified Liberator bomber made flights on 12 and 14 March 1947, and a modified Lincoln on 15 March.

2 Squadron Leader R. H. Gray flew the Sikorsky near the Mertz Glacier tongue on 13 March 1948. He returned in the following August to command the RAAF Catalina emergency flight known as 'Operation Sinbad' from Hobart to Macquarie Island.

3 SMH, 30 April, 6, 7 May 1947. ANARE — the Australian National Antarctic Research Expedition — was the name announced by the Executive Planning Committee for the Antarctic after its March 1947 meeting in Melbourne. On 8 May 1948 the Federal government established the Antarctic Division of the Department of External Affairs, thus giving permanent status to ANARE. Stuart Campbell was the first chief executive officer.

4 Dr Phillip Garth Law was born in Victoria in 1912. He trained as a physicist and lectured at Melbourne University. He served as senior scientific officer on the *Wyatt Earp* cruises of 1948 and as an observer in the 1950 Norwegian –British–Swedish ('Maudheim') expedition. In January 1949 he was appointed leader of ANARE and director of the Antarctic Division, from which he retired in 1966 to become head of the Victorian Institute of Colleges. He made 15 visits to Antarctica, and was leader of 11 expeditions.

5 Leckie, D. W., Report to Dept. of Air, Canberra, on RAAF participation in ANARE, 1954. Doug Leckie returned to Antarctica in 1971–72 as commercial pilot of a chartered Pilatus Porter.

6 *Aircraft*, October 1948, p.18.

7 From notes by John Seaton.

8 Somov, M. M., *Co-operation of Scientist In the Antarctic. Vestnik* (Herald) the Academy of Science USSR, January 1966.

9 From notes by John Seaton.

10 Dept. of Air Report on 1956 RAAF Antarctic Flight.

11 Bob Dovers, first leader at Mawson, heading a three man surface party sighted and named the Prince Charles Mountains in December 1954. John Bechervaise, second Mawson leader, made the first visit to the mountains with a surface party in 1955. The mountain chain, 200 kilometres (125 miles) southeast of Mawson stretched in a north-south direction for some 600 kilometres (375 miles).

12 The RAF aircraft were Auster Mark VI, fitted with a Gipsy Major 7 engine of 142 hp. The aircraft cruised at 85 knots with an endurance of 3 to 4 hours. Dr Law subsequently purchased the aircraft, which were stored at Cape Town for the start of ANARE.

13 Three Australians participated in the expedition. One was Phillip Law, an observer with the 1950 summer party. The two other physicists were G. de Q. Robin and J. E. Jelbart. Robin, who had served with FIDS, developed an effective seismic sounding technique to determine the depth of the ice

cap. Jelbart was one of the three men drowned in the accident on 24 February 1951.

14 Law, P. G., 'Establishing Davis Station', in *Aurora*.

15 On 4 September 1957, Peter Clemence with passengers Mather and Goodspeed made the first 1,280 kilometre (800-mile) flight from Mawson to Mirnyy. They reported that 160 expeditionaries were living at the Russian base and the air detachment numbered 16 planes; they returned on 10 September. The RAAF flight covered 100,000-kilometres (62,500 miles) this year.

16 Dept. of External Affairs press release, Canberra, 17 August 1958.

17 Included in Phil Law's group for the hand-over was Mr Bruce Coombes of the Dept. of Civil Aviation who inspected the area around Wilkes as a possible landing site for aircraft flying from Australia.

18 Phil Law was able to say 'no important rock features now remain undiscovered...on any part of the coast of Australian Antarctic Territory.' ANARE explored 6,400 kilometres (4,000 miles) of coastline and accomplished 28 new landings. The dream of Mawson had at last been realised.

19 In seeking improved airstrip sites (Gwamm being too exposed for sustained flying operations) ANARE in February 1960 selected a plateau location known as Rumdoodle close to Mt Twintop at the foot of the Masson Range, 19 kilometres (12 miles) from Mawson. In 'Operation Icefield' four caravans and a diesel-electric generator were taken to the site to form a field camp. At Rumdoodle wind velocity was reckoned to be 20 knots lower than Mawson because of the barrier effect of the mountains.

20 *Antarctic*, March 1960; Blizzard and Fire, pp. 215–233. The loss of the two Beavers with associated airstrip equipment was estimated at £100,000 (more than $200,000).

21 The Dakota was equipped with two Pratt & Whitney 14-cylinder twin row engines; it had a cruise speed of 145 knots and a four-tonne payload. The cabin had been modified to seat 10 passengers, allowing space for an equipment bay and large cargo space. The equipment bay housed a Wild R.C.9 vertical camera and two K17B oblique cameras. Navigation equipment included a Polar Path compass, a Kollsman sky compass, a Kelvin Hughes periscopic sextant and a Marconi doppler navigator to provide ground speed and drift as well as distance flown. A radar altimeter provided elevation above the bedrock to enable computation (from a known altitude) of ice thickness.

22 *Aurora*.

23 Dept. of External Affairs press release, Canberra, 13 December 1960.

24 On 4 May 1959 the first Russian aircraft had landed at Wilkes on a mercy mission to treat an ANARE member suffering a serious nervous illness. Delayed by bad weather the party stayed three days. Another Russian aircraft made a goodwill visit in June 1963.

25 *Antarctica*, March 1960. The U.S. flight of 3 December 1959 enabled the patient treated previously by the Russian doctor to be finally returned to Melbourne.

26 During 1979–82 seasons, RAAF C-130H 'wheel' aircraft made supply flights between Christchurch and McMurdo. A study was made at Davis to determine the possibility of installing an ice free gravel runway in the Vestfold Hills. In 1989 a spokesman for Senator Richardson, Minister for the Environment, confirmed that the RAAF had been instructed to report on commencing a direct service between Hobart and Casey, using C-130 aircraft. Both proposals appear to have lapsed.

27 The *Thala Dan* flight was commanded by Squadron Leader Norm Ashworth. Some 1,600 kilometres (1,000 miles) of vaguely known coast was photographed. At 130 kilometres (80 miles) south of the coastline, Ashworth reported an ice cap elevation reaching 1,650 metres (5,000 feet) and continuing to rise.

28 The 1965–66 expedition suffered another aircraft mishap when the chartered Beaver lashed to the deck of the supply ship *Nella Dan* was struck by a huge wave in stormy seas. Serious wing damage ruled out the proposed trimetrogon camera flight program. In January 1975, a chartered Pilatus Porter was destroyed in a blizzard that again struck Mawson's runway.

Chapter 10

1 *Antarctic*, September 1963 (quoting ANARE Club's *Aurora*). The Russians were en route from Mirnyy to the new Molodezhnaya station site.

2 Ibid, December 1959.

3 *Medical Journal of Australia*, 6 March 1965.

4 The earlier mercy flight to assist a sick Australian was that of 4 May 1959 when a nine-man Russian party reached Wilkes (later Casey) station from Mirnyy. The Russian doctor treated a member of the base who was ill with a serious nervous disorder. The Li-2 commanded by chief pilot Boris Osipov landed on the plateau ice about eight kilometres (five miles) south-east of the base; departure was delayed by three days after the onset of a storm with 60 knot winds.

5 The Li-2 is a medium-range low-wing transport designed by Lisunov. It is, in fact, a Russian version of the DC-3, built under a licence obtained from the Douglas Aircraft Company in the late 1930s; some 2,900 were produced with Russian engines installed. The An-2 is a single-engine cabin biplane, designed by A. K. Antonov. The IL-12 is a longer range twin-engine passenger and supply plane, resembling the Convair 400, designed by S. V. Ilyushin. The IL-14 is a popular redesign and update of the IL-12. An American icebreaker crew visiting Mirnyy in 1958 reported seeing eight aircraft parked on the station airstrip; five were Li-2 type 'which had been built in the U.S. in 1938'. The bay ice runway measured 2½ kilometres (1½ miles) next to McDonald Bay.

6 The Russian aviators left evidence of their passing. South of Wilkes station a surface party found a steel cylinder containing a note, a vodka bottle and an area map deposited during a flight of October 1956.

7 *Operational Problems of Antarctic Aviation*, Journal of the Royal Aeronautical Society, October 1967. Writer John Grierson commented that Russian polar aviators, possibly from their Arctic experience, had an uncanny sense of dead reckoning. He attributed their navigational accuracy to being able, at reduced altitude, to take frequent drift sight readings of sastrugi (hard wind-formed snow ridges) or whatever else they could identify as surface features.

8 *Antarctic*, June 1960.
9 One Russian pilot visiting McMurdo told his American hosts he had landed his plane on ice no greater than 10 inches thick. 'The problem,' he added, 'was that once I stopped, I sank.'
10 Molodezhnaya, now the main Russian base, has a snow compacted runway, begun in 1977–78, located 20 kilometres (14 miles) east of the station. Aircraft from Moscow reach 'Molodezh' by way of Mocambique, the first taking place in the 1978–79 season. Mirnyy lies 720 kilometres (450 miles) to the east.
11 The first men in history to winter-over on the polar ice cap were the four Russians who established Pioneerskaya station 376 kilometres (235 miles), and at an elevation of some 3,000 metres (9,000 feet), south of Mirnyy.
12 *Antarctic*, March 1959.
13 Ibid, March 1960.
14 The Russian expeditionaries who manned Sovietskaya station at 4,000 metres (12,300 feet) above sea level spoke of suffering headaches, shortness of breath, pounding of the heart and low blood pressure. At night they awoke with the feeling of being choked. Despite increased rations, they lost weight alarmingly during the first month's residence.
15 *Vestnik* (Herald) Academy of Sciences, USSR January 1966. The late Dr Somov, a planner and leader of the Soviet IGY expedition, had been active in polar research since 1938. In 1950–51 he commanded the drifting ice floe station North Pole 2 and was subsequently made a Hero of the Soviet Union. As a foremost Russian geographer, he received numerous international decorations for his work as a polar explorer.
16 Dept. Defence News, Washington D.C., 4 January 1960.
17 U.S. Antarctic Research Program news release, Washington, D.C., 16 February 1965. U S. scientists and construction workers 'flew to Vostok (a position located close to the centre of the earth's magnetic field) in January 1965 to install geophysical instruments and aerials as part of an international upper atmosphere research project The visitors were met by 14 station personnel who flew the flags of the USSR and USA above the small station building which carried a 'welcome' sign above the door. Forty Russians awaited the third American aircraft visit to Vostok on 25 January 1977. The only woman visitor, Lieutenant Elaine Roberts, administrative officer at McMurdo, received a bouquet of fresh cut flowers, including a carnation. The Russians said they had been growing radishes, tomatoes and flowers since 1974 by the hydroponic method — the nearest solid earth at Vostok is some 3,700 metres (11,000 feet) straight down.
18 *Advertiser*, 4 August, 7 September 1955; *Argus*, 11 January 1956.
19 *Age*, 7, 11, February; 8 June 1957; also Dewart, G., *Antarctic Comrades — Antarctic Journal of the United States*, March 1986.
20 U.S. National Science Foundation news release, McMurdo Sound, 7 December 1963.
21 *Antarctic*, June 1958.
22 *Polar Record* , No.6, 1951.
23 *Argus*, 11 February; *Age*, 3 July 1957. Also, *New Commonwealth*, October 1956 in which Illingworth wrote: 'It should be stated that some of these South Polar outposts will have purposes closely associated with the extension of civil aviation, and also of strategy. The IGY has given the Soviet Union the opportunity of establishing herself in the far south, one result being that four of Australia's major cities are now within range of Soviet bombers.' The American journal *Missiles and Rockets* of June 1959 also reflected the scare mentality of the times when it stated 'At the frozen bottom of the earth Russia is moving into a position from which its missile squadrons could outflank the free world. Half of Antarctica is rapidly turning from white to red . . . the missile submarines, then the missile sites, could come at any time.' In 1966 a group of Soviet nuclear submarines was reported to have cruised south of the Antarctic Circle.
24 *Antarctic*, March 1962.
25 One of the Soviet's serious air losses occurred in February 1986 when an IL-14 crashed near the Philippi Glacier some 240 kilometres (150 miles) from Mirnyy, killing all six crew.

Chapter 11

1 *Polar Record*, May 1956.
2 *The U S. in Antarctica, 1820–1964*. FIDS later became 'BAS' — the British Antarctic Survey. The Survey suffered a number of aircraft casualties among its fixed-wing detachment: 1960, a Beaver lost in an ice hole at Adelaide Island; 1963, two Otters damaged in a gale at Deception Island; 1963-64 season another loss, though without serious injury, in a poor visibility landing at Adelaide Island; in 1977, another Otter crashed into a snow slope.
3 *Antarctic*, June 1957; *The United States In Antarctica*, pp. 7–8.
4 *Antarctic*, March, June 1962; *Dakotas in the Antarctic*, Appendix B.
5 Argentina suffered its worst Antarctic air disaster on 16 September 1976 when 11 men died in the crash of a Neptune on Livingstone Island in the South Shetlands group.
6 Like Byrd in 1930, George Dufek was promoted by special Act of Congress to Rear Admiral on the retired list in order to take command of Task Force 43, Operation Deep Freeze.
7 The ships of Deep Freeze I were the icebreakers *Glacier*, *Edisto* and *Eastwind*, the attack cargo ships *Arneb* and *Wyandot*, the freighter *Greenville Victory* and the tanker *Nespelen*; 4,200 tonnes of cargo were unloaded. Some 1,800 men were in the summer expeditions, 93 remained for the winter at McMurdo and 73 at Little America.
8 *Nine Great Flights*, as told by Admiral Dufek to Joseph Oglesby in *Pegasus*, October 1956, reproduced by the U.S. Antarctic Projects Office.
9 Setting up camp at Hut Point was the first task of Deep Freeze I personnel. Then followed the snow ploughing and scraping of the 1,850-metre (5,600-foot) landing strip, on the bay ice. In the first season, aircraft taxied close to the tanker *Nespelen* to refuel from a pipeline which had been laid across the ice.
10 The American government was reportedly anxious to win prior knowledge of the Antarctic interior, ahead of other IGY expeditions, ie, the Russians. The outbreak of the Korean war had upset a proposal by Admiral Byrd to have the Americans return permanently to Antarctica in the early 1950s.

11 Aircraft on the nine long flights carried three months' emergency rations for each crew member. However the men believed they stood a very slim chance of rescue if forced down on the plateau ice. 'No big plane could land here for rescue and get off again — the air is too rarefied to provide buoyancy,' said Lt. Cdr Henry Jorda of VX-6.

12 The westward flight which reached the Knox Coast hoped to sight the landing place of the Soviet expedition. However, owing to ice conditions the Russians had moved further west to the vicinity of Haswell Islets where Mirnyy was established.

13 The American press noted a 'we saw it first' ring to the message which Byrd radioed to the Soviet expedition: 'Welcome to Wilkes Land. Hope you are having good luck finding your IGY base site. We recently flew over interior in vicinity of your planned inland bases. Surface does not appear rough, but glacial plateau ranges between 11,000 to 13,000 feet elevation. We would like to exchange weather information . . . best wishes for success in our international effort in science.'

14 In 1955, two respected members of the New Zealand Antarctic Society, R. A Falla and A. S. Helm, wrote to Prime Minister Holland urging the government to establish a base in the Ross Dependency. The letter stressed the ease with which any country could establish valid claim to the territory. Argentina, Russia, the United States or any other nation setting up a base in this region could put forward an effectual claim . . . (however) if 'a [N.Z.] scientific station is set up, even with token administrative facilities, our sovereignty will be greatly strengthened'.

15 *Antartic*, December 1959.

16 Ibid, March 1960.

17 Before beginning the trans-Antarctic trek, the expedition's Otter and Auster aircraft were engaged in exploration of the area surrounding Shackleton base and reconnoitring the trail for the Fuchs' surface party. On 20 September 1957 the Auster, piloted by Gordon Haslop, while on a medical emergency flight with Dr Allan Rogers as passenger, was forced to land 'somewhere on the ice edge' off the Vahsel Bay coast. After 10 days of waiting, silence was broken with a radio signal received from the missing pair; both were uninjured, living on iron rations and sheltering in a hole dug in the ice. Urgent work at Shackleton brought the Otter from its snow covered winter pit. On the third day of fruitless searching along the ice edge, Lewis and Stratton sighted a Verey light. The Otter landed and refuelled the Auster, enabling both aircraft to return on 4 October.

18 Major Jim Lassiter of the U.S. Air Force figured in American aviation exploits in the Peninsula and Weddell Sea regions of Western Antarctica. He was chief pilot in Ronne's 1946–47 expedition and then headed the 1957–58 air force detachment which made a 3,200-kilometre (2,000-mile) fly-in with two C-47 Dakota aircraft to Ellsworth from Ushuaia in Argentina, testing an electronic positioning system en route. He was involved in the wreck of a Beechcraft aircraft at Robertson Island, on the north-east comer of the Peninsula on 6 December 1958. Lassiter with two other Americans and an Argentine lieutenant were on a scientific mission. A seven-man Argentine rescue party set out from the transport *Bahia Aguirre* using a Weasel tracked vehicle. After the Weasel fell into a crevasse the party marched across the ice to reach the wreck on 8 December. Lassiter and one of his crew were reported to be in an exhausted condition with frost-bitten feet. The rescuers brought them to the ship on 15 December.

19 The TAE Otter was bought for US$70,000 by the US Navy. Purchased later by RNZAF, it was not operated but sold to an airline in Ontario, Canada, and was subsequently used on charter service in Edmonton, Alberta.

20 A lesser-known RAF flight to Antarctica occurred in November 1969 when a Comet aircraft reached Adelaide Island from Punta Arenas while on a navigation and radio test mission.

Chapter 12

1 George Dufek, trained as a naval aviator, was navigator of the *Bear* during the USAS voyages of 1939–41; in Operation Highjump he commanded the Eastern Croup from USS *Pine Island*. As Rear Admiral, he commanded Task Force 43, known as Operation Deep Freeze, until his retirement in 1959, aged 56. He died in Washington in February 1977, aged 74. William 'Trigger' Hawkes had commanded the air detachment at Little America during Highjump. He had flown in the Alaskan theatre and claimed his enthusiasm for the polar regions came from his boyhood reading of the exploits of Scott and Shackleton.

2 *Aerospace Historian*. Spring edition 1967.

3 The C-124, a heavy supply and transport aircraft for U.S. military forces, built by the Douglas Aircraft Corporation, Long Beach, California. Maximum payload was 35 tonnes. Range with a 27-tonne load was stated as 3,200 kilometres (2,000 miles). Four Pratt and Whitney engines gave a 200-knot cruising speed.

4 Budget for Deep Freeze I was stated to be US$322 million. According to Finn Ronne, every 1 dollar spent on Antarctic science required an 8 dollar outlay on logistic support.

5 Kainan Bay, named by Lieutenant Nobu Shirase who commanded the Japanese Antarctic Expedition of 1912. His ship was *Kainan Maru* — a 'ship to open up the south.' Admiral Byrd, as Officer in Charge of Deep Freeze I attended the commissioning of Little America V on his last Antarctic visit.

6 The American government order of 1 July 1955 also directed Deep Freeze, apart from scientific and exploratory goals, to provide for the establishment of 'permanent stations in the Antarctic as directed by competent authority, in support of United States rights in the area.'

7 The Great Antarctic Horst is the mountain chain (the Trans-Antarctic Mountains) that rims the western side of the Ross Sea and the Ross Ice Shelf, extending north-south for some 1,900 kilometres (1,200 miles).

8 When summer melting of the ice airstrip threatened the aviation support schedule, a U.S. Army civilian expert was hurriedly flown to McMurdo. He ordered the filling of melt-water holes with a mixture of ice chips, snow and water that froze solid. The 'ice concrete' as it was termed

allowed 'wheel' operations to continue.

9 Deep Freeze 11 of 1956–57 was supported by 12 ships and a force of 3,000 men, of whom 317 were to winter-over at the 7 bases (including McMurdo) which America established in Antarctica for the IGY.

10 The P2V Neptune, an anti-submarine and maritime patrol aircraft, manufactured by the Lockheed Aircraft Corporation, in Antarctica, was modified to perform resupply and aerial photo reconnaissance missions. Powered by four engines (2 piston and 2 turbojet) it had a speed of over 300 knots and a range of 4,800 kilometres (3,000 miles). The R5D, the navy's version of the DC-4 Skymaster, manufactured by Douglas had 4 Pratt and Whitney engines, giving a maximum speed of 243 knots across a range of 2,590 nautical miles. For Antarctica, the R4D had fuel capacity increased to some 1,800 gallons, together with the fitting of JATO racks. The UC-1, a single-engine Otter manufactured by the de Havilland Corporation of Canada was taken to Antarctica aboard ship and operated on skis. Early in Deep Freeze, Admiral Dufek considered bringing all shorter-range aircraft to Antarctica aboard an aircraft carrier, as had been done in Highjump.

11 The first Hercules in Antarctica was the C-130D type of the U.S. Air Force 61st Troop Carrier Squadron. The first navy Hercules was the C-130BL delivered for Deep Freeze (with strengthened tricycle ski landing gear) on 17 August 1960.

12 The American mercy flight was on 4 December 1959. The Russians, in an Li-2, had visited Wilkes seven months before. The navy R7V was a Lockheed Super Constellation passenger and cargo aircraft, powered by four Wright turbo-compound engines. Two air force C-135 aircraft reached the Antarctic coast during geomagnetic and cosmic radiation measuring flights from Melbourne to the South Magnetic Pole in 1965.

13 Despite 'cold war' uncertainties, one of the numerous co-operative ventures developed with the Soviet expeditions was the erection in January 1964 of a tall antenna at Vostok station for the international cosmic ray counter program. Three landings were made by navy C-130 Hercules to deliver the equipment together with a force of nine Seabees who installed the automatic receivers after completing a similar task at Pole Station. Despite acclimatisation, the Seabees suffered symptoms of hypoxia (oxygen starvation) at Vostok's high altitude; they had to wear face masks fed from oxygen bottles.

14 *Antarctic*, September 1964.

15 First supply flight by the largest U.S. Air Force transport, the C-5B Lockheed Galaxy reached McMurdo in October 1989. In two trips, the giant aircraft delivered four fully assembled UH-1N turbo-helicopters.

16 *Antarctic*, December 1958. The cost of the C-124 losses was put at $8 million.

17 Ibid, March 1961.

18 *History of Air Development Squadron Six* (VX-6), p.25.

19 On 4 June 1958 the U.S. State Department announced that 11 nations had accepted the American invitation to attend informal talks in Washington on the future of Antarctica.

20 Powered by four Allison turbo-prop engines, the Lockheed Hercules is able to operate in temperatures down to –54°C (–65°F). Under reclassification in 1962 the C-130BL became LC-130F. Maximum payload is about 15 tonnes and with maximum fuel load, range is given as 5,184 kilometres (3,250 miles); average top cruise speed is 544 kpm (340 mph). Eight 1,000 lb thrust JATO units (4 per side) can be fitted to boost take-off in heavy gross weight/high altitude operations.

21 *Antarctic Journal*, March, June 1987; National Science Foundation annual report 1988.

22 *Antarctic*, Winter 1987. An earlier mishap occurred on 28 December 1984, when the ski gear of an LC-130 became wedged in a giant crevasse during taxiing for take-off near Starshot Glacier. The aircraft was repaired two weeks later.

Epilogue

1 The first 'wheel' landing by an LC-130 Hercules on an interior permanent unprepared blue-ice runway took place at the Mill Icefield, near the Beardmore Glacier on 28 January 1990. Utilisation of an interior blue-ice runway promised to enhance the support of American scientific programs.

2 Dramatic advances have been made in navigation accuracy and capabilities through the use of Omega, and of Litton inertial navigation systems on American C-130 aircraft and the introduction of the satellite-related Global Positioning System (GPS) for air and surface movements. The Soviet expedition introduced inertial navigation on the IL-76TD four-engine jet transport which began flying the Moscow–Mocambique–Molodezh route in 1985–86.

3 Melbourne *Sun*, 9 September 1928. Ten years after Mawson's statement, the foreign Antarctic whaling fleets returned with a record kill of 46,000 whales, equivalent to 84 per cent of the world's catch.

4 Scientists estimated that some 220 minerals, in varying degrees of intensity, had been identified in Antarctica since the IGY; others noted included chromium, nickel, cobalt, platinum. Some 16 were said to have 'commercial value'.

5 Dr Law's paper (Adult Education Board of Tasmania, 1964) did not go as far as did a post-war statement by Admiral Byrd in which he mentioned the possibility of using controlled nuclear explosions to melt the ice cap for the extraction of minerals or oil from bedrock.

6 The Antarctic Treaty was signed in Washington on 1 December 1959, initially by the seven claimant nations, plus Belgium, Japan, South Africa, USA and USSR. By 1992 the number of signatories reached 40.

7 At the 1992 conference of the International Whaling Commission (IWC) the trend was possibly reversed with certain nations, notably Norway, Iceland and Japan recommending a resumption of commercial whaling. Japan has continued to hunt the minke whale, ostensibly for scientific purposes. An IWC spokesman said the ban on hunting endangered species, particularly the blue and humpback, would not change. At the 1993 conference, Japan and Norway confirmed their intention to continue whaling.

8 In the 1991 summer, 31 cruises carrying some 3,000 passengers were scheduled to visit the Antarctic Peninsula. Japanese tourist cruises visited the Ross Sea region. During the earlier ANZ and Qantas flights, 10,000 people travelled. A Chilean crash on King George Island on 1 January 1985 took 10 lives .

9 Two Otters of the Chilean Air Force reached the South Pole

on 30 November 1984. In the following year, with Chilean support, Air Network International (ANI), latterly with a DC-6, began operating from South America to the blue-ice runway in the Patriot Hills situated 1,056 kilometres (660 miles) from the South Pole On 11 January 1989 the first ANI Twin Otter flight reached the Pole. In January 1989 an ANI-led surface party comprising two women and seven men travelled on skis to the Pole.

10 Smith: 79, 85, 87. *Antarctic Journal of the United States*, March 1986, p.9.

11 Ibid, p.10.

12 On 3 November 1986 an LC-130 was flown across Antarctica from McMurdo to Queen Maud Land, via the Pole for refuelling to bring out a sick South African expeditionary. On 4 June 1991 another Hercules flown by a navy crew evacuated a seriously ill member from the New Zealand base. This was the fifth emergency flight to reach McMurdo outside the normal Deep Freeze summer transport season, and first mid-winter rescue made from Christchurch in 24 years.

13 The C-5B Galaxy which first landed on McMurdo runway in 1989 has three times the carrying capacity of the C-141. The use of heavy transports reflects America's annual investment in Antarctic operations, running at around US$150 million.

14 Reprinted by kind permission of the Berrima District Historical Society.

15 Through No. 36 Squadron, of Richmond base, the RAAF returned to Antarctica in the 1979–82 seasons for a series of C-130H supply flights between Christchurch and McMurdo to supplement the work of American and New Zealand C-130s. In return, the American (National Science Foundation) ski-equipped aircraft made supply runs from McMurdo to Casey station. The first RAAF Hercules reached McMurdo on 30 November 1978; the first VXE-6 crewed flight with an LC-130R landed on Lanyon skiway at Casey on 24 January 1979.

16 On 4 October 1991 the United States and 22 other Antarctic Treaty consultative states signed the Protocol on Environmental Protection to the Antarctic Treaty. This agreement seeks to designate Antarctica as a natural reserve, devoted to peace and science, and prohibit all mineral resource activities, except as related to science. Australia and France disagreed with the Protocol on Minerals and suggested a different form of agreement.

17 Since 1988, American ER-2 reconnaissance aircraft (the former U-2 spy aircraft) have been gathering air samples above Antarctica to assist scientific investigation of the annual summer depletion of the south polar ozone layer; later, this work may be undertaken by the Perseus unmanned remotely-controlled powered glider.

Picture credits

ANARE: 190, 193 (below), 197(above), 204, 207, 208(above), 209, 211, 2291, 294
Argentina — Dirrecion Nacional del Antarctico 238
Australian War Memorial: 173
Author's Collection 9, 11 (below), 12 (centre),13 (centre),19, 26, 28, 31, 46, 55, 110, 123, 146, 148, 158–160, 164, 166–168, 230, 235, 239, 241, 243, 245, 257
Jonathan Chester (Extreme Images) 10 (lower), 45, 86, 87, 89, 91, 194 (lower), 201, 210,211
Fuerza Area de Chile 236, 237, 289 (lower)
Elizabeth Chipman Collection 109, 113
John Fairfax 12 (lower), 35, 47, 52, 56, 71-73, 84, 102, 106, 121, 123, 187, 293
John Hopton Collection 13 (below)
P.G. Law 5, 8, 16-17
Lockheed Aircraft Corporation Collection 3, 279, 276, 277, 278 (lower)
Lufthansa 142-143, 150-156,199 (inset)
Mawson Collection (Barr Smith, Library University of Adelaide) 11, 76-78, 80, 81, 92, 93, 99, 102, 103
Mortlock Library, Adelaide 44, 162
Colin Monteath (Hedgehog Productions) 283
National Archives (US) 13, 37, 38, 40, 42, 46, 53-55, 57-60, 66-68, 111, 112, 114, 116, 118, 131, 133, 138, 252, 253, 264, 276
National Library, Canberra 79, 80, 82, 96, 101, 107, 125-129, 133-137, 140, 141, 173, 192, 193, 225
News Limited 290
Norsk Polarinstitutt 95, 145, 147
Russell Pardoe 218, 219
Royal Geographical Society 1, 10, 14, 19, 147, 242
John Seaton 14, 187 (lower), 189,182, 194 (upper and inset), 196, 197, 203 (lower),207, 221, 232
Dick Smith/Australian Geographic 231, 287
Smithsonian Institution 32-33, 41, 51, 62, 64-66, 140, 164, 165
Soviet Antarctic Expedition 13, 213, 220, 225, 229
Dick Thompson 194, 198, 203, 208 (lower)
U.S. Air Force 254, 279, 286, 289
U.S. Army 175
U.S. Navy 12, 14, 15, 18-25, 27, 29, 69, 70, 171, 172, 274, 176-186, 202, 215, 219 (lower), 223, 226, 227, 241 (lower), 247-249, 253, 254 (lower), 255, 256, 258-263, 265-272, 274, 275, 277 (lower), 278,279, 284, 286 (lower), 287, 290, 291

INDEX

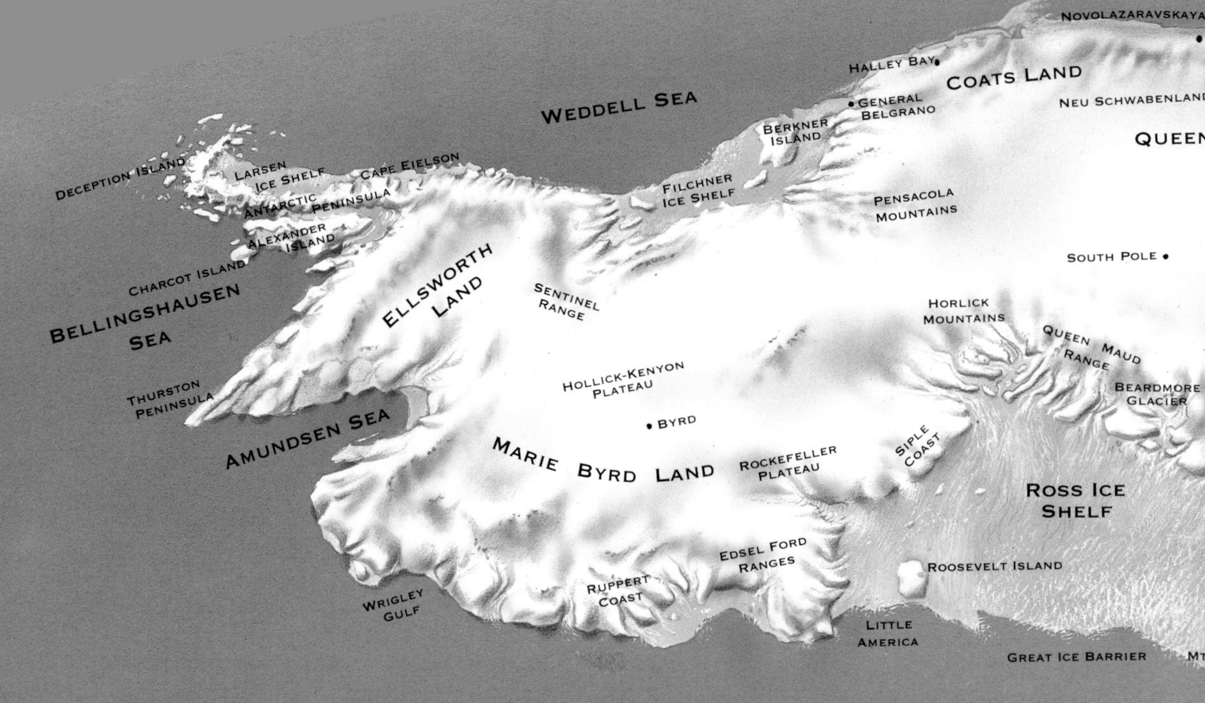

Russian IL-14 loads at Mirnyy

Among the ice floes, finding the ship?

Veteran Antonov cabin biplane waits at Mirnyy

Deep Freeze LC-130 lifting NZ field party

US Navy neptunes pause at South Pole

DC-4 tourist flight lands in Patriot Hills